D37/6

The Social and Religious Plays
of Strindberg

The Social and Religious Plays of Strindberg

by

JOHN WARD

THE ATHLONE PRESS
LONDON 1980

Published by
THE ATHLONE PRESS
at 90–91 *Great Russell Street London* WC1

USA and Canada
Humanities Press Inc
New Jersey

British Library Cataloguing in Publication Data
Ward, John
    The social and religious plays of Strindberg.
    1.   Strindberg, August – Criticism and interpretation
    I. Title
    839.7'2'6   PT9816

    ISBN 0 485 11183 7

Printed in Great Britain by
WESTERN PRINTING SERVICES LTD
Bristol

Preface

Despite the increasing number of translations of his plays, there is no satisfactorily comprehensive book on Strindberg's drama in English. Of the existing studies, F. L. Lucas's *Ibsen and Strindberg* contains a vicious critical parody, Mortensen and Downes's *Strindberg* is little more than a cursory summary, while Gunnar Ollén's *August Strindberg*, though excellent, is only a brief introduction. The rest are either largely biographical (Sprigge, McGill and Campbell), specialised (Madsen and Dahlström), dated (Lind-af-Hageby), or psychological and tendentious (Brustein's widely read *The Theatre of Revolt*). Walter Johnson's two fine studies differ notably in approach and aim from the present book and the recent American translation of Martin Lamm's Swedish classic *August Strindberg* provides the *starting point* of a modern analysis of Strindberg's work. Most recently, Birgitta Steene's *The Greatest Fire* (1973), though competent, attempts to cover far too much in too few pages, while Gunnar Brandell's classic *Strindberg In Inferno* is necessarily restricted in its subject matter. There is then a clear need for a full length critical book which will not only re-affirm the value of such popular plays as *The Father, Miss Julie* and *The Dance of Death*, but which will also analyse, and place in context the later experimental dramas from *The Road to Damascus* to *The Great Highway*. Nevertheless, though the project is both urgent and worthwhile, in the case of the present writer a doubt persists; for there seems an undeniable presumption about someone who does not read Swedish attempting such a specialised task. Strindberg scholars, in particular, will be naturally and perhaps justifiably suspicious of an outsider, with such an important disqualification.

The disadvantages of being unable to read a word of what Strindberg actually wrote are formidable. Clearly, there can be no profession of original scholarship, nor would a detailed stylistic analysis based solely upon translations be particularly credible. Equally important is the inaccessibility of his thousands of letters, few of which have been translated and most of which are reputedly very revealing of both his personal and literary life. (Although those which are available are often so inconsistent, and even self-contradictory that they might confuse a critic as much as they would instruct him.) Finally the bulk of Swedish criticism and scholarship, which is the bedrock of our understanding of Strindberg's work, is not yet in translation. Nor, since this book is intended for the English reader, has untranslated German and French criticism been quoted.

All these factors constitute major obstacles which cannot be surmounted. All that can be done is to plan one's course in order to avoid them, and, fortunately, the present requirements of the literary public in England encourage one to do so. The most obvious lack of understanding of, and sympathy for, Strindberg's plays is not among academic specialists, but among theatre-goers and the theatrical establishment. Ultimately, these people will only become Strindberg enthusiasts when there are more intelligent productions of his work on radio, television and in the theatre. But, before this is likely to occur, managers and producers, critics and students, actors and designers must be educated about his attitudes and ideas. It is at this level of instruction, that of completing an up-to-date programme of serious critical groundwork, that the present book is aimed.

It is intended to provide a general account of Strindberg's ideas and dramatic themes and to give a detailed examination of each of his translated social and religious plays in terms of them. At the same time, this will not simply repeat established theories and interpretations but will present a personal view of a foreign writer's achievement. In those cases where previous discussions of particular dramas are acceptable, they will be assimilated to the analyses given. Although even there an attempt will be made to remain faithful to the philosophical perspectives of this book.

The emphasis on the playwright's themes is deliberate. We possess sufficient material in English from Strindberg's plays, novels, short stories, essays, diaries and letters to get a clear understanding of his thought and its development throughout his career. Moreover, thematic discussion, though finally dependent upon textual evidence, is less likely to be invalidated (especially on a philosophical level) by the various nuances of individual words and phrases that different translators offer. Fortunately, thematic understanding is particularly important in Strindberg's case because an appreciation of his ideas constitutes the best means of appreciating his overall dramatic achievement. This is so because his constant experimentation in the theatre was almost invariably prompted by his urge to express his changing social, philosophical and spiritual insights. In Strindberg's writings, more than in any other dramatist of his time, style, form and structure are functions of his thought. Indeed, his attachment to so many different schools of drama was caused less by his acceptance of their theatrical credos than by his attraction to their historical, social, philosophical or mystical views.

For this reason perhaps the major obstacle to a richer appreciation of his merits among British audiences is their almost total unfamiliarity with his ideas. The average playgoer could probably give some account of the principal ideas of Ibsen, Chekhov, Pirandello or Brecht, but he would be unlikely to know anything about Strindberg, other than that he was a misogynist. And for the appreciation of a playwright whose work communicates a densely textured, developing body of thought, this is fatal. Furthermore, if what has been said above is correct, it follows that ignorance of his ideas will be accompanied by a failure to understand the sources and the nature of his dramatic innovations as well as his need for them.

A further requirement of a book on Strindberg at this time is that it should include some attempt to place him in the context of nineteenth- and twentieth-century drama by examining his sources and influence. The purpose of this would be to counteract the curious prejudice that Strindberg is some kind of literary anomaly outside the main current of European arts. It might also, if successful, help to persuade our contemporaries that Strindberg is not the poor relation of Ibsen; that he is in fact the most modern of all nineteenth-century dramatists and that the present under-performance of the bulk of his plays and the widespread ignorance of, and prejudice against, what he achieved is a major literary injustice.

Even within its range though, the present book does not pretend to be exhaustive. Strindberg wrote many bad plays which do not possess any extra-theatrical interest. In this study, I have discussed only what I regard as either good or significant plays. However, as these comprise over eighty per cent of Strindberg's social and religious dramas, it seems unlikely that anyone's favourite play will have been omitted. No attempt has been made in the text to summarise the plots of the plays discussed. Although it is to be hoped that the reader will be able to follow the references to dramatic narratives, this book is essentially a work of criticism not of description. It is designed for readers who have read or are about to read Strindberg's plays. To get maximum value from it, it will be necessary to be familiar with a dozen or more of them. Even so, the perceptive reader will know that, whatever the pretensions of authors, no book of criticism is so perfectly integrated that it cannot be dipped into for specific illumination.

Finally, the account of the ideological influences on the plays has itself necessarily been selective. Strindberg had a magpie mind. Virtually everything he read had a conscious impact on his thought and his creative work. So, while attempting to provide a balanced reconstruction of his ideas by analysing the most crucial influences upon his dramatic writings, it has been impossible to offer detailed discussions of such diverse mentors as Wagner, Byron, Sar Peladan, The Rosicrucians, Goethe, Baudelaire, Hofmannsthal, Hugo, Linnaeus and so on. What follows is not intended to be comprehensive but is offered as a consistent and sustained effort to understand Strindberg's theatrical work through the medium of his most important philosophical and religious themes. Some critics will undoubtedly find the omission of explicit discussion of his Manicheism regrettable, but it is hoped that this is implicit at least in the theological account of the post-Inferno period. Others will find the emphasis on Swedenborg's influence too insistent, but I feel that the constant reference to Swedenborgianism invariably illuminates Strindberg's later and best plays.

J.W.

Contents

Acknowledgements

Extracts from *Twelve Plays of Strindberg* translated by Elizabeth Sprigge are printed by permission of A. P. Watt and Constable & Co Ltd; extracts from *The Plays of Strindberg*, Volumes 1 and 2, translated by Michael Meyer are printed by permission of the author and Secker and Warburg Ltd. My thanks are due to both. I also wish to thank my wife for her constant encouragement and for her careful correcting and typing of the manuscript.

Introduction

Of all the writers whose work is an imaginative recreation of their lives, Johan August Strindberg is among the most obsessive. Literature was for him both a safety valve and a means of therapy. He used his plays to wrestle with his emotional problems, his novels to settle private antipathies and to compose his autobiography, his diaries to pour out his soul's torment and his scientific researches to establish his intellectual status. As a result, critical discussions of his work have tended to centre on biographical information. A mass of detail correlating his life and work has been uncovered and, while this has been valuable in enabling us to understand the man and his creative processes, from a critical point of view it is arguably barely a preliminary to assessing the quality and importance of his writing.

Nevertheless, not only have certain critics appeared to believe that a biographical approach to Strindberg is sufficient but some have also believed that the content of his life so informs the quality of his work that the obvious flaws of one are inevitably reflected in the other. The classic statement of the biographical position has been provided by Martin Lamm:

> When one has portrayed Strindberg's personality one has already given a descriptive account of his authorship. In world literature there are assuredly very few writers in whom life and literature so wholly intertwine. If his personality is nothing else than the disemboguement of his violently vital and intense temperament, then his literary product is essentially nothing more than the image of his temperament on paper. The explanation of the powerful influence he has exercised both among us and in foreign countries rests in no small degree in his astonishing immediateness. To read him is the same as to live with him.[1]

While Lamm has been prompted by such a conviction to explore the relationship between the man and his work with great subtlety and understanding, actively unsympathetic critics have exploited it for their own purposes. From Strindberg's contemporary, Carl David af Wirsén (who prevented his being awarded the Nobel prize), to F. L. Lucas, they have used it to justify brutally personal attacks on the plays. Thus despite its early value in uncovering the social and psychological origins of Strindberg's work, the biographical approach has widely inhibited serious criticism by being used to buttress the belief that the literary product of a man so hysterical and so obsessive must contain characters and ideas equally uncontrolled.

The most effective way of rejecting the censures of biographical critics is not to attempt to prove that Strindberg was not an hysteric or a bigot, but to expose the inadequacies of their method. Even if we accept that he lacked control over his emotions and his behaviour, we can still argue perfectly plausibly that his literary style was not his life style. Certainly, even the finest of Strindberg's plays contain moments which are at least eccentric but we might show that these frequently add to their artistic value. Instead of causing the play to topple over into literary insanity, these touches might transform a scene into something quite extraordinary, precisely because the bulk of the play has been created by a mind fully in control of its material. However, such examples will not satisfy someone who maintains that no matter how well Strindberg writes, his beliefs that women are agents of man's destruction (or salvation?), that marriage is an appalling battlefield and that life is literally hell on earth, are obsessions that can only produce drama of a fanatical and unrepresentative kind.

To argue in this way, though, is to assume that the value of a theme can be fruitfully isolated from its dramatic presentation. Yet the whole point about Strindberg's ideas is that they only begin to acquire any real significance, apart from their extra-literary value as inroads into the man's mind, when they are embodied in his plays or his novels. Only there do they gather the nuances and reverberations which transform them. By being concretised in complex situations Strindberg's prejudices tend to lose their brittleness and surprisingly become not only adequate but often uniquely valuable to an appraisal of what human beings are and do. The apparent contradictions are reconciled when we realise that Strindberg's cast of thought was dialectical. Only then do we see that the tensions between his beliefs helped to drive him towards conclusions of dramatic and human importance.

His apparently unsystematic philosophising was at a deeper structural level characterised by variety without radical change, by 'unity among a multiplicity'; as indeed was his supposedly haphazard emotional life. The basic structure of his ideas did not develop, it was merely revealed in all its forms by the gradual pressure of changing circumstances. His purpose, albeit unconscious, was apparently always to fit his loves and hates, his successes and failures, his insights and confusions into a theoretical framework which had a fixed infrastructure. Throughout this study it is this theoretical framework that will be examined in the light of the plays. And, if we discover that it is coherent and profound, then his tortuous emotional life will be secondary to an evaluation of his work. The theoretical structure of the plays will be found to have contained the psychological frustrations that prompted their creation. Indeed, the ideal critical work on the plays at the present time would probably not only ignore his life completely but also all his informal writings, concentrating solely on the dramas, his essays and his theoretical works. Whereas current Ibsen criticism certainly needs a deeper understanding of the man behind the work, the time has come to forget Strindberg the man for a while.

THE DRAMATIST AS INNOVATOR AND OUTSIDER

When discussing the well-made play against which he had reacted so violently in the late 1870s, Strindberg wrote a few lines that sum up for us his long-term vision of the theatre and imply his practical attitude to dramatic forms long exhausted. 'There was much that was sensible and just in this version of *The Poetics*. But like other styles in art this one, too, ran its course and degenerated.'[2] The perspective of these remarks is historical and teleological. Generally, for Strindberg, there was no right or wrong artistic form but a great and increasing number of forms suited to different purposes. Part of the skill of an artist consists in selecting the most appropriate form or style for his particular purpose and since one artist may in his life have many goals, he must needs adopt many styles. Even so, Strindberg believed, we can discern some direction in the proliferation of new forms. As our modes of thought are altered by social and philosophical developments, so our modes of communication must be enriched and extended to encompass new truths and insights.

Old forms do not become valueless. We might still be able to revitalise them but they can be exhausted and become, at least temporarily, obsolete. Thus, while Strindberg never *rejected* his naturalistic experiments, he did come to see that they were inadequate to the expression of his later spiritual philosophy. Yet, significantly, he was able to evoke the structure of *Miss Julie* as a paradigm for the Chamber Plays; '*Miss Julie* (without an intermission) has gone through its ordeal by fire and shown itself to be the kind of drama demanded by the impatient man of today: thorough but brief.'[3] Doubtless, he would have agreed that the hereditary-environmentalist determinism of the play was antiquated, but he saw too that the tight structure and the dramatic economy might profitably be used as models for his later chamber sonatas. Strindberg never allowed theoretical preconceptions to prevent him from borrowing techniques and ideas from 'obsolete' traditions. His very eclecticism partly explains why he was, throughout his life, a theatrical innovator. He was restlessly in search of new ways to express his emerging philosophy. He neither prized the new for its own sake nor despised the old on principle. Whatever techniques there were available to him were judged by their effectiveness in expressing his ideas at any particular moment. And when existing techniques were inadequate, he invented new ones. Temporarily, under Zola's influence, he became a strict theoretician but for the rest of his life he was an experimenter and a pragmatist. As a result, he pioneered a more varied range of dramatic forms and styles than is normally presented by half-a-dozen playwrights.

Whether or not we like his plays it is hard to deny that they represent the most varied and persistent attempt at experimentation in the modern theatre. Throughout his life he tried out and developed virtually all the theatrical innovation of his time. He wrote naturalist, expressionist and symbolist dramas, black comedies and comedies of manners, histories, quart d'heures, religious allegories, boulevarderies, social, sexual, folk, fairy, dream and chamber plays. His themes were drawn from Western and Eastern philosophy, the latest social and psychological data, theology of many types, the occult in numerous forms, mythology, the history of Sweden and, most of all, from his own abnormally complicated life. He was a born synthesist who fused an immense variety of styles, forms and experiences into a series of plays that in most cases, transcended the influence which had germinated them. Beside him Chekhov appears narrow in his range and ideas, Ibsen seems to have aged prematurely as a dramatist, while Pirandello's experimentalism is dwarfed. And yet in comparison with them (even Pirandello in view of their respective output) he is grossly neglected; under-performed, under-translated and rarely discussed. Generally, only his fellow playwrights have responded profoundly to his work.

Other important dramatists have been neglected because their work stands outside the central liberal-humanist tradition of the theatre but only Strindberg has the stature to be an embarrassment. Jarry, Claudel and Wedekind, for example, can be condescendingly revived, then shelved until once more the need is felt to prove that the British theatre is the liveliest around. Strindberg, however, wrote too much and too well to be plausibly represented by a couple of revivals every five years. Yet, if we remove *The Father, Miss Julie, Creditors, The Dance of Death* and *The Ghost Sonata* from Britain's theatrical repertoire he would be virtually unknown over here. There are a number of reasons why this is so.

A Strindberg production in this country is a risky enterprise on several counts. Unfamiliarity and lack of knowledge breed lack of interest and this is a difficult circle to break. From recent productions, it has become clear that Strindberg's plays, as much as Ibsen's, demand a fully developed tradition of performance. Every major playwright poses a unique complex of problems at every level of presentation. So it is hardly surprising that British producers and actors have chosen to perform Strindberg's most easily accessible naturalist plays. And when occasionally they have approached the later plays, the result has been ill-informed and unadventurous. For example, in the National Theatre production of *The Dance of Death* an ignorance of the diabolic and Swedenborgian substructure of the play was apparent. Anyone who can interpret the play as a kind of turn-of-the-century *Who's Afraid of Virginia Woolf* (Albee's dramatic origins are not denied) shows small knowledge of Strindberg's ideas and temperament. Yet, can they be blamed when a scholar of Michael Meyer's status writes of the 'straight realism' of *The Dance of Death, Easter* and *Erik the Fourteenth*?[4] And is it not inevitable in such circumstances that when his plays fail to be convincing in such terms, the layman puts the blame on Strindberg's bizarre personality?

Again, the appeal of Strindberg's plays to actors is limited. Although he wrote many great set speeches, created magnificent dramatic sequences and helped to revolutionise our ideas of theatrical characterisation, many of his major roles defy virtuoso performance. The protagonists of *To Damascus*, *A Dream Play* and *The Great Highway*, for example, are not the neatly delineated, well-structured, psychological entities that actors are likely to appreciate. *Prima facie*, they are amorphous, inconsistent and dramatically implausible. What Strindberg termed the rejection of static characterisation does not give a conventional actor much chance to build up dramatic tension or to establish a rapport with his audience. Strindberg equated traditional characterisation with stasis, and what he wanted was fluidity. Whether driven by his naturalistic ideal of a multiplicity of motives or by his post-Inferno conviction that men are the playthings of the Powers, he created characters that are constantly changing. Moreover, this dynamism does not easily appear as growth; often the protagonists are so mercurial, so evidently lacking in rationality, that their behaviour seems to lose all consistency. It is not so much that they are irrational but rather that their fears and ambitions change so frequently and so rapidly that we find it difficult to keep track of them. It is only after deeper study that we begin to grasp that Strindberg is trying to project a new concept of human personality and human relationships.

Partly as a result of this notion of character and partly owing to Strindberg's mania for authorial analysis, his plays often appear to the newcomer to lack tension. A playwright who insists on constantly making his own, and his characters' surface attitudes explicit is hardly likely at first sight to evoke a sense of mystery in his audience. But then the compensations of his emotional directness together with his emotional complexity endow his plays with a power rarely glimpsed in the modern theatre. What Strindberg sometimes (though by no means always) loses in the excitement of plot and the tensions between characters, he gains in the force of introspective questioning, and through face to face confrontations. But these advantages are strong meat and not always immediately appealing.

Then again, Strindberg had not an entirely attractive sense of humour except possibly in the sketches and stories. Even his *theory* of humour in the theatre might put many people off: 'People think that the purpose of humour is fun. No! It is very serious business. An author does not dare state truth nakedly, it is too appalling. He must mask it; he must serve it up under the less dangerous label of humour.'[5] Thus the humour in his plays tends to be either black or satirical, but even these cases are exceptional. Although he was a man of ready wit and charm, both in his life and work, these tended to be swamped by his more morbid characteristics. His plays rarely allow the audience to relax. They are permeated with a totally serious and abnormal anguish which appear to reveal the playwright as not merely melancholy like Ibsen or sadly disillusioned like Chekhov or cruelly harassed like Pirandello, but as nearly demented. In his later years, he regarded existence as disgusting, human happiness as an illusion and his fellow-men as, for the most part, corrupt. In *The Dance of Death* (1901) man is 'a barrowload of filth', 'Mankind is to be pitied' forms a leitmotif of *A Dream Play* (1901), decay, foul odours and vampirism are used to describe the human condition in the Chamber Plays (1907), while his last drama, *The Great Highway* (1909), completes his ascetic withdrawal from life. Human beings who would divert the man of God from his chosen path are vilified; pride, vanity, avarice and deceit are all we can expect from them. The world is variously seen as a dungheap, a madhouse and a drunken orgy. Only after death will everything be justified when the workings of Divine Providence will be revealed in all their inexorable logic. Until then we must accept whatever suffering is imposed on us by Providence, humbly believing that we shall be redeemed and enlightened after death. To step outside the Providential Design by killing ourselves would involve asserting our own ego at the expense of God's express Purpose. Clearly such sentiments are not any more welcome to most people today than are the earlier Strindberg's better known misogynistic views. Contemporary theatre places a high value on humour. Whatever the sociological reasons for this, the fact is that total seriousness seems to be regarded as either indecent or boring, and Strindberg has been the victim of this attitude.

A further point against Strindberg as a popular dramatist is that to present-day audiences many of his plays would appear morally repugnant. Throughout his life, Strindberg's thinking was so geared to justifying his own hierarchical morality that now it can seem absurd, if not offensive. Whether he was maintaining the inferiority of women or of mankind, he was essentially asserting his own special status; either as a superman or as a member of a religious elite. He even admitted that the specifically elitist elements in Nietzsche and Swedenborg's thought appealed to him for this reason. 'Not till I read *Heaven and Hell* [i.e. of Swedenborg] do I begin to get help. There is then an object in these mysterious sufferings—the improvement and development of my personality to something greater, something like Nietzsche's imaginary ideal, but differently conceived' (*Legends*, p. 40).[6] That most of the systems of thought which appealed to him were hierarchical or elitist lays him open too easily to the charge of 'fascism'. Yet if this is why he is so neglected, it is unfair. When we think of Wagner, an incomparably more distasteful individual, and of D. H. Lawrence, an arguably more absurd figure, we do not find that suspect ideas necessarily destroy an artist's reputation. Moreover, as we shall see later, Strindberg's thought and feeling contain much that should demonstrate how partisan an unqualified verdict of 'fascist' would be.

Yet, perhaps it is his continual questing after fundamental principles, for dialectical answers to existential and eschatological questions, that is finally so discouraging. There is nothing neat about either Strindberg's thought or his dramas, as there often is about Ibsen's. He did not write plays about specific social problems. His plays were either embodiments of pure disgust or confused journeys with no aesthetically satisfying goal; just the inevitable release of death. And even when he did conclude such plays as *Easter* or *Advent* with a moral or spiritual resolution, the content is too unfashionably biblical to engross modern audiences. Furthermore, despite the emotional turbulence of his characters, Strindberg's plays lack the cynical aggression which has proved so popular in modern drama. His protagonists struggle to achieve self-abnegation; their more self-indulgent outbursts and their attempts to shift blame or to play for sympathy are ruthlessly condemned. They are not even allowed to be positive but are required to be humble and ascetic. Unfortunately for Strindberg's popularity the twentieth century has *not* proved to be the era of those who stand and wait.

More immediately though, it would appear that Strindberg's religious dramas, his dream plays and his Chamber plays have been ignored not just because their subject matter is unfashionable but because their form, their themes and their style are so complex that they present production problems beyond the normal range of British theatrical managements. Few producers in this country seem to have any knowledge of the ideas of Strindberg's post-Inferno period, nor does his exacting experimentalism offer them the easy popular impact of more recent products of the *avant garde*. For instance, the Chamber plays with their tight musical structure, demand a sense of pace and timing at least as precise as that required by Beckett's and Pinter's dramas. They also need the kind of mastery of the presentation of layers of reality demanded by the plays of Pirandello and Ionesco. To say this is not to fault these playwrights' work, it is rather to point out the uncompromising, perhaps even inconsiderate nature of the Swede's theatrical needs.

PART ONE

The Pre-Inferno Plays

I

General Introduction to the Pre-Inferno Plays

Since the publication of Martin Lamm's *Strindberg's Dramer* (1924–6), it has been customary to divide Strindberg's dramatic work into two comparatively distinct periods. Those plays whose composition precedes 1894 have been characterised as largely naturalistic in style and predominantly concerned with social and sexual themes; those written after 1897 as symbolist or expressionist and dominated by religious or mystical ideas. The period 1894–7, commonly known as the Inferno crisis, was a watershed in both Strindberg's personal and creative life. During those years he passed through a severe mental illness in which he was most probably legally classifiable as insane. His work thereafter acquired a new impetus which helped to transform European drama.

However, while Lamm's classification makes a useful general distinction between the earlier and later plays it obscures the fact that Strindberg's work was a developing unity. Most of the ideas and technical forms which are so startling in the post-Inferno plays are to be found in embryo in the so-called naturalistic dramas. Thus, although Lamm's scheme will be retained in this book for the sake of convenience, the similarities and continuities between the two periods will constantly be emphasised.

STRINDBERG'S NATURALISM

The fascination that French culture[1] always had for Strindberg inevitably brought him into contact with the naturalistic movement, which he embraced with characteristic fervour from about 1887 till 1892. Artistically, the great impetus of naturalism derived from Balzac; theoretically from a variety of sources that included Hippolyte Taine and Charles Darwin. Its classic definition was given by Emile Zola who appropriated the 'scientific' method of Claude Bernard's *Introduction à l'Etude de la Médecine Expérimentale*. Zola's definition included the three basic principles of truth, grandeur and simplicity. The naturalist must present a closely documented reality in which character is scientifically portrayed in terms of heredity and environment; both physiologically and psychologically. Decor should accurately represent a realistic milieu within which credible human personalities are created. The structure and style of both the play and novel must be concentrated and simple. Plot, language and setting are to explain and authenticate human behaviour; they are not to be cultivated for their own sakes. On the other hand, the situations and conflicts that form the subject matter of naturalistic writing must contain themes as archetypal as those of the classics. By choosing themes of great importance and, at the same time, portraying them simply through realistically drawn characters, free from the distractions of high style, Zola hoped to synthesise a series of paradigmatic accounts of human behaviour.

As in the case of many artistic movements, there was a strong social drive behind naturalism. Human degradation through poverty and overwork was remorselessly exposed by a careful documentation of social reality, for example, in Zola's novels and Hauptmann's plays. Class structure and the money motive were attacked as corruptive forces which hinder the full expression of human dignity. To these ends, the naturalistic play and novel, which became a kind of sociology of the day, were perfectly suited. 'We also desire to master certain phenomena of an intellectual and personal order, to be able to direct them. We are, in a word, experimental novelists. . . . in this way, we shall construct a practical sociology.'[2]

The naturalistic artist therefore sought to provide a variety of specific case studies by which general deterministic explanations could be exemplified. According to Zola the novelist must 'possess a knowledge of the mechanism inherent in man, show the machinery of his intellectual and sensory manifestations under the influence of heredity and environment, such as physiology shall give them to us, and then, finally [to] exhibit man living in social conditions produced by himself which he modifies daily and in the heart of which he is undergoing constant transformation'.[3] From these bases the naturalistic novelist implied that the terrible lives of his characters might have been ameliorated. While their inherited characteristics could not be changed, social conditions and hence many of their resulting behavioural defects could be improved.

The world of the naturalist was usually Godless. Human development was seen as the result of an evolutionary friction between man's physical inheritance and his psychological conditioning within the social milieu. Thus human behaviour was regarded as being susceptible to scientific analysis. 'We should operate on the characters, the passions, on the human and social data, in the same way that the chemist and the physicist operate on inanimate beings, and as the physiologist operates on living beings Determinism dominates everything.'[4] Zola's final declaration here is a little misleading. Certainly, the naturalists were determinists but they were not fatalists; freedom of will was thought to be severely restricted but was not entirely denied. Since we can, in certain respects, observe and analyse our environment, we can change it, and so must accept partial responsibility for it.

Strindberg's plays of 1887–92 clearly belong to the naturalistic tradition, but in conformity with the theory he laid down in *Vivisections* (1887), the preface to *Miss Julie* (1888) and the essay 'On Modern Drama and Modern Theatre' (1889), his conception and practice of naturalism was, in important respects, peculiar to himself. In the essay,[5] while he concedes that art is a piece of nature, he emphasises the importance of subjective content. For this reason, he dismisses Henry Becque's *Les Corbeaux* as true naturalism.

> This is the objective realism which is so beloved by those devoid of temperament, the soulless as they shall be called! ... It is not the great naturalism which seeks out the points where the great battles are fought, which loves to see what you do not see every day, which delights in the struggle between natural forces, whether these forces are called love and hate, rebellious or social instincts, which finds the beautiful or ugly unimportant only if it is great. (p. 17)

Strindberg, then, contrasted the Zolaesque 'faire grande' of his own naturalism ('This grandiose art which we found in *Germinal* and *La Terre*', p. 17) with mere 'photography' which is non-selective, undramatic and psychologically undifferentiated. His demand for large themes accords well with Zola's theory and practice:

> In the new naturalistic drama, striving for the *significant motif* was felt at once. Therefore the action was usually centred around life's two poles, life and death, the act of birth and the act of

death, the fight for the spouse, for the means of subsistence, for honour. (pp. 18–19)

Where he and Zola parted company (in practice if not in theory) was in their interpretation of the role of the artist's personality. Whatever he might write in theory, it is clear that the following could not plausibly be applied to Strindberg the artist: 'The experimental novelist is the one who accepts proven facts, who points out in man and in society the mechanism of the phenomena over which science is the mistress and who does not interpose his personal sentiments, except in the phenomena whose determinism is not yet settled and who tries to test, as much as he can, this personal sentiment . . . by observation and experiment.'[6] One does not have to embrace biographical criticism wholeheartedly to suggest that Strindberg continually 'interposed' his sentiments, his life and his beliefs into his work.

Significantly, he also rejected Zola's insistence on comprehensive social documentation. According to Strindberg, the milieu of any character could be presented concisely by concentrating on those features which *specifically* affected his post development and present behaviour. As a result, Strindberg's naturalistic dramas are free from the mass of social detail and statistics that bogged down certain novels of the period and lumbered some of the plays of Hauptmann. Moreover, because Strindberg concentrated on crucial human conflicts to reveal individual psychology rather than on precise reportage of contemporary attitudes and disputes, his plays do not seem as contextually dated as Ibsen's *Ghosts* and Hauptmann's *Vor Sonnenaufgang* (1889). While much naturalistic work was 'photographic' and contemporary, Strindberg's was selective and timeless. Even *Miss Julie* which was largely a naturalistic play is not restricted by the archaic social structure and curious morality it presumes but remains permanently valuable in virtue of its psychosexual understanding.

In place of photographic realism and Zola's physiological determinism, Strindberg substituted a mass of *psychological* detail which he proudly described, in the *Miss Julie* preface, as his characters' 'multiplicity of motive'.[7] This he saw as embodying a modern conception of character because it implies that 'an incident in real life is usually the outcome of a whole series of deeply buried motives'

(Preface, p. 101). Previously, realistic dramatists had suggested that one motive or a definite number of them prompted their characters' behaviour. Strindberg, however, argued that many motives play a part and that it is misleading to select any particular one as crucial. (Selection, of course, is involved but it involves choosing groups of motives rather than specific ones.) Human beings are constantly changing; driven by a variety of forces which are more or less transitory. So, we must substitute for that typical product of photographic realism, 'the bourgeois conception of the immutability of the soul', a much more dynamic conception which emphasises the fluidity of human nature. This is why Strindberg's characters are, or appear to be, driven from moment to moment by surges of motives which are constantly rising and dying.

While Zola insisted 'We must admit nothing occult; there are but phenomena and the conditions of phenomena', Strindberg reconciled his naturalistic convictions with his mystical beliefs and his belief in extra-sensory perception. Again, Zola's naturalism is antithetical to expressionism, but Strindberg's is not.[8] Indeed, beneath the numerous theatrical styles he adopted, there is a consistent attitude towards drama which explains the basic continuity of his work. If we compare the foregoing quotations from 'On Modern Drama and Modern Theatre' with the following account of expressionism we shall see that, even in terms of theory, there was no necessary incompatibility between Strindberg's early and later dramatic achievement. 'The weight of the play lies in the lyrical and rhetorical intensity of each scene, condensing the emotions and experiences of a lifetime into moments of utmost significance, which are heaped one upon the other with growing fervour until the climax is reached.'[9]

The reader could be excused for thinking this was a description of *Miss Julie* or *Creditors*. The aims of both Strindbergian naturalism and expressionism were to go beyond the individual example; to capture, in the former, the crucial behaviour of human beings in paradigmatic situations and, in the latter, the flow of a whole reality reflected through a single representative ego. But whatever the route, the goal was the same; the expression of an archetype of some relationship or situation. For this reason, as we shall see, Strindberg was able to combine naturalism, symbolism and expressionism to produce the most emotionally violent of all his later plays: *The*

Dance of Death. We should note too that, in his efforts to dramatise the philosophical and psychological ideas that obsessed him from 1887 to 1892, he diverged even then in important respects from naturalistic practice. The influence of Nietzsche's superman philosophy and contemporary speculation about hypnosis led him to accept the existence of non-naturalistic hierarchies and elites. His interest in psychical phenomena made him employ symbolism to communicate occult ideas. His use of mime, ballet, monologue, incantatory dialogue, dream imagery and suggestion were (to say the least!) additions to Zola's theatrical canon which anticipated his own theatrical experiments at the turn of the century.

STRINDBERG'S MISOGYNY[10]

It is tempting to describe Strindberg as an anti-feminist as though his violent attacks on the female sex were the result of his exasperation with the undue advocacy of women's rights by many of his contemporaries. But while *he* tried to maintain that this was indeed the case, 'You can appreciate that as a creative writer I mix what I imagine with reality and that my hatred of women is completely theoretical, for I wouldn't be able to live without the company of women',[11] neither the tone nor the content of his life and writings support him. Probably only in the stories published in *Getting Married* and to a lesser extent in *Comrades*, did he put forward purely anti-feminist views.

In fact, he was for long periods of his life a misogynist, which is not to say that he was coldly indifferent to women or that he continuously disliked them or even that he did not frequently idolise them. He was that very human hater of whom Arthur Koestler once wrote (in reference to the Trotskyite and the Communist Party), 'he proclaims to all and sundry that his sweetheart is a whore and yet foams with rage at each new proof of it'. His adoration in no way precluded his loathing; indeed, in Strindberg's case, it was virtually a precondition of it. Misogyny is rarely pure or simple, usually it is an highly ambivalent attitude. And certainly, with the exception of his feelings for his children, all Strindberg's emotions displayed a radically contradictory tension. His feelings towards God, the nobility, the lower classes, his work, the future of mankind and even towards himself alternated between extreme love and hatred; extreme optimism and pessimism.

Whether he saw woman as naturalistically or spiritually deter-mined, he usually held to his fundamental conviction that they were generally baser, more cruel and less scrupulous than men. Those intoxicated moments when he was freshly in love were deviations from the norm: occasions when he was so drugged that he tried hysterically to deny his own creed, which was perhaps well expressed in one of his favourite quotations from Chrysostom: 'What is woman? The enemy of friendship, the punishment that cannot be escaped, the necessary evil, the natural temptation, the longed for misery, the fountain of tears which is never dry, the worst master-piece of creation in white and dazzling array. Since even the first woman made a pact with the Devil, how should her daughters not do the same? Created as she was from a crooked rib, her whole mind was awry and turned to evil'. Strindberg liked this description so much that he virtually plagiarised it.

> Woman is to me the earth and all its glory, the bond that binds and of all the evil the worst evil I have seen is the female sex. The hindrance, the hatred, the low calculation, the crudity, above all the inhuman threat to a spirit that wants to grow, to rise. The instinctive meanness as Schopenhauer, the master, says: 'To love a man—to debase him in his own eyes and lift him up in the eyes of the world to meet the needs of her own vanity'.[12]

The *precise* nature of his love affairs was highly ambivalent. His first impulse when meeting a woman was to put her on a pedestal; to transform her from a flesh and blood creature into a frail divinity of innocence and purity far above his reach. By contrast, he felt gross, ugly, coarse and lustful; unworthy of her in every way. So in his fantasies he was able to shift the burden of his contradictory urges on to her idealised image. She became the means by which he could satisfy his desire to flagellate himself and, at the same time, the source of his hope that by association he might aspire to a god-like stature. She was a mother who could comfort him and a graceful virgin whom he could worship. Later in his life, in *A Blue Book*, Strindberg defined these feelings very clearly:

> When I approach a woman as a lover, I look up to her, I see something of the mother in her, and this I respect. I assume a subordinate position, become childish and puerile and actually am

subordinate, like most men . . . Her beauty inspires me, and I have a propensity for beautifying, for seeing more than is there; I put her on a pedestal. She becomes, so to speak, older than I, although she is younger . . .[13]

His physical needs were strong and it was not enough for him to love a woman as a mother and adore her as a female ideal, he must also possess her physically. Unfortunately not even Strindberg could emotionally reconcile mother love, virginal innocence, spiritual adoration and sexual lust. Sooner or later, the tensions between the impossible demands he made of the woman and his sexual guilt feelings would make themselves felt, and she would invariably prove inadequate to his ideal of purity. 'She was no longer the virginal mother with whom I had fallen in love.'[14] If he went on to marry her, the already fatal problems would be exacerbated by the ordinary, day-to-day difficulties of living with a woman (let alone a goddess *manqué!*).

But this description only covers the situation from Strindberg's perspective; it assumes that women are entirely submissive to a man's wishes, which, of course, they rarely are. Both Siri von Essen and Harriet Bosse were actresses who believed that their careers were just as valuable as Strindberg's. Moreover, they were both self-willed and believed that their opinions, and their rights, were as important as his. The mother they were intended to represent soon became for Strindberg not a source of comfort but a force which sought to undermine his manliness. On several occasions he hints that he was periodically impotent and not unnaturally he was predisposed to blame his failures on Siri and Harriet.[15] Thus he found his ideal female companion had turned into a monster and his marriage had become a hell. But, of course, it was not fortuitous that he married aggressive women. They were precisely the kind of dominant females he could grovel before and who would thus feed his sense of personal injustice, and it is clear that either at some murky level of his consciousness or deeper in his unconscious he understood this fact only too well.

Thus Strindberg came to believe that, through sex, man can *initially* be a conqueror but before long woman will exploit his love of the mother to reduce him to the status of a child (compare Tekla and Adolf in *Creditors*). Men resist this at the risk of alienating women's love, losing their children and possibly becoming insane. Marriage, therefore, becomes a battleground in which women fight for their own and their children's interests without any consideration for their husbands. They use men to sire their children and to provide them with an income, then as Laura says in *The Father*: 'You have done your job as a father and a breadwinner. Now you are no longer needed and you can go' (Act 2, Scene 5). Or as Nietzsche put it: 'For the woman, the man is a means: the end is always the child.'[16] If women fail to dominate their husbands, love will turn to hatred and the marriage will disintegrate.

However, there was one temporarily cohesive factor, at least in his first marriage; his deep and usually abiding love of his children. They were for him archetypally innocent, capable of giving and receiving love with complete spontaneity. They did not threaten him, so he could love them and be loved by them without becoming suspicious. For them he was prepared to endure much. Unfortunately though, there was one person to whom the children were more attached even than to himself; their mother. This was not important while the child was a baby but as it grew older and could respond to specific stimuli, Strindberg would become increasingly suspicious of his wife's influence. He would be overcome with panic that she was trying to alienate it from him or was using it to bring him to heel. If a child was nervous in his company or did not quite show him the affection he thought it should, Strindberg would decide that this was the result of his wife's influence. And the more he watched for wifely intrigue, the more the children were likely to feel uncomfortable in his presence. Thus his antagonism towards his wife would precipitate a battle over their children.

The above account of his marital relationships is not intended as a description of his extremely complex personal life or as a complete analysis of his sexual psychology. It is no more than a behavioural model which will serve to explain the literary expression of his misogyny up to his Inferno experiences. To complete the model, we must mention the determined rationale Strindberg gave of his emotions in the form of anti-feminism. The fact that it was essentially a rationale does not mean that Strindberg's views about the place of women in society were not held with fanatical conviction. Nevertheless, these views were the *effects*, of which his personal sexual frustrations were the cause.

From the early 1880s onwards, he saw himself as the lone obstacle to the wave of feminism emanating from the 'famous Norwegian male blue-stocking', Ibsen, whose 'scandalous attacks on the male sex' in *A Doll's House*, a play 'sick like its author',[17] he wished to countercharge in *Comrades* and *The Father*. He was convinced that 'in ten year's time when we shall have these women devils over us with their right to vote and everything, downtrodden men will dig up my trilogy but will not dare to stage it'.[18] The feminist movement was certainly sweeping Scandinavia and Strindberg put himself forward as 'the last man' who 'shall fight as long as I have a nerve left in my body' even 'if they peck me to death'. Because there was a prevailing fashion for women's rights, he was able to dignify what was essentially a response of personal despair as a case of social martyrdom. Strindberg, the noble hero, fighting not merely for his own sanity, but selflessly for the freedom and dignity of *all* men. And, sure enough, before long he was able to play the role in reality when he was socially crucified in the blasphemy proceedings against *Getting Married*.

After the Inferno crisis, his underlying misogyny remained but it was transformed. Physical disgust had always characterised his descriptions of sex but, in his later years, his imagery became more violent and was applied to the whole of human life. Notable examples of his later intermittent aversion to sex which taints love are the Tempter's great speech in *To Damascus*:

> I've never been able to understand how a kiss, that's an unborn word, a soundless speech, a quiet language of the soul, can be exchanged by means of a hallowed procedure for a surgical operation, that always ends in tears and the chattering of teeth. I've never understood how that holy night, the first in which two souls embrace each other in love, can end in the shedding of blood, in quarrelling, hate, mutual contempt and LINT. (p. 266)

and, from an *Occult Diary*:

> It was my soul that loved this woman, and the brutalities of marriage disgusted me. For that matter I have never really been able to understand what the not very elegant act of procreation has to do with love for a beautiful female soul. The organ of love is the same as one of excretory organs. (p. 47)

In the latter quotation we can also detect an idea that was to occupy Strindberg's mind more and more as he grew older; the notion of salvation through a pure woman. This gradually replaced his earlier longing for a mother ideal but ultimately it was to give him no more satisfaction. His disappointments with women (in particular with Harriet) as a source of religious inspiration gave rise to the same anguish and the same longings as his earlier sexual disillusion. Once again the structure of his emotional life and its dependent beliefs was constant; only the content changed as he grew older.

What, then, are we to say of the quality of Strindberg's misogyny as a basis for worthwhile drama? Must we agree with F. L. Lucas that 'It is in Strindberg alone that one finds this hatred for half the human race becoming the obsession of half a lifetime as if he had been possessed by some devil or his bloodstream poisoned by some rabid bacillus, so that he grows both odious and tedious, both boor and bore' (p. 356)? No! Lucas's description is oversimplified and ultimately bigoted, because it does not take note of the despair Strindberg felt about his relationships with women and in later years with man in general. The sense of disgust that accompanied his failure to find a lasting sexual and spiritual companion constitutes a tragic statement of defeat in a man who had so desperately wanted to fulfil himself in heterosexual love. Strindberg could not for long gloat over his misogynistic beliefs. Whatever the virulence of his outbursts, he was constantly aware of his ambivalent attitude to women and struggled to overcome his antagonisms in a loving relationship. While he was always capable of blaming others for his own inadequacies, his bouts of self-deception never destroyed his awareness of his own prejudices and their roots in his childhood. 'If there had been as many girls as boys present in class, innocent friendships probably would have been formed, the electricity would have been carried off, the madonna worship brought within its limits and his false conception of woman would not have followed him and his companions through life' (*Son of A Servant*, p. 55).[19]

Even later when he was giving way to more grandiose feelings, humiliation and pain are apparent beneath the bombastic phrasing.

All women hate Buddhas, maltreat, disturb, humiliate, annoy them with the hatred of inferiors, because they themselves can never become Buddhas. On the other hand, they have an instinctive sympathy for servants, male and female, beggars, dogs, especially mangy ones. They admire swindlers, quack dentists, braggadocios of literature, pedlars of wooden spoons—everything mediocre (quoted by Sprigge in *The Strange Life of August Strindberg*, p. 151)

This is clearly the kind of outburst that Lucas has in mind but its tone is of a man in misery, flailing wildly at an invincible adversary. Perhaps the briefest précis of Strindberg's intolerable dilemma appears in a letter written by his self-portrait, Arvid Falk, in *The Red Room*:[20] 'There was no hell on earth until paradise was completed, that is to say until woman was created' (p. 250). Each of these quotations exposes the painful tensions within Strindberg and affirms the power of his feelings.

Unfortunately Lucas plays on the curious prejudice that misogynistic or even anti-feminine opinions are somehow diseased *a priori*. But the belief that women are more properly objects of hatred or contempt than adoration has a long and respectable literary history, if not social status. And as such it should not be ignored or rejected out of hand. If it is, then the work of the following writers must be repudiated in part or whole since they either despised women or regarded them with lofty contempt: Euripides, Plato, St Paul, St Jerome, John Knox, Milton, Swift, Schopenhauer, Nietzsche, Kafka and Hemingway.

As long as heterosexual relations are confused and difficult, there remains the possibility that we can learn from such men as Strindberg who challenge our premiss that men and women are ideal partners. So long will there be a case for examining the destructive ambitions of each sex as well as their more loving qualities. Although, clearly, there is something compulsive about an attitude that condemns all women on the basis of a narrow personal experience, statistical assessments of the plausibility of misogynistic attitudes miss the point. Most men, including Strindberg, who come to see women as corruptive forces in human society do so for psychological reasons, not because they have completed a programme of empirical or market research. They oppose the *idea* of women thrown up by their needs and fears and perhaps confirmed by their jaundiced experience rather than that of *all* women as such. Whether or not we shall value this idea and their reaction to it will depend upon the skill with which they are both developed to throw light on human psychology and human behaviour.

Strindberg's sexual views are finally interesting because of the fine dramatic portraits that issued from them in such plays as *The Father, Miss Julie, The Dance of Death, Creditors* and *To Damascus*. His personal integrity in respect of the female sex is redeemed by the fact that, although he frequently gave way to the most hysterical abuse, he never ceased, throughout his life, to fight his prejudices and to try to conquer the sense of insecurity which gave rise to them. And that unending personal struggle is at once a key to his artistic greatness and the source of a lasting paradigm of human sexual relationships:

Philosophical Influences[21]

Schopenhauer, Kierkegaard and Nietzsche have influenced the course of Western literature more than any other nineteenth-century philosophers.[22] Either directly or indirectly their writings have been sources of inspiration for artists of all types and nationalities. Even today their ideas can still be discerned in novels, plays, poems and literary theories. In view of the continuity of their influence, it would be strange if their relevance to Strindberg's work was limited to his pre-Inferno period. Actually, their vision of the world struck a chord in him which resounded sometimes softly, sometimes deafeningly throughout his life.[23] Essentially, the lasting appeal of these irrationalists to Strindberg owed less to the details of their philosophical doctrines than to the nature of their own characters and personal problems. Between them they characterised and tried to answer the discontents and demands that tormented Strindberg almost every day of his life. For this reason the general structure of their beliefs will simply be outlined and only their points of similarity with Strindberg will be emphasised.

Unfortunately the cases of Schopenhauer and Kierkegaard are problematical. Although Strindberg read them both when he was young, their most striking influence is on his post-Inferno work. Their significance in his earlier work is either oblique and partial or is most striking in his prose or historical writings. In view of this, the discussion of their general ideas will be delayed to the second part of this book (i.e. Chapter 5). Here, their thought will simply be examined peripherally to fill out the ideas he derived from the naturalists, from Nietzsche and from contemporary 'psychology'.

NIETZSCHE (1844–1900)

Strindberg's intellectual debt to Nietzsche is clear but the date and source of his acquaintance with the German's writings must be defined with care. Although Strindberg did not read *Thus Spake Zarathustra*, according to Harold Borland,[24] he did read reports of Brandes's lectures on Nietzsche in *Politiken* of 17, 18 and 25 April, and 2 and 9 May 1888. He also read *Jenseits Von Gut und Bose*, *Menschliches Allzumenschliches, Der Fall Wagner* and *Götzendämmerung*. Borland sums up as follows: 'There does not seem to be sufficent evidence to show Strindberg had first-hand knowledge of *Zarathustra*. No doubt he had good second-hand knowledge of the work through Brandes and Ola Hansson. Brandes, in his lectures, had given an exciting introduction to Nietzsche's prose poem and Ola Hansson's ecstatic Nietzsche essay had a particularly hectic section on *Zarathustra*. But however impressive these reports, they must be regarded as a poor substitute for personal experience of the original' (p. 20). A point worth making as an extension of Borland's remarks is that Nietzsche's ideas were very much in the air throughout Europe after the mid-eighties. Ola Hansson, Georg Brandes and Heidenstam all became acquainted with Nietzsche's work in the 1880s and Carlyle, Emerson, Max Nordau and de Tocqueville had earlier propagated ideas which were in various respects similar to those of the German philosopher. Moreover, Dostoievsky's novels *Crime and Punishment, The Possessed, Notes from the Underground* and *The Brothers Karamazov*, all written by 1880, contain almost clairvoyant statements (and criticisms) of Nietzsche's views on the Death of God, Slave and Master Moralities, the Superman and the Will to Power. In view of this, it seems inconceivable that a modernist and polymath like Strindberg would not have come into day-to-day contact with such ideas as the Superman philosophy, eternal recurrence, the will to power, the 'death of God' and the slave mentality.

Nietzsche's influence on *Creditors* is direct, on *The Father* and *Miss Julie* second-hand and in other cases vicarious, through the writer Max Nordau who despite his vicious attacks on Nietzsche's ideas produced an elitist psychology that strikingly resembled that of the philosopher. Without dogmatically asserting direct influence, it can be argued that there are four chapters of Part One of *Zarathustra* which are most helpful to a study of Strindberg's pre-Inferno sexual attitudes and rationalisations; 'Of Chastity', 'Of the Friend', 'Of Old and Young Women' and 'Of Marriage and Children'. Others though have gone further, so that Elizabeth Sprigge can write 'Nietzsche had finally destroyed Strindberg's first marriage.'[25]

In what obviously must be a schematic presentation of Nietzsche's philosophy, we can follow through seven of its central ideas which are relevant to an understanding of Strindberg's plays. With the *Death of God* which Nietzsche notoriously announced, teleological meaning and absolution sanctions of morality are removed from the universe. We can no longer find any justification for the Christian conformist ethic which demands human obedience and humility. Instead we can see men as they really are; ambitious egoists trying in their various ways to dominate each other. Here we can detect Schopenhauer's influence on Nietzsche (and on Strindberg). He, too, portrayed life as a source of unceasing conflict: 'the life of the individual is a constant struggle, and not merely a metaphorical one against want or boredom, but also an actual struggle against other people'.[26]

For Nietzsche, the majority of mankind is characterised by a *slave mentality*. This is an ethic of resentment which rejects new experience and inhibits man's creative drive. Its principle qualities are subservience, meanness, sympathy, timidity and humility. It is the morality of the herd that tries to impose its values on all men through Christianity. Socialism and democracy are its typical socio-political forms. Kierkegaard exhibits a similar distaste for moral systems, which seek to impose uniformity on human beings, whether they are expressed by the Established Church or by the State. For him, they involve an intrusion between the witnessing individual and his God; for Nietzsche, a restraint on the free man's self-expression.

Since the *Death of God*, Nietzsche maintained, the slave ethic has become increasingly untenable. Hereafter, each man of worth must begin to create his own values and meanings by taking control of his world (as must Kierkegaard's religious man). If he is to achieve true stability and fulfil his creative potential, man must forget his old morality and devise a new basis for authority. 'Indeed, who can feel with me what it means to feel with every shred of one's being that the weight of all things must be defined anew.'²⁷ Christianity must be rejected and man must become his own god; the slave morality must be replaced by the *Master Morality*. This will grow out of a triumphant assertion of oneself and will say 'yes' to life and to new experience. To the slave, it will appear terrifying because it will be individualistic and challenging. Its virtues will be generosity, independence, imagination and self-reliance. Ultimately its embodiment will be in the new man of the future, *the Superman*. As the end product of human striving, he will transcend good and evil, but, even so, will not turn away from this world (as the Christian hero does). He will accept life in all its tedium, but will distinguish himself by escaping from the enervating effects of life's most definitive characteristic, *Eternal Recurrence*. Nietzsche agreed with Schopenhauer that life was, for the vast majority, a tedious affair but whereas the latter saw this as an inevitable consequence of the Will to Live, Nietzsche blamed it on eternal recurrence.

Life without God is irrevocably transient; an eternal, repetitive cycle without purpose or meaning. Realisation of this fact is supremely enervating; Zarathustra calls it 'my most abysmal thought', for it applies to the great man as unavoidably as it does to the mediocre. It is an intolerable burden which endlessly affirms man's finitude and lack of values. In this respect Nietzsche's concept is entirely different from Kierkegaard's. The latter maintained that 'Repetition is and remains a religious category.'²⁸ For the aesthetic man, who is concerned with transitory pleasures, life is a process of continual change and the past is irretrievable. Repetition for him is a pointless series of fleeting, discrete instants. Since this does not involve personal fulfilment, it produced despair. By contrast, repetition in the life of the religious man is forward looking. It enables him to grasp the continuity of his existence; his 'becoming'. Spiritual repetition is transcendent and eternal because it brings man face to face with himself before God. Thus Kierkegaardian Repetition is eminently desirable.

Yet recurrence also has a positive value for Nietzsche. It serves to define the Superman because only he has the strength to accept the endless cycle of being enthusiastically and without recourse to illusory hopes. The means by which he is able to do this is through his *Will to Power*. 'What is good?—all that heightens the feeling of power, the will to power, power itself in man. What is bad?—All that proceeds from weakness. What is happiness?—The feeling that power increases—that a resistance is overcome.'[29] For Nietzsche, this will is the ceaseless process of becoming; the drive by which (in a typically existentialist sense) man creates his own essence. The Superman achieves freedom by self-assertion; the Kierkegaardian religious man, by a leap of faith to God. Like Schopenhauer's destructive Will To Live, the Will To Power characterises all reality. 'The World is Will to Power and nothing else', though it is epitomised in the Superman. *Unlike* Schopenhauer's Will which is responsible for all human suffering, Nietzsche's Will is the source of his escape. Through it, the Superman organises the chaos of his passions, transcends feelings of resentment towards life and, by rising above the masses, fulfils his potential. In this way he creates his own being and he destroys the stifling, cosy image that the ordinary man cherishes of himself.

How exactly does the Superman's Will to Power transfigure the pain of Eternal Recurrence? He accomplishes this by using his will to overcome *himself* rather than others; he strives for power over his own nature and once achieved this will automatically give him power over others. The means by which he accomplishes this is *Sublimation*; that is he transforms his animal passions into the highest human qualities. 'Once you had passions and called them evil. But now you have only your virtues: they grew out of your passions. You laid your highest aim in the heart of these passions: then they become your virtues and joys. And though you came from the race of the hot tempered or of the lustful or the fanatical or of the revengeful: at last your passions have become virtues and all your devils angels. Once you had fierce dogs in your cellar: but they changed at last into birds and sweet singers. From your poison you brewed your balm: you milked your cow affliction—now you drink the sweet milk of her udder.'[30] This is why the Superman is characterised by the strength of his passions; the stronger the sublimated drives, the greater the final achievement (cf. Gustav in *Creditors* or at least the author's initial image of him).

Since everything is endless repetition, there is no purpose to (or God in) the universe and man's state of being becomes everything. The Superman's goal therefore lies within himself; the meaning of life is for each man to become the end and purpose of Eternal

Recurrence. Thus the Superman aspires to be the supreme combination of intellect, character, creativity and physical perfection. 'The Roman Caesar with Christ's soul'; Goethe and Napoleon in one. While Kierkegaard would have rejected Nietzsche's irreligion, he would have supported his emphasis on the role of the individual. He too believed that man had to create his own essence (though not as a Superman) and that he must do this alone in a *personal* dialogue with his God. Social, political, even religious props must be rejected in favour of a journey into self towards the Divine.

Once the Superman fulfils his potential and realises that the will to power is the essence of life, a *Transvaluation of Values* occurs; that is, values are firmly reconstructed on the basis of man's freely asserted will. Although individual moral precepts might not change, they are now based on entirely new attitudes and spring from entirely new motives. Thus these new values, which issue from the Superman's unique vigour and power, will provide him with a new sense of purpose in his life and so enable him to transcend the miseries of eternal recurrence. Nietzsche envisaged the transvaluation as involving the replacement of Christian norms with a Greek individualistic ethic.

Strindberg develops (distorts!) Nietzsche's philosophy by importing into it three other doctrines which obsessed him in the late eighteen eighties; Darwinian evolutionism, anti-feminism and the battle of brains formulated in various psychical terms. Nietzsche's thought can be *made* to accommodate the last two notions but not Darwinism without definite distortion. While Nietzsche was undoubtedly influenced by evolutionism, Darwin was one of his *bêtes noires*. He firmly rejected Darwin's emphasis on external circumstances; changes for Nietzsche stem from the Superman's inner potential. The notion of eternal recurrence, too, as interpreted by Nietzsche is strictly incompatible with biological evolution; the former is pointlessly repetitive, the latter is characterised by adaptive change. Nor did he believe that natural selection favours the strong; indeed the masses, by objectifying their slave mentality in established institutions, usually triumph and destroy all that is worthwhile in human kind.

It was by identifying the Superman as a higher stage of a makeshift Darwinian evolution, particularly in *Creditors* and the Quart d'Heures plays, that Strindberg transgressed both the spirit and letter of Nietzsche's beliefs. Without specifically intending to do so, R. J. Hollingdale perfectly sums up Strindberg's error in this respect: 'Undoubtedly the word [Übermensch] was not well chosen, because it led to the misconception of the Superman on Darwinian lines: as a form of life destined to supersede man as man has superseded the ancestor he has in common with the apes Nietzsche specifically repudiated this interpretation in *Ecce Homo*—but he is none the less responsible for it.'[31] In particular, this confusion has involved paying homage to Lamarckism and Strindberg is no exception in this respect.

While Martin Lamm is mistaken in regarding Nietzsche's Superman as simply an instinctive predator,[32] he is certainly correct in contrasting him with Strindberg's conception of the new man. Strindberg's Superman is narrowly intellectual; Nietzsche's represents the whole man. Nietzsche was, in fact, anti-intellectual in his prejudices. In many respects Strindberg's ideal human being is a far less appealing figure and curiously lacking in obvious dramatic potential. His Superman was a somewhat unemotional character; at best a sufferer, far from the joyous creation of Nietzsche. Indeed in a play like *Pariah* the superhuman X is almost an automaton. This appeal of the disciplined, cerebral genius was almost certainly an attraction of opposites; Strindberg projected himself in this role as a wish fulfilment. It was something he could not even approximate in life. Fortunately, in his more profoundly realised plays, his own uncertainties intruded and, instead of cerebral superman or the godlike creatures of Nietzschean mythology, he produced profound characters with superhuman ambitions such as Gustav in *Creditors*.

So far as anti-feminism was concerned, Strindberg found an approximate confirmation of his personal prejudices in both Schopenhauer and Nietzsche. If we compare the following quotations from the two philosophers with any number of the misogynistic outbursts of Strindberg quoted throughout this book we can see this.

Schopenhauer

'Women remain children all their lives, never see anything but what is closest to them, cleave to the present moment, take appearance for reality and prefer trifles to most important affairs.'[33]

'. . . the fundamental defect of the female character is a lack of a sense of justice. This originates first and foremost in their want of rationality and capacity for reflexion, but it is strengthened by the fact that, as the weaker sex, they are driven to rely not on force but on cunning: hence their instinctive subtlety and ineradicable tendency to tell lies.'[34]

'Only a male intellect clouded by the sexual drive could call the stunted, narrow shouldered, broad hipped and short legged sex, the fair sex: for it is with this drive that all its beauty is bound up. More fittingly than the fair sex, women could be called the unaesthetic sex.'[35]

Nietzsche

'In a woman's love is injustice and blindness towards all that she does not love. And in the enlightened love of a woman, too, there is still the unexpected attack and lightning and night, along with the light. Woman is not yet capable of friendship: women are still cats and birds. Or, at best, cows.'[36]

'Let man fear woman when she hates: for man is at the bottom of his soul only wicked, but woman is base . . . The man's happiness is: I will. The woman's happiness is: He will.'[37]

'Ah, this poverty of soul in partnership! Ah, this filth of soul in partnership! Ah, this miserable ease in partnership! All this they call marriage; and they say their marriages are made in Heaven. Well I do not like it, this Heaven of the superfluous! No, I do not like them, these animals caught in the heavenly net.'[38] Strindberg might have made any of these remarks at various stages of his life, and particularly from 1885 to 1892.

At least from *Creditors* onwards to the Inferno crisis, Strindberg used semi-Nietzschean and Darwinian ideas as a loose framework to accommodate the 'psychological' ideas of Charcot's Paris school and Bernheim's Nancy school.[39] Charcot used hypnosis for therapeutic purposes but his main interests were neurological. He investigated the neurological symptoms of hysteria but showed little concern with its psychological implications. He rejected the view that hypnosis was a form of suggestion and tried to design experiments showing that hypnotic induction may be elicited without verbal contacts. Moreover, he drew parallels between hypnotic trances and hysterical states which may have contributed to the dramatic development of Miss Julie's breakdown. Clearly what makes her susceptible to hypnosis is her unstable emotional condition; though as an example of hypnosis or auto-hypnosis her final exit hardly conforms to Charcot's model.

Bernheim, on the other hand, was concerned with maintaining that hypnosis was merely extreme suggestibility induced by artificial means. His emphasis was psychical whereas Charcot's was physiological. Suggestion was seen as a means of exposing the spiritual lives of men and the vicious battle of brains that takes place beneath the camouflage of social compromise. In *De la Suggestion* (1884), Bernheim argued that hypnosis was a normal phenomenon which could be regulated completely by psychological factors. Again, before the Convention of the French Association for the Advancement of Sciences in 1883, he stated: 'To obtain these suggestive phenomena (without sleep), I do not need to hollow my voice with an authoritative tone, nor flash my eyes to overwhelm my subjects: I talk to them very simply, smiling, and obtain the effects, not from people deprived of their will, but from well-balanced individuals, who reason well, who make full use of their own will, some of them even revealing a spirit of insubordination.' All individuals it was claimed, could be hypnotised, though in varying degrees. This was important to Strindberg since it allowed him to extend Bernheim's views to everyday social intercourse (cf. Gustav's hypnotising of Adolf in *Creditors*).

Max Nordau went even further than Bernheim by arguing in *Paradoxes*[40] (1885) that suggestion has a physiological basis; being a transfer of molecular movements between the brains involved. In a way that was quite compatible with Nietzschean thought Nordau contended that there was an aristocracy of intellect exercised through suggestion. Strindberg very probably took many of his views about the Superman from Chapter Five of *Paradoxes*, 'The Psycho-Physiology of Genius and Talent'. Nordau puts forward an evolutionary elitism that is quite compatible with Nietzsche's ideas as interpreted by Strindberg. 'Each step of progress that humanity makes is the work of some man of genius who performs for his race the same services that the chief brain centres perform for the individual' (p. 187). The exceptional man manipulates the masses: 'The man of genius it is who thinks, judges, wills and acts for humanity at large' (p. 187); the ordinary man is totally passive. 'The general mass of mankind does nothing else but imitate the man of genius; it merely repeats what the man of genius has done in a better way' (p. 187). The means by which such elitist domination takes place in cerebral, '... the individual of more perfect develop- operates by way of *suggestion* on him that is of a less perfect type' (p. 195).

Strindberg defined his own position in regard to these various theories in the essay 'The Battle of Brains': 'Dr Charcot assumes the possibility of suggestion only in hypnotised hysterics; Dr Bernheim goes somewhat further and admits that all who may be hypnotised are susceptible to suggested ideas ... Without being a professional or an authority, I seem to have found that suggestion is only the stronger brain's struggle with and victory over the weak and that this procedure is applied unconsciously in everyday life ... All political, religious, literary controversies appear to me only to be a question of the individual's or the party's struggle to attempt to impose the suggestion ... which is nothing but the struggle for power, but that of the brains nowadays since the physical battle is becoming obsolescent.'[41]

As he portrays it in the pre-Inferno plays, however, this battle is more than orthodox social manoeuvring, it is a life or death struggle: '... one now creates a majority against him i.e. the victim, converts him, exposes his intentions, attributes to him different intentions from those he actually has, deprives him of his means of subsistence, denies him his social standing, ridicules him, in one word tortures and slanders him to death or drives him mad instead of killing him.'[42] By means of hypnosis, superior will power and suggestion his characters wage deadly wars to show off their super- human abilities.

The outcome of the battle of brains is not seen by him as merely the triumph of one will over another; it is a physical conquest. So Strindberg goes further than Bernheim and Charcot towards the more bizarre ideas of Nordau. In *Creditors*, Gustav by force of his intellect hypnotises Adolf into having an epileptic attack, the vampire characters drain their victims of physical energy and the power to concentrate, while the supermen reduce the weak to little more than puppets in their hands. In *Pariah*, X totally crushes the criminal Y and, in *Simoon*, Biskra by force of will and suggestion so hypnotises Guimard that he dies of fear. While these ideas of Strindberg are undoubtedly odd and even dangerous, they can best be understood in an evolutionary framework. What he was saying in an extreme dramatic form was that the higher man would evolve as a result of the struggle between human beings at social and personal levels. And when the Superman appeared he would be characterised by superior cerebral power which would enable him to control his fellows by a variety of psychological means. His success would depend, ultimately, upon his intelligence, his strength of will, his ruthlessness and his capacity to adapt to a wide range of social pressures (cf. Gustav in *Creditors* and Madame X in *The Stronger*).

In practice, Strindberg's fascination with psychical phenomena during this period of his life more often than not resulted in the intrusion of theory upon art. So far as the quality of his drama was concerned the consequences were often unhappy. He was convinced that he himself possessed extra-sensory abilities[48] and often they were sources of terror and shame for him. Increasingly he became convinced that if he used them, supernatural Powers would take their revenge upon him in some way or other. 'By playing with those mysterious powers out of pure folly I had given the reins to my evil desires, but they, guided by the hand of the unseen, had struck at my own heart' (*Inferno*, pp.58–9). So, whenever he wished to hint at something too bizarre to contemplate, he found refuge in such resources. Telepathy, hypnotism and clairvoyance evoked huge responses in him and he appears to have asumed that they would have the same paralysing effect on everyone else. This is why, often, when he employed them in his plays, they appear as crude devices which explain little other than the mechanics of his own intelligence. For example, the inclusion of hypnotism and suggestion in *Miss Julie*, whatever his intentions, functions as means to *avoid* explanation.

2

Two Early Plays

LUCKY PETER'S TRAVELS (1882)

Strindberg's earliest fairy play was clearly inspired by Ibsen's *Peer Gynt*, though it is none the worse for that. While not of the stature of the Norwegian masterpiece, it is still an interesting play. Its light-hearted irony and optimism together with the indulgent affection of the author for its hedonistic young protagonist, distinguish it from Strindberg's later essays in the genre, *The Keys of Heaven, Swanwhite* and *The Bridal Crown*.

Lucky Peter's Travels[1] dramatises the gradual education through experience of a young man who learns to conquer his own egotism and escape from man's hypocrisy by devoting himself to selfless love and hard work. A motto for the play, as well as a description of its central character's progress, could be taken from the closing words of Strindberg's autobiographical novel *The Son of a Servant*: 'Sensitivity to pressure. That's why he tried to lessen this pressure first by rising in the world and secondly by criticising and exposing the higher level to show that it was not so high, and consequently not worth striving for. So he stepped out into the world! To evolve, change, develop—and yet to remain for ever the same as he was' (p. 204).

The play betrays a variety of artistic influences. Maurice Valency[2] has suggested a number of sources including Wagner's *The Flying Dutchman, Candide* and the Prologue and Book IV of *The Decameron*. More obviously the first act with its Scrooge-like Old Man, its tableaux of Christmas scenes, its spirits of good and evil and its optimistic hero reflects the influence of Dickens's *A Christmas Carol* and Hans Andersen's fairy tales. In fact, Strindberg wrote the play very much with children in mind and, like Dickens, he employed exaggerated contrasts, magical transformations and grotesqueries to appeal to a youthful audience.

When we first encounter Peter, he is an innocent but eager for experience and pleasure. His misanthropic father has locked him up in the Church tower 'to protect him from the evils and temptations of men', but Peter does not understand this. In his eyes his father is just being spiteful and dictatorial, so when the malevolent Hobgoblin persuades the fairy Godmother to release him into the wicked world Peter is elated. However he soon discovers that worldly pleasures pall and that even the most beautiful flower has thorns. As he carelessly throws himself into life, nothing seems to live up to his expectations. This is Kierkegaard's aesthetic stage. Before long he declares that simple pleasures 'are quite good, but not as good as I expected' and inevitably quite soon more sophisticated vices begin to attract him. He is unable to accept the faithful Lisa's advice, 'Do not always believe your eyes Peter', 'Everything is imperfect in this life Peter. Remember that and take the bad with the good.' His nature and youth do not admit of caution. He is eager for the experiences that have long been denied him, 'The devil take the bad. I want the good' (Act 2 Scene 3). He thinks he knows what he wants and is determined to get it. Like Peer Gynt (another Kierkegaardian character) he is an outright egoist and is in danger of pursuing a life of naive amoralism.

Faced with the choice between men and nature, he chooses the former; the creators of sin. His decision is the prerogative of youth which has yet to encounter social corruption. No matter how much good advice an inexperienced youth like Peter is given, he will only learn the lessons of life by living it and living it involves experiencing both good and evil. What particularly bores Peter about Nature is that for all its beauty, it is static. 'Don't the trees stand in the same place as they did fifty years ago and won't they stand there for another fifty years ... I want to see movement and hear noise' (Act 2 Scene 3). Youthful vigour demands of life a corresponding vitality; so Peter prepares to enjoy 'Palaces and dishes and wine, and horses and carriages and servants and gold, gold.'

With the aid of his magic ring he creates an opulent mansion for himself but even there he finds his will to pleasure obstructed by the demands of etiquette. Moreover, his new-found wealth is threatened by the Tax Collector; even money brings responsibilities and anxieties. So Peter learns his first lesson about human society, 'Etiquette, taxes, taking the case, keeping house and street clean, hunger and thirst—if that is the lot of the rich man, then I had rather be a street-sweeper' (Act 2 Scene 7). To comfort himself, he summons up a Lady Friend, who proceeds to cajole him, and two male Friends who gluttonously devour his food and squabble mendaciously among themselves. Their friendship is shallow, sycophantic and unreliable. As soon as they have got his gold, they lose interest in him. Worst of all is the Lady Friend who seduces him in order to steal his ring. As a result, he discovers that gold, friendship and women are worthless. Even life itself seems 'thoroughly rotten'. But just as he curses everything Lisa returns to prove to him that 'It is in times of need that we find our friends' (Act 2 Scene 14). With this proof of true friendship as comfort he can at last leave his youth behind and become a man. Ostensibly he begins to seek happiness in the right places; that is, by helping his fellow men rather than by pursuing his own selfish interests. This is Kierkegaard's ethical stage. Lisa acts as his Solveig, comforting him in sorrow and encouraging him to face the reality of life, instead of escaping into fantasy.

Then, in Act 3 fantasy takes over as a Pillory converses with a Statue. These are symbols through which the dual representatives of social order, the Law and the Government, are exposed as corrupt. Social honours and institutions are revealed as shams behind which each man uses society for his own advantage. Peter learns that even a dedicated social reformer who puts general welfare before his own will be persecuted. By a series of absurd economic arguments, Peter's conscientious attempts to improve the town's paving facilities are misrepresented by the powers that be as a threat to the working man's livelihood. Democracy, it appears, rarely works in favour of the dynamic forces in society because the reformer must oppose the powerful minority interests of those capitalists who benefit from the poverty of the masses. And this is a struggle he cannot win. The rulers will misrepresent the reformer and mislead public opinion about him. So Peter is pilloried for his efforts because government is corrupt and concerned only with preserving its own privileges, while the public is gullible and mindless.

To ensure that he learns from his mistakes and does not sink once again into apathetic hedonism, Lisa appears before the pillory in the guise of an Old Woman. She points out that he has become famous as a great reformer but still he is not happy. Honour and glory are as empty as all other human values. In reply, Peter totally rejects capitalist society. Lisa agrees but insists that it can be reformed for the good of all, though apparently Peter is not the right man for the job, unless, perhaps, he acquires Power. Consequently, having rejected democratic reform, Peter next aspires to be a benevolent dictator. But he still has much to learn because he desires more to be great himself than to do good for others.

To experience the fruits of power, Peter goes to the Orient where he becomes a Caliph, though both his lineage and his conversion to Mohammedanism are sham. There he is told that 'it is not fitting for a ruler to be selfish, he must in all respects sacrifice his private interests and tastes to the public welfare' (Act 4 Scene 3). In Peter's eyes 'Life is cruel indeed; Always demanding, but never giving.' So despite all his 'sacrifices', he discovers that his power is limited since the Caliph has no legislative function. Even his contact with the people is indirect, for ruling 'is done in writing'. Real power resides with the government. A Caliph is merely a figure-head surrounded by sycophants who praise him in order to distract his attention from matters of state. Even history itself is manufactured to satisfy the needs of the court. And when Peter is presented with a bride, she is not Lisa whom he loves but a consort chosen for purely economic reasons. Disgusted with the hypocrisy of his position, Peter quits the court to 'go out into nature among my people and see if there does not exist some honesty and honour' (Act 4 Scene 8).

On the seashore, among thrown-up wreckage, Peter surveys the debris of his own life. Here at last he feels free from the contaminating influence of human relationships. His initial desire for human intercourse has been satiated, and he seeks peace in Nature, which he had once rejected. But just as he rests he is menaced by the very elements he embraces. Wild beasts and sea monsters attack him ['Ha nature, you too are a wild beast' (Act 4 Scene 9)]. Horrified, he pleads for Death which, to his surprise and alarm, appears. Unnerved by the confrontation, Peter decides he is not yet ready to depart from life; he still has hope. He meets a Wise Man who tells him that until he has married a faithful wife, his father will not be able to die in peace. Unknown to Peter this Wise Man is his father in disguise.[3] In a flash, Peter understands the reason for his father's apparent hardness of heart. While the Old Man might have been mistaken in trying to cocoon Peter, he was not cruel for he had the boy's best interests at heart. Equally importantly, Peter realises that he truly loves Lisa. At this relatively early date, Strindberg could not only postulate but believe in the ideal of happiness through women. So with hope, love and understanding in his heart, Peter can challenge even the ocean which separates him from Lisa. Never again was Strindberg to have such total confidence in heterosexual relationships.

Act 5 portrays Peter's return to home and contentment. The supernatural forces, represented by the Fairy and the Hobgoblin, feel responsible for his recent misanthropy and decide to engineer a happy ending. Experience has made Peter less self-seeking but, as Lisa says, he will not be a mature, worthwhile human being until he has 'shown that he could make a sacrifice for something other than himself . . . the most we can give for a cause is our dear regard for ourselves; and that the higher powers demand' (Act 5 Scene 2). To facilitate this sacrifice Peter finally learns the truth about his life from his own Shadow. He is informed that he has never experienced real life but has merely pursued his own dreams which have been exposed as illusions. He must learn to face life as it is, not as he would wish it to be. Only hard work and involvement can bring rewards. To attempt to be a saint or a reformer is arrogant, for 'it is not our virtues but our faults that makes us men' (Act 5 Scene 4). With the advice that it is impossible for a man to be complete without a woman, Peter is able to turn his back on his youthful vanities, and endure the evil in life for the sake of the good. He confesses to Lisa that he no longer loves himself above all else and so is redeemed by his love for her. Now he understands that love is man's greatest possession and social (selfless!) obligation his highest duty.

So ends this highly didactic piece which combines moral exhortation with social criticism and a psychological understanding of human vanities. In addition there is a seam of broad satire running through it which attacks religious martyrs (cf. the vanity in their own suffering of St Laurentius and St Bartholomew), religious observances (Act 4 Scene 3), lyric poetry (Act 4 Scene 4) and sycophantic poets and courtiers who indulge in empty rhetoric to gain their ends. Act 3 is particularly impressive. With its social criticism, its use of didactic song, its characters defined by their social roles, their suitability for being played with masks, and its use of dramatic metaphor for comic, critical and alienatory purposes, it can be seen as one of many precursors of Brechtian epic theatre.

Throughout the play Strindberg employs a variety of techniques to express his early socialist views, as later he embodied Swedenborgianism in the fairy play *Swanwhite*. These socialist principles were initially deeply held, stemming from the fantasies he wove around his mother's inferior social status, but they did not survive long into his maturity.

Beneath the surface of *Lucky Peter's Travels* there is much of the bitterness against Swedish society that is so evident in the novels, *Son of a Servant*, and *Red Room*. What differentiates it from them is the coherence and skill with which he manages to parallel serious social criticism with almost lighthearted fantasy, all within the form of a young man's search for his mature identity in the world. As such the career of Peter serves as an allegory of youthful error as well as of the corruption of human society. It is an early example of his 'wanderer' plays and pioneers the circular dramatic structure which was to become so important later. And yet with its richness of imagery and scene, its vigorous development, its humour and general gaiety, it remains eminently entertaining. Nor is it weighted down with the religious seriousness that marks Strindberg's later fairy plays. All of this makes it difficult to explain why it is so rarely performed; although it is far from profound, and the character of Lisa, which needs to be more than an allegorical device, is lifelessly pure, the play as a whole is theatrically appealing.

COMRADES (1886–7)

In contrast with the three great naturalistic plays which startle an audience by their emotional power and the virulence of their characters' attitudes, *Comrades*[4] is a relatively restrained statement of Strindberg's views about the sexes. This is not to say that it is not seriously intended, characteristically prejudiced or even bitterly personal; it is all of these. But it exhibits an emotional control, almost a subordination of dramatic feeling to the communication of social and sexual ideas, that Strindberg could not have produced a year or so later.[5] Nevertheless, despite its undoubted quality, this does not make it a better play than say *The Father*.

Comrades is less an attack on women and married life than a condemnation of *modern* woman (the blue-stocking) and her emancipated ideas concerning sexual equality. At one level, it can be interpreted as a reply to Ibsen's *A Doll's House*. Strindberg implies that too often women confuse sexual equality with their identity as women, with the result that the delicately contrasted balance between a man and a woman, which finds its most perfect consummation in marriage, is degraded into either a passionless commercial transaction or a competitive union of 'equals'. In view of this theme, we can describe *Comrades* as an anti-feminist rather than as a misogynistic play.

To argue his case Strindberg takes the marriage of two young artists. Axel and Bertha have arranged their relationship on the basis of complete equality. They are 'comrades' rather than lovers and they have rejected the traditional roles of the sexes in favour of a shared total experience. But by the time we are introduced to them, equality has been replaced by female exploitation, freedom by licence and unity by rivalry. The fundamental reason for this rests with Bertha whose ambition, egged on by the arch blue-stocking Abel, has led her to exploit Axel's affection and tolerance for her own egotistical purposes. As a result, he finds himself menaced by a dangerous conspiracy of women, which is exacerbated by Bertha's increasing egotism, her willingness to help Mrs Hall and her intrigues with the maid.

Strindberg assumes that while men may enjoy the fruits of comradeship heterosexual relationships, if they are not disciplined by the duties of marriage and the responsibilities of children, will be motivated by feelings of jealousy, pride and even hatred. Once women are allowed to become emancipated blue-stockings with their short hair and 'progressive' ideas, they lose all their femininity and aspire to be the masters of men. As Doctor Ostermark says, marriage involves compromise, which usually means that men have to give in to the demands of women.

When the play opens, Axel still believes his own propaganda: 'We have arranged a sort of comradeship, you see, and friendship is higher and more enduring than love.' This trust even extends to Axel allowing Bertha to use a naked male model. Such ideas awakened the prude in Strindberg despite his proclaimed freethinking during this period of his life. Yet, even in his servitude, Axel can see the way the women are threatening him and it is this essential realism that enables him eventually to triumph over Bertha —'It may seem strange, but to me it's as if you women were intruding and plundering where we have fought for so long while you sat by the fire.'⁶ His agreeing to adopt a 'modern', liberated attitude towards his marriage is inspired more by generosity than by stupidity. And it is his goodness that Bertha finds so insufferable, not his masculinity. It is an indication of his commonsense that when Bertha's calumny is finally revealed, he is not particularly surprised but prepares skilfully to regain control. Early on he senses the snare into which women have drawn him: 'I feel that what you people are saying is false, but I haven't the time or energy to answer you now, but there is an answer!' Yet he is always in contact with reality and when the occasion to act comes, he knows what he must do. 'But you wait if only I free my hands, I'll get out my knife and cut the meshes of your net!'

For a time, Axel and Bertha's tensions are expressed vicariously through their mutual ambition to have a painting exhibited at the Academy. Bertha is intelligent enough to understand this and to realise that when the choice of paintings is made, 'things won't be right between Axel and me again'. While she is jealous of Axel, he wishes only to help her, even to the extent of submitting his own superior work in her name. But despite this magnanimous and somewhat incredible gesture, the strife of competition destroys their comradeship. Axel's sacrifices in the long run count for nothing, because men and women can never be comrades.

> A comrade is a more or less loyal competitor, we are enemies. You women have been lying down in the rear while we attacked the enemy. And now, when we have set and supplied the table, you pounce upon it as if you were in your own home.⁷

In Act 2 the conflict between them reaches a climax. The role of catalyst to this already unstable mixture is filled by the blue-stocking, probably lesbian, Abel, who smokes, has short hair, speaks French and hates men. Simply to cause trouble which she hopes will degrade him further, she tells Axel that he has become like a woman in his own home. 'You beg money from her and she puts you under her guardianship.' But although she is antagonistic to men, Abel is no Machiavelli. She is just confused as all aggressive women must be, according to Strindberg, because they are cut off from their natural social and domestic functions. However, Abel and Bertha are determined 'to tame him so that he'd come back crawling'. To this end, they insult him by ridiculing his paintings and dressing him as a woman; humiliations it is difficult to imagine Axel tolerating. Even their aggression is cowardly. Bertha wishes to destroy him and yet by assuming the mantle of Pilate wants to remain innocent of the doing of it. Significantly, such fastidiousness does not characterise her dealings with the less formidable Willmer whom she has encouraged and can repulse with typical crudity: 'You should have a thrashing, you lying little snipe, always hanging around the petticoats. Don't you suppose I can squelch you?' Throughout the struggle, Bertha reacts emotionally, often making tactical errors as a result of the spontaneity of her responses. Abel, on the other hand, is always cool and thoughtful in pursuing her campaign against the male sex. Yet she is completely debarred from normal relationships, while for Bertha there might still be hope.

In Act 3 Axel asserts his masculinity and provides the antidote to the poison of sex equality. And, most importantly, he does so without losing the sympathy of the audience. He understands that Bertha has never loved him and that she married him only 'because you were hard up and because you had the green sickness'. He proceeds not only to expose Bertha's particular deceits but to attack the social system which has allowed such falsely progressive ideas to prosper. Bertha, he insists, has become strong through *his* strength. 'You were a rubber ball that I blew up, when I let go of you, you fell together like an empty bag.' And once he has demonstrated his superiority (his masculinity according to Strindberg's comforting sexual logic), she falls in love with him. 'Be a little evil, rather, but don't be weak.' This is what women really want; the superman. But why then do they choose weak men or try to reduce normal men to child status in the first place?

Contrary to what we might expect, *Comrades* does not end with a reconciliation. Normally in a Strindberg play we should expect the hero to fall on his knees before the woman he has made to grovel. But Axel remains aloof despite Bertha's 'humiliating' declarations of love for him. The reason for this is that in this play Strindberg is less concerned with dramatising his personal frustrations than with developing a general case against certain prevailing feminist theories. Undoubtedly, *Comrades* is packed with data from his relations with Siri but the writing has an impassive quality far removed from his later misogynistic works. The mere fact that the man can triumph so consumately suggests that this is a play more deeply thought than felt. Here he is working out his philosophy of the ideal marriage and as a result his two central characters are curiously muted in comparison with those of *The Father* and *Creditors*. So Axel exacts just revenge, not merely *personal revenge*. Thus he is not allowed to express what would normally have been Strindberg's feelings by embracing Bertha but is made to reject her so that he might communicate Strindberg's ideas about divorce, prostitution and remarriage. 'Feel now how millions have felt, when they have begged on their knees for the mercy of being allowed to give what the other accepts. Feel it for your whole sex and then tell them how it felt.' From quotations such as this we can see that Axel is much closer to the Superman ideal (albeit before Strindberg's acquaintance with Nietzsche's ideas) than say Gustav in *Creditors* who was intended to be a dramatic representation of the new man.

The play's conclusion is left for Axel to pronounce: a comrade is one thing, a wife is another. Now Bertha, like Abel, has become for him a comrade, to be treated or ill treated as an equal; worthy of no special courtesy or favour. Axel will meet her in the cafe for a drink and a joke, then, at closing time, he will return home to a real woman; the wife who will be waiting for him. Such, concludes Strindberg, are the deserts and possibly the fate of all blue-stockings.

Obviously *Comrades* is a thesis play and must be judged as such. The ideas and attitudes it expresses will undoubtedly seem bizarre or even paranoid to most people today but we must remember they were specifically designed in response to the feminist movement which was fashionable at the time. And in many respects, Strindberg's case is not implausible. Where his play does seem somewhat absurd as a thesis play is in his portrait of the wife and the lesbian blue-stocking conspiring against the husband. At the very least, here he seems to be overstating his fears of feminism. Nevertheless, *Comrades* is a drama with definite merits. On the whole its case is argued with restraint and skill. The characterisation is impressive and convincing despite the *moral* one-sidedness of the protagonists. Strindberg allows even Bertha and Abel an emotional sympathy that enables an audience to understand their behaviour. Throughout, Bertha remains a credibly attractive woman (if she were not, Axel would hardly have tolerated her behaviour for so long), while even Abel has a conviction to her cause that makes Axel respect her. Finally, the play is plotted with economy and the theme is developed with dramatic clarity. In sum, *Comrades* is the kind of play that points irresistibly to the future greatness (as well as to a number of the failings) of its author.

3

The Great 'Naturalistic' Plays

So much has been written about *The Father*, *Miss Julie* and *Creditors* that there seems to be little that is new to say about them. But while it is as difficult to write anything original about them as it is about, say, *Hamlet*, it is very easy to be mistaken or one-sided in one's analysis. This is why the following discussions will concentrate on correcting certain prejudices that have been fostered partly by Strindberg himself and partly by various critics. In the circumstances, the reader must be on his guard lest, in his desire to provide a counter-balance to orthodox misinterpretations of the plays, the present author exaggerates his case.

Most importantly, the plays will be revealed as psychologically complex investigations of male–female relationships which cannot be categorised as morally simple. In each of them we shall discover that, whatever his initial intentions, Strindberg has created dramas which are by no means crudely misogynistic or even anti-feminist. This does not mean that his female characters are not often repellent, as are Laura and Tekla, or fatally flawed like Miss Julie, but it does mean that they are not without arguments on their side and that they are not *solely* responsible for the tragedies in which they feature.

THE FATHER (1887)

With the exception of the historical play *Master Olof*, the first indisputable demonstration of Strindberg's theatrical genius occurred in *The Father*[1] written when he was thirty-eight years old. Behind it are two drives which derived from the disintegration of his first marriage: doubts about his being the father of Siri's children and doubts about his sexual potency. The one is expressed directly and obsessively throughout the play, the other is hinted at obliquely.

Central to the play is the view of love and marriage as a battle ground. Within this context Strindberg portrays the destruction of a powerful, talented man beset by the forces of female cunning. In respect of this conflict and its outcome *The Father* has frequently been criticised for not being credible. To find a succinct amalgam of naive and popular critical prejudices, we can always turn to F. L. Lucas's *Ibsen and Strindberg*. He describes the Captain as a 'neurotic weakling', a most untypical soldier with 'his scientific dabblings and his weepings' and suggests: 'But reader or audience may grow a little incredulous of a middle-aged cavalry Captain who is naive enough to be suddenly so upset by a trooper's truism about the un-certainty of all paternity. Had he never thought of that before? One would think he had spent his life in a nunnery rather than a barracks. But of course, this strange character can be understood only if it is grasped that he is not a real soldier, but simply the neurotic Strindberg disguised in uniform' (p. 345). However, the Captain has been brought up solely by women, and for Strindberg, and many naturalists this would inevitably produce an insecure man. Furthermore it would motivate the captain's desire to remove his daughter from a household of women.

And again 'It may be that if Laura wants to drive this Captain mad, she has not far to drive. For, with such absurd exaggerations, he seems half-demented already. Nor is it easy to see why, after seventeen years married to this she-devil, he should be so staggered at the idea of her being unfaithful' (p. 345). The plausibility of Lucas's arguments here comes from regarding both the Captain and Laura as simplified character-types who are 'essentially a noble, virile, admirable man' (Madsen, p. 59) and a 'scorpion-woman' (Lucas, p. 359). Seen in this way, the Captain's downfall does seem improbable for surely, as Lucas says, after a long married life, he would have known what a she-devil his wife was.

To correct these and other misunderstandings we must analyse the complex characters of the protagonists, remembering that their milieu is *the family*; and remembering also Strindberg's opinion of that institution 'Splendid, moral institution! Sacred family! Home of all social evil . . .' (*Son of a Servant*, p. 35). For instance, the Captain's military and scientific impedimenta partially define him. His references to the Hercules myth, his physical violence and his verbal style reflect the military man, while some of his fascination with the infernal logic of paternity is that of a scientist. Part of his problem is that he falls between two extremes; the physically active man of powerful emotions and the reflective man whose irresistible self-destroying logic feeds those emotions. Similarly, Laura's character is negatively defined by the Captain's milieu; her lack of understanding of his experiments is but one example of her lack of logic. But their *mutual* milieu is the family. The play gains considerable power from the authenticity with which Strindberg portrays brutality beneath conventional domesticity. With great economy, he evokes a family and a family's social context. The Nurse spans the generations, providing a time framework; the Captain with Nöjd and the Orderly comprise a masculine dimension within the home, Doctor Ostermark gives medical and the Pastor clerical and moral advice. While all this was not specific enough to satisfy Zola's extreme sociological demands, it would seem to constitute a perfectly naturalistic milieu.[2]

Against this background, Strindberg depicts a basic battle of brains which is defined by Laura in Act 2 Scene 5, though without the usual psychological determinism associated with such a conflict. Everyone connected with the marriage in *The Father* has dual, moral roles to play; roles which at once hold the parties involved together and yet, by making their lives intolerable, sunder them. This applies as much to the Captain as to any other character in the play. The Captain is highly conscious of his masculine role and is jealous of any attempt by the women in his household to undermine it. His views about the rights of a wife are autocratic, demanding a strongly paternalistic arrangement, whereby a woman sacrifices her independence and her individuality in exchange for financial support. By putting such opinions in the Captain's mouth, Strindberg is able to criticise the man and to condemn those bourgeois notions of marriage for which he felt both contempt and intense longing. The Captain, with or without Laura's incitement, is prejudiced in favour of his own sex. He is inclined to give Nöjd, his subordinate, the benefit of the doubt about Emma's child when he knows quite well that Nöjd has been guilty of the same offence before. For Strindberg, this is fair enough, since if a man cannot know definitely that he is the father of a particular child, then no-one can surely determine his paternal responsibilities. Ironically, here the Captain seals his own fate by admitting that a man's uncertainty about his being the father of a child can be used as a tactic in the sex war.

His failure to compromise hints at some of the pressures that may have compelled Laura to fight him with any means at her disposal.

For example, the ritual of having his wife render her accounts to him seems partly to be his method of humiliating her. Nor does he try to understand her feelings for Bertha which, whatever else can be said about her, are completely genuine.

> LAURA   So she (a wife) has no rights over her own child?
> CAPTAIN None whatever. Once you have sold something you can't get it back and keep the money (p. 39)

The Captain here reduces marriage to a kind of legalised prostitution that would have appalled Strindberg himself. Indeed, in *A Madman's Defence* he 'proposed a modern arrangement in keeping with our views' which was expensively designed to prevent his wife from being a drudge. He may have been a misogynist but he believed, unlike the Captain, that a woman should have equal *respect* with her husband *within* marriage.

Again, the Captain shows his lack of humanity in the following scene with the Nurse.

> NURSE   Why don't you go half way to meet madam about the child? Remember, she's a mother.
> CAPTAIN Remember I'm a father, Margaret.
> NURSE   Now, now, now! A father has other things beside his child but a mother has nothing.
> CAPTAIN Exactly. She has only one burden, but I have three, including hers. Do you think I'd have stayed a soldier all my life if I hadn't been saddled with her and her child?[3]
> (p. 46)

Such a man could not have been easy to live with and one can understand that a woman would rebel. Nor is there any evidence that Laura is initially responsible for the Captain's attitude. In view of the discrepancy between the Captain and Strindberg's outlook, we can conclude that, in the scenes quoted, the author is criticising his central character and trying to provide reasonable motivation for Laura's behaviour.

Nor is Laura herself utterly devoid of decency. She is not presented as a manifestation of pure evil; the play would be a trivial melodrama if she were. She is not even an irredeemable character, a female Iago, nor is she capable of the sheer wickedness of Goneril and Regan. She is a rather stupid, rather unpleasant female animal fighting for its young, and in this she is not qualitatively worse than the Captain; she is simply more successful and perhaps more unscrupulous. Both are understandably afraid and neither is able to give way. This is their mutual tragedy, the misery of being a man and a woman in close proximity of an adored object; their child. Laura might be capable of using her daughter somewhat callously to further her own ends, but so is the Captain (cf. Act 1 Scene 8 and Act 3 Scene 6).

Certainly Laura takes some pleasure in destroying her mate, yet even this is not wholehearted. In her own way she has loved the Captain, he was her child, and when she confronts him, helpless, in Act 3 Scene 7, she feels sorry for him. Perhaps it is the easy magnanimity of the victor but, for no selfish motive, she tries to assure him that Bertha is indeed his daughter. She does not gloat over her triumph, as a woman motivated solely by personal spite would do. And, although at times she appears to despise her husband, she plots against him solely to defend her rights as a mother. She does nothing just for the sake of hurting him. She is far removed from Iago who enjoys the spectacle of his victim's agony or from Alice in *The Dance of Death* who considers dumping her dead husband's body on the rubbish heap. Then again Laura only gradually formulates the manner in which she will destroy the Captain. Indeed, even her precise intentions are slow in maturing. When she originally tells Doctor Ostermark that her husband is mentally unbalanced, she is trying to win the Doctor over to her side and generally make mischief for the Captain. She even appears to believe that the Captain is ill when, quite ignorantly, she asks, 'But is it reasonable for a man to claim to see in a microscope what is happening on another planet?' Only later in Act 2 Scene 1, when the Doctor warns her that such an accusation 'could result in a man being certified as incapable of managing his affairs', does she actually conceive the idea of depriving him of his paternal rights by such a method.

Throughout the play, she receives her ideas in this way. Ironically, the weapon she uses most devastatingly, the inevitable uncertainty all men have regarding the paternity of a child, is presented to her by the Captain himself. The Doctor unwittingly assists her further when he tells her: 'A sick man is receptive to the slightest impression, and can therefore be made to imagine anything'. She takes this

Bernheimian insight seriously and immediately acts upon it, indicating even at this early stage that she really believes the Captain is ill. She makes no claim to be a mastermind but freely admits: 'I don't know that I ever planned or intended what you think I have done.' She perfectly sums up the situation when she tells the Captain that her plot 'just glided forward on rails which you laid yourself'.

The tendency of some critics to fault the play on the grounds that Laura is not a convincingly drawn she-devil fails to take account of the extent to which she is a woman trapped in a situation that compels her to an aggressiveness which is not entirely self-chosen. Certainly, as the Pastor reveals, she was self-willed as a child but this does not prepare us for the lengths to which she eventually goes. Strindberg's attack on women in *The Father* is extreme but because Laura is a credible character rather than an embodiment of a single idea, an ordinary woman fumbling for ideas about how to get what she wants, his anti-feminism is not hysterical. She does not possess the slightest trace of nobility, she is stupid, she is vicious, but she is a flesh and blood character who can be confused, miscalculating and driven by recognisably human motives. She is not entirely free, but neither can she escape completely from the moral responsibility of what she does. Through her, Strindberg is able to express his anti-feminist feelings without making facile moral judgements.

Given that she is inferior in intelligence to her husband, how is Laura able to destroy him? Why does the Nietzschean slave morality triumph? The answer is to be discovered primarily in the man's character. The Captain resembles a Shakespearean tragic hero, in particular Othello. He was intended as an Agamemnon to Laura's Clytemnestra but the Shakespearean play is a more helpful model to explain such a modern figure.[4] Greek tragic heroes are destroyed in spite of their psychologies; they compare more valuably with Strindberg's fatalistic protagonists of the post-Inferno period. But the Captain's fall can only be understood as can Othello's, Macbeth's and Hamlet's in terms of his own mind.[5] Like Othello, the Captain has a self-destructive urge which virtually compels Laura to torment him. Unconsciously he places the weapons in her hands and delivers himself up to madness by throwing the lamp at her, boarding himself up in his study and allowing his nurse to put the straitjacket on him. Even before either Laura or the Nurse appear on the stage, the Captain feels threatened in his own home which is 'like a cage full of tigers—if I didn't keep a red-hot iron in front of their noses they'd claw me to the ground the first chance they got' (p. 34), and although we can imagine that his resentment has good cause the tone of this outburst resembles the hysteria of persecution mania rather than the irritability of a father who is being thwarted about his child's upbringing.

Furthermore, once the Captain has acquired from Nöjd the idea that a man can never be certain that he is the father of his child, he forces Laura to torment him with doubt. Apart from the single occasion in Act 1 Scene 9, when she introduces the idea, the doubt is always brought up by the Captain himself. The damage has been done, she does not have to refer to it again because the Captain, being the obsessively insecure individual he is, will torment himself. His urge to self-flagellation is clear when we consider that all he has to concern him is a problem that in theory, faces *all* men not just himself. Moreover, Laura quite openly uses the idea against him; so openly that a man of his intelligence must realise she is using it for her own purposes. She never says that Bertha is not his child, she just postulates the possibility: 'Suppose I were prepared for anything—to be driven out, despised, anything—rather than lose my child? Suppose I am telling you the truth now when I say to you "Bertha is my child but not yours"'' (p. 52). She could not be much plainer than this without actually saying that she has made up the whole story. The Captain *knows* that she is lying but he does not *believe* that she is.

We have to conclude then that the Captain is the efficient cause of his own ruin and Laura merely its condition. This judgement becomes inevitable when he refuses to accept any story but that of her adultery. She offers to 'swear by God and all that is sacred that you are Bertha's father' but, caught in his own inexorable logic, he cannot believe her because she has told him that a woman will commit any crime, perjury or blasphemy for her child. He wants her to tell him 'everything', whether it is true or not does not matter, as long as she tells him he has been betrayed:

LAURA   Those suspicions of yours about the child are completely unfounded.

CAPTAIN   That's just what's so horrible. If they were real, at least one would have something to grip on, something to cling

to. Now there are only shadows hiding in the bushes and
poking out their heads to laugh. A real betrayal would
have acted as a challenge, roused my soul to action.
(p. 85)

The exquisite self-torture of the Captain is not a typically jealous
response; there is something too passive, too tormented in his
behaviour. Moreover, his jealousy is highly dramatised; he compares
himself to Shylock and Hercules, destroyed by women to whose
breasts he will return, emasculated, a child. There is something
wholly self-indulgent in his outbursts:

'Oh, my brave lion's skin that you would take from me! Omphale!
Omphale! O cunning woman, who so loved peace that you discovered the art of disarming men. Awake, Hercules, before they
take your club from you! You would rob us of our armour and
have us believe that it is only cardboard. No, it was iron before it
became cardboard. In the old days it was the smith who forged the
soldier's tunic; now it is the seamstress. Omphale! Omphale!
Strength has been vanquished by craft and weakness. Curse you,
damned woman and all your sex.' (p. 86)

The Captain here melodramatises his position, and it is difficult to
believe that he is not enjoying the role. 'May I rest my head in your
lap? So. That's warm! Bend over so that I can feel your breast.
Oh, it is sweet to sleep at a woman's breast, whether a mother's or a
mistress's, but sweetest at a mother's' (p. 86). The Captain relin-
quishes his adult male responsibilities and identifies himself with the
mighty Hercules, betrayed by women, while satisfying his need for
comfort at a woman's breast. Nevertheless, we must not suppose
that, in Strindberg's eyes, this self-indulgence makes the Captain
unmanly. 'To me he represents especially here a manliness people
have tried to disparage, taken away from us and awarded to the third
sex. It is only in the presence of woman he is unmanly, and that is
how she wants him and the law of accommodation forces us to play
the role our mistress requires.'[6]

Throughout the play, the Captain's relationship with his women
folk conforms, at moments of crisis, to a child-mother pattern.
When he wishes to beg Laura to remove his doubts, he naturally falls
into a childlike role which he contrasts with his role of mate.

'Don't you see that I am as helpless as a child, can't you hear me crying for pity like a child crying to its mother, can't you forget that I am a man?' (p. 67). She is moved because this is the only way she can respond to him and because his childlike desperation awakens memories in her. But now that she has Bertha, a child of her own, she no longer needs him and she tells him 'I loved you as my child' but when 'The mother became a mistress—ugh!'. This, of course, has the desired effect on the Captain; it makes him conscious of his deficiencies. 'I thought you despised my lack of masculinity, and I wanted to win you as a woman by being a man.' In Strindberg's eyes, Laura confirms the wickedness of her sex when she tells the Captain: 'The mother was your friend, you see, but the woman was your enemy.'

Bertha is the focus of the Captain's roles both as victim and provider. She represents the ideal to which women try to reduce him and to which he must aspire to receive the undiluted love of the wife-mother. She also crystallises the strife between husband and wife to the latter's advantage since the mother has a special relationship with her. Not only is she more involved in caring for the child and so able to influence its attitude far more profoundly than her husband, she is also secure as a mother in a way that no man can ever be sure as a father. Bertha is the battlefield of their marriage and she represents (as it were) Laura's home front where her husband can have no hope of winning. This is why Laura is not boasting when she says she is stronger than the Captain and why he condemns himself when he makes the Nietzschean point that the stronger is in the right because he is the one with power.

However, Strindberg is careful to deny women the nobility of evil; they are merely bitches on heat who pursue their ends with minimal animal cunning. When Laura says that the Captain realises that her intelligence is equal to her will, this does not mean that her intelligence is exceptional but that a perfect congruity between the intellectual and volitional aspects of human personality, which is the real source of human strength, is more often found in women than in men, who are rarely single-minded enough to compete with women. The broader, the more varied a person's feelings, abilities and interests are, the weaker he will tend to be.

Frequently in the theatre, Strindberg's condemnation of women is blunted by productions which seek to make the Nurse a totally

sympathetic character who has to trick the Captain into the straitjacket because she realises that he is mad; a menace to himself and
others. Consequently, the Captain's instability is exaggerated and
Act 3 Scene 6 is played with a tragic sentimentality which moves
the audience's attention from the suffering of the Captain to the
suffering of his Nurse. Such an interpretation misses Strindberg's
point that the Captain is not insane but reduced to a state of total
despair because he realises that Laura is stronger than he and that his
conflict with her is too much for him. This is tragic because in spite
of what has been said above, Laura is inferior to her husband and
with less justice on her side. Strindberg makes it clear that Bertha
will not benefit from her mother's suffocating supervision. Thus,
although he shows the Nurse to be a woman capable of motherly
affection who is genuinely disturbed by what she feels compelled to
do, he also shows us that, in the last resort, she too is not very
different from the rest of her sex. She expresses contempt for the
father of her child, and after she has betrayed the Captain all she can
do is urge pieties on him: 'Humble your proud heart and pray to
God to forgive you' (p. 83). When the Captain, her 'child', dies in
her lap, her satisfaction is complete: 'he prayed to God in his last
moment' (p. 87). Like any other woman, she can respond to a man
who agrees to become her child but once he begins to assert his
manhood she will leave him, 'caught, cropped and cozened as surely
as any Delilah' (p. 83).

The Captain then is more than a victim, he is flawed as a
Shakespearean hero is flawed and so he transcends what was
probably Strindberg's original conception of him as a noble man
destroyed by a wicked woman. Thus *The Father* is not primarily a
naturalistic play but a complex psychological drama in which
characters transcend the ideas they were conceived to represent.
And because the Captain has tragic dimensions, he lends to the
portrait of male–female relationships a sense of inevitable disaster,
of *a priori* failure, that it would not have acquired in an anti-feminist
tract. This transforms Strindberg's bitter, unreasonable misogyny
into a powerful expression of pessimism in face of the fatal conflict
supposedly inherent in all heterosexual unions.

Consequently, together with *Creditors* and *The Dance of Death*,
it is the blackest theatrical statement he ever made against women
and marriage. A woman is like a praying mantis, she devours her

husband when he is no longer of any use to her and a man is lik
male of that species, he almost wants to be eaten. Complex psy
logical motives operate in the cases of both men and women but the
net result is an instinctual urge to destroy and be destroyed. The
conclusion of this marital battle of brains is a compound of psychic
manslaughter on Laura's part and psychic felo-de-se on the Captain's.

MISS JULIE (1888)

While it is an historically important document as well as a superbly
combative theatrical manifesto, the Preface to *Miss Julie*[7] is not a
reliable guide to the theme and content of the play. It was written
after the play and in some senses is a rationalisation. Certainly it
offers an interpretation which is both stimulating and coherent but it
is more relevant to a discussion of Strindberg's intentions than to his
achievement.

Miss Julie is Strindberg's first tragedy about a woman and his first
purely *sexual* tragedy. The other plays of this period dealt with the
difficulties of male–female relationships, marriage as a battlefield and
the role of children but Julie is the only Strindbergian character so
far who is destroyed by her sexuality. Still she is not the corrupt
human being, that Lind-af-Hageby variously describes as a 'weak,
neurotic, aristocratic Miss', 'the useless, unnatural, pleasure-loving
hysterical woman of the leisured classes whom he detested' and 'the
pretty, neurotic sexual useless woman, blue-blooded and empty-
minded, destined to total extinction in the process of natural selection.' Nor, *pace* F. L. Lucas, is *Miss Julie* simply 'an exposure of a
decadent woman'.

The evidence for this critical abuse of Julie's character, and the
implied praise of Jean, is to be found principally in Strindberg's
Preface. There he declares that Julie is 'a relic of the old warrior
nobility which is now disappearing in favour of the new neurotic or
intellectual nobility' (p. 104). She is an aristocrat whose role and
function is being superseded by the evolutionary process. She is a
member of a virtually extinct class who is destroyed by the representative of a lower, more dynamic class.[8] This was certainly
Strindberg's conception but, as the play developed and he delved
deeper into the characters, the moral and psychological issues became
more complicated. In the Preface he was concerned to provide a

purely naturalistic account of the play that would serve both as a reply to Zola's criticisms of *The Father* as insufficiently naturalistic and as a declaration of the aims of naturalism. But, in practice, his Darwinian prejudices faded before the complexity of the characters and both Julie and Jean emerge as much more than the class stereotypes described in the Preface. Julie is more sympathetic, while Jean is more contemptible.

The analysis contained in the Preface will be rejected because, as we shall see, it makes *Miss Julie* a poorer play than in fact it is. Certainly Julie and Jean are imprisoned by class bonds and their relationship is crippled by social prejudices but it is far too simplistic to conclude: 'Thus the servant, Jean, lives; but Miss Julie cannot live without honour. The slave has this advantage over the knight, that he lacks the latter's preoccupation with honour' (Preface, p. 105). This theme can be found in the play but it provides neither a sufficient, nor an unambiguous, explanation of the drama as a whole. Julie, especially, is too complex to be the symbol of a class or to be a pawn in a Darwinian strategy. Jean, too, emerges most powerfully as an individualised human being rather than as a social type. The dramatic force of the play is to be found precisely at those points where it goes beyond social theory and portrays the passionate inter-relationships of the characters stripped of their incredible pretensions.

In fact, in the process of composition, neither Julie nor Jean turned out to be plausibly typical of their class. She is déclassé as a result of her sexuality, while he is uneasily class conscious as a result of his vague ambitions. In view of the text, it seems strange that so sensually vital a woman was ever intended to represent the last of an etiolated aristocratic line or that such an insensitive, swaggering lackey as Jean should be regarded as the successful representative of the newly emerging dominant class. To explain this we must remember that Strindberg prudishly regarded Julie's hypersensitivity and morbid sexuality as evidence of her decline, while he saw Jean's hard-headed materialistic ambition as a source of social power. The anomalies between Strindberg's declared intentions in the Preface and his much greater achievement in the play reflect the way in which the psychological conflict centering on Julie took over in his mind from his original concern with class issues.

Unlike his other protagonists of this period, Julie is not and has not been married; this fact alone would make the play unusual.

Unexpectedly, Julie is in many respects a sympathetic and certainly a pitiable woman; though this should not make us suppose she is fundamentally different from the rest of her sex when her interests are threatened. In common with Strindberg's other women, she can be cruel, as when she takes Christine by the nose and makes fun of her; superior ('I, the lady of the house, honour my servants by attending their dance'); domineering, as when she tries to force her fiancé to jump over her riding whip like a dog; and contemptuous ('Quite the little aristocrat, aren't you'). By exploiting the allegiances of her own sex, she tries to enlist Christine against Jean. Given the chance, her pride and conceit would compel her to dominate any man as she tries to dominate Jean. But in his case there are two things which prevent her from being successful; her class and her strong sexuality. The one makes marriage out of the question, the other inspires a fatal attraction. Fatal because for a woman to compete with a man outside marriage is dangerous and, for an aristocratic woman, disastrous. As Strindberg has shown us, married life is a woman's home front; there she has all the advantages. But it is not too difficult to conceive of a situation in which a man has the odds. And this is precisely what Strindberg does in *Miss Julie*.

Julie is a woman of strong sensuality who is repressed by social convention. She is essentially a modern woman in a feudal setting. There is nothing domestic or abashed about her; she possesses none of the modest 'virtues' of her time. Rather she titillates Jean unmercifully during the first part of the play. She is self-assured, self-opinionated, sensual and considers herself the equal of any man and the superior of most. Although she is likeable in many respects and sexually appealing, we must be careful not to overlook her failings or to exaggerate Jean's brutality. But equally, we must realise that the driving force of the drama is Julie's character. The play is not entitled *Jean the Valet*. Julie is the more interesting and complicated character into whom Strindberg has poured much of his own contradictory nature. Jean articulates attitudes of social resentment, ambition and humility which were, at the time, part of his creator's nature but the sexual conflict that constantly dominated Strindberg is primarily to be found in Julie not in Jean.

By making her a single woman who had not been corrupted by marriage, he was able to invest her with that gaiety and enchantment he had always sought in women. Nevertheless, Julie presents a problem. When presented with a sensual woman Strindberg's feelings of insecurity usually reasserted themselves. Yet he does not vilify Julie. He presents her with all her shortcomings but there is no edge to his voice when he portrays her. The explanation would seem to be that Julie is not directly a dramatic portrait of anyone from his own personal life. She is a projection of his personal needs and fears, of course, but in general he distanced his life from the characters of this play more than he did normally.

Julie is an aristocratic Estelle and Jean is a plebian Bentley Drummle[9] but she is also a nineteenth-century Connie Chatterley and he is her Mellors. In a long Rousseauesque speech Julie tells Jean how her mother brought her up as a '*boy* of nature' so that I might stand as an example of how a woman can be as good as a man', wihle 'on the estate, all the men were set to perform the women's tasks and the women the men's' (pp. 143–4). To this degree she is a victim of her upbringing. Quite naturally, she wishes to join uninhibitedly in the peasants' Midsummer revelries and escape from the restrictions of her social position, so that she might 'burrow my way deep into the earth'. But she has also had passed on to her a deep hatred of men which though normally suppressed is blatantly revealed at times of stress. So she humiliates her fiancé and generalises from the example of Jean, after he has butchered the greenfinch: 'I'd like to see all your sex swimming in a lake of blood' (p. 154).

Rousseau like Strindberg would blame this on her childhood education. In *Emile*,[10] the French philosopher offers some advice which was very close to Strindberg's heart: 'Love childhood, indulge its sports, its pleasure, its delightful instincts.' In *Miss Julie* to point up the truth of Rousseau's doctrines, Strindberg has Julie's mother wilfully misinterpret them. Instead of bringing her child up in a state of nature appropriate to its sex, she provides Julie with a natural environment and then imposes an unnatural series of human relationships upon her. Rousseau warns that 'a perfect man and a perfect woman should no more be alike in mind than in face' and so 'it follows that their education must be different'. Julie's mother ignores this and instead literally puts into practice a remark that Rousseau intended to be ironical. 'Who is it that compels a girl to waste her time on foolish trifles? . . . What have men to do with

the education of girls? What is there to hinder their mothers
educating them as they please? ... Well then, educate them like
men.'

Thus, at one level, the tragedy of Julie is a demonstration of the
truth of Rousseau's educational ideas and a dramatic realisation of
his theory that the more women are like men, the less influence
they will have over men, and that everything which cramps and
confines nature, for example, in girls the development of grace, is
in bad taste. This interpretation is confirmed by Strindberg in the
Preface; the half women, the men haters 'are a poor species, for they
do not last, but unfortunately they propagate their like by the
wretchedness they cause; and desperate men seem unconsciously to
choose their mates from among them ... but fortunately they go
under because they cannot adapt themselves to reality or because
their repressed instincts break out uncontrollably' (p. 103). Here
Strindberg suggests that the feminist conspiracy of women, which
aims at undermining human society, endeavours to gain strength
and continuity from a conspiracy of mothers which hands down to
daughters a desire to dominate and humiliate men, while creating in
sons a need to be the victims of women.

However, Julie's position is not quite as simple as this because,
as she admits, when asked if she has ever loved her father:

> Yes, enormously, but I've hated him too. I must have done so
> without realising it. But it was he who brought me up to despise
> my own sex, made me half woman and half man. Who is to
> blame for what has happened—my father, my mother, myself?
> Myself? I haven't any self. I haven't a thought I didn't get from
> my father, not an emotion I didn't get from my mother ...
> (p. 159)

From her father she has inherited her urge towards self-abasement
and her lack of emotional control. Most of the time she is her
mother's child but occasionally she is her father's weakling; from the
one she derives her will, from the other her tendency to make a fool
of herself over men. Julie, then, is a psychological hermaphrodite,
torn between an urge to power and a need for humiliation, between
passion and caution, love and hate, grossness and refinement, the
masculine and the feminine: 'tenderness and contempt, ecstasy and
irony ... erotic desire and chaste modesty'.[11] Without Julie, Jean

would have remained an ambitious, resentful, common man whose life would never have touched the heights of tragedy. By contrast Julie would have been a tragic figure with any man.

From the perspective of sex, Jean is a much more straightforward person; his complexity lies in his class attitudes. He is a daydreamer who is almost completely cowed by his social environment. When he resists Julie's advances and warns her of the danger, at one point ordering her to leave him, 'For your own sake I beg you . . . if they find us together you are lost' (p. 133), his concern is double edged. An innate sense of what is socially, and therefore morally, proper makes him think it inconceivable that the lady of the house should make a fool of herself with a servant. But he also fears for his own skin.

> JEAN (*frightened*)   You must go away at once. I can't come with you—then we'd be finished—you must go alone—far away —anywhere. (p. 147)

These are the words of a desperate man who is placing responsibility on a woman because he is hamstrung by 'this damned lackey that sits in my blood'. Without Julie's encouragement he would never have had the courage to sleep with her (though once aroused he is a very passionate man), let alone the will to make her kill herself. The notion that Jean hypnotises Julie is both unconvincingly portrayed and artistically inappropriate. Nothing in the play leads up to its introduction and when Julie mentions hypnosis, she uses it as an example of the power of command. She tries to will Jean to behave like a man, like an aristocrat. To explain the suicide, it is more natural to discuss her hysteria which is apparent throughout the play. In a sense, Julie decides to kill herself; Jean merely says the words. If anyone is controlled or conditioned, it is Jean by the bell, not Julie who, for reasons that will appear, makes her own decision. Yet Strindberg intended that the stronger will of Jean should be the determining factor in Julie's suicide, so the ambivalence of the final scene would seem to be misplaced. On the other hand, the play acquires both credibility and subtlety if we largely discount hypnotism and explain Julie's decision in terms of her psychology.

Jean's essential feelings towards Julie are rooted in fantasy. Although he suggests later that his story of his childhood encounter with her is false, the intensity with which he relates it indicates, at least, that it represents a profound yearning on his part. Julie is the ideal, the beautiful girl in 'the Garden of Paradise' who is to be worshipped, but once she has 'soiled' herself with 'a peasant's child', his sense of social order and morality are destroyed. When he discovers 'that the eagle's back was as scabbed as our own, that the whiteness of those cheeks was only powder, that those polished fingernails had black edges, that the handkerchief was dirty though it smelt of perfume' (p. 140), all his disappointed puritanism bubbles over—'Servant's whore, lackey's bitch . . . Have you ever seen any girl of my class offer her body like that? I've only seen it among animals and prostitutes' (p. 140). The beautiful Turkish Pavilion turns out to be a latrine, his ideal woman becomes a slut and his Eden is degraded into a Gomorrha.

On different occasions, Jean manifests casual brutality, animal sensuality and a rather pathetic tendency to daydreaming which is devoted to evading the need to act. He is a most un-Nietzschean character; his power is simply the brutal failure of a born peasant with resentments he is unable to live out. The framework which holds these qualities together and unifies them is class, though even in Jean's case it is not the basic driving force of his behaviour. He is an embodiment of the myth of working-class virility in which such artists as Strindberg and Lawrence seem to have believed. The myth did not haunt Strindberg permanently as it did Lawrence, but in *Miss Julie* he had his peasant display more overt sensuality than any of his more sophisticated characters in the other plays: 'You are like hot wine, strongly spiced' (p. 141). Jean's memory images are insistently sensual. 'Have you ever noticed how beautiful cats are? Soft to the touch like human skin' (p. 131). Indeed, it is his coarseness, his brutal sensuality that Julie finds sexually appealing. In contrast to the attitudes expressed in the vast majority of his plays, Strindberg writes in the Preface: 'Jean has the whip-hand of Miss Julie simply because he is a man. Sexually he is an aristocrat by virtue of his masculine strength, his more finely developed senses and his ability to seize the initiative' (p. 106).

Their mutual social and sexual roles are schematised by the two dreams they narrate. Julie's dream does not simply mean that she wishes to escape from the isolation of her social position, it is also a symbolic expression of the sexual needs that Jean can satisfy: 'I long to fall . . . I know I shall find no peace till I come down to the ground. And if I get down I should want to burrow my way deep into the earth' (p. 127). For Julie, Jean's attraction is that he is 'a great strong lout', who in her mind is the opposite of her weak fiancé. Although she knows that an affair with Jean will degrade her, her ambivalent personality draws her to him. Time and again, in outbursts that are the product of despair and regret, she demands to be punished: 'Hit me, trample on me, I've deserved nothing better'. 'Kill me too! Kill me!'. 'Hurt me more' (p. 140). Of course, she wants him to help her, she desperately wishes she had not 'fallen', she is afraid of her father and ashamed of the social disgrace but it would be a simplification of her character to ignore the element of self-indulgence in her degradation, which is expressed so superbly in her dream speech.

In a similar way, Jean's dream expresses his will to power and his desire to ascend the social ladder, while at the same time communicating his masculinity in specifically phallic terms. 'And I climb and climb, but the trunk is so thick and slippery' (p. 127). Alone he cannot escape from his class; his ostensibly virile self-confidence is not sufficient. This is evident in his encounters with Julie for his masculine bravado and cynical cruelty alternate with a sense of kinship and affection for her. Moreover, every occasion on which she makes him feel powerful is balanced by another occasion when she makes him feel inadequate. He can never be content with being 'just your animal' and is painfully aware that he can never make her love him. So eventually Jean admits defeat. Julie is altogether too complex for him, the class situation too overawing and his ambitions too fragile for him to be socially effective. Beneath the virile role he plays is a servant who conquers the world in his dreams and causes havoc among the ladies from time to time. But when he finds the waters too deep, his puritanism asserts itself and he self-righteously abuses Julie and primly admonishes Christine: 'Kindly express yourself more respectfully when you refer to your mistress' (p. 157).

Contrary to F. L. Lucas's opinion, the unimaginative Christine is the perfect mate for the valet. She will be impressed by his smattering of French, his 'refined' tastes and his physical vigour. She will remain a solid support who will listen to his stories without leading him into danger. Christine is too stupid to see through him, too much of a peasant to tempt him to realise his ambitions, but enough

of a snob to appreciate his pretensions. We can imagine, after years
of married life when they are still valet and cook, Jean self-pityingly
blaming his failure on Christine's inhibiting lack of drive and
imagination. She is the perfect excuse for his inadequacies and the
perfect foil for his self-esteem. That he should choose her as his wife
is conclusive evidence of his class conservatism. For once, Strindberg
is correct when he writes in the Preface: 'She is a female slave,
utterly conventional, bound to her stove and stuffed full of religion
and morality which serve her both as blinkers and scapegoats'
(p. 106). She is a perfect embodiment of Nietzsche's slave morality,
herd mentality. This insight suggests that he was not entirely un-
perceptive about the qualities of her natural mate.

Even though she exhibits a slave mentality, Christine is a far
more decisive and self-willed character than either Julie or Jean.
For instance, Julie's decision to commit suicide is stimulated less by
Jean's brutality than by Christine's pietism. Underlying the perfectly
adequate account provided by Julie's hysteria, the sexual and class
impasse and her deep sense of personal shame, Strindberg suggests
that her death has a religious context, which is provided by Christine.
In the servant's character he embodies much of the narrow-minded,
ungenerous pietism embraced by his stepmother and which, after a
brief conversion in his youth, he found utterly distasteful. In words
which could equally be applied to Christine he has written of his
stepmother: 'John saw how she had succumbed to the sin of pride.
She really believed she was far ahead of others on the road to
blessedness and already a child of God' (*Son of a Servant*, p. 127).
In Christine, the pietistic self-righteousness of the Nurse in *The
Father* is made even more extreme and unattractive by the insularity
of the peasant. By portraying Christine so unfavourably when it
would have been quite easy to show her as the long suffering victim
of class conflict and other people's vices, Strindberg effectively
condemns pietism and peasant conservatism.

Christine is more responsible than Jean for Julie's death because
she is stronger than he is. Jean, at least, has the excuse that he is
paralysed by fear of 'his lordship' because he knows that in terms of
the class morality he has done wrong, but there is nothing to prevent
Christine from helping Julie. Yet when Julie desperately appeals to
her as another woman to help her against Jean, all Christine can do
is moralise.

CHRISTINE	The blessed Saviour suffered and died on the cross for all our sins and if we turn to Him with a loyal and humble heart, He'll take all our sins upon Him.
JULIE	Do you believe that, Christine?
CHRISTINE	With all my heart, as surely as I stand here . . . And where the sin is exceeding great, there His mercy shall overflow.
JULIE	Oh, if only I had your faith! Oh if!
CHRISTINE	Ah, but you can't have that except by God's special grace, and that isn't granted to everyone.
JULIE	Who has it then?
CHRISTINE	That's God's great secret, Miss Julie. And the Lord's no respecter of persons. There shall the last be first.
JULIE	Then He has respect for the last?
CHRISTINE	(*continues*) And it is easier for a camel to pass through the eye of a needle than for a rich man to enter Kingdom of Heaven. (p. 158)

After piously affirming her own comforting theology, confident of course that she has 'God's special grace' and that the Lord does respect *her* person, she concludes with a cold-blooded act of class propriety:

That's how it is, Miss Julie. Well I'll be going—and as I pass the stable I'll tell the groom not to let any of the horses be taken out before his lordship comes home, just in case. Goodbye (*goes*). (p. 158)

In the scenes quoted above, Christine signs Julie's death warrant by suggesting an image of redemption after death without in any way trying to comfort her as a woman. If she had shown Julie by an act of kindness that someone could sympathise with her, the girl might have had some hope; but provided with such cold comfort, all Julie can do it despair. Julie's final words, 'And the first shall be last', ironically supplement Christine's self-satisfied, 'There shall the last be first', and clearly remind us of the servant's moral responsibility for her death.

In terms of mood and style *Miss Julie* is ostensibly a hybrid play which falls into two separate parts. Once Julie and Jean have slept together, the midsummer magic dissipates, the scents and the sounds of revelry fade as if the sun had indeed set, their pretences are torn aside and Strindberg depicts a furious sex battle to the death. At the same time, the class war is joined with a bitterness we had rarely glimpsed in the earlier half where both Jean and Julie play out their class/sexual roles without revealing the two rather desperate human beings behind them. At first, Jean plays his part as the virile young servant who is handsome, ambitious and daring enough to distinguish himself among his class while remaining securely within it. By contrast, Julie is the Lady who believes she can occasionally join in peasant fun and games without demeaning herself and falling from aristocratic grace. They both enjoy living a little dangerously but remain and wish to remain what they are; a peasant, who despite his fantasies, knows his place, and an aristocrat, who despite her taste for social slumming, remains the Lady of the Manor.

But when they make love the danger becomes real and what was originally a game develops into tragedy. They are thrust out of the class roles which have shielded them; he from the painful discrepancy between his ambitions and his servility, she from her perilous sensuality. They find they have committed themselves not merely sexually but socially. They have rebelled against a sexual code that is part of a wider social code and a very important part. Their intimacy has been witnessed, if only circumstantially, and they can do nothing together but live beyond the social pale or die. The inevitability of their tragic situation is portrayed by defining the social conflict in terms of increasing sexual aggression. Neither of the latter forces would be sufficient to account for Jean's brutality or Julie's hysteria but together they make inevitable such scenes as the butchery of the greenfinch,[12] the suicide decision and Julie's outburst against the male sex. The conclusion of the play is reached by an intensification of those social and psychological factors which had been established earlier. So, although the surface texture of the play changes, its deeper emotional structures remain constant.

Yet there are definite stylistic differences between the two halves, even though their social and emotional drives are continuous. And curiously enough it is the first part of the play, the least intense and volatile, which is stylistically more experimental. While the closing sequences of *Miss Julie* are clearly naturalistic, the first half presents critical problems which are unusual among the pre-Inferno plays. These problems can best be introduced by recalling the dream speeches (pp. 126–7). In a predominantly naturalistic play we might suppose that such lyrical invocations would be out of place.

There is something incantatory about Julie's repetitions, 'drifts, drifts on and across', 'it sinks, sinks', 'I long to fall, but I don't fall', which is echoed in Jean's dream speech. In fact, these are stylised dream speeches uttered mesmerically for theatrical effect so that Strindberg can carry the audience with him, while he makes a number of points in a highly succinct and ostensibly undramatic manner. The rhythms of the speeches are designed to suspend the disbelief which would be a normal response to such a blatant cancellation of naturalism. If we examine the extract closely, we shall hardly fail to notice how precise it is, much too neatly juxtaposed to be real, much too full of pastoral imagery to be more than a lyrical expression of Jean and Julie's experiences, and much too tightly constructed to be part of natural dialogue. In about twenty lines of dialogue Strindberg presents Julie's misanthropy, her sensuality, her class discontents, her sexual ambivalence, and precisely contrasts them with Jean's class ambitions, his Eden fantasies, his phallicism, his aggression and his inevitable sense of failure. The contents of these two speeches are models of stylised simplicity but they are no more like actual dreams than they are like actual dialogue.

The first half of the play is impregnated with non-naturalistic effects. Up to the ballet sequence that is contemporaneous with their love-making, the play is written as a subtle mixture of lyricism and realism which might be seen as metaphor of Strindberg's view of courtship. Even the physical setting combines the mundane with the bucolic. Kitchen utensils mingle with 'a statue of Cupid, lilac bushes in bloom and tall Lombardy poplars', the tiled stove meticulously provided 'with a section of an overhead hood to draw away fumes' is also decorated with birch leaves; this kitchen contains as well as a sink and an ice-box 'a big Japanese spice-jar containing flowering lilacs' (p. 117). These contrasts are justified by its being Midsummer eve but the fact that Strindberg chose this time of year gives the earlier section of the play a magical quality. The mood is heavy with heat, lust and gaiety. No one, except Christine, behaves conventionally, as the mood of the festival heightens their responses.

And yet there are numerous realistic touches which anchor the play. Strindberg asked for a realistic decor in the kitchen without 'painted saucepans' (p. 110). The 'filthy mess' Christine is cooking to abort Julie's pug, Jean's butchering of the greenfinch and Christine's reference to Julie's 'monthly' to account for her crazy behaviour, must have been quite shocking to nineteenth-century audiences. But even these 'realities' play a dual role. The symbolism of the pure-bred pug's sexual association with a mongrel prefigures Julie's fall, while the greenfinch has several symbolic overtones; as a beautiful caged bird denied its natural freedom it represents Julie but as the present of her former fiancé it represents his and Jean's servitude and hence Julie's aristocratic authority (which Jean eventually destroys).

But Strindberg is not content merely to contrast reality and fantasy, he orchestrates them into movements which lyrically express his characters' yearning for some ideal. The magic of Midsummer Night intensifies Jean's longing for the ideal aristocratic life and Julie's desire for an Arcadia where she can behave simply as a woman, without incurring the social stigma that would normally be attached to such conduct. Their flirtation scenes, by remaining at the level of romantic parody, safely express a sporadic desire to become each other's equals. Julie can drink beer and allow a servant to kiss her shoe and Jean like a young gallant can flirt with her. Both can interpret these scenes to suit their own fantasies; but such an ideal is possible only because it is the creation of a special occasion and something utterly apart from social realities. This indeed is an unusual evening when everyone (even Christine during her mimed soliloquy) is affected by the strange, undefined longing created by song and dance, scent and flowers.

A further example of the way Strindberg uses unreality to heighten real psychological and social conflicts is in Jean's long childhood reminiscence (pp. 129–31).[13] The story he tells is real enough (whether it is true is irrelevant) but the style in which he narrates it is extremely high-flown. One has to be careful here because this is not simply a description of a childhood experience by an adult, it is an attempt on his part to recreate the experience as *felt* by that child. Strindberg is portraying a grown man's recollections of his childhood attitudes. Most of us tend to fall into an exaggerated, rather stilted, consciously literary style of speaking when we try to express our childhood feelings, as if we believed that a child's mind was full of palaces and kings, absolute beauty and ugliness, pure good and evil. And this is precisely the habit that

Strindberg is exploiting through Jean's speech; but for purposes beyond those of verisimilitude.

As before, the contrasts are too neat, the social and sexual references too appropriate to the present situation, the imagery too typical of the speaker's role and the narrative too much under control, to be Jean's natural reminiscence. This speech with its romantic evocations ('the Garden of Paradise and there stood many evil angels with flaming swords to guard it', 'a Turkish pavilion in the shadow of jasmine trees and overgrown with honey-suckle'), the self-conscious drama, the Dickensian pleading for pity and the religious overtones, serve the functions of allegory as well as those of psychological revelation. Certainly, it is a very romantic outburst bereft of the bitterness we should expect of Jean. The emotional discharge, 'Oh, Miss Julie! Oh! A dog may lie on the Countess's sofa, a horse may have its nose patted by a young lady's hand, but a servant . . . !', is too self-consciously literary to be genuine class bitterness; it is much closer to romantic despair.

In view of these lyrical qualities, to what extent do Strindberg's naturalistic techniques determine the impact of the play? Zola had criticised *The Father* for the absence of particular milieu. In *Miss Julie*, Strindberg sought to remedy these 'failings' and, as he admits in the Preface, 'I have therefore not suggested that the motivation was purely physiological nor that it was exclusively psychological' (p. 102). Apart from the psychological drives, which have been examined in detail, a multiplicity of motives is given. Physiological (Julie's menstruation), hereditary, physical (presence of the razor), mental (hypnotism, the stimulus of the count's bell and the blood of the bird) and environmental (the Midsummer night, the odour of the flowers etc) causes supposedly impel Julie's sexual fall and suicide. Certainly each of these factors plays a part, but they are not separately or jointly what makes *Miss Julie* a unique, profound and credible drama. The psychological naturalism of the play, as it blends social and sexual frames of reference within an economical physical setting, is what raises the play to the level of great writing and great theatre. If each of the causal elements, enumerated by Strindberg in the Preface, were to take full effect, they would distract from the concentration of the piece. *Miss Julie*, indeed, has a background of references that gives it body but they are not each fully-fledged causes. These are to be sought in the characters of Jean and Julie, which

Strindberg has developed with even more complexity than those of the Captain and Laura.

The milieu in *Miss Julie* defines character in broad outline but not in detail. Christine's environment is the kitchen, the domain of a peasant. Jean, the servant with noble pretensions, occupies the kitchen and the master's bedroom. Julie, the slumming aristocrat, commutes between the manor house and the kitchen. These parallels neatly relate character, social class and location to each other but they are not allowed to dominate the play. In *Miss Julie* the born dramatist fortunately triumphed over the theoretician. In fact, Strindberg followed his own injunction to seek out those points in life where the great conflicts appear (*faire grande*) and, as a result, neither Julie nor Jean are loose bundles of responses untied by a firm personality. Whatever Strindberg intended, he created eminently rounded, flesh and blood people. This is the principal reason why *Miss Julie* is arguably his finest pre-Inferno play and, for its size and scale, one of the great masterpieces of the Western theatre. This is also why Julie's death is convincingly tragic, contrary to the following incredibly wrong-headed assessment by Dahlström: 'Julie's fall is not a moral one, rather it is a superficial social disturbance . . . Even for Strindberg, Julie's fall is not genuine. He gave her nothing to lose but false pride and nothing to stain, but an already badly stained name. *Miss Julie* cannot succeed as a tragedy because the author failed to give it adequate tragic substances.'[14] Against this, as a conclusion of the foregoing analysis, we can simply state that she is a character for whom an audience can feel sympathy, whose social and sexual dilemma is convincing and whose considerable potentiality as a human being is tragically wasted.

CREDITORS (1888)

In *The Father* we saw that Strindberg portrayed male–female relationships as a battle between pairs of alternating opponents; mother and child, lover and mate. This essential pattern is maintained in *Creditors*,[15] a play equally misogynistic, and the first of Strindberg's plays to be influenced directly by the writings of Nietzsche. As such, it tends to be more philosophically rigorous than either of the other two great naturalistic dramas.

Structurally, *Creditors* is the simplest and most economical of the great naturalistic plays. Like the Chamber Plays, its theme is exposed, developed and resolved in line with the classical sonata form, while the three central characters are strictly permutated without appearing on stage all together until the final tableau. The development of the theme also roughly approximates to an Hegelian dialectic, which is defined by Adolf in terms which suggest its compatibility with naturalistic determinism: 'Yes, I'm afraid of what is going to happen now. But I can't stop it happening. The stone is rolling, but it wasn't the last drop of water that set it rolling, nor the first one either. It was all the drops together' (p. 193).

Thus we can discern the following dialectical thematic structure:

THESIS   Woman steals from her mate, his manhood, his ideas and his moral strength.

ANTITHESIS   The voracity of woman contains the seeds of her own destruction. Once she has drained her man of all vitality, she feels contempt for him; turning to other sources for her pleasure. As a result, she makes an enemy of him, and, by insulting his pride and arousing his jealousy, she provides him with a purpose (i.e. revenge) and a potential source of energy with which to accomplish it.

SYNTHESIS   By her own behaviour woman has laid down all the conditions necessary to generate a superior race of men, of indestructible supermen. The renewed man impervious to her wiles returns to render her victim-less and harmless, and to swell the noble rank of anti-feminists who will work to ensure that never again shall women emasculate the superior sex. Most men, Strindberg pessimistically grants, will be fooled by a woman at least once but among the many creditors she leaves behind her, there might be one who will return to claim payment. As Gustav says: 'One only gets fooled once; after that, one goes round with one's eyes open. You've never been deceived—beware of those who have. They're dangerous.' (p. 182)

Thus Adolf represents the whole of Scandinavian manhood corrupted by feminism. Tekla is a Strindbergian *femme fatale* who has the habit of making her husbands into dolls—a fitting misogynistic reply to Ibsen. Gustav is the superman who destroys Adolf's illusions about his painting and about his wife.

In *Creditors*, Strindberg extends his indictment of women and marriage in two ways; by introducing the theme of female *intellectual* parasitism and by comparing two marriages of the same woman. This enables him to link his pessimistic anti-feminism with his ideas about the power of mental suggestion, while developing a more optimisitic view of male regeneration in Nietzschean terms. Tekla is an archetypal Strindbergian woman who has emotionally crippled her husband, Adolf, as she had his predecessor, Gustav. When Gustav questions Adolf, we learn how Tekla has drained him of his virility, his dignity and his ideas. As Gustav says: 'The woman has eaten your soul, your courage, your learning' (p. 185). Tekla no longer treats Adolf as a lover worthy of respect but has 'managed to usurp the male prerogative' and has transformed their relationship into a pseudo-incestuous brother–sister association; referring to him as 'Little Brother' and to herself as 'Squirrel'. She clearly loves him but as a child not as a man. She finds him inadequate to her female needs, which she satisfies in casual promiscuity. Moreover, by stealing his ideas and taking them as her own, she has destroyed his artistic vigour and developed her own meagre writing ability at the expense of his genuine talent for painting. As Gustav says: 'You educated her. But she was clever enough to make you think that it was the other way round' (p. 186). Having exhausted his talent and destroyed his manliness, 'The snake is full. Now she vomits up her victim', and chases 'clean young men', leaving Adolf who 'can't live without something to worship', little more than a slave who must wait for her patiently at home. 'Your wife will be bringing home your heart soon' (p. 189). In *A Blue Book*, Strindberg defines the kind of woman Tekla is. 'She desires his virile power in order to become a husband and make him into a passive wife' (p. 188).

With great skill, Strindberg suggests that Gustav has experienced exactly the same kind of humiliation at Tekla's hands several years before. Their marriages have been so similar that Gustav can anticipate how Adolf feels and what he has suffered. Gustav does not have to be told that 'She calls you "brother". Do you still act that little comedy?' or that 'Her capillary power has sucked her up to your level.' Through the two marriages, Strindberg gives us a dramatic representation of the idea of eternal recurrence which was so central to Kierkegaard's and Nietzsche's philosophies. And through it, he is able to transform his one-act play from an examination of the lives of his three protagonists into a universal statement about the nature of marriage and female sexuality.

For the first time since *Comrades*, Strindberg purports to show us the successful male in action, though now he envisages his dominant hero as a Nietzschean Superman. Through Gustav who has survived his marriage to Tekla, we are shown that married men can rebuild their lives, despite all that women can do to them, and such revitalised men, it is argued, will form the vanguard in the struggle against female domination. Supermen (like Gustav) will use ordinary men (like Adolf) who have become women's slaves, to wage war on the female sex in general. On an individual level, the play features a battle of brains. Gustav the strong man flexes his muscles on Adolf as he prepares to tackle Tekla. Through force of will and superior mental discipline, he implants idea after idea into the brain of the weaker man; making him agree to abstain from sex with Tekla and working him up to an epileptic attack merely by describing the symptoms of his 'younger brother'. By a process of suggestion and hypnotism, Gustav fulfils his promise to 'pass some electricity into' Adolf. Gustav now appears so 'terribly powerful' that physical contact with him makes Adolf say 'It's like gripping an electrical machine' even though Gustav was once as weak as he. Adolf too was once a powerful man who influenced Tekla; in those days *he* was 'The mesmerist who instilled new energy into her flabby muscles and charged her empty brain with new electricity.' He is therefore Tekla's creditor, as well as Gustav's debtor.

Since the break-up of his marriage to Tekla, Gustav has changed so much that Adolf cannot recognise him from a portrait which was painted when he lived with her. He has become a different person, but how? What has sustained him so that now he can return as a creditor for the payment of the emotional debt which both Adolf and Tekla owe to him? Although it is not made explicit an answer to this question rests in the pages of *Thus Spake Zarathustra*. Gustav has taken heed of Zarathustra's basic advice to the man of the future: 'he who cannot obey himself will be commanded'. Through harsh experience he has learned too that 'even when he commands himself then also must he make amends for his commanding. He must become judge and avenger and victim of his own law'.[16] Past suffering has enlightened and strengthened him. Moreover, he acquires strength from the fact that he has right on his side. He has been the victim of Tekla's calumny and Adolf has stolen his wife from him. So he can justifiably claim recompense for the debt of suffering she owes him, even though he realises that to do so will probably involve destroying Adolf. In Nietzschean terms he has transformed himself, transvalued his values by the assertion of his own Will to Power.

Aware of its Nietzschean overtones, Madsen has described the play as violent and one-sided. This curious assessment comes as usual from reading Strindberg's life unrestrainedly into his work. It implies that Tekla is too crudely a figure of evil and that Gustav is an idealised superhuman hero. In fact, while he intended to make Gustav the spokesman of his anti-feminism and Tekla its victim, once more Strindberg does not portray a black and white situation. Gustav is neither benevolent nor all powerful. On the contrary, he is unscrupulous and, in comparison with Tekla, not particularly impressive. Admittedly, he toys with Adolf convincing him that his wife is wicked and that he is a 'yellow corpse' in her care. Then after persuading him to take up sculpture, he ridicules the weaker man for putting any faith in 'that *passé*, abstract survival from man's infancy' (p. 186). Mercilessly he torments Adolf; at one moment offering him hope, at the next smashing his illusions. But too often he displays petty-minded malice rather than destructive grandeur. Vindictively he confesses that he 'felt a desire to take [Adolf] to pieces and jumble them up so that he couldn't put them together again', for no other reason than that quite unwittingly 'he began to rub up my old wounds'. Gustav plays the part of the superman and so, in strict Nietzschean theory, he is above morality, but nonetheless he is the immediate cause of Adolf's death.

He cruelly exploits the weaker man's epilepsy, his gullibility and his love of Tekla, for purposes of personal revenge. Throughout the play he seems to pervert his Will to Power in a number of ways which hardly seem to constitute the motivation or behaviour of the man of the future. Even granted that he tries to cast himself in the role of reformer, at the end he shows little or no concern for Adolf, who is apparently beneath contempt. Again, although Gustav delights in his own power, is he so perfectly superhuman? Certainly he is mercilessly skilful in compelling Adolf to submit completely to his will, even to the point of persuading him to collaborate in testing Tekla's integrity. Indeed he is so successful, he even believes at one point that 'I shall haul you up again'; that is, he will transform him into a superman. However, a closer examination will make it clear that he is by no means a dramatic realisation of Nietzsche's Übermensch.

Gustav is a Strindbergian (that is to say an approximation of the Nietzschean) superman. He is presumably the closest that Strindberg, at this point in his life and with his dramatic integrity, could imagine anyone living up to Nietzsche's ideal. If the Captain is a projection of Strindberg's mania for persecution, his desire to be destroyed by women and his need to justify his misogyny, Gustav is a projection of his delusions of grandeur, of his desire for revenge and of his need to think himself capable of exacting revenge. Through Gustav he tries to become the Superman who describes his intentions towards a woman as confidently as follows: 'Don't be afraid later when you see me at work dissecting a human soul and laying out the bits and pieces here on the table. It sounds nasty if you're a beginner, but once you've seen it you won't regret the experience' (p. 192). He is the woman-tamer who can say: 'But do you know why you two drew the short straws in this context? Why you were fooled by me? Because I am stronger than you and cleverer. You and he were the idiots not I' (p. 217).

Characteristically, Gustav is a superman who has to be humiliated before he can conquer, who has to have what Nietzsche would denounce as vulgar moral right on his side before he can act and whose whip is not his inherent superiority nor even his phallus but the insidious nastiness he has learned from women. To justify his treatment of Adolf, Gustav has to provoke him into unwittingly vilifying him, a motivational ploy which hardly seems to indicate any transvaluation of values. Moreover, Gustav destroys Tekla not by facing her in a battle of wills but by trapping her; using the Shakespearean device of provoking her to reveal her true character in the presence of the person she has deceived. This is not the way of a man let alone a superman but it is the best Strindberg can conceive in a struggle against woman. However, we should be grateful that *Creditors* is not successful as a dramatic illustration of the superman cult because what we have instead is one of the finest one-act plays Strindberg ever wrote.

Gustav is much more complex than a mere cold-blooded superman intent on revenge. A sense of injustice motivates him but so does a lingering passion for Tekla and a feeling of inadequacy which is revealed in aggression. Even the demonstrations of his power are not as impressive as they might at first appear. Adolf is a broken man long before Gustav meets him. If anyone is to take 'credit' for destroying him, it is Tekla. And in fact Gustav soon realises that Adolf is beyond his aid. As this wreck of a man rightly says: 'I am like a legless child and my brain lies open', while Gustav is 'a teacher of dead languages and a widower' (p. 189); the only one who can speak the language of masculinity in a feminist world. Nor is Gustav's method of handling Tekla exactly domineering. Whenever he confronts her, he takes refuge in irony, flattery and reminiscence designed to induce her to reveal herself to the eavesdropping Adolf. Even when he has accomplished his purpose: 'I have come to take back what you have stolen from me not what I gave you freely. You stole my honour, and the only way I could get it back was by robbing you of yours' (p. 218), he has not succeeded in really hurting her. She is not humiliated as he was. Her reaction is at the comparatively mild level of anger ('You're a vindictive beast. I despise you'), self-excuse ('How can you who must regard me as innocent because my heredity and my environment drove me to act as I did, how can you think yourself entitled to take revenge on me?' (p. 210), and an almost casual acceptance ('Can't we part friends?'). He has not conquered her. Only when she learns of Adolf's complicity and death does she break. By comparison with Tekla, Gustav is weak. Unaided, she virtually destroyed two men but Gustav required the unwitting assistance of another man to harm her. As Nietzsche says: 'Let man fear woman when she hates: for man is at the bottom of his soul only wicked, but woman is base.'[17]

Nor is *Creditors* as *morally* one-sided in its treatment of women as Madsen suggests. Tekla has certain qualities in her favour just as Gustav has his faults. She is both attractive and charming. And we must remember that the only evidence we have that she has harmed Gustav and Adolf is their own somewhat biased testimony. What we do know from the *action* of the play is that she is capable of genuine affection. Thus, eventually, Gustav realises that he did not understand Tekla as fully as he had believed and that much to his surprise she does love Adolf. He has had his revenge in a way he did not imagine possible, because he had seen their brother–sister relationship as a parody of love, without understanding that it was an outer form of something deeper. 'In woman a slave and a tyrant have all too long been concealed. For that reason woman is not yet capable of friendship: she knows only love.'[18] If he had known this Gustav would have deduced that their sibling relationship was passionately incestuous; a notion which is developed when Gustav (Tekla's first husband) becomes a father figure to Adolf (her second, child-like husband).

Tekla is not just looking for excuses when she insists that she cannot be blamed for what is after all her basic nature. In an important sense, she is not free and she does not understand herself. Walter Johnson correctly calls her an instinctive rather than a calculating vampire.[19] One minute she will pour contempt on Adolf, pitying the wretch because he still loved her, ridiculing his love and revelling in his weakness; yet when his life is in danger she is genuinely terrified. Strindberg acknowledges Nietzsche's precept that 'Everything about woman is a riddle', and implies its complement, which was expressed in *The Father*: 'And everything about woman has one solution: it is called pregnancy.'[20]

Tekla is a far more complex creation than Laura but curiously she is characterised chiefly through the responses of the two men. On the basis of this fact, Madsen mistakenly argues that apart from them she has no real identity. She is supposedly quite unoriginal, receiving all her ideas, gestures and attitudes from her husbands. She is 'a phonograph only which repeats your and other people's words. slightly diluted'. Even her child by Adolf so resembled Gustav that they had to send it away. This image of Tekla as a *tabula rasa* on which a compound of the two men's personalities has been imprinted is a corollary of the image of Tekla as a vampire who drains the vigour from her husbands. Although there is truth in this interpretation, it does not completely define Tekla's character. Primarily, she is a woman who is thrown exclusively into the society of men. Her normal maternal instincts, which would have allowed her to develop independently through her child, are turned onto her husband whom she wishes to dominate. Adolf admits how successful she has been. 'I couldn't tell if she were I, or I she. When she smiles, I smile: when she weeps, I weep. And when she—can you imagine it?—when she was giving birth to our child, I felt the pains in my own body' (p. 178). But a child also influences its mother. She assimilates the influence of her husbands but she also discards them when they have been of use to her. Indeed, the point of the ending is that she remains in some way inaccessible to masculine influence and understanding. Yet Tekla is not without justice on her side. She has had to stand up for herself in a world of men, yet in her own way she is capable of loving a man. Her character would best yield to an analysis that concentrated on her childlessness and the manner in which she has tried to compensate for it.

Creditors is significantly different from its immediate predecessors in the physical disgust that pervades it; a distaste which resembles the post-Inferno dramas and which, in the pre-Inferno period, was taken to a ludicrous extreme in *Simoon*. Strindberg's imagery throughout the play is far more dehumanised and violent than previously: 'yellow corpses', 'capillary level', the simile of the disembowelled saint, the horrible description of epilepsy and, most relevantly, the grotesque portrait of woman: 'Have you even seen a naked woman? Yes, of course. A half-developed man, a child stunted in mid-growth a youth with udders on his chest, a case of chronic anaemia who has regular haemorrhages thirteen times a year' (p. 187). Corresponding to this disgust is an attitude of sexual cynicism that has replaced the sexual despair of *The Father*. In *Creditors*, bitterness has completely taken over; Strindberg is less tormented and can envisage his revenge on women. Sexual love which once represented an ideal has now become an object of contempt: it is 'carnal excess', 'boils that are being lanced', 'a withered fig leaf'. Now quite cynically, he can write: 'For woman, love is injustice and blindness towards all that she does not love' (p. 83).

Such cynicism is rarely restricted to one relationship, one sex or even one species. It tends to be all-devouring and assuredly the anti-feminism of *Creditors* merges into a vague misanthropy which was not apparent in *The Father*. Gustav feels contempt for Adolf as well as for Tekla ('perhaps someone has left a dog in there') and shows no compassion when Adolf dies. Life itself is being condemned: 'Don't you realise there are false notes in life which can never be tuned? The only thing to do is to stop your ears with wax and work. Work, grow old, pile as many new impressions as you can into the cupboard to keep the skeleton from rattling' (p. 181). When Tekla blames her cupidity, and Gustav his desire for revenge, on the forces of heredity and environment, Strindberg as a naturalist is prepared to concede the point, but whatever Strindberg's opinions about free will and human responsibility, he does not appear to feel any of the affection for these characters that he showed towards the Captain. When he described *Creditors* as 'human, lovable, with all three characters lovable', we can assume that he was either being ironical or was talking about the play he *wanted* to write.

Creditors is by any standards a fine play; more bitter but not as emotionally powerful as *The Father* and more controlled but not as lyrical as *Miss Julie*. In many respects it is identifiably naturalistic. It begins in mid-sentence, the milieu reflects the central notion of the play that, within a metaphorical and real framework of commerce, human relationships are degraded. 'Such terms as creditors (and debtor by implication), bills, payment, first mortgage, accounts, settling, tearing up bills and dun are basic.'[21] Even Adolf and Tekla's 'Little Brother-Squirrel' routine which is a superbly effective indictment of man's childlike debasement at a woman's feet, is perfectly explicable in real terms. ' "Brother and sister", "little mother", "playmates" and so on, covers under which lovers are accustomed to hide in order to abandon themselves ultimately to playing the beast with two backs.'[22]

However, as in *Miss Julie*, there are traces of near expressionism. The portrayal of Tekla as a vampire, the epileptic image of Adolf's condition, the omniscience of Gustav which is almost clairvoyant and telepathic, Gustav's great creditor speech which so resembles the Doctor's curse in *To Damascus* (Part II Act 1), all anticipate distinctive features of Strindberg's post-Inferno work. The creditor image itself has a psychological menace which acquires much of its force from the mental and emotional unity of the three characters (cf. *Easter*). There is not a great difference between the role of Gustav in the psychological world of Adolf and Tekla, and the Doctor's in that of The Stranger/Lady. In common with *The Father* and *Miss Julie*, the dialogue of *Creditors* becomes, on occasions, highly stylised and non-naturalistic; for instance the allegory of the saint, the brutal description of women and Adolf's long account of his relationship with Tekla.

A weakness of the play, to a post-Second World War generation at least, is that Strindberg seems to share Gustav's moral conclusions; namely, that superior cerebral power and volition confer greater personal rights. This is unfortunate enough but its corollary that the weak and helpless, such as Adolf, have no rights whatsoever, is even worse. It may or may not be reasonable to suggest that moral value is in some way related to intellectual or aesthetic worth but to suggest that there is a one to one correspondence between them is simply *inhuman*. If there is any conclusion to this pessimistic yet perfectly balanced tragedy of three complex characters, it is that a 'woman is a man's child, and if she isn't that, he will become her child and then the world's upside down'. Or perhaps Nietzsche was closer: 'That man sought a handmaiden with the virtues of an angel. But all at once he became the handmaiden of a woman, and now he needs to become an angel too.'[23] Adolf died a handmaiden while Gustav became an angel of sorts.

4
Miscellaneous Plays (1889–92)

In 1889, Strindberg wrote three Quart D'Heure Plays which were the culmination of the urge to dramatic economy that was evident in the great naturalistic tragedies. Martin Lamm quotes a metaphorical explanation Strindberg gave in November 1888 of his aims in writing such limited plays.

> In France I always ate five lamb chops, to the great astonishment of the natives. You see, each chop consisted of a half-pound of bone and two inches of lard, which I left on the plate. Within was a back muscle—la noix. This I ate. 'Give me the nut!'—is what I want to say to the dramatist.[1]

Or, as he argued in 'On Modern Drama and Modern Theatre', every play seems to have been writen for the sake of a single scene so why not exclude the periphery of 'exposition, presentation, entanglement, disentanglement, peripeteia and catastrophe'. Whether or not such theatrical asceticism was purely the result of a theoretical conviction must remain an open question. Perhaps his theorising was a rationalisaton of the *fact* that during this period his inspiration was fragmentary.

Two of the Quart D'Heures (*Pariah* and *The Stronger*) were miniature masterpieces but it soon became clear to him that the genre was necessarily limited and what was being gained in concentration was being more than lost in thematic and character complexity.[2] All of the Quart D'Heures are riddled with the influences of Darwin, Nietzsche, Poe,[3] Charcot and Bernheim. Their themes range over the varieties of pyschic and semi-mystical phenomena that obsessed Strindberg at this time. These ideas, which appear more or less peripherally in the naturalistic masterpieces, are now treated centrally. To a greater extent than at any other stage of his career, he wrote thesis plays which often avoid being theatrically sterile, only by becoming melodramatic.

PARIAH (1889)

Pariah[4] is a succinct Nietzschean piece developed along the lines of Poe's detective fiction (e.g. *The Gold Bug*), though it was in fact an adaptation of an Ola Hansson short story. It concerns a 'battle of brains' between X an archaeologist and Y a forger but their individual psychologies are not rigorously analysed. Instead, Strindberg produces a number of moral and social statements, together with an analysis of criminality. The outcome of the two men's conflict is determined by their contrasting standards of personal honesty, which are seen to affect their respective cerebral power. Y may be the more devious and unscrupulous but X is more clever and gains strength from his integrity. Being honest, X is invulnerable whereas Y is easily trapped within the mesh of his own deceptions. Unlike Nietzsche, Strindberg agreed with the Italian criminologist, Caesare Lombroso, that the criminal was not a strong man but a degenerate; a stupid weakling.

Technically both men have committed crimes but while Y has been punished for forgery, X has murdered a coachman without being punished. The differences between them (which in Strindberg's opinion justify this state of affairs) consist of X's personal superiority, the unintentional nature of his crime and their contrasting attitudes to what they have done. In existentialist terms, X's behaviour is authentic, Y's is a case of bad faith. X is fundamentally a worthwhile member of society, happily married and hardworking. His researches have been successfully carried out without him having to break the law to live. Although he has accidentally killed a man, he does not have a criminal mentality; rather he is painfully honest. He is unable to steal any of the valuables he has discovered, although he could do so without danger, and even though the money would pacify his landlord and enable him to illustrate his treatise. Yet he does not regard his honest behaviour as a merit, instead he recognises that it is as much a necessity for him as dishonesty is for a criminal. Honesty and dishonesty are beyond free will.

What is a question of choice, however, is the individual's attitude towards his crime *after* it has occurred. Y, a shifty opportunist, tries to deny all personal responsibility by putting the blame on unconscious forces and self-hypnosis. When X sees through these excuses and exposes his true nature, Y tries to blackmail him.

Y defends this new crime on the grounds that X deserves to suffer because he has not been punished for the murder he committed. Y simply does not understand that one should, 'feel exonerated, washed clean, raised to the old level, as good as anybody else, when you have suffered your punishment'. In this respect he is more fortunate than X, for while X has felt no guilt about ending the coachman's 'allotted period of vegetation', he has suffered, even more than Y, from fear of detection and from poverty.[5] Y forged a signature to benefit himself and now once more commits a crime to extort money from X, under the guise of administering the law. But X gained nothing from the coachman's death; he merely refused to allow its consequences to wreck his scientific researches and the lives of his parents, his wife and children. Unlike Y who is criminally minded, he will commit no other crime. This is presumably one indication of his superiority as the superman type.

As usual during this period, some of Strindberg's dialogue and ideas are offensive. X describes the supposedly inferior Y with the words: 'Your ears come so close together behind that sometimes I wonder what race you belong to.' The coachman, too, proposes a kind of class fascism. He seems to suggest at times that criminals, kitchen-maids and women-lovers are essentially inferior, and can be used for their own purposes by those who are cerebrally powerful. What would be justified as pure description begins to sound ominously like exhortation. The further Strindberg goes beyond naturalism towards didactics, the more he lays himself open to the charge of fascism. This impression is strengthened by the fact that as a superman X resembles Poe's Dupin, rather than a moral giant or a powerful personality. With his considerable perspicacity, he easily demonstrates the dominance of the Master over the Slave mentality but his moral insights are hardly profound. For example, he initially suspects Y merely because (echoing a sentiment shared by Strindberg) he always mistrusts people with whom it is too easy to be friendly. They must, he believes, be insincere since they are forever tailoring their own personality to fit those of others. In the section entitled 'Affable Men' of *A Blue Book*, written eighteen years later, Strindberg warned against such persons, concluding that 'it is dangerous to be affable, and it is dangerous to consider men simple'.

The artistic value of *Pariah* lies in the skill with which Strindberg integrates a 'battle of brains' with the detective story formulae.

Its development relies, as does a Dupin or a Holmes story, on the acumen with which the superior intelligence acquires and interprets the clues (in this case, to Y's true nature) and uses his stronger will to suggest ideas to his victim which force him to expose his sordid personality. The compression and clarity with which Strindberg achieves this give the play a dramatic tension that compensates for the brutality of its protagonist and the absurdity of its ideas. Strindberg builds up the conflict with great ingenuity and none of the tedious and improbable detail which is often associated with the mystery genre in the theatre. The play is worth its place in any theatre group's repertoire for its overall dramatic rightness, for the impact of Y's speech on prisons, for its model structure in a highly restricted form and for its verbal style, described by F. L. Lucas as 'the gaunt, bleak prose of Strindberg's naturalistic plays':[6] though what Lucas considers to be a failing, here, others would applaud.

THE STRONGER (1889)

In his greatest naturalistic plays, Strindberg had depicted a 'battle of brains' in which one combatant emerged triumphant not through innate superiority but because he or she was more adaptable. Neither sex nor class decide the issue finally, but the *ability* of Laura, Jean and Gustav to use existing conditions to their own advantage and to accept the ravages of 'war', with greater equanimity than their victims.

In his next play, Strindberg dramatised the naturalistic principle of 'the survival of the fittest' as simply and as explicitly as would seem possible. *The Stronger*[7] is a thesis play, pure and simple. In common with its predecessors, it is not completely in the naturalistic mode although both characters are defined by their physical belongings. Mademoiselle Y's life is conjured up with admirable concision at first sight. Alone in a café on Christmas Eve reading a magazine with a half empty beer bottle in front of her, she is an independent spinster not too well off, who has nothing to celebrate and no one to celebrate with. She sits in the café, idly passing her time, perhaps unwilling to return to her solitary room. On the other hand, Madame X, in her winter clothes, carrying a 'delicate Japanese basket' and drinking hot chocolate, represents the comfortably married woman for whom Christmas is a time of presents and parties. She conforms to the role, envisaged by Strindberg as the natural state for all women; that of the mother, the basis of the family.

Yet, contrary to Michael Meyer's opinion that *The Stronger* is one of the very few examples of Strindberg's work which contains a sympathetic portrayal of his wife',[8] neither character is appealing. Y, whose promiscuity is revealed in X's long monologue, is Strindberg's *bête noire* amongst women, the potential home wrecker. 'Unfaithfulness is a cosmic crime which brings the one or other member of the married pair into perverse relations with their own sex' (*A Blue Book*, p. 176). Moreover, Y is a man-eater who has recreated X's husband in her own image. Nor is Madame X much better. She is compulsively spiteful towards Y, disdaining her for being single ('Yes, Amelia, my dear—home's best after the theatre— and children you know—no, of course you don't', p. 230), then hypocritically pretending to be friendly only to turn upon her when she begins to suspect her husband's infidelity. X is a typical Strindbergian woman, intemperate, cruel and competitive. She ridicules her own husband, imitating the supposedly effeminate way he walks. Her imagery is violent: 'I'd have scratched her eyes out', and her language coarse: 'I queered your pitch that time' (p. 231).

The play accurately portrays Strindberg's belief that women rarely like members of their own sex; mistrusting them as social and sexual rivals. The extent of their communication is to pursue their own ends and to ridicule the absent male, but the outcome of their struggle will not ultimately depend upon which of them possesses the man or the home or the child but who is the more pliable and resilient. Confronted with X's flexibility even Y's vampirism ('Your soul crept into mine like a worm into the apple, ate and ate, dug and dug, until there was only skin left with a little black powder', p. 233) is ineffectual. X triumphs because she learns to benefit from the situation. She vindictively interprets the influence Y has had over her husband to her own advantage. 'Thank you for teaching my husband how to make love! Now I shall go home and make love to him' (p. 234). She can ignore the truth of her predicament and concentrate upon those practical considerations that make a love relationship work. So she comes, perhaps half-consciously, to realise that love is a question of fantasy, compromise and adjustment, rather than of romantic ideals.

The play works initially at a level of appearance. X is an actress who adopts a number of roles; the married woman extolling the virtues of domesticity, the jealous wife, the doting mother, the performer (e.g. the firing of the cork) and finally, the stronger. At first, we might think her sudden conversion from jealous wife to determined realist more of an act of defiance than a genuine conviction. Yet when we remember that she is an actress whose personality changes are exhibited most profoundly in her ability to take on new roles, it makes more sense. The conclusion is not a moral one, but supposedly Darwinian, though we could argue that Madame X, like X in *Pariah*, triumphs because she represents stable domestic virtues.

However, the above discussion makes *The Stronger* appear to be an unproblematical play. In fact, the problems of its interpretation radically divide critics. Against the view stated above that Madame X is the stronger,[9] there is a powerful body of opinion that sees Mademoiselle Y in this position. And certainly when we consider her persistent silence, it is a pleasingly ironic interpretation. Anthony Swerling writes: 'If the wife is seen to be the "stronger", then the work is "comic"—cheaply so: one rival bawling at another. If, as is Strindberg's more covert and ironic meaning, the silent protagonist (of aristocratic dignity before the impotent vituperations) is the victor, then the work is not comic but bitter, not vaudeville but tragic humour.'[10] We can agree with everything Swerling says in this argument from dramatic depth and still consistently maintain that in the last quarter of the play Strindberg adds a final twist that makes X the stronger. In this way, the play would acquire a further ironic reverberation; that X's apparent weakness is a source of strength or rather that a movable object can often evade the irresistible force.

Egil Törnquist has devoted a whole article[11] to proving Y's greater strength. Much of his case is, unfortunately, biographical, but he also argues persuasively that X's accusations against Y are, in fact, manifestations of her own insecurity; that she is describing herself when she scorns Y, that Y's silence intimidates her because it is a sign of Y's self-confidence and strength. Again one cannot see why this should not be conceded, while accepting the turnabout at the end of the play as proof of X's dominance. It has never been asserted that, throughout the bulk of the play, X does not reveal her insecurity, only that finally she is able to make her vulnerability a source of strength, by accepting it.[12]

Selected Plays from Cynical Life

The six Plays from Cynical Life were written as a result of Strindberg's increasing dissatisfaction with the compressed 'naturalism' he had developed in the late 1880s. The economy of the Quart D'Heures had been achieved at the price of stifling his theatrical inventiveness. Then, in the early 1890s he began once again to write full-length one-act plays seeking greater dramatic flexibility to express more fully his sardonic attitudes towards society at large. Primarily, the Cynical Life plays contain less regular tempos and more disparate scene lengths than their predecessors. In embryo, these structural irregularities are developments contributing to his liberation from linear narrative which was to result in expressionism and the theatre of dreams.

The dominant theme of the six plays is disillusionment; with motherhood, with the courts and even with children. Misogyny, more or less virulent, permeates all of them with the exception of *Debit and Credit*. The degrees of cynicism that result vary from play to play. *Mother's Love*, *Playing with Fire* and *First Warning* are bitter whereas *The Bond* is anguished but relatively restrained. A quotation from *A Blue Book* sums up the general attitude they express.

> Life is not beautiful, on its animal, domestic and business sides it brings us into many ugly situations. Life is cynical since it ridicules our nobler feelings and flings scorn on our faith. Therefore it is difficult to use fine words in the stress of everyday existence; one hides one's better feelings in order not to expose them to ridicule. One might therefore say that men are partly better than they appear to be. One is forced to play the sceptic in order not to perish and one is made cynical by life's cynicism. (p. 267)

Since only two of the plays are dramatically interesting, the following discussion will be restricted to them.

PLAYING WITH FIRE (1892)

Up to scene eighteen, *Playing with Fire*[13] promises to be a fine synthesis of naturalistic and symbolic theatre; less powerful but more succinct than *The Dance of Death*. Unfortunately the last four scenes represent the triumph of Strindberg the misogynist over Strindberg the dramatist. This judgement is backed up by the evidence we have of the difficulty he had in rounding off the play and by the unusual extent to which he revised it. In fact, it has three different endings, none of which is dramatically satisfactory.

As the ambiguities of the title suggest, Strindberg creates an atmosphere of heat, both climatic and sexual, in which to depict a cynical comedy of social and marital disillusionment. The setting and the action which is pushed on by the characters' reactions to inertia and boredom resemble a cross between the plays of Chekhov and Tennessee Williams. Knut, the son, is a hedonistic weakling who is ready to seduce his self-centred, man-eating cousin Adèle but remains extremely jealous of his wife Kerstin. At the same time, there is a fatal contradiction at the centre of his character which drives him to thrust Kerstin into the arms of his friend Axel. When he does so, Kerstin becomes all the more attractive to him as she is desired by Axel. Knut is ultimately contemptible; he is parasitic in his affections and emotions. Even the idea of seducing Adèle only occurs to him after his wife has remarked on her vivacity. Within a marital menagerie Knut has become dominated by women and suffers, in a less advanced form, from the disease that destroys Adolf in *Creditors*. He even admits himself that 'I've been going around here for so long among petticoats that I've become like a woman' (p. 268). As an expression of her contempt for him, Kerstin dresses Knut in clothes resembling those of Axel.[14] Knut is, in fact, a Strindbergian portrait, less lurid than Adolf, of the deterioration of Scandinavian manhood under the tyranny of women.

Yet Knut is no worse than the rest of his family. His father is a pious, mean old hypocrite,[15] Adèle is a slut, and the mother, who is the sole relative with whom we can sympathise, is decidedly fey. Moreover, by marrying into this family, Kerstin has herself been infected by its manners and values, though she has the advantage that she is much stronger than her husband. An attractive, highly-sexed woman, her crucial vulnerability is that she is dangerously bored by her present life. She confesses: 'I feel so desperate that I long for something dreadful to happen—a pestilence, a fire—that my child should die! That I should die myself' (p. 262). This terrible feeling of frustration is the ultimate cause of her downfall. Like her husband she is a parasite and feels that she might only fall in love with Axel when he is with Adèle. While establishing a neat parallel between the parasitic adultery of both Kerstin and Knut, this also underlines the catalystic role of their lovers. As Axel realises: 'Miss Adèle and I seem to act as firelighters' (p. 263). Nevertheless, Kerstin is far from being a Strindbergian devil woman and, dramatically, cannot be made to bear the weight of blame forced on her in the last four scenes. Much of the implicit criticism directed against her by Axel is undermined by the fact that *he* is not so much a character as a code of honour; and an intolerable one at that.

His sense of honour extends almost solely to his own sex. A man of some experience, he is portrayed as knowing women for what they are. He professes to be under no illusion about their cruelty and the mortal strife involved in marriage. He has been with other women and distinguishes between adultery and marriage merely in terms of 'consecrated' and 'unconsecrated' dirt. But while bitter experience has taught him to dislike marriage, he cannot be called a woman-hater; he is just woman wary. Like Strindberg himself, Axel is not satisfied with promiscuity, he cannot 'bear to live in this house on crumbs from the rich man's table' (p. 273). To do so would not only be dishonourable, it would also be unsatisfying and un-manly. However, we suspect he would not decline on moral grounds to seduce Adèle if he was more than superficially attracted to her. Yet he does not attempt to approach her although he knows that 'she's got an exquisite figure', and even though Knut and Kerstin try to provoke an affair between them. He demands more than sex from a woman and cannot be satisfied by just a casual affair. So it would be misleading to argue that his fear of marriage *alone* drives him away from Kerstin at the end of the play. His cynicism is skin-deep as his basically romantic attitude to women indicates. We must then con-clude that he finds the specific prospect of marriage to *Kerstin* undesirable; and that the reasons for his revulsion are intended, by Strindberg, to constitute a criticism of *her*.

Hidden beneath the social conventions is evidence of unrest; sleeplessness, intrigue, matchmaking and gratuitous personal insult. Each character in the play (with the exception of the Mother) is trying to conceal his own feelings, while searching out and trying to exploit those of the others. The fire referred to in the title is the feelings of the characters. Knut plays with the feelings of Kerstin and Axel, Adèle with those of Axel and Knut, Kerstin with those of Axel and Knut and so on. Ultimately, the pressure of frustration becomes too intense for Kerstin who confesses her love for Axel. How far she is responsible for this is unclear. Certainly, she urges Axel to ignore Knut's feelings and to deceive him but Knut, by his constant masochistical playing with fire, his desire to feed off Axel's feelings for his wife and by his own infidelity, has encouraged their affair. Axel, the Strindbergian man of the world, acts honourably and rejects Kerstin's suggestion that they should continue as they are; controlling their feelings except when alone together. He knows that, for him at least, this would be both ignoble and impossible, though for a Strindbergian woman it would be natural. For this reason, they decide to tell Knut everything.

At this point Strindberg very skilfully interposes two short, relatively unimportant scenes which serve to intensify their passion and fears as they sit apart, on the edges of their chairs, waiting for their fate to be decided. Then, in Scene 18, Knut enters and the play disintegrates. Quite insufferably, the son now plays the role of the injured party: 'Consider my feelings a little, since I am comparatively innocent, and am always the one who suffers'—and we are not at all sure that Strindberg does not agree with him. 'Honourably', he decides to give up his wife to Axel who, surprisingly for a man of his experience, is overcome by this 'noble offer'. Here the play works at a shallow psychological level but what is even more dramatically unacceptable is that Strindberg is also writing dishonestly. Throughout the play, Knut has been portrayed as an ambivalent character who can only respond to his wife when someone else wants her. Thus, to intensify his desire he masochistically thrusts his wife into Axel's arms. Yet when the inevitable happens Kerstin is made the scapegoat for the whole affair. Moreover, Axel is attracted towards Kerstin because she is forbidden fruit (though he is capable of recognising the ephemerality of his feelings). Yet she alone is made to bear the blame. Now, for a man who, while adhering to a stern code of honour, can see through himself and through Kerstin (and by implication the whole female sex), it is curious to say the least that he cannot recognise Knut for the charlatan *he* is. The so-called nobility of the son's gesture would embarrass a gigolo let alone 'a gentleman', yet Axel feels guilty. Has the formerly forbidden fruit lost its attraction now that it has been offered? If this is the explanation of Axel's retreat and of his pretence to respect Knut's declaration, then it certainly is not realised dramatically.

By comparison with Knut, Kerstin is quite sympathetic. In Scene 2 with the Mother she particularly gains by contrast with him. Certainly, she is hysterical and self-seeking but she is not hypocritical and self-deluded. We can easily sympathise with her for being married to the son and having to endure the rivalry and spite of Adèle. Although she does not blame herself for the affair, she does validly criticise Axel in the 'Or from you . . .' speech in Scene 19. Indeed, throughout that scene, she appears more human than Axel; his sense of honour is snobbish, his self-righteousness dishonest.

Structurally, *Playing With Fire* is typical of Strindberg's cynical plays, possessing the fast flowing, temporally continuous narrative structure of the genre. In common with *Debit and Credit*, it contains coarse humour (e.g. 'the breast' *double entendre* in Scene 2), brutal wit (cf. the son's several attempts to take over his father's proverbs), malice (the mother is variously called a 'freak', an 'old frump' etc.) and a mood of boredom and disillusionment. It departs from the naturalistic tradition in creating a highly stylised character in the Father, in rejecting deterministic explanations and in its symbolist use of leit motifs. The most dominant of the latter is the use of 'fire' and related terms ('Ignite', 'matches', 'burns', 'dynamite') to describe the emotional tensions and impending explosions within the family. The sexual undercurrents create an atmosphere as vividly oppressive as in *Miss Julie* where again the characters are immersed in tides too powerful for them. But, unlike the earlier play, *Playing with Fire* predicates a universal degradation of love to a selfish uncontrollable impulse.

THE BOND (1892)

Strindberg wrote one other misogynistic drama, *The Bond*,[16] before his Inferno crisis of 1894. It is a fine play but it adds only a little to the views we have already discussed. Written about a year after he and Siri were judicially separated, the play is a savage attack on the legal system and on female intransigence. Throughout his career, Strindberg was to pillory the legal system (*The Road to Damascus*, *The Pelican*, 1907), lawyers (*A Dream Play*, 1901) and judges (*Advent*, 1898). He refused to accept that anyone, just by donning robes and a wig, should presume to take on the God-like role of a Judge. He could not understand how twelve men who are as weak and irrational as the rest of mankind, suddenly became competent to analyse the incredibly complicated relationship between a husband and wife, just by being sworn in. 'Marriage is a blood-bond and more—it is a sacred transaction. It is so tender and so fragile that a hasty word—a joke as one calls it—can make an end of it for the whole of life' (*A Blue Book*, p. 268). And most of all he questioned how anyone but God Himself could have the power to take a child from its parents and decide what its upbringing should be.

The setting of the play is a courtroom in which divorce proceedings between a Baron (an idealised self-portrait of Strindberg) and his wife are to be heard. The divorce is not in dispute but the custody of their son is. For the child's sake, the Baron nobly compromises with his wife; agreeing that there shall be 'no recriminations in Court' and that 'you keep the child during the year of separation, with the provision that it visits whenever I please and that it is brought up according to the principles I have laid down and you have approved' (p. 179). He makes these concessions although it is apparent that the Baroness was largely to blame for their quarrels. In the interests of his son, he subdues his pride because he knows that 'if we wrangle about the child and challenge each other's claim to have charge of it, the Judge can order it to be taken from us both and handed over to pietists to bring up in hatred and contempt of its parents' (p. 180). Initially his wife agrees with him but the law will not allow them the dignity of parting amicably. As a result of its insensitivity and inadequacy and by using their child as bait, the court compels the Baron and his wife to re-enact their marital strife in public. Like Miss Julie's mother, the Baroness has tried to reverse the sexual nature of her child, 'she has wanted to bring the boy up to become a woman instead of a man' (p. 189). She has also used her sexuality to gain her own financial ends. For the first time in the theatre Strindberg *explicitly* propounds the view that marriage is most often a form of prostitution.[17] Such a view was implied in *The Father* when the Captain described marriage as a legalistic arrangement but in *The Bond* the Baron states categorically that 'she introduced prostitution into my marriage, first for power, then for gifts and money' (p. 191). This theme is a natural development of Strindberg's earlier views in that, having promised to 'love, honour and obey', a woman's only weapons on the battlefield to which marriage decays, are her body and her child. And the universal excuse for her cruelty is always, 'I shrink from nothing where my child is concerned' (p. 193); in the Baroness's case perjury in Laura's manslaughter.

What is essentially new in this play is the way Strindberg destroys once and for all the opportunity for critics to misinterpret his view of women as simple figures of spite and Machiavellian evil. Unlike Laura, Tekla and even Julie, the Baroness is an *obviously* pathetic figure. She is clearly a victim. Her unthinking disregard for anyone but herself and her child wounds the very objects she is most concerned to protect. Invariably her intelligence tells her that the Baron is right. For the sake of their own interests and that of the child, they must appear to agree in court and indulge in no recrimination, yet she *cannot* control herself despite the Baron's attempts to smooth things over. As soon as the judge suggests that she might have been 'the cause of dissension', she cannot resist quarrelling with the Baron, although she realises that to do so is disastrous. She is so overwhelmed by hatred of him, by her self-righteousness and by her jealous regard for her child that she cannot even use her common-sense in her own interests.

The Baron is portrayed as a man of utmost dignity and the blame is placed squarely upon the Baroness, yet it is impossible to despise her completely. At the end, she is a pitiable creature, reduced to near dementia and able only 'to scream myself tired against God who has put this devilish love into the world to torment mankind (p. 207).[18] All in all, though, she is only partly responsible for her unhappiness. The real villain of the piece is the law. Strindberg's horror of the miscarriage of justice is encapsulated in the trial that opens the play where the farmer Alexandersson, a palpably honest man, is persecuted by the court because he does not have any witnesses to support his accusation of Alma's dishonesty. In Strindberg's opinion, this is typical of those cases in which the intricacies of legal procedure seemed designed to convict the innocent and free the guilty. Trammelled by technicalities which they enforce so pompously, lawyers cannot allow their common sense to influence their judgements. In this respect Strindberg's dramatic opinion of the law did not change greatly over the years as is clear in *The Pelican* (1907).

I could never be a lawyer. I don't believe in the legal system. The laws must have been passed by thieves and murderers for the benefit of criminals. One truthful witness proves nothing, but two untruthful witnesses is proof positive. At noon I've got a clear-cut case, at 12.30 I've lost it. One slip of the pen can put a blameless man behind bars. If I take pity on some scamp, he sues me for defamation. (Scene 3)

The Bond eventually rises above marital strife, that is the struggle of two people *within* a marriage, and aspires to discuss the problem of human existence itself. The court scenes have been a one-sided indictment of the Baroness, a necessary catharsis for Strindberg to release from his system the bitterness described in *A Madman's Defence*, but once the judgement of the court had been pronounced the question of blame is cast aside and the much more elevated theme of the human condition itself is touched on. Reverting to the naturalist's hereditary-environmentalist explanation, Strindberg gives the Baroness the speech:

> Yes, but did I make myself? Put the evil tendencies, the hatred and the wild passions into myself? No! Who denied me the power and the will to fight them? When I look at myself at this moment I feel I should be pitied. Shouldn't I? (p. 206)

Her husband agrees with her. He admits that they did everything 'to avoid the rocks of marriage', even 'living in sin'. Neither of them wished to be brought to the present nemesis; circumstances just seemed to be beyond their control. They were in a maze from which there seemed to be no escape. 'It is as if we have been dragged into a mill and got our clothes caught in the mill. And all these malicious people stand looking on laughing' (p. 195). But who or what then was to blame?

> Do you know with what, do you know with whom, we strove? You call him God, but I call him Nature. And what power incited us to hatred, just as he incites mankind to love. And now we are doomed to lacerate each other so long as one spark of life remains in us. (p. 207)

Strindberg's decision to put the blame on God or a pantheistic Nature provides an extreme contrast to his post-Inferno thought. After 1898 he would have deemed this speech of the Baron's to be a particularly vile kind of blasphemy. Moreover, the Baroness commits the same sin when she vows to 'scream myself tired against God'. It is perhaps symptomatic of the uncertain state of Strindberg's thought at this time, that he should excuse his characters on the grounds of some cosmological conspiracy. The Baron, Baroness and Strindberg himself are like the Stranger in *To Damascus*; they are unable to understand the whole sphere of Divine Justice and so arrogantly condemn God for what they take to be His specific injustices.

The ending of *The Bond* is perhaps the most despairing of all the pre-Inferno plays because it dramatises Strindberg's worst horror; that of losing his children to foster parents. This fear is made all the more harrowing for him since the new parents are unintelligent peasants whose 'coarse ways will gradually torture the child to death'. The manner in which the Baroness is to be tormented for her treachery here is not so far removed from the Swedenborgian notion that evil is its own punishment, because she does in fact bring the loss of her child on herself. She and the Baron squabble over him until he is taken away and now they will continue to hate each other because they are inescapably linked by him. The child will remain the persistent reminder of their love and their hate and their loss. 'Because he is our love which took flesh. He is the memory of our most beautiful moments, the bond which unites our souls, the meeting-place where we come together always, whether we will or no. And that is why we can never be parted, even if we are divorced' (pp. 196–7).

Several commentators have remarked that the logic ('God' or 'Nature'), which drives the Baron and his wife through the purgatory of their marriage, has a mystical quality reminiscent of the later work (cf. Lamm *Strindberg's Dramer*, p. 409, Madsen, *Strindberg's Naturalistic Theatre*, p. 151). *The Bond* is seen by them as the transitional semi-spiritual play that its date of composition would suggest. This is obviously an attractive point of view because it enables us to trace the continuity of Strindberg's thought. However, we must not overstate the mysticism of *The Bond* and ignore the fact that this play is largely a clear development of the naturalism of *The Father* and *Creditors*. What Madsen calls, 'Strindberg's conception of nature as a mysterious power or an anthropomorphic force' (p. 151), seems to be nothing more than a mixture of naturalistic determinism and the notion of the married state as being an inevitable state of conflict; perhaps made rather murky here by the author's personal doubts and confusions. Extrapolating from his previous analyses of male–female antagonism, he now argues that beyond the tactics the sexes choose to employ, the essential larger strategy is outside their control. Thus whether we blame nature or nurture or transcendent forces (and it is significant that in so far as Strindberg makes a choice, through the character of the Baron, he plumps for Nature) we must accept that human beings have little more choice about their destiny than puppets.

While perhaps not scaling the heights of *Miss Julie* and *Creditors*, *The Bond* is a brilliantly constructed piece of theatre in which the familiar court scene is not merely the usual stage within a stage but an analogue of life itself. It provides the stimulus for the Baron and his wife to re-enact (or more exactly relive) their marital disharmony in public. By removing his focal position outside the relationship, Strindberg is able to extend the references of his analysis to society as a whole. The highly personal struggle of this couple is used to indict the legal system, to question the right of anyone to interfere with (let alone judge) the *private* affairs of individuals, and to draw parallels between the helplessness of the protagonists and that of the Judge who has to punish where he personally knows he should reward. The marriage of the Baron becomes a microcosm of larger social issues such as the implicit conflict between the Church and the Law, between master and servant, between justice and the legal system. Strindberg magnificently integrates these numerous issues within the central relationship and in the case of the Baroness presents a profound and biting psychological study. In this more than almost any other play he wrote is his dramatic control in evidence. The gradual pressures of the legal and marital trap within which the couple squirms compel them to reveal themselves in all their emotional nakedness. As the personalities of the Baron and his wife are completely displayed, Strindberg transforms what was an existentialist theme to an essentialist one, thus managing to raise what would have been bitterness to utter despair and what might have been cynicism to a profound pessimism.

A Transitional Drama

THE KEYS OF HEAVEN (1892)

Of all the pre-Inferno plays, *The Keys of Heaven*[19] most clearly anticipates the style, themes and mood of the later religious allegories.

Dream sequences, mental scenery, circular-'station'-structure, dopple-gangers and expressionistic parody are exploited rigorously in order to examine the nature of man's spiritual destiny. Although *A Dream Play* and *To Damascus* are much more rich in imagery and complex in theme and structure, they are not necessarily more profound in their moral questioning than *The Keys of Heaven*. Its final act is deeply ambiguous, reflecting the emotional confusion that, by 1892, was hastening Strindberg to the spiritual crossroads of his life. Naturalistic beliefs continued to influence his outlook but they no longer convinced him. And, as he had not yet read Swedenborg, he could find no other explanation for the suffering and the mysteries of his life. Consequently, the idea of heaven became important to him even though it appeared to be surrounded by impossible intellectual difficulties.

He knew that ideals can act as palliatives; means by which we might endure for a while longer the anguish of living. But, once surrendered to, they become illusions; drugs which are the source of even greater misery. The promise of heaven seems to make this life bearable but what eathly reason can there be for believing in it, when innocent children are slaughtered, when man is too base to deserve salvation and when the Church seems to be concerned only with its own temporal power? In these circumstances, is not belief in heavenly bliss yet another illusion which sooner or later will let man down. Since this question is central to the play, the concepts of the *ideal* and the *illusory* are the twin moral notions of *The Keys of Heaven*. It examines a number of false ideals (heavens) by which men seek to live and the personal vanities that inspire them. In the course of this, most human aspirations are found to be inadequate; merely self-indulgent hopes which serve less to improve man than to reveal his weakness and arrogance. Ultimately, then, *The Keys of Heaven* is an attack on self-deception and illusion; a hard-headed plea for a sense of reality.

Characteristically the play opens on a note of despair. In a smithy, suitably decorated with Christian paintings representing salvation and the protection of the innocent, three children have died. Surrounded by the tools and products of his trade, symbols of earthly toil and physical restraint, their father, a blacksmith, laments his existence. Now that he has been deprived of 'all that is most dear and precious' (his personal heaven) he can no longer tolerate the idea of

living alone. The Physician, who is Strindberg's principal mouthpiece in the play, tries to persuade him that even the greatest sorrows
are temporary, and that every loss can be replaced.

> The remedy's not always like the affliction,
> for poisonous burn is soothed by cooling salve;
> You know that they who've lost their sense of sight
> must learn to see with ear and hand;
> You know that when your helpmeet died,
> you soon forgot her for your children (p. 81)

And he goes on to offer further comfort,

> what bliss to die when one is young
> before the evilness of life has touched us (p. 82)

These attitudes to personal suffering, of course, are at best desperate
sources of comfort and, in *The Keys of Heaven*, Strindberg investi-
gates their implications by asking what in life can replace genuine
love and whether we have any reason for believing that death, by
saving us from the miseries of life, can transport us to something
better. The sceptical conclusions to which he came were, by 1892,
paradoxically a sign of his need to believe in something beyond the
here and now.

Prompted by the Physician, the Smith reveals his desire to travel; an
ambition which gradually takes his mind off his loss. In true expressionistic style, the scenery conforms to the protagonist's changing
mental state. Furniture and clothing associated with the dead
children slowly disappear as their memory image leaves the Smith's
mind. His forthcoming pilgrimage will achieve three things: forgetfulness, an examination of what life has to offer in place of love and,
through the symbolic search for St Peter's lost Keys, an understanding of the reality of heaven. St Peter is, in part, a figure of fun
through whom the ineptitude of religious prophecy is exposed and
also an object of compassion whose muddled desire to do good in a
brutal world which he does not understand is extraordinarily
moving. He varies between harshness and gentleness; between the
conventional pamphleteer and the saint who naively believes in
human goodness. Through him Strindberg maintains the belief that
sanctity is more often than not a historical accident rather than a
spiritual decision. Throughout the play, in fact, orthodox religion

receives quite a battering. Clearly Strindberg was ripe for the non-conformities of Swedenborg.

The development of the play is defined by the Physician who signals scene changes and engineers the Smith's forthcoming experiences. For example, he forecasts that the Smith will meet and love an ugly woman, that he will see his children once more in heaven, and he also transforms the Smith into the giant of the Mountain. The Physician declares his function in a speech of almost Brechtian alienation;

> I am the master of the art of magic
> but my enchantment is quite rational.
> It's nothing but a setting that you see;
> its mechanism is a trifle complicated
> and must be mastered thoroughly,
> its common name is 'change of scene'. Let's go. (p. 88)

He is an expressionist device; the narrator, the puppeteer. As such his role is very much like those of the Beggar-Confessor in the Damascus trilogy and Indra in *A Dream Play*.

Act 1 Scene 1 is a fanciful satire on human vanity which teaches the Smith one of the major lessons of the play, namely, 'know yourself'. By discovering that external appearances are unimportant and that the soul is the reality of self, the Smith is prepared for his encounter, and subsequent love affair, with the ugly Courtesan. But before he can truly know himself, he must first understand life. This he begins to do when, in Act 2, he experiences the sensual life which he must transcend before he can fulfil himself. His meeting with the Courtesan makes him realise that there is no correlation whatsoever between physical appearance and spiritual worth. The beautiful may be either good *or* evil, as may the ugly.[20] So the Smith's persistent love for the hideous Courtesan can be interpreted by each character according to his own lights. To St Peter it represents a proof of the heavenly kingdom; to the cynical Don Quixote it is a proof of the madness of mankind.

Don Quixote is not at all as Cervantes conceived him. He attends the belated wedding of Romeo and Juliet which is the centrepiece of a fantasy sequence dominated by literary characters. No longer an absurd idealist, the Don has become a disillusioned cynic who can see only the misery and deceit of human life. Sancho Panza, on the other hand, has been converted by his master's former optimism. Quixote's new realism enables him to condemn the Smith's naive love for the Courtesan. He also exposes the bizarre activities of his fictional companions at the wedding; the sexual misdemeanours of Romeo, the hypocrisy of Bluebeard's marriage to Lady Macbeth, Othello's illusions and Hamlet's vanity. In Quixote's brilliant set speech, which is permeated with irony and misanthropy, Strindberg anticipates much of the despair that was later to compel him to turn away from life. According to Don Quixote, all men can do is 'stuff each other full of lies—so full that you have to go behind the stable and take a look to see how you appear inside' (p. 99). This is perhaps the finest scene in the play and Don Quixote's disgust is the most intense feeling expressed by any of its characters.

As if to justify Quixote's cynicism, the Smith's love for the Courtesan withers. Although it had survived Quixote's jibes, it fails to survive the Smith's own temperament. And with the loss of love comes disillusion. As Quixote says: 'the power of illusion is mighty' (p. 101), it can explain everything, love and hate. So, like Strindberg in his later life, the Smith has 'lost all illusions of finding a heaven on the earth, having come to the conclusion that it's hell to live' (p. 102). The Physician finds such sentiments difficult to argue with so he gets rid of the fantasy character with words that might almost serve as a poetic revelation of religious expressionism: 'You shadow creatures! I called you forth from earth to clothe your thoughts in visual form and image—return below ... And turn again to will-o-the-wisps in dried-up wells of putrid vapours' (p. 102).

By now thoroughly infected with Quixote's pessimism, the Smith wishes to become a giant so that he can dominate and, if he wishes, destroy the world he has come to despise. Consequently, in Act 3, the Physician transforms him into the Old Man of Ho Mountain. This giant can see clearly the petty egoism of men from the vantage point of his height and is inclined to annihilate all that irritates him. His size makes him an object of loathing, though in fact he is no worse than anyone else. The dwarves who torment him are no better than he is; they represent human pettiness and are both selfish and dishonest. For instance, they rob St Peter who naively believes in their innocence. Yet while everyone hates the huge bully, nearly everyone fails to notice the greed and cruelty of these tiny creatures. In this way natural prejudices (illusions) and gullibility govern our lives and distort our undesrtanding of people and society. The scene, in sum, warns against the rule of the masses; against democracy.

Meanwhile, Don Quixote has fallen in love and has recovered his ideals. As he says: 'it is through change and variation that we attain true stability' (p. 113)—a truth to which the experience of the Smith will testify. Power has made him destructive, intolerant and isolated. Alone, he now must experience the aridity of so called perfection. Thus Act 4 takes place in Schlaraffenland,[21] a land literally flowing with milk and honey—most people's idea of heaven. But as, Sancho Panza realises, it is enervating. Even at this stage, Strindberg was temperamentally close to Swedenborg's unorthodoxies. Work and strife are needed to revitalise man but unfortunately once these are introduced all the old human ambitions arise and destroy all hope of peace. Once again human ideals degrade into human illusion. The dilemma is inescapable for, as Sancho Panza suggests, 'one ought never to survive one's ideals' (p. 118).

Having exhausted all temporal paths that might lead to heaven, the only other hope would seem to be the established Church, but this, too, proves to be illusory. The Pope is arrogant and full of his own importance; rejecting Peter himself when the saint exposes the legend which the Catholic Church has created for him. The illusions of organised religion are extremely potent but they can be transcended by men of decision. So at last St Peter realises that the way to heaven is not via power or love or even the Church but the Kierkegaardian individualistic 'way of the Cross . . . I mean through suffering' (p. 125).[22] At the foot of the Cross both St Peter and Don Quixote find peace. Playing agent-provocateur in the guise of the Wandering Jew, the Physician causes Quixote to defend the truth of Christ's life and to embrace the one ideal that will not decay into illusion. Now the Don can die and his life provides a model of the way that salvation can issue from personal insecurity. St Peter, too, has found the key to his heaven in the Cross. Only the Smith cannot end his quest here, because he has a cross of his own to bear; the cross of his morning. He must rebuild his life; his own heaven on earth.

The last scene takes place in the Tower of Babel where the arrogance of those who seek to trespass on 'celestial paradise' is shown; Icarus, Prometheus and Jacob are each criticised. Afterwards when the Smith climbs up Jacob's ladder, he discovers that *his* heaven contains his long-lost children. Now, enlightened by his numerous experiences he discovers the ladder that leads not to heaven but back to earth. In view of what has gone before, we might imagine this as hardly an edifying prospect but this time the glimpse of his children will give him courage to face life, while the memories of his pilgrimage will preserve him from the arrogance of seeking heaven prematurely. 'I had sinned out of arrogance, hubris, the one vice that the gods do not forgive' (*Inferno*, p. 79).

The Keys of Heaven is a considerable achievement which occupies a transitional place in his corpus. Its value, at least in part, depends on the skill with which Strindberg fuses a wide variety of moods, attitudes and styles (expressionism, allegory, fairy tale, dream and satire) to testify on the dramatic level to the truth he quotes on the moral level: 'All movement forward is like a wave—undulating—first up and then down' (p. 113). These words are worth remembering when studying the later masterpieces, *To Damascus* and *A Dream Play*. Like them, it is an expressionistic attempt to convey a unified, subjective vision of man's existence. If we insist upon regarding it as a satirical fantasy resembling *Lucky Peter's Travels*, we shall conclude with Lamm that the satire is uncontrolled and pointless. If, however, we realise that the ostensibly satirical scenes must be interpreted from the Smith and the Physician's joint subjective position, we shall appreciate the spiritual depth of the play and also the significance of its experimentalism.

PART TWO

The Post-Inferno Plays

5

General Introduction to the
Post-Inferno Plays

During the 'Inferno' period (1894–7), Strindberg suffered an emotional and spiritual crisis which led him to the very edge of insanity and from which he emerged intellectually a changed man. He was partly saved through the influence of his mother-in-law, Maria Uhl, who induced him to read Swedenborg's *Heaven and Hell* and *Arcana Coelestia*;[1] books which had an immediate therapeutic effect on him and, in the long term, formalised his essentially religious nature. Although his personality did not radically change— he remained the tormented neurotic he had always been—one cannot read his post-Inferno work without noticing the metamorphosis that had taken place in his thinking.

From the secular playwright of the eighties who constantly projected his guilt feelings on to such external forces as the female sex, the class structure, the legal system and the Church, he became a primarily religious author, still obsessed with his own guilt, but able for the first time to explain his sufferings in terms of the supernatural; in particular, in terms of Providence, the Spiritual Powers and the doctrines of Original Sin and Divine Retribution. Having begun his literary career as a misogynist and a social rebel he turned, in middle age, to misanthropy and spiritual stoicism. Much of the despair of his later work was plainly the result of his terrible 'Inferno' experiences which would have strained the most resilient of men, let alone someone with Strindberg's hypersensitive temperament. But the nature of his struggle throughout the rest of his life to resign himself to the human condition and to achieve spiritual peace can only be explained *fully* by examining the curious combination of philosophical and religious ideas he embraced. He had been familiar with the ideas of Schopenhauer and Kierkegaard from his early days; what is new is the way he used them and accommodated them to Swedenborgian mysticism. For anyone interested in the formation and development of Strindberg's ideas during the Inferno period,

Gunnar Brandell's classic *Strindberg In Inferno* is required reading. A glance at that book will reveal how selective the following treatment is though this does not necessarily mean that it is misleading.

SCHOPENHAUER (1788–1860)

Schopenhauer's influence on Strindberg can be detected in three doctrines; the phenomenal world as illusion, life as a kind of purgatory and the possibility of respite from suffering through asceticism and aesthetic contemplation. In both writers these views are combined with a generally pessimistic attitude to mankind and are underpinned by impressive psychological observations. Again, they both universalise and variously modify these doctrines by locating them within a context of Hindu-Buddhist mythology and mysticism.

Schopenhauer is the only totally pessimistic Western philosopher of modern times who is of great stature. For him the world in which we live is a world of appearance; the Hindu Maya, the Strindbergian dream. Beyond it is true reality, the noumenal world, which is the Will. Will is blind, endless striving utterly without purpose; as such it is both cruel and meaningless. The phenomenal world is merely an expression of the Will and so is a place of pain and pointless misery. 'If the immediate and direct purpose of our life is not suffering, then our existence is the most ill-adapted to its purpose in the world: for it is absurd to suppose that the endless affliction of which the world is everywhere full, and which arises out of the need and distress pertaining essentially to life, should be purposeless and purely accidental. Each individual misfortune, to be sure, seems an exceptional occurrence; but misfortune in general is the rule.'[2] This perfectly sums up Strindberg's later vision of life on a non-religious level.

Inevitably, men try to hide life's misery by interpreting the Universe as Divine Creation; that is, by devising theories in which human suffering appears as transitory and, ultimately, redeemable. For Schopenhauer, these efforts are merely further indications of the Will's determination to endure. The Will to Live determines all our thoughts and behaviour; our minds and bodies are objectified Will, so even our rationalisations and our religious beliefs are characterised by a blind, egotistical striving. Strindberg himself was only too aware of this self-centred urge to survive; this urge to assert oneself at the expense of God and one's fellows and he struggled constantly to free his religious yearning from the apparently inevitable taint of vain-glory. Even the desire to procreate is seen by Schopenhauer as selfish. 'If the act of procreation were neither the outcome of a desire nor accompanied by feelings of pleasure, but a matter to be decided on the basis of purely rational considerations, is it likely the human race would still exist? Would each of us not rather have felt so much pity for the coming generation as to prefer to spare it the burden of existence, or at least not wish to take it upon himself to impose that burden upon it in cold blood.'³ While it is difficult to believe that Strindberg would have agreed for long with Schopenhauer's views about procreation (his love of children was too great), it is beyond argument that the suffering of children in his plays usually represents the depths of his revulsion from life. The idea of the innocent con-demned to a miserable existence through an accident of birth caused him deep pain; compare the Strangers attitude to his unborn child in *To Damascus*.

As a result of their subservience to the Will, men are resolutely egotistical creatures who make of the world a battleground in which each individual tries to dominate and exploit his fellows. Whatever veneer of civilisation we acquire, we discover eventually that we are all governed by blind, unconscious and ultimately uncontrollable instincts. All our efforts to accumulate knowledge, to plan action and to organise society are simply abortive attempts to persuade ourselves that we are rational agents. It was a similar sense of bleak and helpless despair about man and life that drove Strindberg to account for the evil in life in Swedenborgian terms. Schopenhauer would have understood (though not endorsed!) his response very well; '... religion affords an inexhaustible source of consolation and comfort in the countless and great sufferings of life which does not desert men even in the hour of death but rather only then reveals its full efficacy. Religion may thus be compared to one who takes a blind man by the hand and leads him, since he cannot see for himself and the sole point is that he should arrive at his destination, not that he should see all there is to see.'⁴

Schopenhauer maintains that there are two ways we can escape from our subservience to the Will. Through aesthetic contemplation we can attain temporary release. By this means man becomes a disinterested observer, free at least for a time from the egotistical desires and demands of the Will. Permanent release can only be achieved by continual asceticism which inhibits the Will to Live. This involves self-denial and self-mortification but never suicide which, paradoxically, is seen as a concession of defeat to the Will. Rather, one should struggle throughout life to deny one's irrational desires and unconscious impulses. At various times, particularly in his later life, Strindberg responded to the ascetic ideal. While his difficult personality made his life a terrible ordeal, he rarely considered suicide, but he did, on several occasions, seriously think about retreating from life to a non-confessional monastery where he could devote himself to contemplation. Without the religious overtones, this would conform to the ideal advocated but never achieved by Schopenhauer. The path to personal peace was, for both men, one of suffering which must be accepted, even embraced, in the ceaseless struggle to overcome the self. '. . . Also we see those who have once attained to the denial of the Will to Live, strive with all their might to keep upon this path, by enforced renunciation of every kind, by penance and severity of life, and by selecting whatever is disagreeable to them, all in order to suppress the will, which is constantly springing up anew . . . Then we see the man who has passed through all the increasing degrees of affliction with the most vehement resistance, and is finally brought to the verge of despair, suddenly retire into himself, know himself and the world, change his whole nature, rise above himself and all suffering as if purified and sanctified.'[5]

The Stranger's decision to retreat from the world into a life of silence and contemplation (according to one interpretation!) at the close of the Damascus trilogy would represent for Schopenhauer the only way to escape from the turbulently egotistical life he has endured. Again, the Hunter in *The Great Highway* resembles a Schopenhauerian ascetic who learns that the struggle against the Will can never cease. High in the Alps he can attain relative peace but as soon as he descends to the world of men the old longings, the inevitable stirrings of the Will disturb his tranquillity. The progress of Strindberg's later protagonists is perfectly summarised by Schopenhauer in *The World as Will and Idea*. 'Therefore every suffering coming to him from without, through chance or the wickedness of others, is welcome to him, every injury, ignominy and insult . . . he bears such with inexhaustible patience and meekness, returns good for evil without ostentation, and allows the fire of anger to rise within him just as little as that of desire. And he mortifies not only the will itself, but also its visible form, its objectivity, the body . . . he practises fasting and even resorts to chastisement and self-inflicted torture, in order that, by constant privation and suffering, he may more and more break down and destroy the will which he recognises and abhors as the source of his own suffering existence and that of the world.'6 With the probable exception of self-chastisement this describes the kind of life Strindberg strove to adopt increasingly after his final break with Harriet Bosse.

Both Schopenhauer and Strindberg were attracted to Hindu-Buddhism. The philosopher saw the phenomenal world as Maya, the veil of illusion and pain; a distorted reflection of higher reality. In *A Dream Play* Strindberg portrayed man suspended in a dream, condemned to suffer by the indifference of the Hindu deity, Indra. Essentially, the notion of Maya, mutable and impermanent, behind which eternal reality lies, is the idea so brilliantly defined in the Preface to *A Dream Play*. In both Hindu and Buddhist thought there is a demand for escape from the drives of the ego. Man only attains spiritual identity, total self-knowledge, transcendental calm, when he has gone beyond not only the desires of the flesh but all desire. For Schopenhauer, this Nirvana or Samadhi or Mukti was equivalent to temporary aesthetic bliss or permanent self-denial. For Strindberg, it constituted variously the despairing rejection of life in *To Damascus*, the world weary but finally hopeful self-immolation that climaxes *A Dream Play*, the lifeless purity of the Young Lady in *The Ghost Sonata* or the patient, resigned vigil of the Hunter at the close of *The Great Highway* as he awaits the release that death alone can bring.

Eduard von Hartmann (1840–1906) was a follower of Schopenhauer, whom Strindberg *originally* read before 1880.7 In his magnum opus *The Philosophy of the Unconscious*, Hartmann argued that ultimate reality is the Unconscious from which the cosmos developed by chance. At the time of the Fall of Man, the Unconscious became separated into Will and Idea; roughly emotion and intellect.8 The Schopenhauerian Will To Live provides the motive force of the world but cannot *explain* it. The Hegelian Rational Idea gives order to the world but cannot create it. The Will produces pain and suffering and inhibits human evolution. The Idea produces reason, purpose and progress; its dominance is man's only hope of survival as a mental and spiritual unity. So the end of the cosmic process is the liberation of the Rational Idea from the servitude of Blind Will. This produces consciousness which introduces meaning into the World.

However, Hartmann's conclusion is not optimistic because he argues that refinement and civilisation bring an increase of suffering as well as a growth of consciousness; 'consciousness is pain'.[9] Also, cultural progress is only achieved at the expense of repressing spiritual values. Thus, ultimately, man's only hope is for him to become so conscious of the nature of the universe that he freely chooses cosmic suicide. This is man's destiny and, at the same time, his finest hour. Until this time, he must actively support social evolution by behaving as unselfishly as possible; that is, by submitting to the Will as little as possible.

The influence of Hartmann's pessimism on such dramas as *To Damascus* and *A Dream Play* is considerable. Also, by his emphasis on the Unconscious as the primary source of cosmic reality and on conscious motives as artefacts built upon darkly hidden impulses, the German philosopher expressed many of Swedenborg's insights in a secular, more psychological form. And this influenced the development of Strindberg's dramatic expressionism. Moreover, his sympathy for Hartmann's theory of universal destruction served to determine the tone and themes of his later pilgrimage dramas and perhaps, paradoxically—since Hartmann eschewed Oriental philosophy—caused him to find consolation in Eastern idealism. On the whole, the tensions within Hartmann's philosophy between Will and Idea were more congenial to Strindberg's temperament than the black pessimism of Schopenhauer. More importantly, the conjunction of the two German pessimists' philosophies with their psychological insights provided him with the comfort that his own emotional problems, though extreme, were not unique.

KIERKEGAARD (1813–55)

The voluminous writings of the Danish philosopher Kierkegaard had a strong influence on Strindberg throughout his life.[10] From his early pietism to his final phase of mystical pessimism his outlook betrays the religious unease and need for spiritual commitment that is typically associated with Kierkegaard. The all or nothing attitude of the first 'official' existentialist remained permanently attractive to him. Compromise was always difficult for Strindberg; it must be either love or loathing, God or the World, Art or Life, self-assertion or self-abnegation; never both nor anything in between. His life was a constant testing of the truth of Kierkegaard's demand that we choose: 'either–or'. This is particularly evident in his attitude towards Christianity.

> One must consume it all: the impure, the long and the short, the dogmas and miracles. One should swallow it uncritically, naively, in great gulps, then it goes down like castor-oil in hot coffee. Open your mouth and shut your eyes! That's the only way.
>
> (*A Blue Book*, p. 114)

Both the notion and the irony is reminiscent of Kierkegaard.

The central concept of Kierkegaard's philosophy is *choice*. Having rejected the view that there can be any objective criteria for moral values, he urges that man must subjectively choose his own moral and spiritual commitment. Like Strindberg, he regarded orthodox theology and the established church as obstacles to the attainment of true religious faith. Nothing must be interposed between the individual and his God. A man must select the kind of life he will lead unaided and, since there are no criteria, this cannot be a rational choice, it must be a blind leap of faith. Strindberg would have agreed with this but he would have qualified its implications somewhat by a psychological point. 'The truths of religion never contradict reason until the latter has been clouded by an evil will. But then the discoveries begin and then every religious truth "contradicts" reasons' (*A Blue Book*, p. 72).

There are three ways of living available to a man. *Aesthetic* life is defined by the goals of pleasure and the avoidance of pain. Its archetype is Don Juan, the supremely hedonistic, sensual man (an Epicurean), though the range of aesthetic pleasures can encompass both sexual lust and the enjoyment of great art. *Ethical* life is characterised by a variety of determinate moral rules and duties which give it consistency because they are accepted as universally binding. The ethicist transcends the self-centred aestheticism of the first stage and accepts the responsibilities of community membership. The model ethical man would be Socrates; a Stoic. *Religious* life, for which the ethical is a necessary prologue, is distinguished by an irrational obedience to God: who, for Kierkegaard, is essentially the Christian God. 'Without risk there is no faith. Faith is precisely the contradiction between the infinite passion of the individual's inward-ness and the objective uncertainty.'[11] The kind of leap of faith necessary to live religiously is that of Abraham's 'sacrifice' of Isaac which seems counter to one's ethical duty and one's rational instincts. Thus the intrusion of the Divine makes demands upon one that seem absurd and even criminal.

The motive forces of the leap from one stage of life to a higher level are despair and dread. Dissatisfied with the aesthetic life we are leading but not knowing the nature of the existence to which we are committing ourselves we feel *dread*. The burden of our freedom of choice and the consequent fear of the unknown precipitate a feeling of paralysis. 'One may liken dread to dizziness. He whose eyes chance to look down into the yawning abyss becomes dizzy.'[12] We cannot remain at the aesthetic level once we have glimpsed the intimations of eternity within us, so eventually the tension produced by our dread compels us recklessly to leap forward; to live out our terrifying freedom. This ambivalence explains why Kierkegaard describes dread as 'sympathetic antipathy and antipathetic sym-pathy'. Only when we have passed through this acutely painful state are we able to make the qualitative transition to a higher stage, but even when we have made the leap into the religious life we are not at peace, for the leap cannot be made once and for all. It must be renewed every day of our lives. For this reason, the religious path is one of constant hardship, beset by conflicts and contradictions. The struggle to preserve a truly religious attitude demands faith and perpetual vigilance; a continual reaffirmation and renewal of one's religious being. This involves facing and transcending *despair*, 'the sickness unto death'.[13] Despair arises from the uncertainty of our lives and takes the form of a refusal to be oneself. Since there are no clear rules governing our relationship with God, we feel utterly weak and seek to evade the total reality of our freedom. This results in our denying God. Once we have realised that we have the eternal within us, any attempt to reject ourselves necessarily involves a repudiation of our relationship with God, and ultimately of God Himself. Only the Christian can transcend his despair and trust with total humility in God's Mercy. The true Christian is he who commits himself to God *in spite* of the evidence. Yet even so this is not a decision of desperation; it remains a silent, personal decision to suffer before God. It is an act of totally trusting, totally personal, witness. By contrast, many men who lack faith convert their despair into defiance; relapsing like the Stranger in *To Damascus* into a self-obsessed solitude. This is why Kierkegaard says 'I counsel you to despair . . . not as a comfort or permanence but because every man who has not tasted the bitterness of despair has missed the significance of life'[14]—a truly Strindbergian sentiment!

A definitive category of the religious life is *Repetition*. Unlike the repetitive search for pleasure of the aesthetic life (which in fact has no continuity but is constantly changing so that the past can never be recaptured), genuine repetition gives identity to the religious life. When the man of faith achieves repetition, he is able to integrate the events of his life into a personal, highly subjective perspective. While the life of the aesthetic man 'is like a plot of ground in which all sorts of herbs are planted, all with the same claim to thrive; his self consists of this multifariousness, and he has not self which is higher than this',[15] the religious man is truly an individual, totally himself and his life is uniquely the continuous expression of his faith in God. Through repetition man is able to define himself and his world and realise his freedom. 'Who could wish to let oneself be stirred by everything that is fleeting and new, which every day newly delights the effeminate soul? If God himself had not willed repetition, the world would never have come into existence . . . therefore the world endures, and it endures for the fact that it is a repetition. Repetition is reality and it is the seriousness of life. He who wills repetition is matured in seriousness.'[16]

Time and again in his later plays, Strindberg embodied the Kierkegaardian notion of repetition in their structure. It is there in *A Dream Play*, *The Great Highway* and the Chamber Plays, but most notably in *To Damascus*. As he himself wrote of the trilogy in a letter of March 1898 to Geijerstam:

> The artful point lies in the composition, which symbolises 'the Repetition' that Kierkegaard talks about: the action unfolds itself towards the Asylum; there it knocks against the pricks and then kicks back, the pilgrimage, the turned lesson, the reiteration; and then it starts again at the same place where the playing ends and where it began. Perhaps you have not noticed how the settings

unfold backwards from the Asylum, which is the book that closes itself and encloses the action. Or like a snake biting its own tail.[17]

Strindberg was almost a living embodiment of Kierkegaard's theories. In passing through the three stages of life, he was not particularly unique; many men have done the same, but few have passed through them in a *manner* so similar to that laid down by Kierkegaard. Despair at the irrationality of life, dread before the future's uncertainty, defiant isolation, total, often unreasoned commitment to doctrines and faiths and the almost daily struggle against doubt, egoism and anguish typified him. He saw himself (and his most characteristic religious protagonists) as, in Kierkegaard's words: 'witness to the truth—a man whose life has brought him profound inner conflicts, fear and trembling, temptations, spiritual distress, moral suffering . . . he bears witness to the truth in poverty, in humiliation and contempt, misunderstood, hated, mocked at, despised, ridiculed. A witness to the truth is a martyr.' Indeed, like Kierkegaard's religious man he struggled unceasingly after the Inferno crisis to hold on to his faith against all the evidence around him that seemed to confirm his belief that life is hell on earth. And, it was only because he was able to resolve theism and demonism in Swedenborgian terms that he was able to survive as a religious man. His belief in God was not rational, it was the product of a Kierkegaardian leap of faith. After he had passed through the aesthetic and ethical stages of life, he saw that there was nothing to put in the place of faith. Life was too unpleasant and his fellow men too disappointing for him to accept the permanent value of sensual, social or political activity. Neither the established church nor orthodox theology appealed strongly to him; he was therefore left with the necessity of coming to terms with God on his own.

His plays frequently depict men who insistently demand logical explanations of the meaning of life and demonstrations of God's existence, but, sooner or later, they all discover that faith must be a personal commitment for which there can be no rational basis. And, typically, these Kierkegaardian protagonists achieve enlightenment only after they have been stripped of all earthly vanities and have passed through the vale of tears and the chasm of despair. *To Damascus, There are Crimes and Crimes* and *Advent* in particular reaffirm Kierkegaard's notion of salvation through suffering and the need for constant vigilance in the struggle against dread and despair.

Emanuel Swedenborg was a scientist of considerable ability and an intellectual eccentric who was nonetheless extremely important to the development of subsequent literary and mystical thought. The range and fertility of his mind were rivalled only by its idiosyncrasies. Fortunately, only a small part of his work is relevant to a study of Strindberg's ideas after 1894. In particular, we shall consider the unique eschatalogical dimension of his thought, which adds to the basic structure of the philosophical ideas and attitudes already discussed. Perhaps, though, to begin we should mention that in *Legends* Strindberg professed to have 'abandoned Swedenborg's ugly vengeful Christianity' after 1897 (pp. 233–4).[18] The present writer prefers to trust the implicit evidence of the plays and to note that Strindberg contradicted this testimony in later statements.

According to Swedenborg, God is the only unique substantial reality and all life emanates from Him. For this reason, life is essentially spiritual. Yet Swedenborg rejects the implication that such a view commits him to any kind of pantheism; 'although God has created the universe and all things of it from Himself, yet there is nothing at all in the created universe which is God' (*Divine Love And Wisdom*, no 283).[19] Matter is derived from the spiritual world and, ultimately, from God. How this is possible is explained by the *Doctrine of Influx*. Force or motion ('the only existing force which includes all others, namely Motion, the incomprehensible Breath of the Sovereign Maker of the Universe')[20] is the origin of both inanimate and animate matter; the latter being differentiated from the rest of the physical world in possessing life which comes directly from God Himself. The universe, both natural and spiritual, was created and is conserved by God who communicated His Infinite Life to what was originally not alive. He was able to do this because there is a tripartite correspondence between the Divine, the spiritual and the material. The Nature of the Infinite invigorates the spiritual world which becomes structured and, in its turn, determines the structure of the material world. By means of this structural correspondence the Will and the Love of the Divine can simultaneously infuse all levels of creation. Swedenborg sees God as gradually having reduced the intensity and complexity of His life and Love to bring into existence the upper reaches of the spiritual universe (spiritual substances and atmospheres), then with diminished intensity the lower reaches (forces and motions), until through them He was able to breathe life into organic matter and finally substantify inanimate matter. Such is the process of *influx*; the gradual scaling down of Divine essence or vitality so that it becomes communicable to existence at any level of the spiritual and natural hierarchies.

Swedenborg postulated a finite cosmological system in which time and space, mind and matter, the living and the inanimate constitute various interconnected levels. The relationships between these levels is defined by means of two central doctrines: those of Series and Degrees and Correspondences.[21] According to the former, the development from one level to another and, most importantly, from the spiritual to the material is analogical rather than causal. The progression from say the inanimate to the animate consists of a number of qualitative steps or 'leaps'; we cannot logically predict the nature of any given level from a knowledge of its immediately prior level. Only among the items on particular ontological levels are there causal connections to be discerned.

The analogical links between different levels are, however, susceptible to human understanding even though they are not strictly causal. In a note to Part I to 293 of *The Animal Kingdom*, Swedenborg writes that he will 'treat of both these symbolical and typical representations . . . throughout nature and which correspond so entirely to supreme and spiritual things that one would swear that the physical world was purely symbolical of the spiritual world'. Logically, for Swedenborg, these detailed and precise correspondences between different levels of the ontological hierarchy[22] must exist since everything originates from God and 'everything that is represented in the Divine mind, cannot but be carried out in reality in the ultimate parts of nature' (*Adversaria*, no 23). So the natural world is a mirror image of the spiritual world which creates and sustains it because every created entity, be it material or immaterial, embodies some particular aspect of Divinity and is the outward expression of some spiritual principle. Thus we can regard everything in the natural world as an emblem or symbol of the spiritual world which in turn reflects the Heavenly society and, ultimately, God Himself.

In addition to these correspondences between nature and spirit, there are correspondences between man and nature in so far as they both represent aspects of the Divine; nature His Ideas, man His Image. There is a geography of the human mind and soul that parallels natural geography, with its mountains, plains and valleys. The mineral composition of Nature corresponds to what is inert and lifeless in man (his factual knowledge and basic instincts), the vegetable corresponds to intellectual processes and linguistic activities (e.g. '*seeds* of truth', '*Germ* of an idea taking root in the mind', '*flowering*' etc), while the animal stands for the passions and morality. The existence of correspondences between different levels of creation explains the commonness of pathetic fallacy, personification, animal metaphor ('foxy', 'goose', 'cat' etc) and physical metaphor ('turncoat', 'dry old stick' etc) in our language. As we shall see, examined in this light, Strindberg's settings in *To Damascus* and *A Dream Play* take on startling significance.

In similar ways, the three levels of Heaven (the celestial, the spiritual and the natural) correspond to various levels in man; but whereas nature reflects the more primitive qualities of the human soul, Heaven is reached only through man's most refined aspirations. His soul and mind are spiritual substances which are the media of God's love. His physical body in the natural world has its counterpart in his spiritual body which will live on everlastingly after his physical death in heaven. In this way, although God remains totally distinct from man, it is the reflection of Divine love—the spiritual— within us that makes us uniquely human and capable of salvation. The notion of a separate spiritual world from which the human soul (spirit, mind) came and to which, after death, it must return was further complicated by the theory that souls in this natural world could communicate (if they belonged to exceptional individuals) with dead or eternal spirits. Every plane of life then is related to every other: 'There is a correspondence of sensuous things with natural ones; there is a correspondence of natural things with spiritual ones; and there is a correspondence of spiritual things with celestial ones; and, finally there is a correspondence of celestial things with the Lord's Divine' (*Arcana Coelestia*, no 5131). By this gradual ascent, God's Will is revealed to man, but because he is, as it were, so many removes from reality, man can only understand Divine Purpose imperfectly. Even after death, there are correspondences—between the spirit's environment and its former life and nature so evil spirits live in dark, filthy caves; truthful spirits live in bright, beautiful places, scientific, rational men dwell after death in symmetrical, precisely designed gardens.

Turning to the nature of God, Swedenborg affirms, somewhat circularly, that since the universe which is a reflection of the Divine, has life, form and substance, He too must possess these qualities. The essence of God, however, is Love; the love of others not of self. This love expresses itself through the creation of the universe in which it flows and persists to the benefit of all who are able to receive it. It is precisely because God possesses Infinite Love that He created the universe. But what is the purpose, the end of Creation? The cause is Infinite and the purpose is Infinite; God has created the universe to realise His Infinite Purpose through a finite creature, man. Man is the end of the universe. Man is the only creature 'that can comprehend the end, that can acknowledge the end, and acknowledge also, in the fulness of faith, that the end is infinite'.[23] Without man the universe would be merely a beautifully constructed machine, capable of fulfilling no function beyond its own internal processes. And the quality of man that enables him to serve the Divine end is his faith; that inherited endowment that makes us acknowledge the Existence and the Love of God, even though we understand little of His Nature.

Alone in creation, man has the reason, the faith, the love and the freedom to apprehend, if not comprehend, the Infinite and to respond to Him in love. All God's creation exists for man to become the means to His End. Their failure to understand this is the basic flaw of Strindberg's tormented protagonists. Unable to see that the universe was created for them, they shrink into egoism. As a Swedenborgian, Strindberg would assert that until they accept the existence and purpose of God, they will never lose the self-pride and arrogance that compels them to torment themselves and others. Hubris was, for Swedenborg, the major obstacle to human progress because he felt that he himself suffered from it. 'There was something in me that prevented my submitting myself to God's grace as I ought to have done, thus suffering Him to do with me according to His good pleasure (quoted in Trobridge, p. 102). This could serve as a motto for all Strindberg's rebellious and recalcitrant protagonists after the Inferno crisis.

Swedenborg's doctrine of human 'psychology' presents man as having several natures, any of which can be dominant. In the ideal man, the soul or spirit presides, suffused with the Divine Spirit. At a lower level, located in the cortex, is the intellectual or rational mind to which are attached the functions of understanding and willing. Still lower is the animus or sensuous mind of the cerebrum, responsible for sensuous desire, imaginings and passions. The anchor position is filled by the five external senses which are independent of the lower mind. (Obviously while not the same, these 'natures' are not unlike Kierkegaard's three stages.) Within man there tends to be violent conflict between the rational mind and the lower, animal self, between mind and body, spirit and passion, spirit and intellect, the soul and the Divine Spirit.[24] Man has free will to resolve these conflicts and to choose the kind of life he will lead. By rational decision he can will himself to lead a Godly life. There is no *necessary* conflict between the spirit and the intellect; in fact, the one uncontaminated by the lower self, points to the other. To be able to retain not only a balance between spiritual demands and physical sensations but also to allow the former to triumph, requires love of the End as well as understanding. However, man's supreme advantage is that as soon as he shows the faintest interest in, or love of, God's Purpose, he will be helped.

As it is the creator of the body, the soul, can exist independently of it and survive death in a non spatio-temporal world. In *Heaven and Hell* (1758), Swedenborg describes in detail the topography of this other world which he had claimed to frequent. During the first stage of its life in the spiritual world, a newly released soul[25] will be much the same as it was in its natural life. It will be greeted by the souls of its 'dead' friends, relatives and acquaintances with the same pleasure or distaste as they had displayed towards it in life. Gradually, however, the external character (or life style) of the soul, which was created by the compromise between its intrinsic nature and the social and physical pressures of natural life, will wither away until the real life of the soul is revealed and it enters the second stage of spiritual life. The time this takes, of course, depends upon the hypocrisy shown, and the degree of compromise undergone, by each individual soul. Sometimes this process of sloughing off the social persona can be effected only by punishing the soul. Indeed this is almost always inevitable, as the Stranger in *To Damascus* discovers, since 'Every evil brings its own punishment with it. They are inseparably connected.'

Once the individual soul has been stripped of its social mask, it will reveal its true self, showing whether it is possessed of Divine Love or is corrupt. When this second stage has been reached, there will be no need for Divine Judgement, because the evil soul will inevitably be attracted towards Hell, while the good soul will naturally aspire to the Love of God in Heaven. The evil spirit is condemned to inhabit the 'lower earth' where infernal spirits convince it that it still possesses a body so that they can torment it. In this way, they will increase the soul's corruption until it is ready to enter Hell; a place of total egoism (cf. the old couple in *Advent*). There is no Devil, just an infernal society in which utterly egotistical souls torment each other with their own evil. By contrast, good souls must endure a period of purgation to *remove* all those blemishes that might be exploited by the infernal spirits (cf. the role of the Tempter in *To Damascus* Part III). When this has been achieved they enter a third, preparatory, stage in which they are instructed by angels (cf. the function of Paters Isidors, Clemens and Melcher in *To Damascus* Part III) before they enter Heaven itself. This is conceived by Swedenborg as the exact opposite of Hell; that is, it consists of a society of completely selfless souls in which all is kinship and love.

Thus, essentially, a man determines his own spiritual destiny by the kind of earthly existence he leads. The main characteristics of the good soul, as defined by Swedenborg, appear to be remarkably conventional. Though he does not reject the possibility of a rich man's soul entering heaven, the good soul must have rejected wealth as an end in itself together with fame, honour, sensual pleasures and self-love. Now although man is free, during his life, to choose his own code of conduct, he is acted upon by spirits whom he partly resembles. These spirits are almost always evil or are 'middle' character spirits who are neither good nor bad, but are instead extremely confused about their condition because they are still in the first stage after death and cannot resist exploiting what is evil in man. Thus man is encouraged in his immorality and so he needs to be constantly on his guard. Curiously, the evil spirits do not normally realise that they are associating with men. God has prevented them from knowing this because if they were aware of their power the spirits would immediately try to destroy any human being with whom they came into contact. Spirits can deceive us by projecting mental images or apparitions of themselves; they have no conception of natural space-time but possess some private sense of duration and have access to the conscious and unconscious memories of men. By this latter means they are able to use the memory data of living men to hallucinate them or to confuse them by impersonating their friends and acquaintances alive or dead (cf. *To Damascus*).

How, in view of all this, is man to live his life? Briefly, Swedenborg argues that man's purpose must be to become the tool of Divine Will; and this he can achieve only by making himself a receptacle of God's love and by resisting the influences of evil spirits. Yet, strangely enough, evil spirits can help on occasions; by forcing a man's evil tendencies to become overt and thus making him aware of the dangers inherent in his own temperament. This is the role of the Tempter in *To Damascus* Part III. Ultimately, the quality of a man's life is not to be judged solely by what he does; the nature of his motives and will are important too. To perform the right action for the wrong reason is not to be worthy of salvation. The man who is worthy of Heaven must love his neighbour, subjugate his own ego and welcome all manifestations of the Divine in whatever religious guise. But merely conforming to the codes and practices of Official Christianity is no guarantee of goodness; the heathen might live a much better life than the practising Catholic (another Kierkegaardian resonance!). Essentially, Swedenborg argues that man must accept the authority of Divine Providence and submit his will and reason to it. If he does not, he will be appropriately punished with full Old Testament harshness but the 'punishment' will result automatically from his crimes. It will not be externally imposed. Strindberg maintained that 'My former fatalism [i.e. of his naturalistic days] has thus been translated into providentialism, and I realise completely that I have nothing and can do nothing by myself', though he understood himself well enough to add the rider, 'But I shall never arrive at total humility, for my conscience would not permit such self-destruction.'[26]

Finally, Swedenborg's practical theology, which was published under the title *The True Christian Religion* only two years before his death, was a logical consequence of his previous work. He rejected justification by faith; true salvation could only come with a reformation of character, a spiritual regeneration in accordance with the Divine laws of order. In other words, man approaches God by means of rational self-examination which will enable him to reject the influence of evil spirits. Man is absolutely spiritually free since God keeps a balance between good and evil forces, allowing man himself to decide which course he shall choose. 'Evil spirits arouse in the memory of man all the evil and falsity which he has thought and practised since childhood; but the angels who accompany him produce his goodness and truth, and in this manner defend him. It is this conflict which produces pangs of conscience.'[27] Man's choice must be inspired, not by hope of reward or fear of punishment[28] but by love of God and an understanding of his Purpose.

There are six stages in Swedenborg's vision of human regeneration in life: man's consciousness of sin and his realisation that there is spiritual life beyond worldly existence; separation between the internal man who is 'of the Lord' and the external, earthly man; repentance which involves pious discussion and good works; full acceptance of the principles of love (Sun) and faith (Moon); reception of certain spiritual truths; and finally emergence of the true, dutiful life. Essential to this process is understanding which must not be swamped by faith. The goal of regeneration is the annihilation of ego which is the greatest hindrance to goodness. As we shall see, these stages of spiritual rebirth are experienced in full detail by the Stranger in *To Damascus*, but while the brief description above might seem to suggest that man's progress towards God is a linear development, Strindberg portrays it as a dialectical process. Like Kierkegaard, both he and Swedenborg understood the life of the spirit too well to believe that any triumph of good over evil was clearcut or irrevocable. Significantly, in view of Strindberg's undoubted attraction towards the monastic life and his constant failure to enter it, Swedenborg did not recommend here the seclusion of the cloister. 'The life which leads to heaven is not a life of retirement from the world, but of action in the world; a life of piety without a life of charity—which can only be acquired in the world—does not lead to heaven; but a life of charity which consists in acting sincerely and justly in every situation, engagement and work, from an interior principle that is from a heavenly origin' (*Heaven and Hell*, no 535). Throughout his life Strindberg flirted with the idea of retreating to a nonconfessional monastery but ultimately rejected it for much the same reasons as Swedenborg.

Among the writers who have been influenced by this seemingly bizarre philosophical system are Goethe, Blake, Coleridge, Wordsworth, Carlyle, Balzac, Emerson, Tennyson, Thoreau, Ruskin, Baudelaire, James, Rimbaud, Maeterlinck and Yeats.

EXPRESSIONISM

Contemporaneous with the formation of his new religious outlook and stimulated by his efforts to express a complex of spiritual and personal attitudes, Strindberg forged a new dramatic style. After the Inferno crisis, he wrote a series of plays which involve a new conception of theatrical technique and theatrical purpose. What Strindberg created while struggling to dramatise a Swedenborgian universe was a number of predominantly *expressionistic* plays. These were among the earliest models of a literary movement that has influenced much of twentieth-century writing. To explain how Strindberg became an expressionist before his time, we must keep in mind the main features of Swedenborg's philosophy as we examine the movement.

Initially, expressionism was a reaction against naturalistic conceptions of the universe as a stable system open to objective description. At the same time, it was a reaction against aestheticism; the search for ideal worlds in the past and in legends, free from the sordid obsession with contemporary events. While, in common with most such movements, expressionism borrowed extensively from its predecessors, it was quite unique in its refusal to explain social or psychological processes. Its purpose was to portray the world in terms which allowed no pretence to objectivity but were essentially emotional. The artist's personality was to be wholly absorbed by the act of creation in a fusion that could not be disintegrated. The artistic process was to be ecstatic but also it was to reflect the artist's involvement in the *modern* world. And since urban, industrial society was seen to be stifling, the ecstasy was more often than not anguished. Consequently, at one extreme of the expressionistic movement, arose the social revolutionary theories of the Activists.[29]

Essentially, an expressionist asserts the primacy of the ego as revealed through individual consciousness. The ego is regarded as absolute reality, indeed the only reality: the subject that records all changes both of itself and of the surrounding world and within consciousness moulds them into a ceaseless process of 'becoming'. Through the ego we become aware of unity and perceive the world as it really is; not as an external state of affairs but as a subjectively experienced whole. Subject and object are united in 'ego-consciousness'. Thus the expressionist would argue that the sense-data of a realist or impressionist artist are unsatisfactory, because they are not depicted as having been absorbed and radiated subjectively by the ego. The objectively recorded data of the scientist are regarded as even worse because they exclude entirely the emotions of the individual. On the other hand, Expressionists would tend to reject the random incoherence of the Dadaists or some of the Surrealists, because they allow no interaction between subject and object, no attempt to experience the mutual flow of the unfolding ego and the developing world.

The essential criterion of relevance and understanding for the expressionist is the individual ego; in other words, the personality of the protagonist as it unfolds, responds to, and projects the external world. Since this process must be coherent and comprehensive, Dahlström is mistaken when he writes of Strindberg's expressionist plays (and by implication of expressionistic drama in general) that 'one can select any place and any time for a beginning and do the same for the closing because the experience has been one of action without progress'.[30] The ego structures the experience into an identifiable unit. The means by which one can comprehend this unity of subject and object within consciousness is intuition. Often the content of the conscious mind is not, by itself, intelligible and the expressionist affirms that is is necessary to penetrate, particularly through dreams, to the unconscious, the underlying substratum, to reach the basic reality of which conscious thoughts and feelings are mere effects. Here, more than ever, is intuition vital. Through it alone can we grasp the reality of inner experience which determines our knowledge of the external world. The monistic idealism of the expressionist almost makes him enter the *cul de sac* of solipsism here.

To escape this dilemma, one of the realities which expressionists seek and often find is religious insight. Deeply agonised by their awareness of their insignificance and isolation they turn to (and upon!) God. So, in *To Damascus*, He is blamed by the Stranger for allowing man to suffer and for failing to reveal Himself, though, ultimately, He is seen as providing the justification of Life. Without Him, it is impossible to make sense of our existence, even though the path to God is stony and well-hidden. Such religious tension runs through the whole movement. For example, a later expressionist such as Georg Trakl in *De Profundis* exhibits much the same religious ambivalence as that which is so prominent in Strindberg's trilogy. As H. Maclean notes: 'They wanted to lose themselves in a search for God and to *be* God themselves, to reform the structure of the world and to destroy that structure before it began to solidify around them.'[31] Thus the Stranger's restless search for spiritual identity in the form of some personal conception of God is a typical expressionistic endeavour to escape his egotistical dilemma.

Most expressionists see the universe as threatening, permeated with an evil which conspires to render human existence meaningless (cf. Swedenborg's evil spirits and Strindberg's Powers). Faced with this state of affairs, such orthodox expressionist poets as Gottfried Benn and Georg Trakl strove to create highly personal works of art through which they could humanise a hostile environment. They shared with their naturalist predecessors an instinctive horror of the poverty and the insignificance of man in urban society, but while the latter tried to record these phenomena for posterity, the expressionists articulated their disgust. Their writings and paintings, therefore, tend to be abreactive; the sudden flow of hitherto suppressed emotion which combines ecstasy and disgust in a new vision of the world, which is both grotesque and apparently distorted. But this distortion, so they would say, is the direct consequence of the assimilation of the 'real' within the ego to produce a reality which is both more accurate because it is comprehensive, and more representative because it expresses a common human vision of the way things are. Of course, this common vision is usually achieved by portraying the conflicting illusions to which one or several men are subject and then allowing these to cancel each other out until the audience is left with a residue of personal, subjective truth. This is what Strindberg does brilliantly in, for example, the Banquet Hall scene in *To Damascus*. Here again, Swedenborg has a theory which provides a link between Strindberg's ideas and his dramatic practice on the question of distortion. 'The chastening spirits take possession of the imagination of the man who deserves punishment and effect his moral improvement by letting him see everything distorted' (*Legends*, p. 157).

In practice, the explosive nature of expressionistic art results in breaking down rational formulations of ideas and replacing them with symbolic representations in a dream-like world. As in *To Damascus*, the aim is to destroy universal orderliness of the kind postulated by Swedenborg, in order to show the flux, the unfolding of the artist's personal vision of the world. At the same time that the ostensible unity of the material world is rejected, the flowing patterns of subjective reality are attributed to 'the action of massive, often unseen and incomprehensible forces in their disruption of the static and comfortably established'[32]—an interesting Swedenborgian parallel! This disintegration was achieved by numerous literary devices, for example the juxtaposition of opposites: mechanical with lyrical images of nature, or the holy with the profane as in Brecht's famous use of Verfremdungseffekt in *Mother Courage*. Such techniques as these were used increasingly to challenge existing aesthetic, moral and religious values, which were seen as the trivial attempts of human beings to protect themselves in a vast, alien and incomprehensible universe. In several ways then, the expressionist tries to embody, within his drama, social, existential or theological issues which compel him to reject orthodox pyschological analysis, and to create characters who are paradigmatic types of the human condition itself. These character-types, designated by nouns such as Beggar, Lady, Doctor, are revealed by their dress, by bizarre masks, by their settings and their monologues rather than by social interplay. Similarly, the plot construction of an expressionistic play does not follow a natural or even a chronological sequence but consists of a loose series of episodes linked by mood, metaphor and theme. The purpose of this is to depict the constant flux of subjective reality. Moreover, the episodic plot is well-suited to depicting the individual's confused search for God. In Reinhold Sorge's *Der Bettler* (1912), for instance, the protagonist explores, questions and extends his identity through many levels of experience in an effort to reach his goal of social regeneration. By means of monologues and the alternation of prose and verse, expressionists endeavour to convey the problems lying at the heart of human existence and emphasise the despair which must precede any spiritual release.

In conformity with their general rejection of rationality in favour of the emotions, they assert the primacy of such instincts as love and eroticism over the intellect. Indeed, at times, expressionists appear to accept an almost Swedenborgian correspondence between physical and spiritual love, to the extent of implying that love of any kind, being a creative, self-fulfilling urge, is closer to the Divine than is intelligence, the purpose of the latter being to disintegrate and ultimately to destroy. This partly explains why woman, the creature of instinct, is seen as elemental, capable of raising man to the heights or of utterly degrading him. The most complete expression of this theme was, of course, accomplished in Wedekind's elemental character, Lulu, but it was also an obsession that dominated the life of August Strindberg. For him, too, woman was instinctively more dynamic than man who represents the cerebral which is restrictive. 'Woman is the earth-spirit who effectuates a certain harmony with the earth-life. To this earth-life we must bring our sacrifice . . . and therefore wife and child comfort and protect us against the cold abstraction, life' (*A Blue Book*, p. 166).

As we shall see in succeeding chapters, Strindberg made important contributions to almost all these theoretical, stylistic and technical features of the expressionists. Where he differed from them was in their frequent emphasis, on socio-political values which assert the spiritual brotherhood of man and their often positive, indeed aggressive approach to social issues. Strindberg's work contains little or no drive to change man's world. Rather he extolled or at least tried to extol resignation in the face of suffering and stressed the need to accept that the most important dimension of life, the spiritual, was largely beyond our understanding. By contrast, the expressionists too tended to agree that life inevitably involved suffering, but they sought to convert this fact into a positive force. They were not prepared to rest content with Kierkegaard's conviction that 'all those who have really loved God . . . have all had to suffer in this world. Further, that this is the doctrine of Christianity: to be loved by God and to love God is to suffer.'[33]

On the other hand, the tenor of Swedenborgian thought is, in some respects, expressionistic in its implications. S. Toksvig makes a general point about Swedenborg's psychological interpretation of spiritual enlightenment that might serve as a model of Strindberg's dramatic expressionism: 'The drama of man for Swedenborg, therefore took place in the mind, as he had long ago stated in *The Economy of the Animal Kingdom*. If men could restrain the lusts of their will by means of understanding, not by blindly accepting authority in moral matters, then they could receive the influx of divine love into their wills and the influx of divine wisdom into their understanding.'[34] Also it is not difficult to see that both Schopenhauer's notion of the Will as the unifying force in human life and Kierkegaard's relentless insistence on the primacy of individual choice and the subjective vision, could be communicated in expressionistic terms.

MAETERLINCK AND THE SYMBOLISTS

Without becoming involved in a discussion of the poetry and ideas of Mallarmé and Villiers de L'Isle-Adam, let alone tracing symbolist origins to Baudelaire, de Nerval and Rimbaud, we can still give an account of the movement's aims and achievements adequate to clarifying Strindberg's debts and development. As Haskell M. Block, in his essay 'Strindberg and the Symbolist Drama', makes clear, 'Strindberg's symbolist affinities in the 1890s are primarily mystical and religious rather than literary in origin.'[35] Given the belief in correspondences between material, animal, intellectual, spiritual and angelic universes together with a profound vision of himself as an initiate of the occult, Strindberg was clearly disposed to welcome an aesthetic which sought to transcend conventional ontological distinctions in order to articulate what is considered to be the ineffable mystery of life. He was, in particular, bound to be attracted by Maeterlinck's work: 'I have grown to like Maeterlinck more and more. There is a peculiar elegance about his art that impresses one as being strange at first, because of its originality, but later enchants by its sublime power of giving colour to its mood' (*From an Occult Diary*, p. 28).

Strindberg viewed Maeterlinck's dramatic style as principally a means of communicating their mutual spiritual vision. That these two visions were at once very similar and very different is obvious to anyone who reads Maeterlinck's *The Treasure of the Humble*. Their agreement over such questions as the importance of suffering as a source of spiritual redemption, the inviolable beauty of the divine in life, the inescapable presence of the Powers, the significance of emblems and omens, the existence of occult hierarchies and the intrusion on earth for good or evil of the spiritual world, explains the value for Strindberg of the Belgian's theatrical achievements. But their profound differences explain why their overall dramatic styles are so contrasting. Although Maeterlinck's early fatalistic plays (e.g. *The Princesse Maleine*, *The Intruder*, and *Pelléas and Mélisande*) were largely pessimistic, by 1896 in his book of essays *The Treasure of the Humble (Le Trésor des humbles)* he had evolved a much more optimistic philosophy. He seemed to begin by believing that man's destiny is a source of sorrow, that the unknown is to be feared and that Death ultimately triumphs. Later he became convinced that love can conquer all and that the purity of a man's soul is inviolable. Basically then Maeterlinck's occultism was optimistic, emphasising the beauty, omnipresence and endurance of the spiritual. In *The Treasure of the Humble* he saw himself as living in a great spiritual epoch where the opportunities for human regeneration were greater than they had ever been. He rejected elitism and believed that the numbers of the spiritually pure and the sum of spiritual potentiality had been greatly underestimated. In essence, he believed fervently in a spiritual progress that eventually would at least match material progress. His optimism sprang from his conviction that love had the power to reveal the hidden goodness within the human soul. Thus even the dour exterior of *Pelléas and Mélisande* is permeated with omens of hope.

Strindberg, on the other hand, was a pessimist and a misanthropist for long periods of his life. He accepted that the few would eventually be redeemed but for the mass of his fellows he had little hope. Earthly life, for Strindberg after the Inferno crisis, was not a misery, but a corruptive hell.[36] Endurance and humility, confused acceptance and submission, were the only hope for mankind. This pessimistic fatalism of Strindberg's later years is perfectly summed up in a quotation from a short story by one of his favourite authors, E. T. A. Hoffmann: 'Life seemed to have become for him nothing but a dream and foreboding; he kept on saying that everyone who imagined himself free was really the plaything of dark and cruel powers; it was useless to rebel, we all had to bow humbly to our destiny.'[37]

Again and again, throughout such books as *The Great Secret* and *The Treasure of the Humble*, Maeterlinck urges his reader to resist the impulse to take the world in which he lives for granted. 'There is not an hour without its familiar miracles and its ineffable miracles.' Anyone who accepts that the limits of reality can be probed by scientific or materialistic philosophies will be denied insight into, and experience of, the infinite riches of life, which are nothing less than a mode of expression of the Divine or universal spirit. The lives of all men are illuminated by the Spirit but few of us seem able to discover it and to follow the light which will reveal the inner recesses of our souls. As a Symbolist, Maeterlinck wished to reassert the sense of life's mystery and to reject as mere appearance that concept of reality in which total explanations are inevitably materialist. In love or silence, or even when observing the familiar, we can feel the influence of extraordinary powers which will always be beyond our full comprehension but which we can occasionally half capture through a humble resignation of self and through artistic symbol or metaphor. In his plays Maeterlinck sought to personify spiritual conflict, and the mystical impregnation of life, by means of what Arthur Symons describes as a 'theatre of artificial beings who are at once more ghostly and more mechanical than ... living actors'.[38] These puppet characters parody life as we know it but their very limitations within an unfathomable and magical theatre by extension imply the condition of rational man; the materialist, in a mystical world.

Aware of the pan-spirituality of Maeterlinck's thought, Symons can accurately describe his drama as that 'in which the interest is concentrated on vague people who are little parts of the universal consciousness, their strange names being but the pseudonyms of obscure passions, intimate emotions' (p. 157). While Maeterlinck's definition of the spiritually enlightened is less elitist and more a source of optimism than Strindberg's, his characters are far more remote from experience. The Belgian was capable of loving his fellow men far more spontaneously than the Swede and he had faith in their spiritual potentiality which he tried to transfigure in his art. But too often this involved Maeterlinck in distancing himself from the realities of human life and, as a result, his plays usually lack solidity. While Strindberg remained concerned with concrete moral issues even when he was writing highly mystical dramas, Maeterlinck wished to depict the spiritual nature of man that transcends morality. 'I may commit a crime without the least breath stirring the tiniest flame of this fire'[39] (i.e. the great central fire of our being).

Since Strindberg did not believe that the bulk of his fellow men had much spiritual potential, he constantly fell back, even in *A Dream Play* and *The Great Highway*, on moral diatribe. None of is plays aspires to that objectivity, that absence of authorial comment and bias which characterises Symbolist art in general and

Maeterlinck's best dramas in particular. In this respect they are not inferior; merely different. Strindberg uses Symbolist techniques to communicate spiritual ideas but he is also usually concerned, unlike Maeterlinck, to integrate them into an expressionist understanding of human psychology. It is precisely when he fails to do this, when he is closest to Maeterlinck, as in *Swanwhite*, that his plays, however beautiful, seem curiously etiolated. He actually summed up his theatrical response to the Belgian as follows:

> The term (stylising) became known after Maeterlinck's splendid dramas (not after 'Monna Vanna' when he had deteriorated). Maeterlinck's secret is this. His characters are active on a plane other than the one on which we live; he is in communication with a higher world; his spiritual powers are so refined that he senses (his fate), prophesies his fall (his deterioration) . . . I believe, however, that Maeterlinck is best unperformed. His Inferno world is in the spirit of Swedenborg, but there is light in the darkness, beauty in the suffering, and sympathy with everything that lives. But it is (a world of) despair, disaster, heaviness . . . this poet's marvellous world, where everything has proportions, tones and light other than we have in this world. (*Open Letters to the Intimate Theatre*, translated by Walter Johnson, pp. 299–301)

Here Strindberg makes a valuable point which could serve as a critical introduction to Symbolist drama as a whole. He suggests that Symbolism is essentially a poetic movement and that mystical poetry in the theatre, even at its best, is somehow too fragile to sustain dramatic performance. For example, in Maeterlinck's plays dramatic impact depends too exclusively on the spiritual atmosphere created by extraneous effects. The actuality of the theatrical event demands, at some point, a concretisation of imagery; a realism that is absent from purely Symbolist plays. Admittedly no-one tried more strenuously than Strindberg himself to dramatise the ethereal but, as we have already remarked, he was influenced by naturalism and expressionism too. These generally compelled him to focus his dramatic themes through human characters in recognisably concrete situations, or, at least, situations which were familiar even while they were being heightened or distorted to suggest the noumenal world. If we examine them closely, we shall discover that most of the settings of *A Dream Play* and *To Damascus* are remarkably solid and authentic. The spiritual force of the plays is achieved mainly by a cunning distortion of commonplace locations and by a detailed depiction of the protagonist's developing psychological torment.

In his book *Strindberg in Inferno* Gunnar Brandell accurately summarises Strindberg's differences from the Symbolist: 'What primarily separates [them] . . . is his much greater inclination toward concrete reality and factual reality. The later poets created their symbols by an act of imagination . . . Strindberg found his in the real world, through acute observation' (p. 241). For the Symbolists, characters were little more than shadows, events had no great significance, the real action of the play took place off-stage between spiritual forces. For instance, both the Symbolists and Strindberg used dream material in their work but while he employed it to illuminate both the content and the form of his every-day experiences, they used it to go beyond phenomena. For Strindberg the dream was an important mode of perception, for the Symbolists it was a mode of transcendence. Strindbergian dreaming was closer to Freudian dreaming. Personal narrative, autobiography, psychological conflict and moral exhortation, all of which were anathema to the Symbolists, form the bases of his dream plays. A striking difference between *The Treasure of the Humble* and *A Blue Book* is that in the former the mystical is expressed almost objectively, while Strindberg can only conceive of it through the medium of his own psychology. In *A Blue Book* everything is expressed autobiographically.

6

The Road to Damascus (1898–1901)

The Damascus trilogy[1] which is Strindberg's most complex play, and arguably his greatest, works on many levels. It will facilitate our exposition if we disentangle some of them; though we must remember that the attempt to isolate elements which are so completely integrated into a dramatic whole will inevitably involve some distortion.

Most basically the trilogy contains an autobiographical analysis. Strindberg was not simply interested in telling his life story; he set out to *dissect* the mental and spiritual developments which had brought his life to a point of crisis. In doing so he redefined many of his old attitudes towards women, social alienation, the superman and human destiny. To accomplish this task of self-analysis he chose to enter completely into the mind of his central character and to portray his essentially solipsistic mental universe with all its fears, hopes and obsessions. *To Damascus* can be seen as a multi-charactered play about an external world but it is as a dramatic monologue of the expressionistic type, designed to evoke the inner flow of the Stranger's ego, that it is primarily important and credible. Although the great trilogy is a theatrical expression of the biographical content and the spiritual implications of *Inferno*, Strindberg eschews realistic description of his suffering. Rather he seeks 'To unpick your fabric thread by thread'; that is, he tries to untangle from the fabric of his life the various strands which have led him to his present nadir, to trace them to their source in his childhood and to use them to define his destiny. Finally, he weaves them once more to form a new pattern that takes as its centre, not the ego of man, but the Purposes of God and the Powers. By this means, he seeks to convey the spiritual conflicts inherent in life and to make a definitive statement about man's existential condition.

The only psychology which is significantly revealed is that of Strindberg the Stranger himself. Dahlström clarifies this well: 'At most only one character in an expressionistic drama has anything more than a shadow of individuality; when the author portrays himself and projects all other characters out of his ego as reflections of this dramatic representation of self, then there is opportunity for individuality.'[2] Unfortunately an awareness of this fact can result in critical misjudgement: 'Almost all the action of Strindberg's trilogy takes place within the mind of the protagonist or is seen exclusively from his point of view, so that only where we identify with him, as in the nightmare humiliation of the banquet scene, does the play have any real dramatic power. Even in the first and strongest part, the sufferings of the Stranger are more talked of than dramatised and it is hard to feel . . . that by the close of the trilogy he has earned the peace he hopes for'.[3] This comment entirely ignores the dramatic tension provided by the conflicts between the Stranger's various alter egos, the powerful portrait of a soul tormented by hallucinations and torn by its own conceit and guilt, the religious substructure which offers objective standards against which to compare his progress and the narrative vigour of his convoluted spiritual pilgrimage as it is expressed in powerfully original theatrical terms.

Moreover, there is no reason in principle why an expressionist monologue should not present a complex emotional universe as full of diversity and conflict as any kind of drama. All that is necessary is that the various 'characters' are projected by a single unifying consciousness. There is no *a priori* reason why these cannot be as complicated and as revealing of the human condition as those arising from inter-subjective relationships. Even in a rigorously solipsistic universe there can be as many imagined, highly differentiated characters and attitudes as there are in the world as we know it. Indeed, it is precisely the inadequacy of solipsism that it is radically unfalsifiable, since the universe it postulates as existing in the thinker's mind is, in principle, indistinguishable from the everyday universe. In view of this it seems unreasonable to maintain that an expressionistic universe which in many respects only approximates that of the solipsist cannot incorporate the complexity and variety of the world we all experience. Strindberg's usual psychological understanding then is abundant, even though the Stranger is depicted as an alienated individual. Strindberg rejects *orthodox* psychological analysis because he is trying to go beyond portraying an emotionally disturbed individual. He offers an expressionistic paradigm of the socially alienated man who radiates a private emotional universe which becomes increasingly disturbed as memories of past guilt and consciousness of present unease bombard him.

The Swedenborgian picture of the world as the playground of Dark Powers and evil spirits[4] that juggle maliciously with men's lives constitutes the second important feature of the trilogy. These forces are able to punish man for his sins though they must operate within the general Providential plan. Divine Justice is uncompromising but it balances the power of evil with the power of good, thus allowing man some freedom of choice: 'But I've often thought that two beings were guiding my destiny. One offers me all I desire; but the other's ever at hand to bespatter the gifts with filth' (p. 28). Strindberg goes even further than Swedenborg in portraying the world as subject to a generally evil spiritual invasion. There is a passage in *Inferno* that throws considerable light on the theological status of Part I and Part II.

> I was in Hell and damnation lay heavily upon me. When I subjected my past life to close scrutiny and thought of my childhood, I could see that even that had been like a prison sentence, an inquisitorial court. The tortures to which an innocent child had been subjected could be explained in no other way than by assuming that we have had a previous existence from which we have been removed and sent here to suffer the consequences of misdemeanours of which we ourselves have no recollection.[5] (p. 121)

In the same way, the Stranger feels that he is being persecuted unfairly for crimes, which he is either innocent of or which are beyond his control. 'Judgement has been pronounced. Yet that must have happened before I was born, because even in childhood I began to serve my sentence' (p. 55). He concludes that 'the living can be damned already', for sins they have committed in a previous existence. 'We are already in Hell. It is the earth itself that is Hell, the prison constructed for us by an intelligence superior to our own, in which I could not take a step without injuring the happiness of others, and in which my fellow creatures could not enjoy their own happiness without causing me pain.' It is thus that Swedenborg, perhaps without knowing it, depicts our earthly life when meaning to describe 'Hell' (*Inferno*, p. 120). The bleak pessimism of this vision of the world is, of course, not unlike that of Schopenhauer's view of human life. Remove the religious framework and the differences are minimal.

Once we have accepted that Strindberg is portraying a Swedenborgian world of evil spirits, correspondences, telepathy and interworld communications which comprise a purgatory for the Stranger, together with a depiction of his emotional universe, it seems appropriate that the play should be cast in the form of a dramatic monologue. The Powers are not metaphors or symbols, they are living, charactered beings who reveal their individuality in the way they influence men's lives. Significantly, Swedenborgian spirits too are substantial. To portray this influence, since it is largely telepathic, it is necessary to enter the mind of the person or persons being influenced. Similarly, Swedenborgian correspondences are not artistic or religious symbols, they are *natural* symbols which acquire their significance from structural similarities with the minds of men and spirits. The natural world has meaning because it resembles the mental and the spiritual world. Thus the physical world in *To Damascus* gains significance as an adjunct of the Stranger's mental universe; it is reduced to the mental furnishings of a dramatic monologue. And, to capture the Stranger's desperate struggle against spiritual forces, Strindberg has to resort to dramatising mental entities, delusions and imaginary figments which can change character as the mind of the protagonist unfolds.

A third strand in the trilogy is the picture of a man endeavouring to come to terms with God and the world around him as he passes through all the various stages of pride, illusion, fear, weakness and despair that men commonly experience in their efforts to find spiritual peace. The Stranger tries a number of paths to salvation, without any success, before he accepts the Kierkegaardian insight that the fault lies within himself. This search accounts for the structure of the play and reflects another of Strindberg's (and Swedenborg's!) life-long obsessions: the notion of the recurrence of life which he derived initially from Kierkegaard and Nietzsche.

Each part of the trilogy has a different mood and a different structure. Part I is the most precisely plotted, consisting of eight exploratory scenes that are climaxed in the ninth as the Stranger realises his quest has been illusory and that he must retrace his steps to the crossroads of his life. When he finally arrives back at his starting point, he learns not only that he had taken the wrong fork but that his ostensible reason (lack of money) for moving at all was mistaken. At first, Part I is rather desperately hopeful but after the scene in the convent it becomes more grimly ironic, though there is evidence at the end that the Stranger has made spiritual progress. In view of the circular structure of Part I which is a necessary feature of its narrative, this testifies to the truth of Kierkegaard's declaration that without repetition there can be no moral order, no existential meaning or religious understanding. The second part is much more despairing and, appropriately, its structure is rather disjointed. The only recurring set, the 'Rose Room' serves as the base camp from which the Stranger can make forays out into a hostile world. In this section, hatred of woman reaches a high point, when Strindberg recalls his life with Frida Uhl, and his pessimism is at its blackest and most Schopenhauerian as he dramatises the world's contempt for his scientific experiments. All appears to be transformed; all reality an illusion, all truth relative. Strindberg can go no further in the direction of despair but, at the time he wrote these two parts, 1898, he had nothing more optimistic to offer. Three years later, when he wrote Part III, he had; his love for Harriet Bosse. The Stranger's bitterness against women is modified and the Lady is acknowledged as a fellow sufferer. But the overall mood of this section is weariness; a desire to bring the interminable struggle to an end. The narrative relates a gradual progression from the river bank up the mountain, stage by stage, through distractions and temptations, to the monastery where he can rest and perhaps be born again.

The trilogy as a whole is remarkably well made despite the fact that Strindberg did not initially intend to write a trilogy. Essentially its structure is dialectical in the Hegelian tradition. Part I states the *thesis* that the Stranger is alienated from life and seeks spiritual salvation through woman, the Virgin Mother, who will inspire him to transcend the petty obstacles of his environment. The result is that he begins as a social rebel and ends as a guilt-ridden husband who has begun to accept that his problems are spiritual and personal. Part II states the *antithesis*, that living with a woman inevitably involves a man in a new series of difficulties which are both more enervating and more difficult to surmount even than loneliness. Woman does not remain the Virgin Mother who comforts, elevates and protects, but becomes the mate who ultimately degrades a man.

The result is that he becomes a despairing pilgrim who in a Purgatory partly of his own making is the centre of a conflict for his soul between Swedenborgian spirits of good and evil. Part III describes a synthesis. Man, through his relationship with woman, has so probed the depths of despair that his desire for spiritual peace is even more urgent; being capable at last of compelling him to realise his own deficiencies. Now he can adjust because Woman, through her association with man, has shared his suffering and taken his evil upon herself. Although their union has made him an extreme pessimist, it has also shaken his arrogant assumption that he is the sole victim of the Powers. He now understands that his despair was not solely the fault of the Lady but that their relationship was ruined, at least partly because of his own failings. The result is that by directing his moral scrutiny inwards, ironically the Lady has proved to be the *condition*, if not exactly the *cause* of his salvation.

The dialectic also has Swedenborgian content. In Part I, we are presented with the Stranger at odds with society but attempting to slough off the blame on to forces beyond his control. The thesis under scrutiny in Part I is that a man can solve his own spiritual problems without the assistance of Divine love. The Stranger accepts the first two premises of Swedenborg's programme of spiritual regeneration; consciousness of his sin and awareness of a spiritual life; but he does not relate them to the existence of God. Rather he uses the vague notion of the Powers as an excuse to indulge in self-pity at the way in which he seems to have been specially selected to suffer. And, being unable to justify his suffering in terms of any genuinely religious ethic, he cries out in anguish against the nature of things and the Nature of a God who could allow such injustice to exist. Since he relies totally on himself and earthly illusions, making no attempt to understand Providence, his arrogance and self-pity grow.

In Part II, we are shown this lower animal self gradually being destroyed as the Stranger sees that all natural reality is illusory. The proud, self-pitying individual who aspires to put himself in the place of God, necessarily contains within him the seeds of his own destruction. The more he demands of himself, the more he realises his limitations and the more self-pitying, and subsequently aggressive and demanding, he becomes. The paranoid personality is cumulatively self-destructive. Furthermore, as the Stranger demands

comfort from life, seizing self-glorification first through his relationship with the Lady then through his alchemical researches, he
gradually becomes aware of the illusions of earthly existence. The
conflict between the spiritual/intellectual and lower animal selves,
described by Swedenborg, develops with increasing violence. The
animal in man says 'I want', the spiritual says 'But it's worthless'.
So in Part II, the Stranger is dominated by his animal self which is
exploited by spirits of evil and is purged by suffering until, in the
midst of disillusion, his intellectual, and later his spiritual self, begin
to dominate. But as one conflict subsides, another (between intellect
and spirit) develops. Intellectually he demands to understand the
universe, but not in order to draw closer to God, merely (because the
animal self is not yet dead) to justify himself. In Part I, we had a
predominantly animal-dominated self which used the intellect to its
own purposes. In Part II, we have a conflict between animal and
spiritual selves in which the intellect is the balance, used first by one,
then by the other.

In Part III, the synthesis of the intellectual and spiritual sides of
the Stranger enables him to cast off the animal self and so escape the
radical bifurcation which afflicts Father Melcher's eleven geniuses.
By accepting the illusory nature of the world, he is able to free
himself from the animal, yet the urge to redeem himself remains;
though now, under the guidance of the spirit, it is exhibited in a
desire to come closer to God. When he enters the monastery, the
Fathers, by teaching him the rudiments of spiritual awareness,
satisfy his intellectual demands, and then when he is enlightened
(i.e. beyond carnal desire) he is ready for an angelic rebirth. An
awareness of the Divine has entered his life; his self-destructive
animal nature created a vacuum which compelled him to aspire to
some force beyond the material to provide him with personal well-
being. If he had not, in Part I, succumbed to the grosser elements
of his being but had remained a self-compromising pseudo-intel-
lectual, the personal despair that drove him to God might never have
been reached. Thus, in a truly Hegelian sense, Part III represents a
synthesis of the drives of Part I and the despair of Part II; and, to
that extent at least, a genuine progress. Yet Dahlström can offer the
following shallow reading of the trilogy: 'Even the Stranger in
To Damascus, despite all the wanderings, makes no genuine progress. He enters the monastery not because, at long last, he has been

led there by his deep convictions, but because there are no answers to his questions.'⁶

Part One: Illusion

In Part I Strindberg portrays the inner life of his unnamed protagonist on three dramatically integrated levels. Fundamentally, he *describes* the Stranger's personal and social alienation in a Swedenborgian world that is beyond both his control and comprehension. Next, by using expressionistic techniques to evoke past memories, obsessions and guilt feelings, he traces the *causes* of this estrangement. Finally, Strindberg draws certain *conclusions* from a cathartic emotional experience which has enabled this outsider to make a crucial advance towards the growth through suffering he undergoes in Part II.

DESCRIPTION OF THE STRANGER'S ALIENATION

As the play opens, the Stranger (Everyman) is standing at a street corner, the crossroads of his life, 'uncertain which way to go' (p. 25);⁷ the clock strikes three, it is the mid-afternoon of his years. Despite his hesitation, he is aware, even at this early stage, that there are evil spirits that interrupt one's solitude. And above these there is a Swedenborgian Order which he attributes to the Powers; 'Life, that once had *no* meaning, has begun to have one. Now I discern intention where I used to see nothing but chance' (p. 27). He notices correspondences: 'Once I merely saw objects and events, forms and colours, whilst now I perceive ideas and meanings' (p. 27), and understands 'that the living can be damned already' (p. 26). Anyone who can comprehend so much, whatever sins he might be led to commit, is potentially good, but like most men he has to suffer an emotional crisis (Scene 9 the Convent) before he can deduce from this knowledge the state of his own sin and the existence of his own spiritual life; that is, before he can reach the first stage of Swedenborg's process of spiritual regeneration.

Initially the Stranger is prepared to blame anything but himself for his suffering. As if he were a special case, he cries out against God: 'Why is one born into this world an ignoramus, knowing nothing of the laws, customs and usage one inadvertently breaks? And for which one's punished? Why does one grow into a youth full of high ambition only to be driven into vile actions one abhors. Why, Why?' (p. 75). He has yet to learn that

> When you are persecuted by misfortune and your conscience cannot call it deserved, take it quietly. Regard the endurance as an honour. There will come a day when everything will improve. Then perhaps you will discover that the misfortunes were benefits, or at any rate, afforded opportunity for exercising endurance. (*A Blue Book*, p. 51)

As yet he cannot concede that the workings of Providence may be beyond his intelligence but declares: 'I've never seen a good action get its reward' and concludes: 'It's a disgrace to Him who records all sins, however black or venial. No man could do it; men would forgive' (p. 76). He is guilty of blasphemy. 'I've heard that a man can wrestle with God, and with success; but not even Job could fight against Satan' (p. 77). In a fit of exalted despair, he challenges God and then, in a Strindbergian move to the opposite extreme, he agrees to endure anything for the Lady's sake. He argues: 'If I can't overcome the unseen, I can show you how much I can endure' (p. 54). When he has exhausted his momentary bursts of self-grandeur he turns to self-pity and to self-abnegation; from the blasphemous superman he becomes the martyr-in-apotheosis. As recurrent reminders of his tainted condition, he is haunted by a number of expressionistic symbols and Wagnerian motifs. From time to time he hears Mendelssohn's funeral march, a correspondence to his present mood and to the tragic destiny that awaits him if he does not change. Again the ticking sound he hears repeatedly is defined in *Legends* (pp. 147–8) as a sign of imminent death. The furies pursue him and he flees into the lair of the Werewolf (Doctor) where lightning strikes. Wherever he goes he is harassed by the same signs and symbols; dead Christmas roses, corpses, madness, poverty and even worse, by neurotic obsessions that make him return to the same situations, allowing him a momentary hope before plunging him back into even blacker misery. By these means, the powers torment him with evidence of Nietzschean eternal recurrence. These various symbols of his guilt feelings and the presence of the Powers are drawn together in an expressionistic funeral sequence during which he imagines his own death. A guilty conscience makes him see the mourners dressed in brown, carrying vine leaves and generally celebrating the demise. They reveal that the dead man was a good-for-nothing who deserted his wife and children but the Stranger refuses to recognise himself in this description, accurate though it is. Eventually the good spirits that accompany the Stranger to balance the influence of their evil counterparts appear through the correspondences of the church bells, the sun and the coloured rose window above the church door. The evil fantasy of death is contrasted with the good reality of the church. But the Stranger is utterly confused: 'Things are happening that have no natural explanation'; 'Is this carnival or reality?' (p. 39).

In one sense, the funeral sequence is a psychological projection of his guilt feelings; a daydream[8] in which he imagines his own ignominious end. Unless he can save himself the world will declare him a thief and a coward whose literary fame will count for nothing against his beggarly existence. In another sense, it is a dramatisation of Swedenborg's world of the spirits, communicating (and interfering!) with the minds of men. Although good spirits intervene to save the Stranger from utter despair, the net result appears to be evil because the malicious powers prevent him from collecting the letter which, by solving his financial problems, would have prevented much of his subsequent suffering. Moreover, they thrust him further into the arms of the Lady, who is at this time his source of illusion. But his failure to receive the letter might also be good because his travels are necessary to his spiritual development and his turbulent relations with the Lady are necessary to his eventual salvation? Such irresolvable dilemmas are precisely what the Stranger should not contemplate. 'The presumption of wishing to understand God and His purposes is as though one attempted to steer a frigate with an oar' (*A Blue Book*, p. 72).

In Scene 3, the Stranger and the Lady stay together in an hotel room which they have both visited before with different partners. The cruelty of the powers is apparent but still the Stranger does not feel chastened. 'The devil's in it . . . But I'll be even with him yet' (p. 51). Not until they arrive at the sea which, for Strindberg with his love of the kerries, was always a place of joyful release, do they experience a temporary bliss, free from pursuit, but even then fate does not cease to spin its web; obsessively the Lady's crochet work (a symbol of their journeying, cf. pp. 102–3) reminds him of the web of destiny. Later they are confronted by the sign 'Beggars not allowed in this Parish', which bodes ill for the Stranger who several times has been taken for a tramp. And sure enough they pass through a ravine of rocks forming human profiles and flanked by the red glow of a hellish smithy over which, with 'those two insignia of witches, the goat's horn and the besom' (*Inferno*, p. 121) the smith and the miller's wife (cf. the later sounds of the grinding mill) stand guard. When the travellers approach, these two infernal spirits flee as if recognising a power darker than themselves.

The fact that the Stranger is surrounded by evil familiars which make him appear to be a force of corruption is confirmed by the Mother and the Old Man who, by means of a number of Sweden-borgian correspondences (e.g. shying horses, fierce dogs, a magpie) become aware of the spiritual evil he has brought into their home. 'When a man is tried with respect to his understanding, evil spirits summon up only the evil deeds which he has committed. These are symbolised by unclean animals' (Swedenborg, quoted in *A Blue Book*, pp. 88–9). They both understand 'how Providence has laid hands on him, how his soul is being ground in the mill, ready for the sieve' (p. 71).

EXPLANATION OF THE STRANGER'S ALIENATION

Surprisingly, the Stranger begins with considerable self-knowledge; for instance, he realises that an important reason why he is so alienated is that 'I determined that life should never make a fool of me' (p. 27), a conceit which he admits is close to sin. He resembles Kierkegaard, one of Father Melcher's 'two headed' characters of whom God made a fool, despite all his precautions (cf. p. 281). The Stranger will be deceived, confused and humiliated precisely because he is arrogant enough to demand certainty, enlightenment and dignity. Throughout the play, the Stranger's pride leads him into disaster because the more he demands certainty, the easier it is for the Powers to confuse him. The persistent expressionist illusions to which he is subjected are salutary punishments laid down by Providence which is violated by such human insolence.[9]

Another reason the Stranger conceives for his problems is articulated formally through the parable of the changeling, 'a child substituted by the elves for the baby that was born' (p. 27). This child of the elves (i.e. the Stranger) is flawed at birth and being the destroyer of the human baby, it is associated with Cain; disorientated as soon as it enters the world. 'Life has given me all I asked of it, but everything's turned out worthless to me' (p. 28). In consequence, the Stranger is plagued by guilt feelings that are as inescapable as Original Sin. For Swedenborg man is punished for sins committed in a previous existence. So the Stranger feels damned from birth. Significantly, Swedenborg depicted Cain, the cultivator, as a man of *intellect*, and the correspondences of the intellect are the fruit of the earth. Similarly the Stranger is an uncharitable thinker who kills the child of love (the human baby, Abel the shepherd) within himself.[10] Unable to love God, he is condemned to wander desolately. 'A fugitive and a wanderer shalt thou be in the earth' (Genesis 4: 12). Not until he has shaken off the evil spirits which make him question the existence of God will he rest. Peace will come only with belief.

The Stranger's self-disgust also issues from his guilt feelings for past sins. These are expressed through three dopplegangers, the Beggar (the Dominican Confessor), the Doctor (Pater Isidor) and Caesar (the Pilgrim), who with the Mother represent the Powers, good and evil. 'I . . . saw the Powers as one or a number of concrete living individualised personalities who directed the course of events and the lives of human beings' *(Inferno,* p. 80). In Part I, the Beggar is an alter-ego whose function is to give the Stranger a sense of reality. He denotes the practical man rather than the man of principle, 'Virtus post nummos'. Nevertheless he can help the Stranger to survive without committing mortal sin. He warns him not to risk all for the sake of his pride. If they are not to ruin him, the fates must be bought off with a least a token humility. Although, as the example of Polycrates shows, mere gestures cannot redeem an essentially corrupt individual, they can allow him a respite during which he might reform. When he sees that they both have a scar on their foreheads, the mark of Cain, the Stranger throws away his ring in the form of a coin which he hands to the Beggar; thus sealing their union. From this time on whenever he reappears in the trilogy the Beggar will be identified, even confused (e.g. in the funeral scene) with the Stranger as a fellow outcast and a fellow changeling. In Scene 6 the Stranger follows his advice again when he throws away his last coin to pacify the evil spirits in the Ravine. Most crucially, the Beggar urges him to accept life as it is and to cease demanding to know the purpose of the universe: 'I have always succeeded in everything I've undertaken, because I've never attempted anything . . . Life has given me all I asked of it. But I never asked anything' (p. 32). If the Stranger must search for enlightenment he should do so without arrogance.

The Lady's husband, a Doctor who was wronged by the Stranger when they were both children, is a guilt phantom of the Stranger's past.[11] Unlike the Stranger, he has learned that 'one cannot escape one's fate' and that 'I've wasted time and energy in fighting the inevitable' (p. 42). The Stranger's error is not in struggling for integrity but in failing to distinguish between the Powers of Light and Darkness. He is confused because he does not interpret his experiences in the light of Divine Love but relies solely on the power of reason. Perhaps the Doctor is partly modelled on Henrik Ibsen. He has a portrait of the Stranger in his study[12] and they are instinctive enemies who recognise something of themselves in each other. The brief dialogue on p. 104 between the Doctor and Caesar neatly sums up Strindberg's opinion of Ibsen's moralising individualism; he would prefer the uncompromising 'Nietzsche Caesar'. Caesar signifies the maniacal side of the Stranger's nature which drives him to challenge God like poor mad Nietzsche. The arrogance of his madman exactly contrasts with the humility of the Beggar.

Yet another voice of the Stranger's conscience is provided by the Lady's mother who is modelled on Strindberg's mother-in-law, Maria Uhl, a Swedenborgian seer and a Catholic. The more *orthodox* Catholic view is embodied by the Lady's Grandfather who uncharitably 'will have nothing to do with what seems to me shameful' (p. 167). The Mother, on the other hand, analyses the Stranger's real motives and offers him religious advice; beg God's forgiveness and accept your Destiny. She realises that the only hope for the Stranger and the Lady is that 'they're meant to torture each other into atonement' (p. 67), but not into redemption! She also reveals that the Stranger does not wish merely to create an ideal woman but 'intended to destroy the whole sex' (p. 69). In spite of her understanding, though, she is still a woman with an instinctive desire to protect her daughter and to punish the seducer. So she remains an ambiguous figure whose later seemingly perverse behaviour is explicable only in Strindbergian terms.

THE LADY'S ROLE

In the Stranger's eyes, the Lady represents his immediate destiny, his soul mate, his ideal and his hope of redemption. To her he can confess his utter disenchantment with life and his presentiment that she might be an instrument of Providence. Although she cannot accept his extreme pessimism, she concedes that she might be destined to play a part in his life. With remarkable precognition (if this is *not* a dramatic monologue), he christens her Eve, the temptress, who will destroy any arrogant hope he might have of paradise on earth. But, for the time being, she is his ideal, reminiscent of his mother and so flexible to his purpose that he can invent for her a name, an age, and even a character. She is to be his anchorage in sanity.

As Eve, she represents the curious female who, on reading the forbidden book (*A Madman's Defence*)[13] samples the knowledge which accelerates their mutual fall from grace and destroys their future happiness. According to Swedenborg, the temptation in the Garden of Eden was not created by an external evil, the serpent, but existed within Adam and Eve themselves. Thus the Mother, in representing the Serpent, is not an embodiment of pure evil, but is the instrument of Providence she believes herself to be. Eve succumbs to evil before Adam because, in general, women stand for the emotional, men for the intellectual side of human nature; Eve's lower sensual nature triumphs over her mind which would draw her to God. As an expressionistic female archetype, the Lady tends to appeal to the Stranger's basic animal nature; directing his attention to herself, to money, the family and the child, while encouraging him to abuse his intellect by using it to gain independence instead of Divine Guidance. Whenever his failings are social or personal the cause will be the Lady's influence but whenever they are the result of intellectual arrogance the fault will be his own.

In her dual role as an ideal and temptress, the Lady wears a Christmas rose (p. 34) which has a symbolic *correspondence* both to the forces of deception (the mandragora)[14] and the power of healing (cf. 'Rose Room'). She is in fact an ambiguous figure; at once simpler and more elemental yet more knowing than the Stranger. She is surprised when he bitterly criticises her: 'I feel as if I lay hacked in pieces and were being slowly melted in Medea's cauldron.

Either I shall be sent to the soup boilers, or arise renewed from my own dripping. It depends on Medea's skill' (p. 36). But she is sincere in wishing to help him: 'We must see if you can't become a child again.' He depends upon her because 'When I'm alone, I've no strength at all, but if I can find a single companion, I grow strong' (p. 40). Inadvertently, when she comforts him, she fulfils the Power's purposes by spurring him on to a Nietzschean vainglory. 'Killing dragons, freeing princesses, defeating wolves—that is Life!' (p. 40).

Her immediate function, as a source of atonement, finds its symbolic correspondence in the 'Rose Room', the refuge in which, for a time, she manages to comfort the Stranger. The 'Rose Room' is a spiritual oasis (see *Inferno*, pp. 115–16) but it is also there that she reads his book and there that the illusion of their happiness begins to crumble. The 'Rose Room' of Scene 8 with all its illusory 'reality' immediately precedes and leads to the real 'fantasy' of the climactic Convent scene. In the 'Rose Room' the balloon is pricked, in the Convent it utterly deflates. The ambivalent nature of the 'Rose Room' is communicated by a series of theatrical effects. The view of the poorhouse, a dark, unpleasant building with black uncurtained windows, is a reminder of the poverty to come. It is also a symbol of Hell which is ever present outside the temporary sanctuary of the 'Rose Room' (cf. *Inferno*, p. 120). In such surroundings, whatever her good intentions, the Lady cannot for long protect the Stranger and he continues to feel irritable and persecuted. But she has ushered in one vital improvement. The noise of the funeral march, the symbolic prognosis of his spiritual death, has been replaced by the noise of the Mills of God,[15] predicted by the Old Man (p. 71) as a sign of the Stranger's slow and painful spiritual regeneration. Thus through the Lady's influence he has become alive again to the world and is being chastised so that he will escape from that state of sin which makes 'people I meet cross themselves'. Without her the Convent scene could not have occured because alone he would never have reached such an extreme of spiritual self-disgust.

THE SIGNS OF THE STRANGER'S SPIRITUAL PROGRESS

The ninth scene in the Convent is the climax of Part I and marks the end point of his journeying. The stage directions provide a wealth of emotional connotations that represent the egotistical feelings of the Stranger and are also welded into a pattern symbolic of his spiritual condition. Among them are the amorphous background figures of his imagination; 'damp patches on the walls, looking like strange figures' and 'A painting representing the Archangel Michael killing the Fiend' (p. 78). This latter idea was probably stimulated by a guilt feeling Strindberg had about one of his earlier Nietzschean boasts ('Come! Come hundreds! Come thousands! Come asses! Come scoundrels! Come Devils! I'll smash you all. Come Satan and Hell's legions, I'll slaughter you like bugs for I am the Archangel Michael'). Throughout *To Damascus* the scenic design is perfectly adapted in this way to projecting a Swedenborgian spirit world. Indeed, one of the most noteworthy innovations of Strindberg's post-Inferno drama is the development of a fluid, virtually personified, scenery which reaches its perfection in *A Dream Play*.

In the Convent scene, the Stranger is dressed as a patient about to receive spiritual surgery. Also present are the mourners of Scene 1, the Beggar, his first wife with their two children in mourning and someone who resembles the Lady seated crocheting (the Furies!). These are to be the spectators at the Stranger's spiritual trial. Strindberg, however, allows for the nearly naturalistic explanation that the Stranger really is in a convent (or is it the poorhouse?) after falling and hurting his hip;[16] a reality which occasionally interrupts these comatose fantasies. As a disturbed dream sequence, however, it it brilliantly done. The Stranger himself asks if the spectators are real and receives a reply which neatly fuses the natural and the expressionist: 'If you mean true, they've a terrible reality. It may be they look strange to you because you're still feverish. Or there may be another reason' (p. 80). For the first time he begins to be afraid, realising that he is confronted by all the people he has wronged; all his *creditors* from the past and the present. To him, it is as if he has been in Hell. The Confessor has withheld absolution from him because the sins he confessed to were so great. Now a requiem mass is held for his dead soul; reminding him of what he must face on the Day of Judgement. Finally, the long malediction for disobedience from Deuteronomy 28, which the Lady and the Doctor have used to take revenge on him, is chanted as a warning of what is in store for those who reject God. Aware that he has lost his way, the Stranger takes the advice of the Abbess who tells him to seek charity 'in a rose room' (p. 84) but the Confessor knows that he is more concerned with physical than spiritual wellbeing.

The 'Rose Room' no longer represents an illusion of love and hope; it has been refurnished more practically. Now its function is as a place of work and its correspondence is to reality and disillusioned love. There he meets the Mother who provokes him to confess his inadequacies. As a result of his experiences he has come to see 'that there are forces which, till now, I've not believed in' and 'that neither you, nor any other man, directs your destiny' (p. 87). He has, at last, awakened from the vanity of self-pity to an awareness that he has a spiritual life whose sickness is the real cause of his suffering (i.e. Swedenborg's First Stage). Now his gaze will begin to turn inwards to reveal his own shortcomings. 'Do not consider yourself to have made any spiritual progress, unless you account yourself the least of all men' (*The Imitation of Christ*, p. 70).[17] Although the change gives rise to the sheer despair of Part II, it is a necessary condition of his regeneration; he has 'already gone part of the way' (p. 87), though there is still far to go.

The first symptoms of his new self-knowledge are his failure to write and to sleep. Even the consolation of death is no longer his, 'for I'm no longer sure my miseries will end, with my end' (p. 88). Yet still he cannot humble himself before God, though where before his obstinacy was defiant, now it is acknowledged with regret, even despair. He continues to question but now 'because I yearn for light' (p. 94), not to justify his own wretched existence. (He has reached Swedenborg's Second Stage of Spiritual Regeneration.) Symbolically, this change is represented by the transformation of the Beggar into the Confessor; from a purveyor of worldly advice to a purveyor of spiritual advice. Up until the Convent scene, the Stranger's immediate problems had been 'social' because he was incapable of seeing beyond himself. The task was to enable him to overcome his pride and to this end the Beggar always provided both good advice and a salutary example. Even after the cathartic experiences in the Convent, the Beggar makes one more appearance to bring him and the Lady together again, thereby directing him to the next stage (the purgatorial) of his spiritual development. Thereafter, in Part II, the Stranger no longer requires worldly advice but he desperately needs a spiritual adviser, which the Beggar becomes in the form of the Confessor.

He has left behind him his un-Godly life (Jerusalem) and is *beginning* to move towards spiritual truth (on the Road to Damascus or Calvary?). The Mother tells him, 'Go back the same way you came. Erect a cross at every station, and stay at the seventh.[18] For you there are not fourteen, as for Him' (p. 93). He takes her advice and does, in fact, take refuge in the church after he has made a penance at each stage of his return journey. This time when he passes through the ravine the Smith and the Miller's wife are not afraid because they know now that he is vulnerable. The Beggar, who is carrying a starling in a cage (a captive soul?), tells him to be hopeful, knowing that progress is being made.

By the sea, at a symbolic Calvary, the Lady and the Stranger meet and decide to travel together. He feels the need to suffer for both of them since 'You will not allow Him to suffer for you' (p. 99). He has rejected the path of salvation through a woman's love and, seeing that the deficiency is in himself, he has chosen the equally mistaken course of seeking salvation through suffering. He has begun to imagine himself as a Christ figure (cf. pp. 101–2). For this reason, he must confront the Doctor once more and supplicate the Powers which, represented by the withered Christmas rose and the sound of the grinding mill, continue to torment him. The Doctor, belying his nickname of werewolf, tells the Stranger to forget the past and acutely points out that he should accept things as they are. The Stranger, happy that this is one more creditor he has paid off, returns to the street corner where he collects the money which has been there all the time.

He now realises he was made to journey in circles because he had challenged his destiny, instead of submitting to it. But his experiences have not been in vain for, chastened, he can at last enter the church, with its dark windows, a Swedenborgian chapel. He has made the first step towards expiating his sins; he has admitted them. Nevertheless, we must not suppose that the Stranger is not capable of regressing. Although Lamm's comment on this episode is a misleading simplification, he is certainly correct in his description of the Stranger's vacillating temperament: 'The blasphemer is not very consistent or steadfast; it takes only one letter containing money to convince him that he has misjudged the Unseen One.'[19]

Part Two: Despair

Raymond Williams, in *Drama From Ibsen to Eliot*, writes of the trilogy that 'Each part is a separate work in the sense that *Burnt Norton* or *East Coker* is a separate poem; although the full richness of the work, as in *Four Quartets*, only emerges from the series' (p. 111). This is misleading. The first play states and develops themes that have inevitable dramatic consequences in the second and without which they would be crucially incomplete. The finale of Part I is unresolved and acts merely as a resting stage from which to contemplate the lessons learned. While the form of each section is rounded, read separately, they are not thematically complete. Although Strindberg did not set out with the intention of writing a trilogy, the plays are so richly integrated, so connected by the same leitmotifs, and so logically and dialectically continuous, that any one of them read on its own is considerably less than a third of the whole. Part II, in particular, would neither make sense without its predecessor nor have much point without its successor.

THE DEUTERONOMIC CURSE TAKES EFFECT

As Part II opens the Mother is telling a Dominican Confessor, the doppleganger of the Beggar, that the Stranger has illicitly married the Lady. From this conversation we learn that the curse of Deuteronomy has taken effect and has blinded him with confusion like St Paul; making him understand that 'The ways of Providence are inscrutable' (p. 117). Now, as before, he is beset by evil powers but recently he 'came upon books that taught him that such evil powers could be fought' (p. 118), a reference to the writings of Emanuel Swedenborg. Yet, despite his new spiritual understanding the Stranger continues to evade the responsibility he owes to God for his existence. Symptomatic of the Stranger's persistent self-will is the way he corrupts the Lady so that their marriage becomes a condition of strife, replacing the old social evils with an even more personal misery. From now on, we shall not see the Stranger being tormented by the funeral march, the mill sounds, his various alter egos and past sins, nor by any other external correspondences of the Powers. Now his torturer will be Woman who, having held out the highest promise, will become his greatest disappointment, 'one thing I am sure of; as soon as a man deserts God, he becomes the thrall of a female devil' (*A Blue Book*, p. 117).

In Part II, the hell of complete egoism and indifference to the Divine Will gives way to a purgatory in which the Stranger, having reached the primary level of spiritual awareness through Woman, is chastened by utter loneliness. In this receptive state he will be driven to even greater folly and suffering, as the Curse of Deuteronomy is gradually realised, but he will also be able to detect the workings of Providence and learn through the Confessor to trust the good influences that are evident in his life. Thus he will acquire the strength to turn away from early illusion and reach the middle stages of Swedenborg's process of regeneration, in preparation for the spiritual rebirth of Part III. The foremost scourge in this Purgatory is, of course, the Stranger himself but initially the Lady provides the sharpest *external* spur to his rebellious nature. Yet, although the Stranger regards the Lady as one of the furies whose 'talent for making me suffer excels my most infernal inventions', he also realises her value as a spiritual purgative 'if I escape from her hands with my life, I'll come out of the fire as pure as gold' (p. 121).

In her new role the Lady opens his letters, ironically nicknames him Job,[20] misunderstands his scientific experiments and is aggressive towards her former husband, the Doctor. Like Tekla in *Creditors*, she wishes to make both her husbands as dependent upon her as children and when she succeeds she will feel contempt for them. This transformation from the ideal to the typical woman can be blamed upon the influence of the Stranger's book (*A Madman's Defence*). After reading it the Lady, like Eve, knows the difference between good and evil and uses this knowledge against men. She humiliates the Stranger by persuading him unwittingly to wear a suit that belonged to her first husband. In this way she tries to recreate her husbands in the same childlike image but she is never allowed to become predominantly a force of evil. She is as she sees herself, a source of spiritual retribution in the Stranger's life; her function is to torment him for his own good. She reminds him of his sinful past that he cannot forget despite the Doctor's advice (pp. 106–7); and which he denies even their unborn child can obliterate, sinless though it is.

Next Caesar, the madman, enters and informs them that, as a result of the Stranger breaking up his marriage, the Doctor has become insane and has taken to wandering the countryside like a tramp. So there is yet another burden on the Stranger's conscience, another creditor, and one part of the curse, 'The Lord will smite thee . . . with madness' (p. 83) has come true; even if vicariously. And, if he should try to evade this responsibility, the Lady is at hand to redeem him, by punishing him further. Now he understands the need to suffer: 'You see, at every stroke of the lash, I feel as if a debit entry had been erased from my ledger' (p. 130). The Doctor enters, a man ruined by a woman, who warns the Stranger of the similarity of their fates. He suggests that the clothes the Stranger wears are as fatal as the shirt of Nessus, advises him 'don't forget your stick' when he goes to the Lady (p. 131),[21] and affirms his role both as the alter-ego and the creditor of the Stranger in a speech of great power whose virulent poetry could have come from *Creditors*. It is a curse of psychological torment, well suited to the obsessive guilt memories of the Stranger, and an explicit echo and complement of the spiritual torment forecast by the Deuteronomic Curse. Now, in detail, the latter takes effect.

We discover that the Stranger's first wife has married the Doctor ('thou shalt betroth a wife and another man shall lie with her'), who therefore becomes the stepfather of his children. ('Thy sons and daughters shall be given unto another people'.) This was the Stranger's, and of course, Strindberg's most persistent fear. 'Didn't you know it was his worst nightmare? That his wife would marry again and his children have a stepfather' (p. 123). Now, as the new Saul, 'his sight was blinded' ('The Lord will smite thee with blindness, that thou shalt grope at noonday, as the blind gropeth in darkness'), and he can no longer sleep for fear of nightmares ('thou shalt fear day and night'). The Stranger's condition here can be defined by reference to Swedenborg, 'The operations which constitute the preparation for a spiritual life begin with devastation (*Vastatio*) and consist in constrictions of the chest, difficulty of breathing, symptoms of suffocation, heart affections, terrible attacks of fear, sleeplessness, nightmare' (quoted in *Legends*, p. 107).[22]

The 'Rose Room', too, serves to fulfil the curse ('thou shalt build a house and thou shalt not dwell therein'); in it the Lady gives birth to her child and the Stranger feels an outcast. Although the room has been restored to its original colour scheme, it is marred by the black and white motif of the nun's habits, the hangings of the bed, the

towel and the black clothing of the midwife. Within this room of
life there is a struggle between good and evil hovering over the
Stranger as he reads Swedenborg. He is unwelcome there and when
he receives a letter officially confirming his success in making gold,
he deserts his wife, leaving her to have the child alone. The child,
like his book, has become 'an apple of discord' and he chooses the
illusions of alchemy, 'To protect myself from total destruction'
(p. 146), to those of domesticity. Finally, he is cursed with a marriage
that will weigh him down in a very personal purgatory, when he had
believed it would free him, 'and He shall put a yoke of iron upon
thy neck, until He have destroyed thee'. But the 'thee' that will be
destroyed in Part II is his arrogant animal self.

THE ROLE OF THE CONFESSOR

The Confessor (Ananias?) is a realist like his counterpart the Beggar
and as such is less likely to be swayed by formal declarations than
the Mother. In the first scene he sees that the Stranger's escape
through marriage to the Lady is only temporary because he still has
not 'accepted the love of truth'. Yet, despite the suffering which will
bring the Stranger deep despair, he is in God's hands. He is not
beyond redemption; the sign of the crucifix can stun him and, as
the Dominican observes, 'our prayers will be more powerful than his
resistance' (p. 119). But they will have to pray constantly because the
Stranger has not yet conceded his right to fight against fate. Although
he accepts that Providence directs the lives of men, he refuses to
humble himself before it. 'Can one love what does evil?' (p. 121).
This clearly indicates that he has not so far reached Swedenborg's
fourth stage; acceptance of the principles of love and faith. He
cannot receive the Mother's insight that the fates appear evil only
because we cannot comprehend the whole theatre of their operations.
Not until Part III will he share her faith and give himself over to
what he does not understand.

A modern Prometheus, he continues to challenge even Zeus with
thunderbolts (p. 138). His problem is still to distinguish between
good and evil, for although he knows that 'Nothing remains but to
bear everything, to fight and to suffer' (p. 139) he cannot decide
what should be fought and what suffered. But at last, as a result of
the Confessor's influence, he is beginning to criticise himself and now
the Lady *learns from him*. When he sees the Doctor, the Stranger

understands they must suffer 'as long as he suffers and our conscience plagues us' (p. 139), because 'We've destroyed a soul'. Yet not until after the Banqueting Hall scene does he cease to blame God 'who's so mismanaged the fate of men'; a blasphemy which receives an unearthly reply through his electroscope. He has made gold and for the time being conceitedly imagines how he will use his wealth to upset the tables of the moneylenders 'to paralyse the present order, to disrupt it as you'll see. I am the destroyer, the dissolver, the world incendiary and when all lies in ashes I shall wander hungrily through all the heaps of ruins, rejoicing at the thought that it is all my work; that I have written the last page of world history, which can then be held to be ended' (p. 140). This though is an outburst of disillusionment not evil.

He might be hedged in by evil but at moments of greatest temptation he is protected by the power of the Cross. Thus, in the Banquet Hall, when he is harassed by the company, his adviser appears; though because the controversy is secular, he is in the form of the Beggar who, considering the depths of the Stranger's delusions, is even more decrepit than before. He concedes that the Stranger is deceived but leaves us in no doubt of his worth by insisting that 'This man's worth a better fate than his folly's leading him to' (p. 153). On no occasion in the trilogy does the Stranger fulfil Strindberg's definition of the damned in *A Blue Book*:

> But he who rejoices over every evil deed which he himself has been under no necessity of committing, he who rejoices when the criminal escapes his punishment; who gloats over the misfortune of a good man, he who suffers when goodness and merit are rewarded—that is the evil man. (p. 52)

The Beggar now reveals the full reality of the Banquet. The invitation was not issued by the government or even the Committee of Science but by the Drunkard's society whose sensible motto is that gold is 'mere rubbish'. Even so, this philosophy does not save the Stranger from imprisonment for being unable to pay for the feast, though, of course, his real crime, as the Beggar tells him, was to challenge the Powers. 'Anything's to be expected, once you have challenged persons as powerful as you have! Let me tell you this in confidence. You'd better be prepared for worse, for the very worst' (p. 156). This is good advice as the Banquet Hall is transformed into a prison cell, which while it is guarded by good spirits (being suffused with sunlight and hung with a crucifix) still plunges the Stranger into despair.

THE ILLUSION OF FAME AND WEALTH

Before Purgatory can take full effect and the Confessor's advice influence him, the Stranger must be stripped of every illusion: 'You'll be forced to preach against yourself from the housetops ... to flay yourself alive at every street corner' (p. 176). This, as Swedenborg points out, is a gradual process. 'When a man is to be born again, his desires and falsities cannot be stripped off at once for that would be equivalent to destroying the whole man because as yet he only lives in them. Therefore for a long while evil spirits are left with him, to stir up his desires that they may be dissolved in many ways' (quoted in *A Blue Book*, p. 214). This slow process of purification begins in the Banqueting Hall and is continued in Part III by the Tempter. The Stranger must be made to realise that worldly fame and power are mere shams. In Kierkegaard's terms, he must transcend the temptations of the aesthetic life, but for the time being, he rejects this message and seeks refuge in the fruits of his talent, spurred on by the news that his formula for making gold has been officially recognised.

In Act 2, we learn that the Stranger and the Lady are arranging a divorce and that he is experimenting with electricity; a correspondence for the Powers. Quite deliberately, he has decided to rebuild his life on the illusion of making gold. 'But I've heard that those who serve the Evil One get honours, goods and gold as their reward, gold especially' (p. 89). This is why the Confessor declares that he has misused the revelations of Swedenborg (p. 118). The Banqueting Hall (Act 3 Scene 1) plays a similar role in Part II to that played by the Convent scene in Part I. It, too, is most easily understood as an expressionistic dream sequence in which the unfolding of the Stranger's thoughts is communicated by a kind of mental scenery and through character-types who represent either pure ideas, obsessions or guilt feelings. Once again Mendelssohn's Dead March is heard reminding us that we are present at the mere illusion of life. Unseen by the Stranger, there is a table of 'dirty and ragged figures' who include Caesar and the Doctor; a tableau which is the 'reality' among this fantasy. After a speech of praise of the kind that

Strindberg himself had longed to receive has been delivered, reality asserts itself and destroys all the grand delusions of the Stranger.

Thus the Banqueting Hall scene conforms to the description of hell given in *A Blue Book*. 'The fire of hell consists, he [Swedenborg] says, partly in this, that prisoners are aroused, only to be mocked and punished; partly in the kindling of desires, which really must be gratified, but die away immediately afterwards since suffering consists in missing something.' With a conscious irony, Strindberg directs that 'servants have exchanged the golden goblet for dull tin ones' (p. 149), the splendid food is removed and the well-dressed guests leave. In their place, a peasant gathering is convened.[23] As the set becomes yet more degraded, the company led by Caesar quickly declare the Stranger to be a charlatan; a fitting judgement on a man who cannot demonstrate his own worth but arrogantly demands that God demonstrates His. 'Hell-fire is our desire to make a name for ourselves in the world. The Powers awaken this desire in us and permit the damned to achieve their objectives. But when the goal is reached, and our wish fulfilled, everything is found to be worthless and our victory meaningless' (*Inferno*, p. 120, also cf. p. 127). Psychologically and thematically, the Banqueting Hall scene is summed up in a passage from *A Blue Book* which defines Swedenborgian Desolation:

> When this feeling of fatality strikes an unbeliever, it often appears as the so-called persecution mania. He believes himself, for example, persecuted by men who wish to poison him. Since his intelligence is so low that he cannot rise to the idea of God, his evil conscience makes him conjure up evil men as his persecutors. Thus he does not understand that it is God who is pursuing him and therefore he dies or goes mad. But he who has strength enough to bow himself or intelligence enough to guess at a method in this madness, cries to God for help and grace and escapes the madness. (p. 39)

As we might expect, the Stranger takes the first course. When the Beggar tells him that God is 'throwing out a sheet anchor as an experiment' (p. 159) he rejects Him; so having refused to bow, he must break. He continues to be duped and persecuted until the second Banqueting Hall scene when finally he does summon the 'strength . . . to bow himself' and begins to turn from earthly things.

THE STRANGER IS FORCED TO TAKE
STOCK OF HIS EARTHLY LIFE

When, after the first Banqueting Hall scene, the Beggar with typical practically tells him 'this is going to be reality' (p. 157) the Stranger approaches a moment of truth. The curse of Deuteronomy and the Doctor's curse have come true, the Lady apparently has failed him, wealth and fame have proved illusions and now he learns that he has been officially declared a charlatan and his children have a step-father. All earthly hope has been swallowed up in this Purgatory and the Beggar ironically throws his own words, 'an enlightened man of the world' (cf. p. 123) back at him. The Stranger's life is now at such a low ebb (the lowest of the whole trilogy) that even the Beggar professes disdain at being seen in his company. As the Mother says: 'He who guides your destiny seems to know your weak spots'; now he has nothing left to lean on. For the first time he asks if he could have been wrong and, with this question, spiritual regeneration becomes a probability. But even now he cannot bow. 'If so it's the devil's work, and I'll lay down my arms.' He must be certain. If the Dark Powers govern his life he feels he must defeat them, not realising that by opposing them he challenges God. In the universe of Swedenborg, the Powers have their function which they must not be prevented from fulfilling. 'Evil has no independent power, but is a servant of God, fulfilling the functions of a disciplinary force' (*Legends*, p. 107).

When his child is born, the Stranger does not wish to see it because in the past everything he has loved has been taken and used to wound him; he does not wish to risk further pain by accepting any new earthly bonds that the Powers might exploit. He thinks he is damned like Cain and, as befits an outcast, he returns to the Banqueting Hall and the rabble to 'take a mud bath that would harden my skin against the pricks of life'. But this turns out to be another inferno in which he must spend his sleepless nights until the 'ghosts [spirits of evil, past memories, former sins etc] lie down to sleep again in graves' (p. 170). Enveloped by the smell of death (a man is dying in the Hall)[24] and rejected even by a prostitute, he defends himself against the Ibsen-like Doctor who criticises him for playing with lightning and looking at the sun (i.e. challenging God). The Stranger justifies himself by arguing that the 'deeper I sink, the nearer I'll come to my goal; the end' (p. 171); but he is too worth-while a person to maintain such pessimism for long. Even in this inferno, the power of good, in the form of the Confessor, can terrify him. When he unjustly believes the Doctor's accusations against the Lady, he falsely condemns her.

Next the Stranger and the Beggar pass through the Ravine which is no longer an inferno but, after the Flood ('The old sun was washed away', p. 175), is covered partly by snow and partly by grass; symbols of sterility and life; the present and future of the Stranger's life. In a series of visions, his children appear and reject him. For the second time (p. 159 and p. 179), the Beggar urges him in his despair to turn to God and this time the Stranger takes his advice. As he humbles himself before eternal suffering, Caesar, his mad Nietzschean alter-ego enters and kills himself; signalling the end of the Stranger's deluded self-grandeur. But although one half of his animal nature has been destroyed, the other, represented by the Doctor Werewolf, does not destroy itself. Guilt survives to haunt him, for all his debts have not yet been paid.

When he returns to the Lady, who has been redeemed from his evil influence by the birth of her child, they agree that, since the Doctor will always be between them, they should part; she with the baby, he to a monastery. He has been arrogant to demand the answers to all questions and the judgement of Providence is that he shall be deceived as to his own worth and to the meaning of his life. Therefore, although it is clear that he is a great inventor, he cannot believe it. Life on earth has begun to lose all interest for him. 'Nothing remains for this unhappy man but to leave the world and bury himself in a monastery' (p. 182). The Lady asks the Confessor to lighten his burden but the good man knows that such suffering is the Stranger's only hope of salvation and, in any case, he will not *believe* any good of himself. Nevertheless, when she takes on herself the burden of the Stranger's sin, the Confessor claims his soul for God: the promise of the convent scene has been fulfilled.

Part Three: Reconciliation

When he first sees the monastery the Stranger knows it is his ultimate destination but first he must bid farewell to earthly concerns and cross the river to a place where his life's work and reputation are unknown. This is a relatively easy parting for him after his recent suffering. Coldly, he reviews his past life and concludes 'I never enjoyed anything, for I was born with a thorn in my flesh' (p. 192), but to cut himself off from his pride and his sense of injustice is more difficult. Much preparation is required before he can take the first monastic vow of humility. To this end the Confessor shows him a pageant of the four stages of man which reveals what a truly Christian life can be like. The child, the adolescent, the married adult and the aged testify that he, who fears the Lord, and walks in his ways will be industrous, loved, fruitful and blessed. Unfortunately, the Stranger does not learn from this at first but begins, once again, to feel full of his own power. Now that he has no earthly ties, there is little to restrain him. His sudden rejection of life and the illumination from the sun's rays,[25] make him imagine that he is the confidant of the Divine:

> Because when the Almighty deigns to speak to an insect, and that in a majestic setting, the insect grows in stature, he is inflated by the honour conferred on him and his pride whispers to him that he must be a particularly worthy individual. The truth is that I believed myself to be the Eternal's equal, believed that I formed an integral part of His personality . . . otherwise He would have made the lightning destroy me on the spot. (*Inferno*, p. 146)

When told that his baby daughter Mizzi has died he refuses to console the Lady, 'to comfort my fury, weep with my hangman, amuse my tormentor' (p. 205), but remarks, 'I congratulate the dead child', that is, for sensibly avoiding the misery of life. However, after he discovers that the Lady's life has been as miserable as his own, his sense of duty towards her re-asserts itself and he feels tempted to remain with her on the worldly side of the river. In order to remove this last excuse for delaying his spiritual journey, the Confessor arranges to have a Sister of Mercy care for her. The Lady cannot, as yet, follow him because the memory of her dead child chains her to life and, as she admits, she has never been able to beg; something which the Stranger has learned to do through bitter experience.

The purpose of this first act is to establish that nothing in life interests the Stranger. He is ready to enter the spiritual world not because he is enlightened (that is to come) but because having overcome the flesh, there is nothing else available to him. 'Thus, well prepared he turned his back on life, and departed from all without missing anything. So it should be, in order that nothing should bind one either with longing or with hope, in order that on the other side of the river one may not look back' (*A Blue Book*, p. 253). As Thomas À Kempis writes: 'When a man is perfectly contrite, this present world becomes grievous and bitter to him' (*The Imitation of Christ*, p. 54). Of course, disgust with life is nothing new for the Stranger, but where previously he had blamed God now he will realise that 'The whole of life—politics, society, marriage, the family—is counterfeit' (*A Blue Book*, p. 40) because man behaves deceitfully and deserves to suffer. This is pessimism at its most Schopenhauerian. Basically, the second act of Part III takes place at a spiritual crossroads that parallels the secular crossroads of Part I. Now that the Stranger has crossed the river into the spiritual world, his essential nature will be revealed so that his ultimate destination can be decided. According to Swedenborg, 'there are three states of life through which a man passes before he enters either heaven or hell'. Whether we believe that the Stranger has died actually or metaphorically,[26] the Swedenborgian reference remains the same.

THE FIRST STAGE (ACTS 1 AND 2)

'The first state of man after death is like his state in the world, because his life is still external. He has therefore a similar face, speech and disposition, thus a similar moral and civil life; so that he thinks he is still in the world' (*Heaven and Hell*). The Stranger will meet friends from his former existence but with no more satisfaction than before. The length of his stay in this state will depend upon the time it takes to achieve congruity, or the lack of it, between his real, inner self and the worldly self created by social pressures. The Confessor accompanies him to instruct him in Divine Knowledge and encourage him to reveal his true self by shaking off the conventions (e.g. the fame, the reputation, the bonds of children and women, rejected in Act I) of earthly life. Or, to put it another way, he must transcend the social and family ties of Kierkegaard's ethical life. If he is saved, it will be because he is worthy when seen in his true light not because he promises to improve. He must actually make an effort to reveal himself as he is. 'Do you think you can climb up to that white house *without* preparation?' (p. 193). Significantly, a part of this process will involve an ascetic move, though not for its own sake, 'To renounce the pleasures of life and wealth and power, with the idea of earning heaven by asceticism is a false view' (Swedenborg, quoted in *A Blue Book*, p. 90). The purpose of the Stranger's asceticism is much closer to Schopenhauer's ideal; that is, to subordinate one's ego and to inhibit the Will to Live by denying one's desires and impulses.

When the Stranger next experiences purgatory, the Confessor interprets it in terms reminiscent of Swedenborg's concept of desolation. The Stranger meets people guilty of lechery ('cinnabar red hands') who have destroyed the brightness ('quicksilver') in themselves and are purified at the sulphur springs for 'Cinnabar is quicksilver and sulphur' (p. 213). This is a distinct Swedenborgian correspondence between the physical life and the spiritual fate of man, between chemical and spiritual formulae, between colour in the material and spiritual world! These and similar lessons are taught to the Stranger during his first period of probation. Unfortunately the demands are too powerful for him and the Confessor concludes that he is proceeding too quickly. The Stranger is beginning to find his confessor's spiritual presence unendurable. Swedenborg explains this quite clearly: 'When the soul separates himself, he is received by good spirits, who likewise do him all kind offices whilst he is in consort with them. If however his life in the world was such that he cannot remain associated with the good, he seeks to be disunited from them, and this separation is repeated again and again, until he associates himself with those whose state entirely agrees with that of his former life in the world, among whom he finds, as it were, his own life ... On returning into this life ... such as have been principled in faith towards the Lord, are led by degrees from this new beginning of life to heaven' (*Arcana Coelestia*, no 316). So the Confessor leaves.

Now the Stranger is left alone, the Lady reappears, as beautiful as when he first met her; not the marriage-soiled Frida Uhl, but the virginal Harriet Bosse; not a woman bowed by life's experience but a newly-emerged spirit. Immediately he idealises her, particularly when she confesses that her original impulse to him was maternal. Now, once more inspired by a loving ideal, he can discuss, with unflattering honesty, his previously mistaken attitude towards women and believe once again that he might find redemption through a woman. But she is more enlightened than he and constantly urges him to love God and search in the Bible for the answers to his questions; they are not to be found in human love alone. She has completely transcended her animal self and is so close to salvation that he can say 'Now, now I can see your soul; the ideal, the angel, who was imprisoned in the flesh because of sin' (p. 217). Yet this pure love cannot last any longer here than it did in life because *he* still retains his insatiable urge to ask 'for explanations of the inexplicable'. Despite the favourable testimony of the Lady, Old Maia his nurse, Caesar, the hostess and his daughter, he is still full of self-pity and self-disgust.

The Confessor re-enters and absolves the Lady of any guilt she had incurred when she 'had to suffer the worst pains of hell for his sake, to bring atonement' (p. 223). The Stranger is left behind to continue his spiritual preparation. The Worshippers of Venus, the lechers, claim that they are his children, spawned by his corrupt books. Much to the Tempter's scorn, he believes their accusations. The Tempter's function is to bring out the evil in the Stranger's soul in order to reveal him as a worthy candidate for Hell;[27] so, by subtly criticising one of his major sins, 'his unbelievable pride', he tries to persuade the Stranger to deny his even greater sin of corrupting another human soul. This technique of playing off one of the Stranger's failings against another, one minute appealing to his morbid sense of guilt or self-pity, the next appealing to his arrogance and pride, is used throughout Part III. This is no ordinary tempter who can imagine nothing but simple evils with which to corrupt his victim. He has sufficient understanding to titillate the Stranger's insatiable desire for knowledge while surreptitiously encouraging his emotional weaknesses.[28] Thus the Tempter can communicate a spiritual truth to the Stranger in order to gain his confidence and thereby lead him on to evil.

The Tempter is the dragon in himself which the Stranger must slay before he can achieve salvation in the form of spiritual rebirth, but the Stranger is not yet ready to kill his fiend or to become an angel and fly away. His Tempter tries to turn him against the Lady, not by showing him the attractions of other women, 'That's too old a trick, as old as Doctor Faust!', but by appealing to his pride in his own strength and independence. In relying on Woman, 'who made a hell of paradise', 'You've murdered your own soul' (p. 226). To

complete his work the Tempter argues that the rightful sense of
guilt the Stranger feels towards the Venus worshippers is misplaced
and he summons up the evil spirit of Old Maia to convince the
Stranger that the Lady was always evil and he guiltless. For a time he
succumbs to the Tempter's arguments and temporarily resorts to his
former self but not without suggesting there might be a reason for
the apparent injustice of life: '. . . Don't you think we're sometimes
punished wrongly, so that we fail to see the logical connection,
though it exists?' (p. 220).

Next, there appears a Pilgrim, the doppleganger or rather the
spiritual metamorphosis of Caesar, who relates a complicated life
story to show that he was not mad. Although the ways of Providence
are curious, they are eventually seen to be just. The Pilgrim is about
to receive absolution 'because I accepted my punishment [i.e. the
Caesar persona] with calmness and humility' (p. 232). Having
learned this important lesson, the Stranger is led away from his
rendezvous with the Confessor to a level higher up the mountain.
As Swedenborg predicted: 'a spirit soon after death usually finds
some excuse to depart the good spirits that attend it'. So the Stranger
now moves on to stage two where he will manifest his true self free
from social restrictions.

THE SECOND STAGE (ACT 3)

Now the Stranger is to be 'vastated' of all his deceptions by being
subjected to a series of unambiguous spiritual tests. In Act 3 Scene 1,
the Tempter's arguments are exemplified in a mock trial in which
the Stranger must be judge. The Tempter is clearly his 'inner voice'
and Strindberg is able skilfully to dramatise Swedenborg's assertion
that in this intermediate stage we are our own judges.

We witness an anti-morality play which the Tempter uses to
demonstrate the emptiness of all moral judgements and the invalidity
of ascribing moral responsibility to individuals. At a trial for pre-
meditated murder, guilt is passed back from corrupter to corrupter
until Eve appears and places the blame upon the serpent. Obviously,
the logical conclusion of this is to place blame upon God, who set
the whole process in motion. 'The Accused, however, seems to have
got out of the business! And the Court of Justice has dissolved like
smoke! Judge not, Judge not, O Judges!' (p. 239). Here the Tempter
is encouraging the Stranger to judge God Himself; and indeed if

we insist on posing the fathomless problem of evil, this is the sin into which we shall fall. The lesson to be learned is that it is mistaken to ask such an unanswerable question in the first place; but if any reply is to be made, it should be that the serpent is a correspondence of our own animal nature. In ourselves rests the cause and the responsibility for the Fall.

At this vital moment the Lady appears and shows the Stranger the beauty of the world as it is, stripped of the Tempter's lies. 'When the wicked endure punishment, there are always angels present to regulate its degree and alleviate the pains of the sufferers as much as may be' (*Arcana Coelestia*, no 967). She and the Tempter struggle for the Stranger's soul, and because the Lady's appeal is more personal and appears to be more truthful she triumphs; revealing herself not as she is but as he desires her to be, a Virgin Mother (p. 242). As the Tempter lets slip, she is the 'reflection of your own goodness'. The Confessor enters and presents the case of a drunkard, ugly with sin, who, after he has been delivered, is revealed as an essentially good man. This is what is gradually happening to the Stranger.

In the next scene, the Lady and the Stranger live together and experience the mutual torment we have witnessed in Part I and Part II. We have seen how, in adjusting to his ideal of the Virgin Mother, she was able to help him, but now, in the role of Woman, she will again make him suffer and so provide the stimulus by which he can cast off yet another earthly characteristic; his need for a lover, a home and a family. They are once again bride and groom, ideally happy for a time: 'We resemble two drops of water, that fear to get close together, in case they should cease to be two and become one' (p. 254), and as before 'We no longer have any secrets from one another' (p. 52). 'The two married partners most generally meet after death, recognise each other, consociate, and for a time live together: this takes place in the *first state*, thus while they are in externals as in the world', and later in their second state, if they are 'concordant and sympathetic, they continue their married life; but if it is discordant and antipathetic, they dissolve their conjugal life'.[29] Since it is the latter which applies to the Lady and the Stranger, they soon part. However, it does not follow that their marriage has been a waste of time; God might have ordained it as a means of purging their characters. Next, he meets his first wife[30] and tries, without bitterness, to understand why she left him; concluding sadly that all human love is essentially flawed and so preparing himself for the move towards Divine Love. If, as he says, human love is 'A caricature of godly love', then in order to leave behind him the pain he has suffered from and inflicted upon women, he must continue his progress up the mountain to something greater. From now on he will experience 'what Swedenborg calls the sexless love of those who dwell in Heaven' (*Inferno*, p. 113).

THE THIRD STAGE

So he enters stage three where he will be prepared for heaven. 'And this is supreme wisdom—to despise the world and draw daily nearer the kingdom of heaven' (*The Imitation of Christ*, pp. 27–8). He has rejected his animal self and will now receive instruction from the particular angels fitted for this task. Significantly, for Strindberg, spirits have substantial forms and sensible faculties, as they had for Swedenborg. At last he arrives at the chapter house of the monastery which is garlanded with sunshine and roses and is to be the location of his novitiate during which, in true Swedenborgian fashion, 'you must show yourself as you are; and defend your opinions to the last' (p. 170). A soul worthy of Heaven must be a positive force for good. The Prior, who has a white beard and white hair and is dressed entirely in white, represents the purely good soul who apprehends the unity of all living creation through telepathic communion. This remarkable gift enables him to divine the Stranger's thoughts.

The monastery over which he presides is a place of learning as well as of devotion; so it unites the dual characteristics that Sweden-borg declared to be necessary for communication with the Divine. The Prior, in his examination of the Stranger, makes clear to him the logical inevitability of Providence which allowed him to be punished for a sin of his childhood. The Stranger agrees 'to forget this history of [his] own sufferings for all time' (p. 272) when Father Isidor, the doppleganger of the Doctor, forgives him and reveals that he had himself committed a similar sin. Here the lessons of the Eve episode of Act 3, Scene 1 are made explicit; life is an eternal recurrence, fault breeds fault and most important as the Prior makes clear: 'If we could only stop accusing one another and particularly Eternal Justice! But we're born in sin and all resemble

Adam' (p. 273). The Stranger should know by now that he is not
the sole child of the elves. We are all flawed by the sin of Adam and
we must all take part in an unequal struggle against our own
natures. There is no excuse for failure while some people manage to
triumph in similar situations; we have only ourselves to blame if we
abuse the free will that God gave us.

A common failing among unhappy souls is the cultivation of
knowledge at the expense of belief, as Thomas À Kempis constantly
points out. The story of Father Uriel highlights the futility of the
Stranger's persistent demand to know the meaning of life. He learns
the Kierkegaardian truth that he who must know before he can
believe will never believe and he who can believe before he knows
does not need to know. The story of Father Clemens teaches him
that all worldly opinion is shallow and transitory, appealing only to
the vanity of men. The conclusion of these lessons would appear to
be that human experience is unnecessary and human values empty.
Is then life worth living? For an answer to this question, the
Stranger is placed in the hands of Father Melcher who, by surveying
the lives of a number of tormented geniuses, demonstrates the incon-
sistencies of life. Contradictions even exist in great men but we
do not allow them to affect our appreciation of their genius. Such
paradoxes arise because 'The Powers play tricks on tricksters and
delude the arrogant, particularly those who alone believe they possess
truth and knowledge' (p. 282). This explains why the Stranger
encountered such personal contradictions on the Road to Damascus.
Now he can achieve the Hegelian synthesis by apprehending everything with 'Humanity and Resignation' (p. 283).

Enlightened, and rejecting the Tempter who tries to turn him
back to life, the Stranger no longer desires knowledge or even
speech; they are inadequate to true belief. 'You've lived in the
erroneous belief that language, a material thing can be a vehicle for
anything so subtle as thoughts and feelings. We've discovered that
error and speak as little as possible' (p. 270). The Stranger's decision
to bring his discussions with the Tempter to an end signal true
spiritual enlightenment. Through his discussions in Part III with the
Tempter, the Confessor, the Lady, and the Fathers he has passed
through the final three of Swedenborg's stages and his true, dutiful
and obedient being has emerged. He is laid to rest to be reborn not
as a baby, despite the Tempter's insistence that he will 'be baptised

once more like a new born child', but symbolically as a Swedenborgian angel in a Strindbergian heaven. 'By an "angel" Swedenborg means a deceased mortal, who by death has been released from
the prison of the body, and by suffering in faith has recovered the
highest faculties of his soul' (*A Blue Book*, p. 30).

To forestall the criticism that this interpretation is too dogmatic,
that it ties the last act of Part III to one level, when in fact, it also
works more or less realistically (i.e. non-mythically), we can admit
that the Stranger's journey across the river and by stages up the
mountain could be seen as the prelude to a merely physical retreat
from life. The Tempter and the Lady would then personify the
archetypal vices presented to such religious solitaries as John the
Baptist and, during his forty days and nights, Christ Himself.
The Stranger's ultimate rebirth at the end of the trilogy would be no
more than his emergence as a monk vowed to silence, contemplation
and the service of God. At this level, the trilogy would perhaps best
be analysed in terms of such Kierkegaardian ideas as the emergence
of the protagonist from the aesthetic and ethical lives to the religious. Clearly a realistic interpretation is plausible and can be conceded without invalidating the previous argument which was
expressed exclusively to clarify the basic theoretical structure of the
trilogy.

However, the thesis that the finale of *To Damascus* purely
dramatises Strindberg's cherished ideal of a non-confessional monastery[31] is less easy to accept. The notion described in the novel,
The Cloister,[32] does not have clear relevance to the trilogy.

> He began to dream his old dream of a monastery, within whose
> walls he would find shelter from the temptations and filth of this
> world, a place where he would be able to forget and be for-
> gotten . . . a non-confessional monastery for intellectuals who, at
> a time when industry and finance had pushed themselves so much
> to the fore, could not feel at home in the atmosphere of a material-
> ism which they themselves had been misled into preaching . . .
> The aim of this monastery was to be the training of supermen, by
> means of asceticism, meditation and the practice of science,
> literature and art. Religion was not mentioned, since he did not
> know what religion there would be, or whether there would be
> any religion at all. (p. 131)

It is difficult to sustain such a view of the close of *To Damascus* for three reasons. First of all, the whole dramatic force of Part III depicts the destruction of the Stranger's Nietzschean tendencies which are supplanted by a sense of humility in face of his spiritual fate. Secondly, both his development and the themes of the trilogy are transparently spiritual not secular. Thirdly, the Stranger rejects the ideal of intellectual communication and simply accepts his destiny without expecting self-improvement.

A more convincing account of the source of the monastic ideal in *To Damascus* can be provided by examining a novel which had a decided influence on Strindberg: J. K. Huysman's *En Route* (1895). Huysman's hero Durtal enters a Trappist monastery but does not take vows and is instructed by the holy and learned oblate, Monsieur Bruno. While the lurid (not to say melodramatic) sexual fantasies of Durtal are unlike anything in *To Damascus*, the central Confessor-novitiate relationship of the book, Durtal's ambivalent attitude towards women, his spiritual and intellectual difficulties with the Church's conception of God, his masochistical drive to subject himself to an ascetic life for which he is not fitted, all must have evoked lasting sympathetic responses in Strindberg. Whatever the facts of the case, there are many obvious similarities between the Stranger's spiritual conflicts throughout the trilogy and Durtal's in *En Route*.

In conclusion, Strindberg may or may not have intended the monastery to be his non-confessional ideal but he does not dramatically integrate it. The trilogy reaches its highest and deepest dramatic representations in its spiritual understanding. The semi-Nietzschean element is there but only very superficially; it cannot (as can a Swedenborgian interpretation) account for the detailed development of three plays. What makes *The Road to Damascus* characteristically Strindbergian and his greatest play is the synthesis of a wide variety of myths, symbols and ideas with a profound spiritual analysis in a new dramatic form. There is room in it for many ideas and many interpretations, though of course they are not all of equal importance.

7
Hybrid Plays

The three plays discussed in this chapter cannot be placed in any of the categories used in this book. Although *Crimes and Crimes* was conceived as a companion drama to *Advent*, there are crucial differences between them. As for *The Dance of Death*, it is in many respects unlike any other drama Strindberg wrote. The fact that these two plays are included in the same chapter is not intended to imply that they belong in the same category. This is very much a miscellany.

THERE ARE CRIMES AND CRIMES (1899)

A typically Swedenborgian piece masquerading as boulevard play, *Crimes and Crimes*[1] is Strindberg's first emergence into light (dim though it is) after the darkness of his immediate post-Inferno work. Its central theme is neatly defined by an extract from *A Blue Book*:

> Now for the first time I understood why I had so often in my life thought myself unjustly accused and punished for offences which I had not committed. I confess now that I had committed them in thought. But how did men know that? Assuredly there is a hidden justice which punishes sins of thought, and when men make each other accountable for suspicions, ugly looks or feelings, they are right. (p. 95)

In this so-called comedy, Maurice, bent on a life of pleasure with Henriette, wishes to escape his family responsibilities and is horrified when his thoughts are consummated by the death of his child. Through a series of unfortunate coincidences suspicion of its murder falls upon him and he is accused. Although technically he is innocent, in the words of the Abbé, 'guiltless you were not, for we are responsible for our thoughts, our words and our desires. You murdered in your mind when you wished the life out of your child' (p. 276). His subsequent punishment is to be self-determined; it is to issue more from his own reactions than from external circumstances. Crime, as Swedenborg pointed out, is its own punishment.

The play also contains a supernatural element which Strindberg himself described in a letter of 22 March 1899: 'the last act is Swedenborgian with hell already on earth, and the hero, the intrigue-maker in the play is the Unseen One'. From the moment he appears on stage, Maurice is suitably flawed to be a victim of the Powers. He has chosen worldly success in preference to faith in God. 'God? What is that? Who is He?' (p. 218). He has weakened Jeanne's faith and he intends to use his fame against his enemies 'to see them suffer what I have suffered'. His role is precisely contrasted with that of the Abbé who has restored Jeanne's religious beliefs. Maurice has no presentiment of the Unknown and his lack of vigilance makes him vulnerable. He is a hedonist, while Jeanne is a Christian who believes: 'O Crux! Ave spes unica' (p. 22). As we might expect, his eventual downfall is caused by a 'devil of a woman', Henriette, who unwittingly represents the power of evil. 'Henriette should seduce spiritually; the vampire who drinks souls; and needs no body (Aphasia is without body!). She doesn't know what good and evil are.'[2] Madame Catherine, the café proprietress, senses this and tries unavailingly to counteract Maurice's fear that he is destined to share Henriette's evil future, with the explicit Swedenborgian belief 'in a good God who protects us from evil powers if we ask Him nicely' (p. 222). But he is too proud to humble himself. Throughout, he tries to disclaim personal responsibility. In contradiction of the introductory passage I quoted from *A Blue Book*, he remarks that 'If we had to answer for our thoughts, who would stand a chance' (p. 224). By the end of the play, he will learn that our responsibility towards God is total.

In Act 2, Maurice experiences worldly success, whilst 'recognising its own emptiness, and anticipating disaster' now that he no longer loves Jeanne. At this point one cannot but sympathise with his remark that she is a little too pure (self-righteous) to be alluring company. Again Strindberg has tended to overstate the purity of his spiritually innocent character. To most of us it would seem perfectly excusable that Maurice would wish to celebrate his theatrical triumph with the vibrant Henriette rather than sit at home with Jeanne, bemoaning the temptations of worldly vanity. But not for Strindberg: for him the ominous leitmotif of a Beethoven piano sonata serves to indicate the danger into which his protagonist is falling. And, appropriately for a man who is eventually to be redeemed, Maurice himself confesses that he has a bad conscience at deserting such a loyal friend as Madame Catherine who 'had a special stake in my success'. Then instantly, before he can repent, Henriette symbolically puts Jeanne and the rest of his friends out of sight and mind, by burning the presents his former mistress had sent him. Now he is Astarte's consort plunged to the hilt in her evil: 'But I believe it is your evil qualities which I need. I believe it is the vice in you which attracts me with the irresistible pleasure of the new' (p. 233). Soon he will discover that 'Every bodily pleasure brings joy at first, but at length it bites and destroys' (*The Imitation of Christ*, p. 52).

At this point, it seems pertinent to inquire whether this sense of evil is not a little melodramatic in terms of character. At most, Maurice's sin is one of omission, though, as usual in the Post-Inferno dramas, evil is not so much generated by what the characters are and do, as by the setting and its atmosphere. From the opening scene in the cemetery, with the old woman bending over a grave among the stone crosses, *Crimes and Crimes* depicts a Swedenborgian world of spirits. Death, strife and evil are predicated by means of correspondences; withered flowers, Maurice hurting the child when he embraces it,[3] Henriette's dream of 'coolly dissecting the muscles of Adolphe's chest and the sight of walls hung with armour and weapons'. Within this context, Maurice's foreboding when he first sees Henriette in the Cremerie is not the wariness of a man irresistibly attracted towards a *femme fatale*, but the fear we feel towards someone who perhaps unconsciously can be a force of evil in our life; the fear of someone who can provoke all our worst and most self-destructive impulses. Both the literary and theatrical value of the play depend upon the skill with which Strindberg and his producers create a dark mood that suggests moral licence and depravity. The behaviour of the characters cannot be subsumed to a set of purely psychological descriptions or to an analysis of conscious or unconscious motivation alone; partly the protagonists are victims of their environment, which, being essentially supernatural, affects them extra-psychologically.

Henriette confirms Maurice's opinion that she is a force of evil by confessing to an unnamed crime (abortion, in fact) which 'put me outside, on the other side of life and society and my fellow-beings', so that 'I have only been living a half-life, a dream life' (p. 234). As a result, she has become superstitious and hypersensitive; the perfect foil to his self-doubt. She never touches cards for fear of a bad omen and she believes in ghosts and evil spirits. Obliquely, Strindberg gives her a Faustian dimension, suggesting that she has set herself 'above and beyond the laws of nature' by some kind of pact (i.e. her 'crime') with the Dark Powers.

Gradually with Henriette's encouragement, Maurice's vainglory reaches Olympian heights when, in Scene 2, he imagines, in a powerful anthropomorphic speech, the whole of Paris, indeed the world itself, 'whispering my name'.[4] Predictably, he would now like to die, but like Strindberg, he cannot find a woman to die with him. Henriette has not sold her soul to throw away her life in an empty gesture. After Adolpe's implicit indictment of their behaviour, skilfully embodied in eulogy, they both realise they have fallen from grace and, although this is not exactly a startling revelation to either of them, its confirmation has temporarily a sobering effect. We see for an instant that they are not intrinsically evil creatures but that their all too human failings (e.g. egotism, sensuality) are being exploited by powers beyond their control.

Curiously, it is now at the point of mutual self-contempt that their megalomania revives with a vengeance and, in thought, they commit infanticide. Strindberg makes this clear by having Henriette pick 'the five of diamonds, the scaffold' from a pack of cards. Despairingly she asks: 'Is it possible that our fates are predestined? That our thoughts are led as if through pipes, the way they must go, without our being able to stop them?' (p. 241). Henriette tries to resist the crime they are about to commit. In so doing, she lays the foundations of her subsequent redemption, but this is to be in the future for, at present, they are still following the hedonist's creed; they plan to run away from Paris and their crimes to seek forgetfulness in 'the sunshine and the sea'.

Their conduct is criticised by Madame Catherine in Act 3 Scene 1. After Adolphe has remarked in expiation: 'Maurice felt the danger in the air . . . It's really as if an intrigue had been woven by some invisible power, as if they had been driven by a trick into one another's arms' (p. 244), she points out: 'But, you see, to *let* oneself be driven or tempted into evil like Monsieur Maurice, that's either weakness or wickedness. And if you feel your strength failing, then you pray for help, and you get it. But he didn't do that—he was too stuck up' (p. 244). This is Strindberg's mature statement on the problem of free will and determinism. Without God we are helpless but we have to make the first move towards Him. Thus Maurice is punished for confusing good and evil and for failing to come to God. His daughter has died and the rumour has sprung up that he is responsible. Mercilessly, Providence has used his own thoughts against him, inducing him to be virtually his own judge and tor-mentor.

Having decided to kill themselves (Act 4), Maurice and Henriette rush to the Luxembourg Gardens, an inferno, ironically overlooked by a statue of Adam and Eve.[5] But once there, they are enveloped by a mass of absurd suspicions, projected into their minds by forces of evil. An evocative stage direction establishes the Swedenborgian context—'The wind is blowing in the trees and stirring leaves, straws and bits of paper on the ground'—a correspondence for the evil spirits stirring their minds. In this context Maurice, whose play had affirmed the value of human nature, now concludes misanthropically that 'human nature has not been slandered'. So once more two 'dark angels' pursue them. 'You are in the grip of the demons of sus-picions, and each of you is tearing the other to pieces with your sense of partial guilt' (p. 267). Again we cannot help feeling that a character is being too explicitly knowing; though as Strindberg's mouthpiece Adolphe can perhaps be excused his prescience. Now it is left to him to articulate Strindberg's theme: 'Everything is grace, but one doesn't get it, you know, unless one seeks for it . . . Seek!' (p. 269).

Henriette takes his advice and leaves Maurice, presumably to live a more Godly life now that she has been enlightened about the nature of conscience and redemption. For the first time, she can accept that she is not a special case but has a higher and a lower nature either of which can dominate, according to the path she takes. Under Adolphe's guidance, she rejects the 'gay Bohemian life' to become —a nun? Then when it has been established that his daughter died from natural causes, Maurice is re-united with Jeanne and forgiven, but not before Adolphe and the Abbé have harangued him. He declares that this world no longer has any attractions, but, unlike the Stranger in *To Damascus*, he is not so much indifferent to this world as dismayed by it. He wants to escape: 'Let me hide behind your consecrated walls and forget this appalling dream which has taken two days and lasted two eternities' (p. 274). Almost light-heartedly, he makes what for him is the appropriate compromise: 'Tonight I will meet you at the church to have a reckoning with myself about all this—but tomorrow I shall go to the theatre' (p. 276). Characteristically, he puts God first without denying his own basic nature. He has come to terms with his success and confirms the Abbé's words that 'Providence has granted you absolution', though it is clear that he has not reached Kierkegaard's religious stage.

As James Allen jr[6] has made clear the basic struggle for Maurice's soul takes place between Henriette and Adolphe. Incidentally, his analysis of their roles adds a neat Swedenborgian (and Freudian) dimension to the conflict. Whether as independent characters or as expressionistic emanations of Maurice's ego, Henriette represents the animal, pleasure-seeking self, Adolphe the spiritual, serene self. Significantly, prior to the play, Adolphe and Henriette have been lovers; that is the two forces in Maurice's personality were compatible. Both the combatants have sinned, but Adolphe has made penance while Henriette repeats (or at least adds to) her crimes. Fortunately for Maurice, both he and Henriette are eventually redeemed; that is, the spiritual ideal ultimately dominates his personality. Expiation of one's sins is always possible, even when they are as freely chosen and corrupting as those of Henriette.

Although *Crimes and Crimes* has been one of Strindberg's most popular plays among Continental theatre managements, it is not a complete success. Admittedly, in Henriette he created one of his most compelling vampire women; to be compared with Tekla and Alice. And the scenes of gradual degradation between Maurice and her, which mount to an orgiastic frenzy until both characters treat the world and its morality with a Nietzschean disdain, are among the most theatrically powerful he ever created. The boulevard atmosphere of Paris, so carefully built up throughout the play, is trans-figured at these moments and the hedonism of Maurice and Henriette becomes maniacal as their feelings of guilt impel them to escape from reality. For such moments, clearly many producers would be attracted towards a play, which in other scenes is repetitive, pre-dictable and smug. The character of Madame Catherine seems to be rather superfluous. Apart from provoking some humour in the last few minutes, her dramatic functions are covered by Adolphe and the Abbé. These two men of virtue have carefully differentiated functions; the one, a redeemed sinner represents human understanding and hope for Maurice and Henriette, while the Abbé is an archetypal spiritual adviser, barely distinguishable from the Confessor in *To Damascus*.

However, the finale is dramatically flat, being very predictable as well as self righteous. Although perhaps in an allegory this is to be expected, Strindberg, by choosing the boulevarderie form, leads his audience to believe that even if the theme is to be *conveniently* resolved, at least the emotional confrontations will be powerfully dramatised. A great deal of foreboding and psychological tension is built up throughout the first three acts, only to be deflated gently in the fourth. Without pleading for a theatre of catharsis, we can still require a climax, which would make of the powerful evil we have had preached at us for an hour and a half something more than a slight case of extramarital adventure. The closing scene gives the impression that Maurice has been a 'naughty boy' or a 'cad', when we have supposed he was something approaching a soul in torment, balancing a purgatorial tightrope.

Yet Strindberg has written a comedy and here we are demanding blood and brutality. This appears anomalous but the fault is Strindberg's not ours, because he did not seem to have made up his mind about his intentions or he did not sufficiently think them out. On the one hand, *Crimes and Crimes* contains a boulevard play about a young playwright's personal vanity being engorged by worldly success and the admiration of an enigmatic *femme fatale*. This would have been a fitting subject for a sophisticated comedy of manners in which tragedy was narrowly averted by coincidence or by the intrigues of his friends, and it could easily, in fact profitably, have been veined with black humour. However, Strindberg wished to take it much further, enclosing the black comedy in a rigid moral and eschatological framework. Now it is possible to combine comedy with serious moralising but when a black comedy is united with a plentitude of preaching about hellfire, evil spirits and moral decay, inevitably lightness is totally eclipsed. A very different play emerges in which all the fun (what there is of it in *Crimes and Crimes*) counts for little.

THE DANCE OF DEATH (1901)

Contrary to the widespread opinion, *The Dance of Death*[1] is not a dour prototype of Edward Albee's *Who's Afraid of Virginia Woolf*. It is rather a masterpiece of expressionism and symbolism whose naturalistic base is transcended throughout. Moreover, it is often at those moments when it is most obviously non-naturalistic that its theatrical greatness is most apparent. Any attempt to interpret the play as a large-scale version of *The Father* inevitably results in reducing its dramatic high points to clumsy and grotesque farce.

In their most pure forms, naturalism and expressionism are incompatible, yet in *The Dance of Death*, Strindberg tried to fuse them and, to a large extent, he succeeded. How? As we saw in Chapter 1, the interpretation of the two dramatic theories given by Strindberg emphasised their underlying similarities. Thus, if there is enough of a naturalistic milieu in *The Dance of Death* to further the central conflict in a socially recognisable manner (i.e. if the Captain's military role is used to develop his marital strife), it need not interfere with the overall psychological indetermination or the symbolic undertones: for example, the Captain's extinguished cigar, the storm, the old woman, the changing colour of Alice's hair, the telegraph clicking out diabolical messages. But before we can go any further with this argument, we must expose the expressionistic features of *The Dance of Death*, which are not as obvious as its 'naturalism'.

Neither the Captain nor Alice is intended merely to represent typical human beings rather they are expressionistic amalgams of critical human attitudes. They are not so much people as syntheses of human weaknesses and vices. This is why they function on so many integrated levels.

EDGAR demonic → brutal → superhuman → psychotic
ALICE pure egoist → animal → bitch → neurotic

And even more important from Strindberg's point of view, their marriage is not like those of the great naturalistic plays in which the numerous tensions in *particular types* of heterosexual relationships are simply developed to an extreme.[8] Rather the relationship between Edgar and Alice is the rule under which most marriages are to be subsumed; it is a blue-print of possibilities from which we can explain and predict all manner of marital experience. Or at least this is what it is intended to be. Yet Strindberg is endeavouring to make a statement about more than the essence of marriage; he is offering a definition of the nature of life itself. Of course, his view of human existence was not always as bleak as this, but when he wrote *The Dance of Death* he was at his most Schopenhauerian. The egotistical nature of human beings, their enslavement to the Will to Live and dominate, the inevitability of sexual conflict and the misery of existence, are all definitive of Strindberg's play and Schopenhauer's philosophy.

The method by which Strindberg achieves such universality is not through depersonalising (i.e. de-naturalising) the characters but by diabolising them. That is, Strindberg transposes their identifiably human failings to a conflict whose keynote is extra-human; in fact, devilish. If we examine both Edgar and Alice, we shall find that in their *small scale* encounters, they can be perfectly well understood as an obstinate selfish boor baited by a malicious disgruntled bitch. They respond with the tired unthinking spite of an old and badly married couple; insults roll off their tongues *and backs* almost effortlessly. And in this they are not so very unusual; most of us would not find it too difficult to discover partial real life models or to imagine the long years of disappointment leading up to their present nemesis. But before long we begin to realise that such an account is inadequate because, increasingly, they step outside their degraded marital game and break even the few rules it still possesses. 'The day he died I'd laugh aloud' (Alice, p. 363). 'Skinners or scavengers can look after him. A garden plot is too nice a place to receive that barrow-load of filth' (Alice, p. 450). Consider also the cruelty of the Captain's divorce scene (p. 389) and his reasons, or lack of them, for attempting to drown his wife.

At times such as these our experience begins to fail us. Malice has given way to evil, defence responses to murderous instincts and disappointment to self-destructive, world annihilating despair. On the surface, the playwright seems to be at fault in creating attitudes which he has not adequately motivated; situations he has not explained. And then suddenly it becomes clear that apart from each separate segment of dialogue Strindberg has made no real attempt to motivate. The Captain and Alice (Edgar, in particular) are not rounded characters whose minds can be probed in order to uncover the sources of their behaviour. They are 'dehumanised' by being unmotivated,[9] or at least whatever motivation they might have is totally inadequate to the viciousness of their behaviour. Indeed, the effect is more diabolic if huge crimes are given trivial motives than if they are given none at all; the classic example is that of Iago. If an audience is totally at a loss to explain a person's behaviour they quickly lose interest, the character is regarded as either insane or a machine. But, if someone reacts monstrously to a moderate stimulus, the action becomes even more monstrous and unexpected; beyond all reason, perhaps even diabolic. This is exactly the case with the Captain.

This lack of clear or consistent motivation transforms the obstinacy of Edgar's character into something akin to the malevolent unreason of a minor devil. Vindictively, he torments himself and his wife for no other reason that he can articulate than a delight in destruction. Since we cannot explain his behaviour, we inevitably and correctly believe that he is like a child (cf. his childlike pride when he receives flowers and letters from his men) who has 'the devil in him', and because he has the power and the intelligence of a grown man, but none of the scruples, he becomes a disturbing, indeed a terrifying figure. Even his physical characteristics make him somehow non-human as Kurt notices: 'His ugliness can be pretty sinister. I noticed that, especially when we weren't on good terms. And when he wasn't actually present, his image swelled and took on frightful shapes and sizes, so that he literally haunted me' (p. 377). Nor is Alice a fully explained character, though we can understand her behaviour more easily than the Captain's, if only because she is a more familiar harpy in Strindberg's mythology. But even she goes so far beyond the norm of marital disharmony that her conduct is not merely inexcusable, but inhuman. Incomprehensible in particular human terms, we must interpret her as a composite picture of unpleasant human features. She is not extra human, it is just that she is not *specifically* human. And yet because she is so malicious she is more nearly human than the Captain who rarely indulges in emotional outbursts of any kind. If anything, at times of stress he tends to be terse ('Hyena').

The unavoidable conclusion of this is that the struggle of the sexes typified by these elemental characters does not end with the death of the Captain but lasts endlessly in all of us and our progeny, beneath the layers of social sophistication. Strindberg has stripped off from these two people the compromises and conventions enforced by social living (as described by Swedenborg), to reveal primitive man; the real animal self to which we are tied so long as we deny God. Swedenborgianism then is the theoretical framework of *The Dance of Death*. At this level we are presented with two resolutely *animal* selves struggling without scruples against each other and, in the course of doing so, revealing all that is primitive and unrestrained in human nature. Thus when we remember that Swedenborgian hell is a place of total egoism and that our animal nature is purely self-centred, we can see there is no conflict between the dual interpretation of Edgar as a devil and a brute. Also, as we have seen, he is not motivated, at least not in any sense we can recognise, because the pure animal self does not intellectualise or socialise; it lacks what we would call reasons or purposes.

The play takes place in a 'grey stone' fortress on a Swedish 'devil's island' (nicknamed 'Little Hell'); symbol of mankind's earthly imprisonment. This is to be the setting of the Captain's self-made hell on earth[10] in which he presides as Satan incarnate over his own and Alice's mutual torment. Here their discordant marriage,[11] the antithesis of Swedenborg's heavenly marriage, becomes an allegory in which Strindberg's misanthropy and his pessimism are communicated through a deep sense of life's malevolence. He seems to despair that man will ever rise beyond his earthly nature to the spiritual heights that God intended for him. As befits his blackest play, there are no traces of that evolutionary optimism or even of the excuse that we are not entirely responsible for our conduct which had been evident in the most cynical of his naturalistic works. Nothing can alleviate or even explain Edgar and Alice's condition; it is characteristic of life itself. Like the inhabitants of Sartre's hell, they are condemned to the torment of their own and each other's company. Despite all the reasons in the world they cannot leave each other; they are literally doomed to remain married until death. Indeed, in view of their personalities, not even death will part them, for if, as we might imagine, they are destined for a spiritual hell, what more exquisite torment could there be than that they be attracted once more to each other?

Part I is the more clearly expressionistic and pessimistic half; in it their twenty-five years of misery is crystallised within the space of three days. Throughout it, they exhibit that complete lack of respect for each other's feelings, and absence of tact and of charity, that often characterises disillusioned relationships, but inevitably they go further; for example, Alice clearly enjoys telling the Captain that his health is not good and that he will shortly die. With considerable insight, Strindberg captures the way in which such couples are not only soured in their attitudes towards each other but also to the rest of the world. Irritated by the monotony of their own bickering,[12] card-playing lives (ominously, spades are trumps), they unite for once to agree that other people are scum too. Such misanthropy is a natural concomitant of their unhappiness. Terrible as their marriage is, it would be unbearable if they thought other couples were happy. 'Could one really get used to being entirely alone' (p. 361). The Captain irritates his wife by his grandiose contempt for her, her family,[13] and her career; indeed for everyone but himself. And being dissatisfied, she is defensive and oversensitive at the best of times, let alone in his company. He is the supreme egotist, blind to everything but his own conceit. She is an extreme neurotic who feels persecuted and defends herself with the malevolence of an Iago. She is forever on the raw and he delights in rubbing salt in her wounds. In fact, Edgar is insensitive to other people to the extent of forgetting what they look like. For instance, he so wilfully insists upon confusing Kurt's past role as a mediator between himself and Alice with his own role, that we might suspect that he is psychotic.

Edgar's love of military ritual, the manly life ('Now, I'll have my grog' 'A man should be able to hold his liquor'), and his military textbooks, his vacant staring into space, his dancing mania and his fantasies of good food, make him an unforgettable character. Unlike his wife, he feels the need for laughter, food, entertainment and people among whom he can shine. He is the extrovert who shows a bright face to the world (a man's man) but who, in effect, is a sychophant. 'You cringe to all your inferiors. Although you're a despot, at bottom you're a slave . . . but you can't get on with your equals and superiors' (p. 351). Like Jean, cowering at the sound of the bell in *Miss Julie*, he is conditioned by a bugle call which he cannot ignore. And yet his philosophy of life is distinctly Nietzschean; he believes that once one's strength and will power have disintegrated, 'when the mechanism's done for, nothing's left but a barrowful of filth to tip on a garden plot' (words which Alice uses crushingly against him, after he has died). Meanwhile, he lives by the corollary:

'But as long as the mechanism's intact the thing is to kick and fight for all your worth, with both hands and both feet.' Nietzsche's superman must needs be a psychotic and, through the Captain, the later religious Strindberg is criticising the arrogant, atheistic conception he had once extolled in such plays as *Pariah* and *Creditors*. He now sees the Übermensch as diabolic. The failure of the Captain in Nietzschean terms significantly is not cerebral, he is as successful a superman as Mr X and more successful than Gustav. His failure, like that of all would-be supermen, is one of feeling.

> ALICE Look at those boots! He'd have trampled the world flat with them if he could. He's trampled other people's fields and gardens with them, and other people's toes and my skull. (p. 376)

He destroys Kurt and humiliates Alice at the cost of alienating (or so he believes) Judith, the one person whose love he needs. Thus, according to Strindberg, does Providence punish all who seek to usurp the power of God.[14] They are made to be the cause of their own downfall.

Edgar's superman belief in his own immortality and his complete contempt for mankind make way for a more cautious estimation of his powers once he has stared into the face of death. If his time and energies are limited, he must use them more efficiently to prove his superiority and indulge his rancour. He does not value life for itself but as a means to accomplish his revenge. Symbolically he discovers he has a calcified heart which will be the death of him; a fact confirmed by the appearance of an old woman (death!) at the window of his improvised sick room. Stubbornly, he keeps his soldier's boots on because he anticipates a battle. For the first time, he considers the possibility that 'the wheelbarrow and the garden plot' may not be all and the prospect of immortality, an endless continuation of this hell on earth, disturbs him. He would prefer annihilation but during the night he becomes convinced that the soul endures and this belief changes his subsequent behaviour.

He continues to play his superman role to the end, remaining too self-assured and too skilful for Alice's feminine devices, but now he is more purposive, more determined. He symbolically takes on the mantle of Lear, an old man close to death, suffering at the hands of a malevolent world. He has opened his cape and

is letting the wind blow on his breast' (p. 383). And he begins to
fulfil what Alice terms his vampire nature—'to seize hold of other
people's fates, to suck interest from the lives of others, to order and
arrange for others because his own life is absolutely without interest'
(p. 383). His desire to do this is vampirism, his ability to do it is
supermanliness, and both involve opposing God. As an implied
criticism of Nietzsche this is valid because, according to the philosopher, ability confers right.

The prospect of death has also conferred on him 'a kind of
dignity' (p. 385) as well as having fired his imagination. Now he
will prove that Alice is right when she says he 'knows the art of
intrigue better than anybody' (p. 385). Like a vampire, he tries to
keep himself alive by feeding off other people's blood, by 'sucking
an interest in life from your [Kurt's] existence and eating your
children alive' (p. 386). Superior cerebral power enables him continually to out-wit both Alice and Kurt in spite of their attempts to
dominate him. Cleverly, he even succeeds in making Kurt and Alice
feel guilty about informing on him to the Quartermaster. Moreover
he does so with such a consummate sense of the dramatic. Even his
heart attacks seem so well timed that we might suspect they are not
all genuine. Yet, whatever the reason, his somewhat incredible see-
sawing between perfect self-control in his Nietzschean manoeuvres
and his sudden prostrations is not intended to be perfectly naturalistic but helps to underline his diabolic quality.

During the Captain's long mime at the opening of Act 2 Scene 2,
we learn more about his feelings than in the rest of the two parts put
together. Dramatically this is convincing because he is the kind of
emotional solitary who would reveal himself only when alone. This
is the only occasion when the following, highly perceptive comment
of Lamm does not apply: 'But the Captain's blustering tone of
command, his raucous guffaws and noisy energy are all continued
and his jovial exhilaration which he hopes will be taken for a sense of
humour, is as false as his effusive benevolence. He has, to use one of
Strindberg's favourite expressions "lied together" a character for
himself.'[15] During his mime, his impatience, impulsiveness, potential
violence, his affection for his daughter and his men, and his fear of
death are shown one by one. The numerous objects he throws out of
the window are either harmful to his health or are associated with
Alice (laurel wreaths, love letters etc). This necessary bit of spring-

cleaning enables him to turn his back on the past and make the most of whatever time he has left to him.[16] In desperation, he is compelled to try to alter the unending torment that destiny seems to have decreed for Alice and himself by the only means at his disposal—the urge to power and domination.

At this point, we encounter his famous philosophy of life:

> You may have observed that my practice of the art of living has been—elimination. That's to say, cancel out and pass on. Early in life I made myself a sack into which I stuffed my humiliations, and when it was full I chucked it into the sea. I don't believe any human being has suffered so many humiliations as I have. But when I cancelled them out and passed on, they ceased to exist. (p. 397)

The word 'cancel' is used ambiguously; in reference to his own misdeeds it means 'forget', but in respect of other people's supposed sins against himself it means 'revenge'. A clue to understanding the Captain's philosophy is to be found in *A Blue Book*:

> It is necessary to make oneself deaf and blind, or it is impossible to live. One must cancel and go on! That is generally called 'forgiving', but it may be a device of the revengeful for sparing himself trouble or a scheme of the sensitive for not letting insults reach him. (p. 58)

The Captain manages to combine all these possibilities with great facility, or rather he does until his confrontation with death: 'But there comes a moment when the ability to create in imagination, as you call it, fails' (p. 398). However, his resolution is completely restored once Alice informs him that she and Kurt are lovers.

Alice's development is simpler but no more appealing. Her antecedents in Strindberg's dramas are obvious. She uses her children and her friends against her husband but, whereas Laura and company sought to reduce their spouses to childlike status, she seeks to *destroy* Edgar. Unless she is played from the outset as a partly mysterious and monstrous figure, the sudden revelation of the full extent of her viciousness when the Captain collapses during his dance will not only be inexplicable but incongruous in terms of what has gone before. As long as the character is kept, as it were, open-ended, the jump from marital disharmony to vicious hatred will not conflict with her previous behaviour although of course it will be surprising. The portrayal of Alice on stage is complicated by the fact that she was once an actress whose career came to an end against her will when she married Edgar. As a result, she retains a penchant for dramatic gestures and for stagey vocal delivery. A skilful actress could add an extra-naturalistic dimension to the character by incorporating such pretensions into her performance while accentuating the larger-than-life insincerity of the woman.

In Act 2 Scene 1, Alice begins to flaunt her sexuality which appeared to be dead within her marriage. She sets out physically to ensnare Kurt as an ally against her husband with as little scruple as Edgar himself would show, though perhaps more hot bloodedly. With all the implacable animosity of which the Strindbergian female is capable—'The day I forgave or loved an enemy I should be a hypocrite' (p. 384), she seeks revenge and so, by her lack of faith and charity, places herself in the same moral mire as the Captain. Conceitedly she declares what only a saint could say: 'My life is open and clear and I have always been above board' (p. 384). Yet despite this, her arrogance seems petty at the side of Edgar's and Strindberg, aware of how he towers over her, allows her almost always to put forward *her* viewpoint. Rarely does the Captain speak up for himself; rather his defence is articulated indirectly through Kurt, or is implied by Alice going too far in her attacks on him. As Strindberg writes in *A Blue Book*: 'A man's goodwill and generosity towards his wife stand in direct relation to her behaviour. When therefore a woman is ill-treated by her husband, we know what sort she is' (p. 166).

Alice's technique in combating Edgar's plans is to insinuate her own interpretations of everything he says into Kurt's ear. Indeed, perhaps Strindberg over uses the expressionist device of the aside to reveal Alice's inner experience. But be that as it may, she wins the allegiance, even the love, of Kurt to such an extent that she can tell him that Edgar has never struck her because 'he knows that I should leave him', while later insisting that 'He beats me—he has beaten me for twenty-five years, in front of the children'. And on both occasions he believes her. Staggeringly self-confident and callous, she allows her hair to go grey (i.e. makes no attempt to keep up appearances)[17] when she is certain she will soon be a widow, but once she has seduced Kurt she feels sexually alive once more and darkens it again.[18] There are no excuses for her any more than there are for the Captain. Deprived of the opportunity or the ability to dominate her husband, she uses her sexuality to reduce Kurt to utter dependence; an experience that might make one believe that Edgar was forced into supermanliness merely to avoid the ignominy of being treated as a slave by Alice. When, at the end of Part I, Kurt leaves her, Alice is horrified that she will lose not only a lover but her husband also. While Kurt is with her she can enjoy the idea of destroying Edgar because she has a replacement but the prospect of being entirely alone makes even marriage to the Captain seem desirable. She wants him not for himself but because, at the close of Part I, he is the only person available to share hell with her.

Without Kurt, the third member of this *menage à trois*, Edgar and Alice would have continued tormenting each other until death carried off one or the other of them, but when Kurt appears, he functions as a much needed catalyst: 'But what was interesting in the experiment was how happy we were as soon as we had a stranger in the house—to begin with' (p. 354). As soon as he enters the house, Kurt feels he is being forced to play an unnatural role. When he is there they can use him as an audience but once he leaves they are forced to moderate their outbursts and make the best of each other's company. Kurt feels that he is in a house of evil. 'What's going on here? The very walls smell of poison—one feels sick the moment one comes in. I'd rather be off if I hadn't promised Alice to stay. There's a corpse under the floor . . . and such hatred that one can scarcely breathe' (p. 362). In these noxious circumstances, it is appropriate that Kurt is a Quarantine Master. As Alice realises, he is to be an instrument of Providence (see p. 364); he even articulates a Swedenborgian philosophy of constraint: 'Alice, the moment you stop asking whose fault it is, you'll have a sense of relief. Try just to accept it as a fact, as a trial that must be borne' (p. 364). But she cannot, because their's is 'a quite unreasoning hatred. It has no cause, no object, but also no end' (pp. 364–5). Similarly, he informs the Captain that he is living a hell on earth: 'You've described your hell so realistically that metaphors, however poetic, are out of the picture' (p. 375).

Although there is more of Strindberg, the man, in Edgar, Kurt is the character in *The Dance of Death* who comes closest to being the playwright's spokesman. In some ways, though, Kurt's familiarity with the couple gradually makes him resemble them. We must remember that, in his later years, Strindberg believed fervently in the infectiousness of evil, so, under the Captain's influence, Kurt becomes something of a vampire too: 'Yes, I want to bite your throat and suck your blood like a lynx. You have roused the wild beast in me' (p. 395). And again he confesses: 'It's as if these prison walls had soaked in all the evil of the criminals, and one only had to breathe to catch it' (p. 396). Even the Captain acknowledges that 'Everyone who comes near us grows evil ... Kurt was weak and evil is strong' (p. 405).

Small wonder then that Kurt can say: 'When I came here I bore no malice, and when I felt myself infected by your hatred, I made up my mind to go away. But now I feel impelled to hate this man— as I have hated evil itself' (p. 391). After he learns that Edgar is trying to alienate his son from him, he is reluctant to pursue his revenge because, as a good Swedenborgian, he has 'discovered that retribution comes in any case', but he is helpless against Alice who reveals her full capacity for evil to him. 'Alice, are you a devil too?' (p. 392). There is between them a strong sexual attraction which, for two starved fellow sufferers such as they, is irresistible. Kurt, however, is not a fool and shows, when he resists Alice's prompting, that he would not allow himself completely to be put into any woman's pocket. All in all, Kurt is the catalyst. He is also the medium through which Strindberg articulates the Swedenborgian virtues of patience and humility. By means of him, we are able to measure both the evil and the misery of Edgar and Alice, for although Kurt has had an unhappy life and is to lose virtually everything he possesses at Edgar's hands, he manages to retain something of human dignity and hope. Beside him, both Edgar and Alice appear pathetic creatures of despair.

PART TWO

There is a strong temptation to declare Part II both dramatically and thematically superfluous. Part I seems not only complete but well-nigh perfect on its own. Its final uneasy truce in which each character's motives are ambiguous is well-suited to the theatrical tastes of present-day audiences. Moreover, with its implications of eternal recurrence (i.e. it opens and closes with Edgar and Alice's silver wedding), Part I produces an open-ended hell which is more terrifying than any death.

The new subsidiary theme centres upon the character of Judith
who was based on Strindberg's own beloved daughter and who is the
source of optimism. We might suppose, within such an emotional
hell, it is out of place to dwell lovingly on the trivial hopes and
crises of a pair of adolescents. Unless, that is, Strindberg either shows
how youthful idealism is inevitably destroyed by marital despair or
how it can avoid it in the future. Since he attempts to portray the
latter, it is not surprising that the portrait of Judith is almost the
best thing in Part II. This high-spirited girl with streaks of obstinacy
and feelings of superiority in her character is quite imaginable as the
Captain's daughter. She is by no means a flawless personality but
from an audience's and Strindberg's points of view her saving graces
are her gaiety and the eventual vigour of her feelings. When we first
encounter her she appears hard, confident of her attractiveness and
of her ability to manage people to her own advantage. The assured
way she manipulates Allan and the Lieutenant suggest a recurrence
of her father's vampirism, but eventually she proves herself different
from Edgar by her capacity to love and even to sacrifice herself for
love. When she allows her better emotions to dominate she escapes
finally from the hell that threatens her and, symbolically through her
own father, she kills the devil. Youth and, most of all, love redeem
her.

After the harrowing experience of Part I, the scenes between her
and Allan provide an affectionate comic relief which is, at the same
time, a marvellously delicate study of adolescent sexuality. The
skittishness, the casual cruelty, the fey despair, the argumentativeness
and the sudden passion of an unplanned embrace have rarely been
bettered. Here is Strindberg remembering his youth and forgetting,
for a time, the pessimism and sense of sin which oppressed his later
life. The triumph of youthful love here, as in *Swanwhite*, is an object
of faith for Strindberg, but while in the fairy play the conventions
of the form exclude questions of possibility, in *The Dance of Death*
Strindberg's optimism for Judith and Allan seems to be wishful
thinking. Everywhere hell surrounds them. Even near Kurt's comparatively idyllic home, there are correspondences of the hell outside.
'On this shore there's but goose-grass, cuttle fish, jellyfish and
stingers' (p. 413). They are pawns in the game of very superior
devils, and yet they manage to escape and destroy the principal
demon. How? By a multiplicity of means; Edgar's fatal flaw (his

emotional dependence on Judith), the accident of Judith and Allan's love suddenly blossoming, Alice's intervention and, most of all, the salutary design of Providence. With an effort we can find good reasons but none of them really issue from the characters of Judith and Allan themselves. This, in one sense, is as it should be, because it would be grossly improbable to make either of them a match for Edgar. But neither are we presented with evidence of love and youth's irresistible power in the face of evil; and this is what Strindberg intended and what an audience should demand. All we are offered is a particular portrait of two young people and a vague belief in providential protection.

In Part II, themes which were treated with great subtlety in Part I are more obviously exploited. The result is not an imaginative extension as in *To Damascus* but simply a matter of making explicit what would have been better left implicit. And, furthermore, this attempt to develop thematic continuity is disrupted by the contrast of mood. The light conventionality of Part II seems less a response to formal demands than to Strindberg's desire to dramatise his affection for his daughter. As a result, the Captain's machinations, complex though they are, appear uninteresting, and the relationship between Alice, Edgar and Kurt by being repetitious and off centre is de-humanised in the worst sense. Whereas in Part I it went beyond the human to the diabolic, in Part II it never fully reaches the human but degrades to the mechanical and the earlier dramatic intensity disintegrates.

The continuities of theme which refer primarily to the Captain make it barely conceivable that his characterisation should be so devitalised. By embarking on his campaign of revenge against Kurt he rejects the lesson of humility which should have issued from his intimations of mortality, and ultimately reveals what had already been apparent in Part I: that although he may be cerebrally superior to anyone around him, he is as emotionally dependent on at least one person as the rest of us. And so with all prospective supermen; such people are always emotional failures because however aloof they try to remain, they cannot bear the thought of being entirely alone in their self-made hell. Clearly an argument of this nature would demand a mood as sombre as that of Part I.

Yet successful or not the change of mood and pace is calculated. A new bright setting, the introduction of young characters, the

Captain out of his uniform and almost dandyish, all help to create a feeling of optimism which he so efficiently and completely destroys. With Machiavellian efficiency, he has fooled Kurt, despite Alice's warnings and has led him into the trap that will mean his financial ruin. As she says: 'You're doomed to destruction' (p. 415), because once the Captain has chosen a prey, it rarely escapes; particularly someone like Kurt who has to have every word interpreted for him. Alice's understanding of the Captain, on the other hand, is almost telepathic but still she is powerless now that he has chosen to act the Serpent in the Paradise Kurt has built for himself. Alice, of course, is the Eve who, despite her intentions plays the Serpent's game by whispering confusion into Adam's (Kurt's) ear. (Completing the allegory, the children represent Adam and Eve before the Fall.) Gradually the Serpent seizes Kurt like 'a man-eater, an insect, a woodworm who will devour you internally, so that one day you're as hollow as a rotten pine tree' (p. 421). With complete understanding, Alice defines this Serpent-Vampire: 'It's the soul of a dead person looking for a body to live in as a parasite. Edgar has been dead ever since that fall of his. He has no interests of his own, no personality, no initiative. But if he can only get hold of somebody, he clings to him, puts out his suckers and begins to grow and bloom' (p. 421).

All this is clear enough from Part I but a new factor that seems without explanation is the Captain's desire to marry off his beloved Judith to the Colonel, an old man. Initially, under her father's influence, Judith herself had been willing to marry for advantage, but when her feelings for Allan become clear she reacts violently against the suggestion. Alice, who apparently hates Judith as Edgar's child, schemes to ensure her marriage to the Colonel by trying to discourage Allan's affection. Her reason seems to be that marriage with the Colonel would transport Judith into the same hell as she herself occupies, but if we can explain Alice's conduct in terms of personal malice, the Captain's enthusiasm for the marriage is more problematical. Only when she begins to love Allan does Judith begin to suffer and be redeemed from this hell around her where 'people speculate—in soda and in human beings' (p. 440). Unfortunately the Captain does not know of his daughter's feelings, so it is difficult to decide whether he would have changed his resolve if he had. Strangely enough, on no occasion throughout the play are Judith and her father on the stage together, so their relationship must be pieced together from second-hand dialogue, but the fact is that Judith's action in rejecting the Colonel is what really kills him.

By the end of the play, apart from Judith, Kurt is the only character who can be said to have learned anything. Judith has learned the power of love, Kurt the necessity of enduring one's fate humbly. He accepts that 'there are wolves and there are sheep. It's no honour for a man to be a sheep but I'd rather be that than a wolf' (p. 447). The Captain, however, still believes that 'everyone shapes his own destiny'; a falsehood which is illustrated when Providence, acting through Judith, creates the one problem for which he had not bargained. Like the Stranger in *To Damascus*, he can say: 'a deserving man like yours truly—yes, look at me. I have striven for fifty years against a whole world; but I have in the end won the game through perseverence, attention to duty, energy and—integrity' (p. 447). In this outburst is all the superhuman arrogance and pride that goes before the Fall into everlasting perdition. Even at the moment of death, he is unrepentant. Intoning 'Forgive them for they know not what they do', he imagines himself to be the cruelly treated Christ figure. Edgar's only hope is through Kurt, his major victim, the one person who forgives him because he knows that there are worse people in the world. 'This man-eater has left my soul untouched—that he could not devour' (p. 447)—not as Alice can!

Alice, of course, remains virulent to the end. Unconcerned about anything but revenge, she delights in tormenting her helpless, dying husband. When she appears to pray, 'Oh God, I thank Thee for myself and for all mankind that Thou has delivered us from this evil', she is trying to shuffle off all the blame on to the Captain. Never at any point does she blame herself for anything. Her attitude is that Providence has destroyed the Captain for her sake. Yet, true to her own words in Part I that she would only speak well of him after he's dead, she can now with the magnanimity of the conqueror write him a glowing epitaph: 'My husband, the love of my youth— yes, you may laugh, but he was a good and noble man—in spite of it all' (p. 453). The conclusion for her is pessimistic and misanthropic. Men are a curious mixture of good and evil as needs they must be in such a world of misfortune. Once the tormenter is out of the way and the immediate recriminations are past, this is a world where it is appropriate to bemoan the degradation of human beings in the face of unintelligible adversity. And, as a fellow soul in this hell, Alice can sympathise with the Captain's egotism now he can no longer make her suffer.

As a finale this is much inferior to that of Part I. Edgar and Alice's marriage was made in hell and it is not to be dissolved so easily by death. We were given to believe that they could not escape each other because they were two sides of the same abominable creation. They needed each other to torment. Indeed, the endless torment suggested by the ending of Part I was perfect and even after reading Part II it is almost impossible to believe that Alice can exist after the death of the Captain. Without him, she has no individuality, no presence, because her character is defined almost completely in opposition to his. To survive him she would have to be born anew like the Stranger in *To Damascus*, but of this there is no evidence.

Finally, the deathly dance itself is absent from Part II. As literally defined it belongs solely to the first section and even its macabre allegorical associations are forgotten later. What the dance meant to Strindberg can be gathered from the following informative source quoted in *Inferno*. After reading in the bible of the evil spirit troubling Saul which can be exorcised by music, his mother-in-law tells him that 'quite suddenly within the last hour, a woman of good family had gone mad'.

> What form does the madness take?' 'She dances, that old lady, dances, dances, indefatigably, dressed like a bride. She imagines herself to be Bürger's Leonora ... she weeps too and fears that Death is coming to fetch her'. That dance of death went on all night, the lady's friends watching over her and shielding her from the attacks of her assailant. As she denied the existence of evil spirits, she called him Death. Yet at times she asserted that she was being persecuted by her dead husband. (pp. 150–1)

So too does the Captain seem to be possessed by evil in Part I until, after staring into the face of death, he becomes in Part II a more *rational* vampire.

The Dance of Death has a theme tune which sets the mood of Part I in direct contrast to the tennis and sunshine atmosphere of Part II. Originally to have been Saint-Saen's *Dance Macabre*, Strindberg changed it to the *Entry of the Boyars* when he learned that Ibsen had used the former piece for *John Gabriel Borkman*. In common with many of his plays, both sections are developed on musical lines. Ideas recur and themes are woven into the structure so subtly that they combine the resources of Swedenborg's doctrine of correspondences and the meaningful hinter reality of the symbolists with something approaching the Wagnerian leitmotif. But it would be tedious to note down each time a particular idea or theme or symbol recurred in a single play or group of plays, and although many examples will be obvious in preceding pages it is not a vital critical procedure. Rather they are to be judged in the last resort for their effect which, in the texture of any given piece, is considerable. Once isolated they seem so trivial that any number of repetitions would not make them particularly significant in themselves. Their value is contextual except when they are used for those specifically theoretical purposes which have already been analysed. Continuing the musical analogy we might say that Part II is more of a coda than a movement, despite Strindberg's intention. It rounds off the piece without contributing any very necessary structural development. But what a magnificent work the whole is, despite that!

8

'Christian' Plays

ADVENT (1898)

As its title suggests, *Advent*,[1] written shortly after *To Damascus*, Part II, is a more specifically Christian morality play than the great trilogy. Set in the four weeks preceding Christmas, it is full of Christian symbolism (crucifixes, images of the Virgin, Christ's blood, the stable, crib etc) and biblical references (the parable of the vineyards, Christ's teaching on little children and the Tree of Knowledge). But as always Strindberg's Christianity is permeated by harsh Old Testament retribution. 'The Old Testament comforted but also chastised me in a somewhat confused way, while the New Testament left me cold' (*Inferno*, p. 42). Both his own predilections and Swedenborg's influence (Strindberg called the play a Swedenborgian drama)[2] made him advocate even brutal punishment for those who persist in full knowledge of their sin. Nevertheless his undoubted belief in the reality of hell fire was often tempered by Christian mercy.

The basic text to explain the treatment of the Judge and his wife in *Advent* can be found in *A Blue Book*.

> What is your belief regarding eternal punishments? Let me answer evasively, so to speak, since wickedness is its own punishment, and a wicked man cannot be happy, and the will is free, an evil man may be perpetually tormented with his own wickedness, and his punishments accordingly have no end. But we will hope that the wicked will not adhere to his evil will for ever. A wicked man often experiences a change of nature when he sees something good. Therefore it is our duty to show him what is good. The consciousness of fatality and being damned comes to everyone, even to the incredulous. (p. 38)

So the two sinners in Advent suffer indignities and violence commensurate with their crimes, but once they admit the magnitude of their sins, 'For me there can be no pardon' (p. 177), there is hope for them and even in Hell they can celebrate Christmas. 'Though the sequel will be long and hard', this act of mercy which gives even the worst of men some hope constitutes the differences between Divine Justice and the human justice of the Judge.

Despite the overlay of Old Testament reference and Swedenborgian correspondences, this morality is essentially Christian. When hope of redemption appears, the inhabitants of Hell do not witness signs of Jehovah, but the Adoration. Unlike the Stranger, the Judge and the Old Lady have not committed sins of arrogance against God, their sins are specifically those condemned by Christ in the Gospels. The Old Lady has maltreated the children, the innocents, and her fate is similar to those who are cast into the ocean with a millstone round their necks; she freezes to death after falling into a swamp. The Judge has used his legal rank to extort money from litigants and eventually becomes the victim of a judgement as merciless as his own. He is stoned to death by those whose lives he has ruined. Thus *Advent* contains a discussion about justice and a critique of the legal system as inadequate to deal with more than venial sins. From this we learn that though the old couple have sinned, 'he who has strength enough to bow himself, or intelligence enough to guess at a method in this madness, cries to God for help and grace and escapes the madness' (*A Blue Book*, p. 39).

The irony of Advent is that so potentially (and actually in its greater part) magnificent a conception could be flawed by Strindberg's piety, his self-righteousness and his sentimental treatment of his pure characters (in particular, the children) which seems to resound with the worst influence of Dickens. By contrast, the scenes between the Judge, his wife and various subordinate characters are superb. Their callousness is throwing their son-in-law Adolph out of his vineyard, in locking up the children in the cellar and in making a servant of their own daughter, Amelia, is truly shocking. The ease with which Strindberg first reveals the two central character's hypocrisy in their dealings with the good Neighbour and their ostensibly Christian piety in the Franciscan's presence, which is gradually exposed as pure human wickedness, reveals the restrained skill that so often characterised the writings of this reputedly hysterical 'neurotic'.

The Judge and the Old Lady delude themselves and others that they are virtuous, and that God acknowledges their virtue by welcoming their final resting place in the idolatrous mausoleum[3] and by making their vineyard fruitful while that of their enemy and neighbour remains barren. Uniquely for villains of their type in a morality play, they are credibly human, supporting their illusions of well-being in the face of their palpable inhumanity with just the kind of precariousness that can quite easily change into violence or despair. Whenever they are crossed they work off their frustrations and, more importantly their awareness of their own viciousness, in yet more brutality. A sinful man has secrets, a secretive man is suspicious of other people's interference, and a suspicious man can easily become paranoid. 'When this feeling of fatality [i.e. of being damned] strikes an unbeliever, it often appears as the so-called persecution mania. He believes himself, for example, persecuted by men who wish to poison him' (*A Blue Book*, p. 39). Significantly, both the Judge and the Old Lady suspect the other of trying to poison their food (Act 2).

As their suspicions increase due to the provocation of spirits, Strindberg presents a series of expressionist scenes to reveal their guilt feelings. In Act 1, they witness the Procession of Shadows, a *tableau vivant*, reminiscent of the entrance of the Seven Deadly Sins in Marlowe's *Doctor Faustus*. The Shadows variously represent victims of the Judge's corrupt professional activities; scythe-swinging Death, who will shortly be visiting them both, Amelia's wronged Mother, the Goldsmith who made the Old Lady's counterfeit monstrance, a headless sailor and several caricatures of the Judge. Their past sins, evoked by the Satanic Other One, parade before them giving them an opportunity to accept the inevitability of their damnation. Neatly integrating expressionism and allegory, Strindberg shows in this brief sequence the old couple's criminal past and their future destination. Similarly in Act 4, two extended and complex 'interior' scenes serve as a further warning to the pair of sinners, by projecting an image of what damnation can be like. Led by the witch (an evil spirit who blows a whistle to provoke illusions in men's minds), the Old Lady enters a chasm which resembles the ravine of *To Damascus*. There amidst heathen symbols she meets the condemned who are presided over by the Master of Ceremonies (a doppleganger of the Franciscan, the man of God, and the Other One, the Devil, whose 'punishment is to serve the good', by tormenting sinners 'into finding the Cross', Act 2). This is the Swedenborgian outer Hell; 'the world of spirits lies between Heaven and Hell and appears as an undulating valley, flanked by mountains and rocks'.[4] With this we can compare Strindberg's stage directions in Act 4 (... a rocky, kettle-shaped chasm. It is closed in on three sides by steep walls of black rock, wholly stripped of vegetation'). It is a place of pure egoism in which there is no need for a Devil to spur on the proceedings. Since it is a Swedenborgian Hell the Other One as such does not appear; instead there is a bust of Pan, 'The shaggy Pan who had been a goat and later became a half-man and later the evil one' (*A Blue Book*, p. 206).

In this Purgatory is a newly arrived soul; an arrogant and vain Prince who, having refused the assistance of God, is condemned to bear his own burdens and to become aware of his own ugliness. These punishments are symbolised by his hunched back. Significantly, like Elis in *Easter*, he 'can perceive a connection between my suffering and my guilt, but I cannot see why I should have to suffer eternally, when He has suffered in my place' (p. 153). The general answer to this is contained in the passage from *A Blue Book* quoted at the beginning of this chapter. On the *specific* question we can turn to *Legends*. 'But the cross is for me the symbol of sufferings patiently borne and not the token that Christ has suffered in my stead, for I must do that for myself' (p. 227).[5] In the last act when he is brought to this inferno, the Judge tries to deny this, but, unlike the Prince, he eventually comes to see that eternal torment is well-deserved and so there is hope for him. The Prince, however, must continue to suffer and to torture others until his self-pity turns to self disgust. Similarly, at first the Old Lady too conforms to the egotistical code of the place.

The proximity of this 'Waiting room' to Hell is evidenced by the strong odour of linseed oil which is identified by the Master of Ceremonies as 'that charnel house smell'. This comfortless gloomy place is the natural habitat of the Judge and the Old Lady who have exhibited all those symptoms of conceit, gratuitous cruelty and self-delusion that we see in the Prince. Here they will be safe from the rays of the sun that burn them. 'Further when heavenly light reaches the damned, an icy chill pervades their veins and their blood ceases to flow' (*A Blue Book*, p. 87), and they will be prevented from persecuting anyone more innocent than themselves. Like twin damned souls, the Prince and the Old Lady commit each of the seven deadly sins until they are revealed in all their physical and spiritual ugliness.

Meanwhile, the Judge experiences *his* moment of truth and like his wife fails to recognise it. Appropriately, in a court room, he meets his doppleganger (the ghost he will become) who provokes him unwittingly to judge himself without mercy or pity, thus preparing the way for the auction of his soul to the infernal spirits. The court room scene inevitably reminds one of Dickens's *A Christmas Carol* and is remarkable for the manner (similar to Maeterlinck's in *The Intruder*)[6] in which inanimate objects are used to proclaim judgement and sentence on the Old Man. Perpetuating the correspondence between the Judge's legal career and the nature of his spiritual trial;[7] the victims of his court are brought before him as accusers. After he is rejected by his creditors, the Judge is condemned by the Other One (for whom the Law of Moses is more appropriate than Christian charity) to be stoned to death. Once he is dead, he joins his wife in the 'waiting room' where they are both shown the evil of their lives and where through Christ's sacrifice and their own repentance, they will be redeemed. Instead of the usual lurid illusions, Strindberg portrays this Swedenborgian hell by concentrating on the egoism of his characters. His evil spirits are extensions of corrupt human beings and the despair of the vision is all the more revealing for the absence of Bosch-like horrors.

Unfortunately, not all the dreamlike sequences are as successful as these. When Strindberg turns to depict the maligned children romping with their angelic Playmate[8] in a Heavenly Eden before the Fall, his curiously unrealistic attitude towards children dominates. The coyness of these children, who converse in language which seems designed for a mentally defective cherub, will grate on most sensibilities. When we read ecstatic writing like this, we must confess that from a literary point of view, Strindberg's social and sexual disenchantment was a most fortunate state of affairs. However, apart from its inhabitants, this Arcadian scene provides, in terms of symbolism and Swedenborgian mythology, a neat contrast to the 'waiting room' sections. Luxuriously planted with flowers, trees and vines, with a scarecrow and a statue of Madonna and Child to keep away evil spirits, it is a place where the innocent cast off their worldly suffering and enjoy themselves. Here the sun that burns the Old Man[9] becomes the children's playmate, and Golden Birds perch, providing a marked contrast to the ominous starling that torments the Judge. So forbearance is rewarded and

Amelia rejoins her children. Unfortunately this is unconvincing because, once again, we feel that Strindberg is being too smug for his dramatic good. Allegorical figures need not be psychologically complex but at least we expect an author to be a little disciplined in his admiration of his good characters.

Apart from the greater tendency to invest inanimate objects with symbolic meanings,[10] the major difference between *Advent* and *To Damascus* is the rather cold nature of the allegory of the former which somehow lacks the humanity of something deeply felt. Where the trilogy is a passionate spiritual self-examination, *Advent* appears to be a more didactic exercise in Christian-Swedenborgian myth. Perhaps the explanation for its failure to move the reader, despite the considerable skill with which Strindberg created it, is that Strindberg did not seem to feel any very strong personal involvement. In fact, *Advent*, is one of those few plays in which he himself does not appear predominantly. There are signs of him in Adolph and the Neighbour but these are subsidiary characters whose main relevance is to a subordinate theme.

EASTER (1900)

Easter[11] is an exception that tests a rule about Strindberg's drama. Generally, when he created roles for children who were to represent innocence and love, the result, as in *Advent*, was catastrophic. Only when he came to portray such adolescents as Judith and Allan of *The Dance of Death*, whose emerging sexual instincts seemed to make their behaviour more credible, was he normally successful. Eleanora in *Easter* is an innocent who yet remains affecting and dramatically acceptable. The explanation of this anomaly is perhaps that Strindberg drew Eleanora directly from life (his mentally ill sister, Elisabeth) and from a well-established model, Balzac's Seraphita.

Easter is Strindberg's most Christian morality play and is suffused with a tenderness which separates it from his more violent Swedenborgian essays. Its central image is the Passion and its basic theme is that of suffering and atonement. Dahlström argues that 'it aims to give a picture of Elis's suffering during the Easter days, an intentional parallel to the suffering of Jesus'.[12] However, if this were so, the result would be obscene. To compare the almost judicial humiliation of this whining egotist with Christ's suffering on the Cross is unthinkable. Certainly, Elis associates himself with Christ, betrayed by Peter (Holmblad), but this is a sign of his arrogance not of his good judgement (compare the manner in which Lindkvist deflates this conceit). Elis is in no way a scapegoat; all his chastisement achieves is his *own* improvement, not his family's. This is why when Lindkvist has finished with him, he does not receive any sympathy from Strindberg.

The Christ figure is, in fact, Eleanora,[13] the only character in the play who can sustain the comparison without irredeemable vulgarity. She saves her family not by a specific sacrifice but by bearing, with patience, the sins of her relatives and by tenderly drawing from them the venomous feelings that bitter experience has aroused. Her example is more important than her actions. Elis, in his selfishness, utterly fails to appreciate this. 'The Redeemer has suffered for our sins, yet we have to go on paying. No one is paying for me' (p. 295). Unfortunately, for the artistic success of the play, Strindberg, by using the model of the Passion, requires Eleanora's example to be more specific and final than it actually is. If, however, the parallel is intended to be with Christ's example, his symbolic sacrifice *every* Easter, and not with his sacrificial act two thousand years ago, then these criticisms are not so crucial. However, the references to Christ in the play and the use of Haydn's oratorio compel the interpretation that the Passion model is inappropriately specific to form a reference for Eleanora's example.

At first sight, the Heyst family seems to be tragically destined to suffer disgrace and disintegration. The father has been imprisoned for embezzlement, the daughter, Eleanora, has been sent to a mental hospital, the son Elis cannot shake off the shame he feels for his father's crime, while the mother lives in a world of her own, tragically protesting her husband's innocence. A family of Pariahs, and to add to their troubles (ironically on Maundy Thursday) their principal creditor, Lindkvist, moves in across the road. Throughout the play, his ominous presence hovers over the household reminding them that if he so wishes he can render them homeless and bankrupt. Appropriately, the theme and mood of the three acts are set by selected movements from Haydn's oratorio, 'The Seven Last Words of our Saviour on the Cross', written to be performed on Good Friday and eventually scored for four voices.

Act 1 is scored for the introductory Maestoso ed Adagio; as

David M. Bergson[14] points out, both the oratorio and the play begin in a tempo which is majestic and slow, preceeding a *gradual* rise to the later climax. As the play opens there is a glimmer of optimism, the sun is shining and Spring is approaching, the 'endless winter' is nearly over. The dialogue bristles with seasonal portents of good omen. Lindkvist's name means 'Twig of Lime'.[15] Seasonally and psychologically, the Heysts are emerging into light from the darkness of winter. 'The days are lengthening and the shadows growing shorter.' Ironically, a white dove has dropped a birch twig at Elis's feet and, confidently, he assumes it is a sign of peace, but clouding his happiness is the memory of his father's disgrace and his sister's illness; his sister whose presence was such a torment and whose absence is so unnatural. Elis, unfortunately, has the tendency to elevate his suffering above that of everyone else. Deftly, Strindberg portrays him as being partially infected with the manic depression that afflicts Eleanora. He alternates between desperate melancholy ('He moves as if trying to free his body from this terrible clinging gloom') and a somewhat unconvincing optimism.

When the news breaks that Lindkvist has become a neighbour, their hope dissipates. Elis's pupil, Benjamin, one of the family's creditors, is certain that he has failed his exam and that as a result his instructor's reputation will be ruined. Elis's trouble is that he has nothing with which to comfort himself during his suffering, not even his fiancée, Kristina. When she tells him that 'It is a sign of grace to suffer when you are innocent', it does not help him. He wants to know why the innocent must suffer and, if they must, what then is the meaning of Atonement? The answer to these questions can be found in *A Blue Book*. 'I bow myself experimentally before the folly of the cross since experience has taught me that wisdom can only be received by a humble mind and that obedience is more than sacrifice' (p. 215). Elis will eventually learn this from Eleanora, while from Lindkvist he will understand the mystery of atonement. Again, *A Blue Book* is relevant:

As regards the redemptive work of Christ you can comprehend it by an analogy. You remember, when you owed so many debts, that there were knocks at your door all day long, that you had to go out early in the morning in order to borrow or to escape your creditors. Finally you feared so, that you dared not go home to sleep. You sat on a seat in the park, and said to yourself, 'It is hell!'. Then there came a man who knew you, he paid your debts, you called him your saviour. Do you not see that one can pay for another and deliver him? Yes, but one cannot make an evil deed undone. No, but the Almighty can obliterate it from our memory, and from the memory of others. (p. 47)

However, for the time being Lindkvist is The Creditor 'who has come here to sit like a spider in the centre of his web and watch the flies' (p. 297). He is sounded by Shakespearean echoes: 'They always wear trinkets made of cornelian-like chunks of flesh cut off their neighbours' backs' (p. 298). With images of this kind Strindberg establishes the menacing effect Lindkvist has upon members of the Heyst family who fail, in their neurotic aggression, to regard him with charity. Yet he is to be their material saviour as Eleanora is their putative spiritual redeemer. Small wonder then that the first advice Eleanora gives to Benjamin (and by implication to the rest of the family) is 'stop judging people—even those convicted of sin'! (p. 301).

Eleanora, a girl of sixteen, is introduced to us carrying a daffodil, a symbol of spring. She is an epitome of gentleness and her most significant mental failing is that she treats all living things (animal or vegetable) as God's creatures, with equal tenderness.[16] Her speech is not intended, however, to come from a normal girl of her age. She articulates her feelings: 'I am so soft I can't bear anything hard' (p. 300), and her intentions so directly, with so little guile (though often playfully) that we might suppose her to be retarded. In fact, Strindberg cleverly integrates the simplicity of the innocent and the vulnerability of someone who has suffered a breakdown with something of the unnatural gaiety of a manic. Inordinately biblical in her conversation and possessed of extra sensory powers (e.g. she can distinguish between a 'good' clock that beats like a human heart and a bad one that cannot bear the sound of music), she is a sufferer for mankind. Strindberg conceived of her as the 'Easter-girl who suffered for others', a modern Christ figure who endures a Passion and is resurrected for her family. Perhaps he defined her best in a letter to Harriet Bosse: 'a close kin of Balzac's Seraphitus— Seraphita—the angel, for whom no earthly love exists because he-she is l'époux et l'épouse de l'humanité. A symbol of the highest, most perfect type of humanity, which by some is thought to be coming to earth to live.' She is responsible for bringing a new happiness to her family which enables most of them (Elis is the exception) to endure their destiny with faith and fortitude, but actual redemption is achieved through Lindkvist and is effected by a combination of Easter (the season of forgiveness) and a law of ethical recurrence resembling the Hindu Law of Karma. The family reap because the father has sown; thus they inherit both the good and the evil issuing from his behaviour. 'Every word is written in the book and at the end of time will come the reckoning' (p. 302).

Eleanora is in a Swedenborgian state of spiritual nakedness, untrammelled by the conventions and compromises that hide the soul from public scrutiny. Her faith and her truth are emanations of her true self. She is a simple child of Nature (or of God) for whom it is as natural to speak in the idiom of the bible as it is for a bird to whistle. She cannot be restricted within the confines of human logic, but responds intuitively and more profoundly than the rest of us. So she is able to enlighten the educated Benjamin, as the untutored Seraphita can lecture Pastor Becker, a man of considerable learning. The ease with which she ridicules logic is reminiscent of the Schoolmaster scene in *A Dream Play*. Again, in common with Seraphita she can converse with birds and identifies herself with a flower, the Lenten Lily, which 'has a chalice, full of sunlight and it has the power of soothing pain' (cf. Seraphita's hybrid plant). This is the flower she feels sorry for and which she steals. Like it she too has 'suffered at the hands of the careless gardener'.

Yet it would be mistaken to suppose that Strindberg equated godliness with a kind of madness. He would, though, maintain that certain clairvoyants would be described by society at large as mad because there is no other category for them. Eleanora is not percipient because she is mentally disturbed but disturbed because she is precipient 'My illness is not sickness unto death, but unto the honour of God' (p. 305).[17] It is therefore not surprising that of all Strindberg's characters she has been found the most bewildering by critics, who have generally thrust an unreal saintliness on her. Her tiresome qualities which have been such a burden to her family are too rarely emphasised, but Strindberg quite consistently gives us occasional glimpses of her depressiveness which, apart from being psychologically accurate in someone of manic-depressive tendencies, lends credibility to her visionary tendencies. As Elis remarks: 'Poor Eleanora, she's so unhappy herself and yet she can make others happy' (p. 307).

Basically, Eleanora is a good person, a child of God, whose conversation is a mixture of orthodox Christian and Swedenborgian beliefs.[18] In particular, she has a very strong awareness of sin and punishment which terrify her; somewhat irrationally in view of her advocacy of charity. Indeed she confesses one of her failings herself: 'You see, that's my sickness. I must know everything. I can't rest until I do' (p. 302), but this is a venial sin that can be excused as emanating from her concern for the welfare of others.[19] More serious, is her over-sensitiveness which was responsible for her breakdown in the first place. We might of course argue that she alone can feel the misery of human life because she has taken upon herself the sins of others. Now this apparently was Strindberg's reading of the character and, to an impressive degree, he fitted his creation to his conception. She does impress us as an innocent suffering for man's ills but, to a modern mind, she is flawed by her naive moral sense. She thinks and behaves according to moral and emotional absolutes (coldness, cruelty, evil, hatred, 'vale of tears'), contrary to what Dahlström writes: 'It is nevertheless clear that she is either "beyond good or evil" or else lacking in concepts of both.'[20] This lack of moral complexity means that in certain respects Eleanora cannot, for contemporary audiences, bear the moral weight placed upon her.

Act 2 states the Passion theme: 'Pater, dimitte illis, non enim sciunt, quid faciunt'. Snow covers the streets in a temporary return to winter and suffering. Eleanora, in apotheosis, has redeemed Benjamin, 'that sulky defiance has quite gone' and 'There is something exquisite about her whole nature . . . she has brought an angel of peace with her, who walks unseen and breathes repose' (p. 309). Yet she is still personally tormented by her failure to confess to the theft. Moreover, she is upset by Elis's blasphemy in identifying himself with Christ, Peter with Simon Peter and the Governor with Pilate, and by her mother's blasphemy. 'Everyone has to suffer today, Good Friday, so as to remember Christ's suffering on the Cross' (p. 319). But she is prepared for the future, even to the extent of returning to the asylum, though she derives comfort from the knowledge that if 'today death, tomorrow resurrection'. She has the faith that will pull her family through these black times. She asks for the curtains to be drawn so that God can see them. Light enters, the symbol of new life; of the thaw beckoned in by the child of God.

Act 3 takes place on Easter Eve and its theme is from Haydn's adagio, 'Sitio', but while Christ's distress was increased by the vinegar and gall he was given, the plea of the Heyst family for charity is answered generously by Lindkvist, but not before Elis is forced to drain his bitter cup. As the curtain rises, the flower motif of daffodils has been replaced by a more ominous bunch of liver coloured hepatica. The sun is obscured by mist, Elis and Kristina are estranged from each other and the shop-breaking has been reported in the press. As Eleanora says with true Swedenborgian resignation: 'The whole of life is frightful—but we have to accept it all the same.' For her this is not an easy conclusion because she regards the asylum, to which she fears she will be returned, as hell. 'where the damned dwell, where unrest has its home, where despair keeps watch night and day . . . there you are doomed' (p. 324). She is consoled by her conviction that her destiny is to suffer for others. She has taught the rest of the family to 'bear life's burdens better'. She has brought warmth into the house to thaw Elis's coldness; Spring versus Winter. While she has faith in the future, Elis feels shame for his father, despair for his mother and mistrust of Kristina. Through Eleanora's influence, Mrs Heyst has become able to blame her husband's downfall on his own pride, instead of self-deludedly trying to assert his innocence. But all Elis can do is to whine: 'But why should we who are innocent suffer for his fault' (p. 326). Eventually Eleanora's faith is rewarded, as it must in the scheme of Providence, and she is cleared of stealing the daffodil. The first evidence of Divine Justice has appeared but it is still not time to put the birch (symbol of penance and Christ's suffering) on the fire. Before that, Elis must find the courage to face Lindkvist.

The Creditor turns out to be an instrument of Providence who will administer 'a charity which runs counter to the law and is above it . . . that is mercy' (p. 331). By demonstrating his power, but declining to use it, he gradually teaches Elis humility, revealing the full extent of the young man's faults. 'The pride and wickedness I shall squeeze out of you' (p. 334)—that is, by emphasising the recurrent nature of events, and the impossibility of making absolute moral judgements about human beings (e.g. Peter Holmblad).

Lindkvist does not do this gently. With the full sternness of Sweden-borgian Providence, he emotionally blackmails Elis to conform to required standards of behaviour.[21] Elis is justly punished for his conceit, his pride and his lack of Christian charity and, ironically, this is all accomplished within the auspices of the law. The final persuasion comes when Elis learns that the person who was responsible for Lindkvist's transformation from an ogre into a benefactor was the man of whom he was so ashamed; his own father. Now the price of happiness has been paid and Eleanora can throw the birch on the fire, but ever mindful of future calamities, she keeps it as a reminder, because people, that is, 'Children are so forgetful'.

Easter can fruitfully be seen as a stylistic precursor of the Chamber Plays. Apart from its structure, based on Haydn's *Seven Last Words*, it has a number of leitmotifs that attach to specific characters; Lindkvist and Kierkegaardian eternal recurrence, Elis and Peter's rejection of Christ, Eleanora and the burden of sin and Kristina and mutual trust. Similarly, certain symbols recur throughout the three acts. The various flowers, daffodils, tulips, lilies representing moral qualities, the Lenten birch[22] and the lime twigs, winter and spring, sunshine and snow. *Easter* is so rich in imagery that if it were not for the theoretical possibilities opened up by Swedenborg's doctrine of correspondences its themes might be submerged. It is full of anthro-pomorphism and personification; telephone wires that wail when people speak cruel words, 'red seals like the five wounds of Jesus', a clock unable to bear music.

Easter is a spiritual oasis in Strindberg's post-Inferno dramatic career. For a number of reasons, largely personal, he was able, temporarily, to believe that the naive goodness he called innocence could triumph even over life's endless misery. Consequently, *Easter* is an inspired work of gentle faith, deeply felt and largely convincing. In these respects it is different in kind from those other dramatisa-tions of the power of love; *Swanwhite* and *The Bridal Crown*. The latter, in common with *Advent*, appears as a rather desperate assertion of spiritual conviction, often superbly done, but not deeply moving. *Swanwhite*, on the other hand, is a fairy play, its qualities are theatrical rather than dramatic. *Easter*, however, is the play with which Strindberg had a love affair. It has little in common with the spiritual wrestling, the self-torment and the disgust of his more complex and more typical religious dramas.

9

A Dream Play (1901)

In common with *Miss Julie*, *A Dream Play*[1] has a preface in which Strindberg describes a new conception of the theatre. In twenty or so lines, he defines his later dramatic purposes and lays the foundation of most of what still remains experimental in the theatre over sixty years later.

> In this dream play, as in his former dream play *To Damascus*, the author has sought to reproduce the disconnected but apparently logical form of a dream. Anything can happen; everything is possible and probable. Time and space do not exist; on a slight groundwork of reality, imagination spins and weaves new patterns made up of memories, experiences, unfettered fancies, absurdities and improvisations. The characters are split, double and multiply; they evaporate, crystallise, scatter and converge. But a single consciousness holds sway over them all—that of the dreamer. For him there are no secrets, no incongruities, no scruples and no law. He neither condemns nor acquits, but only relates, and since on the whole there is more pain than pleasure in the dream, a tone of melancholy and of compassion for all living things, runs through the swaying narrative. Sleep, the liberator, often appears as a torturer, but when the pain is at its worst, the sufferer wakes— and is thus reconciled with reality. For however agonising real life may be, at this moment, compared with the tormenting dream, it is a joy.[2]

Despite its exemplary exactness this preface has been made ambiguous by a publishing accident. In the same year that *A Dream Play* appeared, one of the great seminal books of our time, Freud's *The Interpretation of Dreams* was published. In such a context, Strindberg's talk of 'dream narrative', 'liberating sleep' and 'unfettered fancies' takes on the sexual reverberations of psychoanalysis. However, Strindberg's dream theory cannot be equated with Freud's, although in many respects there are resemblances. Strindberg was more interested in the *form* of dreams than in their content.

Even when he used symbols which clearly had sexual dimensions, a more profound reading of his later plays will reveal that his principal motive was religious. This is true even of *A Dream Play*, littered as it is with genital symbolism. Throughout, he used the seemingly illogical, discontinuous structure of the dream primarily as a means of representing the disorientated ego of man in a spiritually determined universe.

But having said this, we must concede that a Freudian interpretation of *A Dream Play* is possible. In his stimulating article 'The Logic of a Dream Play'[3] Evert Sprinchorn argues for a non-ideological reading, preparatory to analysing the play as an essentially symbolic structure: 'the dialogue often diverts our attention from the basic level on which the play operates. The dialogue is an outgrowth of the visions not vice versa. That is as it should be, for the play is no more about ideas than the best music.' Here Sprinchorn makes a reasonable point, then grossly over-emphasises it. Of course, the Symbolist superstructure of *A Dream Play* is more important than in any other play of Strindberg's but to suggest that the dialogue is secondary and that the play is not concerned with ideas is surely absurd, as we shall see.

Sprinchorn's subsequent interpretation though helpful is excessively Freudian. To summarise it briefly, when Indra's daughter, Agnes, takes away the Officer's sabre as he sits rocking in his chair, 'The daughter of the gods is a mother figure in the eyes of the Officer, who describes her as the embodiment of the harmony of the universe and like a good nineteenth-century mother she is telling her son, rocking in his crib, not to masturbate' (p. 356). Again, 'The grotto, the water, and the church are familiar symbols of woman, and the union of organ and cave is an obvious symbol of sexual intercourse' (p. 358), and 'it takes no doctor come from Vienna to tell us what this castle stands for, with its ability to grow and raise itself, with its crown that resembles a flower bud with the forest of hollyhocks that surround it and the manure piles below' (p. 358). Later, we are informed of the symbolism of the id, the superego, the grotto as a uterus, the theatre corridor as a vagina. Phallic symbols, of course, are seen practically everywhere; a gigantic aconite, towering hollyhocks and the linden tree. 'The fire suggests sexual excitement, dying signifies orgasm and the bursting chrysanthemum on top of the Castle is ejaculation poeticised.' 'Christina, the girl who spends her time sealing windows—a perfect representation of the inhibitive forces, as is the Officer's mother who is continuously trimming the lamp.' And so on.

Overall, we can say that the style of the Freudian work of art does not seem to be at all typical of Strindberg's work.[4] In no other drama is there anything like the detailed sexual symbolism that Sprinchorn ascribes to *A Dream Play*. Moreover, nothing in Freudian thought can adequately account for the complex spiritual argument and symbolism of the play. At the very least, Sprinchorn was in error (despite his imaginative insights) when he sought to reduce Strindberg's mysticism to a conflict between pleasure and reality principles; between sexual instincts and death. Each of the symbols interpreted by him could be given significance in terms of spiritual rather than sexual schemata and would appear much closer to Strindberg's purpose. If we want to understand *A Dream Play* in the general context of Strindberg's late work, if we want to probe what would have been for him the deepest levels of the play, we must look to the spiritual structure which derives from Swedenborg, Hinduism and Christianity.

A Dream Play is only apparently formless. Close inspection reveals that it has a tight and impressive logical structure. In *From an Occult Diary*, Strindberg himself provides a brief introduction:

> Am reading about Indian religions. The whole world is but a semblance (Humbug or relative emptiness). The primary Divine Power (Maham Atman, Tad, Aum, Brama) allowed itself to be seduced by Maya[5] or the impulse of Procreation. Thus the Divine Primary element sinned against itself (Love is sin, therefore the pangs of love are the greatest of all hells). The world has come into existence only through Sin—if in fact it exists at all—for it really only is a dream picture. (Consequently my Dream Play is a picture of life), a phantom and the ascetic's primary allotted task is to destroy it. But this task conflicts with the love impulse, and the sum total of it all is a ceaseless wavering between sensual orgies and the anguish of repentance. This would seem to be the key to the riddle of the world. (p. 55—18 November 1901)[6]

So the basic conflict is between the spiritual and the sensual; Swedenborg's spiritual-sensual self and the animal self.

In this Hindu framework[7] we can place the sexual superstructure.

With the union of Brahman (spirit) and Maya (earth), the universe was created and man's dual aspirations were irrevocably established. Throughout the play, the male and female are examined through three corresponding pairs of egos; Daughter and Poet, Bookkeeper and Lawyer, Mother and Officer. But these later fuse into a single personality; the Dreamer. Through the various female characters, Indra's Daughter represents all women (i.e. Maya), while all the male characters, combine to represent the virile force (Brahman). Man's relationship with woman makes him the slave of the flesh so he devotes his life to pleasure. Liberation from the conflict between flesh and spirit (woman and God) can come only through pain. Thus fire is both the instrument of death and spiritual relief; inevitably it requires a degree of Schopenhauerian asceticism to approach God, but this is merely repayment for the Brahman sacrifice which constituted Creation.

The human conflict is intensified by the fact that the beauty of woman deceptively evokes the beauty of Paradise, so that when a man pursues the one he can easily persuade himself he aspires to the other. Sex and marriage with woman therefore are necessary forms of suffering which eventually purify man for his union with God. For example, as an unattainable ideal, the Officer's beloved, Victoria, causes him the suffering that prepares him for spiritual understanding. The lovers on Foulstrand, too, discover the misery of life on earth through the medium of their love and together seek something better in death. Thus life, like sexual relationships, is a 'struggle between opposites'; man and woman, pleasure and pain, ambition and humility, desire and remorse. Through woman, 'sin and death came into being' (p. 586) and strife will continue until we learn to transcend the limitations of the flesh.

Despite its beauty and compassion, *A Dream Play* is pessimistic in a Schopenhauerian manner. Life is illusion, hope is vanity and man is an object of pity.[8] We are condemned to live in pain and conflict. Agnes the heroine soon learns that human life is metaphorically schizoid; conflicts between love and hate, good and evil, personal and social duties, earthly and divine aspirations make it unbearable.

Oh, now I know the whole of living's pain! This then it is to be a human being—ever to miss the thing one never prized and feel remorse for what one never did, to yearn to go, yet long to stay.

And so the human heart is split in two, emotions by wild horses
torn—conflict, discord and uncertainty. (p. 589)

Thus sexual relationships are a torment—'Conflict between the pain
of joy and the joy of pain, between the anguish of the penitent and
the pleasure of the sensual' (p. 586). Within man, 'the conflict of
opposites generates power as fire and water create the force of steam'
(p. 586). Life is a dialectical process driven forwards by the tension
between these contradictions.

Basically, this is the philosophy of von Hartmann embodied in
religious myth. All who exist must endure this fatal dichotomy.
Even the Divine Daughter acquires animal characteristics and feels
suffocated by her earthly existence.

POET   Even so, before you go, tell me from what you suffered
         most down here.
DAUGHTER From living. From feeling my vision dimmed by
         having eyes, my hearing dulled by having ears and my
         thought, my airy luminous thought, bound down in a
         labyrinth of fat. You have seen a brain. What twisting
         channels, what creeping ways. (pp. 586–7)

In particular, she suffers from the conflict between duties to her
child by the Lawyer and to the human spirit as represented by the
Poet. 'There is a conflict in my soul. It is pulled this way and that
until it is torn in two' (p. 584). Now although we cannot escape such
conflicts, there is no reason, other than our own weakness, why we
should submit to them. The Daughter is free to choose the higher
duty even though she cannot avoid the pain of neglecting her child.
Similarly, man can control his animal impulses and aspire towards
the divine, while continuing to suffer.

A new element in the religious theory of *A Dream Play* is that, in
addition to rejecting the world as illusion, as in *To Damascus*, the
Daughter eventually concludes that 'This world, its life and its
inhabitants are therefore only a mirage, a reflection a *dream* image'
(p. 585). In this respect *A Dream Play* reflects the influence of the
theosophists on Strindberg. 'The Theosophists explain it thus:
parallel with the earth life we live another life on the astral plane.
But unconsciously to ourselves' (*A Blue Book*, p. 128). Earthly existence is merely a distorted reflection of the spiritual life to which we

must aspire while patiently suffering the pain of our mundane lives. And it is a dream in which there is no progress, no end but death (waking).

Indra, the most warlike of the Rudras (warrior gods of the Vedic religion), has sent his daughter down to earth, 'the darkest and heaviest of all the spheres that swing in space' (p. 525). By allowing her to take bodily form which is, in Strindberg's view, the necessary *and sufficient* condition of earthly suffering, he reverses the cycle of birth and death. This act of self-sacrifice (the imprisonment of a divine soul in a human body)[9] which inevitably recalls that of Christ, repeats for man's sake the original Act of Creation represented in Vedic thought as a Divine Self-Sacrifice. Physical life symbolised by the Growing Castle is renewed in the dream of the god Indra who, by sacrificing part of himself (his daughter), will share the pitiful condition of man. In this way, Indra will experience the misery he caused when, with his allies, the winds and lightning, he mercilessly punished human evil. This injustice was caused because Indra's excessive vigilance owed less to his moral fervour than to his vanity, pride and ambition.

His attitude towards the human race is harsh and condemnatory: 'Their mother tongue is called Complaint. Truly a discontented, thankless race is this of Earth' (p. 526). (The dialogue of the Gods which opens *A Dream Play* is reminiscent of the heavenly prologue of Goethe's *Faust* (Pt I).) But now with his daughter as the intermediary of his dreaming consciousness,[10] he will be able to experience for himself the nature of man's unhappiness. The Daughter is to enquire 'if their lamentations and complaints are justified'. And only if she intercedes will they be saved from further chastisement. To ensure that her judgement will be fair and mature, she will encounter all manner of men and institutions and she will develop and age like a human being. While everyone else exists in a dream limbo, she changes from an eager young girl into a world-weary woman who has taken the sufferings of mankind upon herself.

Her first encounter is hardly promising. Against the background of a beautiful forest, 'rises the gilded roof of a castle with a flower bud crowning its summit' (p. 527), but beneath its walls 'lie heaps of straw and stable muck' collected by the young Officer who is imprisoned within.[11] The illusion of life may be attractive but its reality is grounded in filth and suffering. Echoing Alice in *The*

Dance of Death, the Daughter asks, 'Why do flowers grow out of dirt' (p. 527). When she has learned more about the persistence of human dignity in the midst of pain, she will understand. For the time being, she must be content with the Beckettian pessimism of the Glazier: 'They don't like dirt, so they shoot up as fast as they can into the light—to blossom and to die.'

Immediately, we confront a Swedenborgian universe where material objects acquire human and animal characteristics. The Castle becomes a vegetable which, according to Swedenborg's curious taxonomy, corresponds to man's intellectual and linguistic functions. Thus the Castle is a symbol both of the soul imprisoned within the body and also of irrelevant verbiage, false theory and clichéd language which cut man off from genuine understanding. In effect, the image is remarkably similar to Ionesco's growing corpse in *Amédée ou Comment s'en Débarraser*. In this dour world where 'every joy has to be paid for twice over with sorrow' (p. 528), Agnes is 'The beautiful which is the harmony of the universe. There are lines in your form which I have only found in the movement of the stars, in the melody of strings, in the vibrations of light. You are a child of heaven.' Yet, as she points out, so are all human beings. Agnes is another of Strindberg's heroines modelled on Balzac's Seraphita, though she is perhaps more dynamically involved in the tragedies of those around her than the others. She is quite practical; acting as well as providing the intrinsic example we might expect of Indra's daughter.

She frees the Officer from the Castle 'to seek freedom in the light' (p. 529), but he remains full of self-pity, blaming life instead of himself for his misery. Certainly, life is terrible but he uses it as an excuse for his own weaknesses. His life is uselessly dedicated to the conceit of his learning[12] and to his hopeless love for the beautiful Victoria. As a result, he is self-deluded and weak; before he can develop he must find the strength to reject his earthly bonds. His dying mother gives him good advice: 'Never quarrel with God . . . You must not go on feeling you have been wronged by life' (p. 530), and reveals that his suffering is recompense for a sin he committed in his youth. But even the Mother,[13] although she is an idealised figure, declares: 'Ah this life! If you do something good, someone else is sure to think it bad, if you are kind to one person, you're sure to harm another. Ah this life!' (p. 531).

Next, the Daughter is transported to the theatre and shown the vanity of man and the emptiness of his pleasures. Like so many fetishists, the theatre-workers live stultified lives obsessed with physical possessions. The Stage Doorkeeper mourns a lost sweetheart and wraps herself in a shawl to protect her from life. The Billsticker's sole ambition is to own a green fishnet and fishbox[14] but once he has achieved this it turns out to be disappointing. As the Officer concludes cynically but correctly: 'Nothing is ever as one imagined it because one's mind goes further than the act, goes beyond the object' (p. 537). Human beings simply cannot learn to accept what they have without questioning the scheme of things. Succinctly, Strindberg exposes the vanity of theatre life, where obtaining a part is considered to be more important than facing the reality of one's own emotional problems. The theatre is a place of illusion and false values represented by the blue monkshood, a poisonous plant symbolising the deceptive nature of worldly desires which promise much only to bring torment.

From this experience, the Daughter must learn that human values are relative. When she takes over the Stage Doorkeeper's job and listens to other people's woes she realises the ephemerality of human emotions. Time, space, beauty and truth are all relative in this dream of earthly existence. They are not important in themselves but only in comparison with man's suffering. If we are in pain, a minute becomes a year; when we are happy, time flies. Strindberg echoes this theme in the narrative structure of the play where chronological time is replaced by dream or psychological time. For instance, within seconds the Officer becomes an old man and then is young again. Spatial relationships too are relative; their mutability provides the physical links which give *A Dream Play* such a fluid structure. A bed becomes a tent, an office a church and an organ a cave. An analysis of the stage directions alone could almost constitute a text book on theatrical technique.

A powerful influence on Strindberg here (as in *Swanwhite*) was the philosophy of Heraclitus (cf. the preface). According to this Greek thinker or rather the popular Aristotelian gloss on his thought, 'everything is in flux and nothing is at rest' so 'you cannot step twice into the same river; for fresh waters are ever flowing in upon you' (fragment 12).[15] This constant flux (in which there are only processes not solid objects) stems from the unity of opposites, and strife; a notion that informs both the theme and structure of *A Dream Play*. The following quotations from Heraclitus respectively define the character and scenery transformations of the play and the phrasing and content of its Preface. 'The same thing is in us as the living and the dead, the awake and the sleeping, the young and the old; these change to become those and those change back again to become these' (fragment 88). 'Conjunctions: wholes and not wholes, the converging, the diverging, the consonant, the dissonant, from all things one, and from one all things' (fragment 10). Yet, for Heraclitus, dreaming brings the soul into a death-like state which does not resemble Indra's Daughter's condition, unless we place her in a Swedenborgian Hell-on-Earth context.

Having borne the Doorkeeper's burden for a while, Agnes becomes more fully the trustee of other people's suffering. The Summer is over and the Autumn of existence will display man stripped of his pretensions. The Officer, now even older is still waiting. During his vigil he draws our attention to the door in which there is a clover-shaped hole.[16] Through this door he expects his love to appear. Each character uses his own interpretation of the secret of the door as a counterbalance to the disappointments and defeats of his own life. It serves as a means of escapism which corresponds to the Officer's actress and to the pure green which the Billsticker had imagined for his fish net. It is the composite of their illusions without which they would be compelled to accept the world as it is. Indeed, although the enigma of the door makes life more bearable over the short term, in the long run it encourages man to be dissatisfied with his lot and to long for something better.

In the next scene, once more it is Spring; the Officer is now a very old man carrying the stems of a bouquet long since decayed. The clover leaf door is about to be opened but this is prevented by a policeman. Watched by members of the casts of *Die Meistersinger* and *Aida*, this was to be a highly dramatic occasion but, as we shall see later, the mysteries of the universe, symbolised by whatever is behind the door, do not admit of pomp and ceremony. Nor can an understanding of Providence be reached in the theatre of illusions. The next institution to be exposed is the Law which is indicted through the Lawyer in Strindberg's stage directions. 'His appearance bears witness to unspeakable suffering. His face is chalk-white, furrowed and purple shadowed. He is hideous; his face mirrors all the crime and vice with which, through his profession, he has been involved' (p. 540). His underlings, like those of Durrenmatt's Madame Zachanassian, are physically and emotionally only half men. Although he has seen a great deal of human suffering, he cannot imagine any means of overcoming it. His answer to life's sadness is to obey the law, but he is by no means an evil man. On the contrary, he is Strindberg's spokesman. He wishes to burn the shawl 'with all its griefs and miseries' (p. 540), as though that would destroy them. In a striking image, the Daughter replies: 'Not yet my friend. I must let it get quite full first, and I want above all to gather your sufferings up in it, the crimes you have absorbed from others, the vices, swindles, slanders, libel' (p. 540).

Both as an illustration of the Schopenhauerian pessimism of this play and of the power of Strindberg's writing, it will be expedient to quote extensively from the lawyer's great speech:

> My child, your shawl would not be big enough. Look at these walls! Isn't the wall-paper stained as if by every kind of sin? Look at these documents in which I write records of evil! Look at me ... Nobody who comes here ever smiles. Nothing but vile looks, bared teeth, clenched fists, and all of them squirt their malice, their envy, their suspicions over me. Look, my hands are black and can never be clean! See how cracked they are and bleeding! I can never wear clothes for more than a few days because they stink of other people's crimes. Sometimes I have the place fumigated with sulphur, but that doesn't help. I sleep in the next room and dream of nothing but crime. I have a murder case in court now—that's bad enough—but do you know what's worst of all? Separating husbands and wives. Then earth and heaven seem to cry aloud, to cry treason against primal power, the source of good, against love! ... the suffering, the agony! All this I have to hear. Look at me! Do you think, marked as I am by crime I can ever win a woman's love? Or that anyone wants to be the friend of a man who has to enforce payment of all the debts of the town. It's misery to be human. (p. 541)

As the Daughter says, courage to persevere can come only from the one 'who feeds the birds' (p. 541). The Lawyer, who has done his best in a degraded profession, receives no accolade from the world, whereas cloistered academics who have spent their lives in useless theorising, protected from the real troubles of mankind, are greeted with pomp and applause. Of all the vanities despised by Strindberg and Swedenborg, that of sterile learning was placed by them at the top of the list. The lawyer is rejected by the universities precisely 'Because you have defended the poor, said a good word for the sinner, eased the burden of the guilty, obtained reprieve for the condemned' (p. 543). Human knowledge is empty, human feelings are vain and hope is in the future, in another world which, at best, men can only dimly apprehend. And the few men who are worthwhile, like the Lawyer, become martyrs—so many minor Christ figures whose words are unheeded and whose actions are misinterpreted.

The most natural and attractive of all institutions, marriage, is also the most disappointing. 'The sweetest which is also the bitterest—love! Marriage and a home. The highest and the lowest' (p. 545). Not until the Daughter has experienced this will she be capable of judging life on earth in all its sadness and futility. Once again Strindberg defines the *essential* conflict in heterosexual unions when he couples the Daughter and the Lawyer; two people who know the pitfalls and have sufficient humility and compassion to attempt to avoid them. Unfortunately, good will is not enough. Here, instead of repeating the precise, naturalistic indictment of Act 3 Scene 3 of *To Damascus*, Strindberg imparts a nightmarish quality to the domestic sequence of *A Dream Play*. Kristen, the maid, whose life-destroying pasting resembles vampirism, is a force rather than a personality. As she ritualistically pastes strips of paper, chanting, 'I paste, I paste', shutting out both air and sunlight, the Daughter withers like an etiolated plant. Kristen sucks the life out of her as surely as any Hummel could, yet she represents not a human tendency, but the stifling restrictions of married life. Kristen *is* marriage; that self-contained domesticity which is warmth, comfort and privacy to the Lawyer, but suffocation to the Daughter. 'My antipathies may be your sympathies' (p. 545). The function of Kristen is to define this statement. Sacrifices, compromises and even adaptation may be possible for a time, but they cannot alter the fact that people are individuals between whom it is well nigh impossible to achieve lasting happiness. The Daughter concludes: 'It is terribly hard to be married, harder than anything. I think one has to be an angel' (p. 548). There is nothing to do but endure. 'And so life together is a torment. One's pleasure is the other's pain.' To pretend otherwise, to force oneself to smile in anger, is hypocrisy. And so the marriage sequences close with Kristen manically pasting and the Lawyer twisting the door handle which to the Daughter feels 'as if you were twisting my heart strings' (p. 550). 'I paste, I paste . . . I twist, I twist'. Strindberg never loses contact with reality in this magnificent scene but he captures at the same time a sublime ritualism that is the essence of the theatre of cruelty.

The next sequence which could be entitled *Fairhaven and Foul-strand*[17] (i.e. Heaven and Hell) is the heart of the play. Highly symbolical, it presents a Swedenborgian eschatology. Foulstrand, which is divided from the idyllic Fairhaven by a strait, consists of 'Burnt hillsides, black and white tree stumps as after a forest fire, red heather, red pigsties and outhouses . . . an open air establishment for remedial exercises, where people are being treated on machines resembling pipes' (p. 551).[18] This somewhat Dante-esque island is presided over by the diabolic Quarantine Master who is 'dressed as a blackamoor'. In typically Swedenborgian fashion, the various sins have corresponding physical ailments and deformities. The glutton has knotted feet which must be straightened out on the rack, the drunkard has gout for which 'his backbone's got to be mangled by the guillotine', and Don Juan is infatuated with a hideous old coquette of sixty.

As he effects 'remedial' cures and disinfects cholera suspects, the Quarantine Master indulges in masquerades and fancy dress theatricals in order to forget what he is and what he is doing. He is a stylised devil who can laugh at his own pretensions. After the idealistic Officer has rescued Agnes from her marital duties, as she rescued him from the fleshly prison of the Castle, they have to pass through Foulstrand before they can reach Fairhaven. Like the Poet, who occasionally deserts the astral plane to take a mud bath in Foulstrand so that 'he doesn't feel the gadflies stinging' (p. 554), they also need its chastening experiences to put their idealism in perspective. Fairhaven can only be appreciated in the context of Foulstrand, and vice versa.

The Poet is humanity's spokesman; an outcast and a wanderer who is cynical about the disappointments of life. This causes him to blaspheme when he accompanies the Daughter to Fingal's Cave, but in other respects he has deep insight into the moral complexities of human behaviour and acts as her guide. Indeed at one point the Daughter describes him as a dreamer who best knows how to live. However, it is not plausible to argue from this to the conclusion that he is *the* Dreamer. It is the Poet who exposes the injustice of life on Foulstrand which under his scrutiny becomes a Swiftian microcosm of conventional morality and (in the critical parable of the Prodigal Son) of biblical morality. Ironically, he revives the 'flowers from filth' motif—'Out of clay, the god Ptah fashioned man on a potter's wheel, a lathe, MOCKINGLY, or some other damned thing' (p. 554). This is hell where everything eventually becomes ugly like the once beautiful Lina—'Look at her now! Five children, drudgery, squalling, hunger, blows. See how beauty has perished, how joy has vanished in the fulfilment of duties which should give that inner contentment which shows in the harmonious lines of a face, in the tranquil shining of the eyes' (p. 554). Such is life which is simply carried to a Schopenhauerian extreme on Foulstrand.

Nor can young lovers escape the implacable logic of decay. Two idealised lovers, He and She, sail along the strait believing they are heading for Fairhaven when, in fact, their relationship is a ruinous test from which neither will emerge idyllically in love. Strindberg might argue that all young lovers set sail for Fairhaven when they marry, only to discover later that they have been marooned on Foulstrand. This is not a planned punishment, it is just the way things are—'You don't have to do anything in order to meet with life's little discomforts' (p. 557). The lovers, through no fault of their own, must endure their forty days and nights of temptation. If their love is powerful enough to bring them through untainted, they will be free to proceed to Fairhaven. Appropriately, despite his occasional cynicism, the Poet believes that 'Love can overcome everything, even sulphur fumes and carbolic acid' (p. 557). Nevertheless, following the well established marital path, when He and She reappear their faces are pale and their clothes bleached.

The scene now changes to Fairhaven[19] which, though more obviously beautiful, turns out to contain *its* share of pain and suffering. Of course, this is a distinctly earthly paradise. Clearly, the Heaven of God would be flawless but Strindberg argues that any heaven on earth can be no more than a very imperfect reflection of the Divine. Its attractions are not defined absolutely but only in contrast to the horrors of Foulstrand and the misery of life on earth.

Consequently, its attractions are soon shown to be illusory; the subjective projection of human vanity or hope. It is the heaven of wishful thinking; of desperation.

Yet the Daughter is temporarily deceived by Fairhaven's appearance of 'peace and happiness', though soon she discovers that there are some who are not allowed to join in the festivities. There is Ugly Edith who, paradoxically, can create beautiful music[20] but who sits alone because no one will ask her to dance. Here, too, the officer is humiliated by being treated as a schoolboy although he has a degree. He is asked seemingly meaningful questions by a domineering schoolmaster who proves to him that twice three is three. This is the logic of nightmare by which the meaningless is proved and contradictions are resolved. Rational thought is revealed as circumscribed by the premisses one accepts. Given paradoxical assumptions, we can proceed quite logically to paradoxical conclusions. In other words, reason and logic leave the really important first principles unaffected. The fundamental question of God's existence can never be a conclusion of logical argument, rather it is the major premiss from which all reasoning must proceed. Without this basic belief, reasoning becomes a whirlpool of contradictions and absurdities. The skill with which Strindberg weaves logical conundrums may not be on the level of Lewis Carroll, but the result is bizarre enough to fit into the dream texture of his play.

When we are introduced to the newly wed couple after their period of temptation which is probably identified by Strindberg with their honeymoon, we find that they have matured in knowledge. They are still happy but wish to die because they realise that 'in the midst of happiness grows a seed of unhappiness. Happiness consumes itself like a flame. It cannot burn for ever, it must go out and the presentiment of its end destroys it at its very peak' (p. 563). They leave determined to drown themselves to escape life's disillusionment. Of all Fairhaven's inhabitants the wealthiest, most envied and presumably the one most likely to provide an exception to the rule that basically all human life is tragic, turns out to be blind. He has come to the quayside to say farewell to his son:

'Meeting and parting, parting and meeting. That's life, I met his mother then she went away. My son was left, now he has gone' (p. 564). No one is exempt from loneliness and disappointment, neither a rich man nor a child, though a child can more often redeem his grief through intuitive understanding than can an adult.

The Daughter is now coming to the end of her investigations, but before she can quit the earth she must learn the Lawyer's Nietzschean lesson. 'You have seen most things but you have not experienced the worst thing of all . . . Repetitions, reiterations. Going back. Doing one's lessons again' (p. 565), from which comes that dreadful Kierkegaardian feeling that there never has been and never will be such a thing as progress. For her, this involves returning to the oppressive routine of caring for her husband and child. Duties are almost always unpleasant but unfortunately they must be carried out. The Lawyer's message is as usual bleak but valid. All we can enjoy is sin and, sooner or later, we shall be punished for this by the torments of hell. Always repetitions, always pain, 'It is a distorted repetition so that everything which was charming and witty and beautiful the night before appears in memory, ugly, stupid, repulsive. Pleasure stinks and enjoyment falls to pieces' (p. 566).

On a domestic level, the Daughter proves herself to be far from saintly. The more we examine her responses, the clearer it is that she takes on many typically human qualities. The Daughter's progress is like a parabola. Up to Scene 8, she becomes more and more infected with human qualities until she is just another human being. After this, she begins her ascension to the spiritual and to death (the curve of sleep?). Although *A Dream Play* is undoubtedly an expressionistic piece,[21] she is herself rather more than a type-character. She is neither an omniscient goddess nor a passive observer. She engages in specifically human roles taking on the appearance and attitudes of each. She is surprised and enlightened by what she experiences and is at no time too lofty to sympathise with the misery she sees. Her limitations, on the other hand, are most clear in the scenes with the Lawyer where she proves herself to be as impatient, subjective and intolerant as the rest of us. Reminded of her domestic duties by him, she declares 'I would rather die'. Almost invariably in their encounters, he is more honest and more noble than she. He has to point out to her that, for a human being, suicide is a major sin. A deity can be heroically self-destructive if it is within its power, but 'it is not easy to be a human being' (p. 566).

Brought to the limits of her endurance she asks herself the ultimate question. If life is pain and to be human is to suffer, what is it all

for? Why did the gods decree existence—maliciously for their sport
or with some inscrutable but crucial purpose that will benefit all?
These questions and their apparent solution are symbolically represented by the mysterious clover leaf door which will be opened
towards the end of the play. To prepare herself for this confrontation
and for her eventual return to her duties or to her father (for presumably if the 'solution' proves that men have been treated unjustly
by Indra, she will reject her father and remain with men), she decides
like Christ to 'seek solitude in the wilderness' (p. 567). Together
with the Poet, she hears the lamentations of 'The doomed at
Foulstrand' but is powerless to help. Christ tried to, and was
crucified as a result! And those who murdered him are the same as
those who denied the Lawyer his degree. The doctors—the Scribes
and Pharisees—little men puffed up with their own learning, status
and supposed righteousness. The kind of men who will kill to protect
their own position in the world.

The next scene contains strange Brechtian contrasts. We are in a
Mediterranean resort with the usual villas, Casino and blue expanse
of sea but in the foreground is a huge heap of coal which two Coal
Heavers are carting in wheelbarrows. It is one hundred and twenty
degrees in the shade. Depending on the way you look at it, whether
you are a tourist or a worker, this can be heaven or hell. The injustice
of the situation is summed up by the first Coal Heaver: 'We who do
the most work, get the least food. And the rich who do nothing, get
it all. Might one not, without taking liberties with the truth, call this
unjust?' (p. 568). It is difficult to defend a world in which circumstances of birth condemn one man to a living hell, while providing
another with all the fruits of his neighbour's toil. Again the
respectable bourgeoisie are responsible, but to blame them is much
the same as blaming the whole human race because the poor would
become rich given the opportunity. Yet this fact cannot justify such
inequality; perhaps all that can do so is an appeal to the workings
of Providence. There might be a reason for the human condition
which is beyond our knowing. But this is not an easy proposition to
offer starving men who hear the wealthy exclaim how they 'must
go out for a little walk to get an appetite for dinner'.

The scene changes to Fingal's Cave, sometimes given the name
Indra's Ear, where 'it is said the King of Heaven listens to the
lamentations of mortals' (p. 570). Here the Daughter will talk with

her father through the medium of the winds. On behalf of mankind she asks: 'Indra, Lord of Heaven, hear us. Listen to our sighing! Earth is not clean, life is not just, men are not evil nor are they good. They live as best they may from one day to another. Sons of dust they walk, born of the dust, dust they become. Feet they have to trudge, no wings. Dust-soiled they grow. Is the fault their's or Thine?' (p. 571). The waves try to conciliate, to cover up the misery that exists on earth. Among the wreckage thrown up by the sea are to be found all man's ruined hopes—'Look what the sea has stolen and destroyed! All that remains of those sunken ships is their figure-heads ... and the names—Justice, Friendship, Golden Peace and Hope' (p. 572). There, too, are the blind man's drowned son, Alice's sweetheart and Ugly Edith's hopeless love. Deprived of an answer to her question the Daughter feels earthbound and disillusioned; cut off from her father. She must leave Earth before it is too late. But first she receives the Poet's petition, on behalf of mankind 'to the ruler of the Universe' (p. 574). Now she can prepare to learn the secret of the door. Unfortunately, the Poet's petition is arrogant. Ironically looking up at the sky and carrying a bucket of mud, he demands explanation and retribution. The Daughter is horrified because she realises 'The work may not condemn the master. Life's riddle still remains unsolved' (p. 574). God's ear will not be won by anger and accusation.

The climactic scene takes place in the theatre where the secret door is to be opened. There the dignitaries, the Chancellor and the Doctors, will supervise the opening of the door which conceals the secret of life. It is Springtime and the Officer is young again, we have come full circle. He is once again waiting for his beloved Victoria who at last appears. In the words of the Poet, we 'seem to have lived through all this before'. Skilfully, Strindberg shows the absurdity of the conflict between the various faculty Deans. Although their disputations are conducted in a parodied medieval fashion, their motives are shown to issue from conceit and arrogance. Each fastidiously employs the form of assertion appropriate to his discipline. As they argue, their respective pretensions and inadequacies become clear. Each claims for his own discipline an absolute truth which is immediately contradicted by the rest. Academic dispute is revealed to have nothing to do with the truth but to be merely a matter of self-assertion which inevitably degenerates into vulgar abuse. When all is considered, there is nothing to choose between them; they are all vain, pompous fools. 'Enough, birds of a feather shouldn't peck each other's eyes out.' Infinitely preferable is the Chancellor who rather cynically concludes: 'I am merely appointed by the Government to see you don't break each other's arms and legs in the Senate in the course of educating the young. Opinions? No, I take good care not to have any. I had a few once but they were soon exploded' (p. 580). As parody, this section is exquisite, but as satire it is much more important for it expresses what was for Strindberg a profoundly significant truth; that whatever flattering guise a man adopts he will before long reveal himself to be motivated by the same egotistical urges that compel all human beings.

The Daughter accuses the Deans, like so many Socrates, of corrupting the youth, but instead of making their Apologia, they self-righteously defend themselves. They condemn her as their predecessors condemned Christ and threaten her with stoning. Before she can depart, the Glazier opens the clover leaf door behind which according to the theologian is: 'Nothing. That is the solution of the riddle of the universe. Out of nothing in the beginning God created heaven and earth' (p. 582). But typically his fellow Deans disagree with him, each providing his own characteristic interpretation. They cannot even agree among themselves about 'nothing'. The reason for this is that they persist in trying to conceptualise what is entirely beyond their comprehension. They will try to explain what it is a sin of hubris to wish to explain. They are to be pitied. Only the Daughter understands the significance of the door and she is called back to her domestic duties by her husband. The Lawyer once more appeals to her conscience but she sees that there are higher duties even than those to her husband and child. She has a duty to comfort and enlighten *mankind*. 'There is a conflict in my soul. It is pulled this way and that until it is torn in two' (p. 584); all men are her children. By facing and transcending earthly duties, sensuality (Maya) and returning to the spiritual realms (to her father, to Brahma), she renews the salvation of mankind. As Indra sacrificed her Divine self for the earthly, she destroys her earthly self for the spiritual.

The closing scene takes place as did the first 'Outside the Castle' —the circle is closed.[22] It is late Spring, the flowers are in bloom and the enormous 'chrysanthemum bud at the top of the tower is on the point of bursting' (p. 584). Now she has learnt the answer to the riddle of existence the Daughter will soon depart from the Earth. To give the Poet faith she relates the creation of the world according to the Vedas; showing him that suffering is inevitable and must be borne with patience and humility. On hearing this truth, each character puts on the sacrificial fire his or her particular woes and vanities. The Stage Doorkeeper burns her shawl of misery, the Officer his rose bouquet, the Billsticker his posters though not his fishnet, Edith her ugliness, Victoria (the doppleganger of She) her beauty. Now that their illusions have been destroyed they all come together; 'When a life is nearing its end, everything and everyone pass by in a single stream' (p. 587).

However, there are those who have learned nothing. The riddle of existence is beyond human words to express so the Dean of Theology, whose business is words, turns on God for failing to reveal Himself. The righteous who claim for themselves a special status are often those of least faith. And Kristen the maid continues to paste—'If Heaven itself were cracked open you would try to paste it up' (p. 588). The Daughter has been like Christ; an example from which men can learn and take comfort, but also one which they can ignore. Ultimately, the choice belongs to men themselves; messiahs, prophets, saints and avatars just provide the *opportunity* for enlightenment and redemption. In Swedenborg's system, the soul after death is made to manifest its true nature, so Indra's daughter, the catalyst in this final scene, causes the pretensions of each character to drop away, leaving the ego nakedly good or evil.

In her final speech, the Daughter summarises all that she has learned during her sojourn on earth. Life is a paradox of ambitions, a contradiction of needs and wants, but she has become like a human being and her parting causes her deep pain. Nevertheless, she has confidence in man's capacity to endure his fate and even eventually to triumph. She will remember what she has learned and 'Where I am going and in your name, carry their lamentations to the throne' (p. 589). At this point, the growing castle of illusions bursts into flame around her, illuminating the agonised and questioning faces of those human beings who stand beneath its walls then, as a final symbol of hope, the giant chrysanthemum bud bursts into bloom. The spirit is liberated from the body. Leta Jane Lewis interprets this same idea alchemically. Derived from the Greek, 'Chrysanthemum' means flower of Gold and its blossoming represents the production of gold from lead, flowers from filth, spirit from body and the consummation of existence (*samadhi*). Another reverberation is that for Heraclitus fire is the basic substance from which everything issues and in which everything is ultimately consumed; 'was ever, is now, and ever shall be, an everlasting fire' (fragment 30).[23]

Compared with such plays as *To Damascus*, *Advent* and *Easter*, *A Dream Play* does not emphasise quite so strongly the overriding need for humility. In this drama Strindberg concentrates on the seeming injustice of the world and on the need to avoid blasphemy, but by casting Indra as the deity, he suggests that God at least listens to the justifiable lamentations of mankind and perhaps makes more clear his Divine purposes. Perhaps, he suggests, there is a need for Him to send His child once more among men, to help them in their weakness. While *To Damascus* is Strindberg's most complex play, *A Dream Play* is his most beautiful. More poetic and allusive than the great trilogy, it rivals it for the title of his greatest work. Never before or again was he to achieve such fluidity of form, such beauty and subtlety of symbolic design or such delicacy of spiritual insight. It is more widely compassionate than *Easter* and is not marred by any discrepancy between myth and reality. Unlike *The Ghost Sonata*, which it rivals for being awarded the appellation of his strangest play, its overall mood is not bitterly cynical or even despairing, but is elevated by a deep compassion. Small wonder that Strindberg called it 'My most dearly loved play, the child of my greatest sorrows.'

10

Folk and Fairy Plays

Swanwhite[1] is a fairy play, written for Harriet Bosse, to demonstrate the power of love to conquer hatred, evil and ugliness. As Strindberg pointed out: 'Eros is not the central theme: the symbolism relates to Caritas, the great Love which suffers everything, survives everything, which forgives, hopes and believes, no matter how much it is betrayed.'[2] As a result, it is full of optimism, despite the brutality of its evil characters. Hardly surprisingly, the milieu of *Swanwhite* consists of fairy castles, wicked stepmothers, magic horns, good spirits and handsome princes. As a setting for the triumph of love in adversity, *Swanwhite* is more or less what we might expect; no intense psychological realism, for in Strindberg's scheme of things reality meant conflict, betrayal and degradation; no social naturalism, for this would be more appropriate to depicting the misery of life on earth than heroic or spiritual triumphs. Strindbergian love at its height was worthy of better things; dragons to slay, princesses to rescue, witches to transform, and ultimately, death to transcend. In view of the pitfalls into which its theme and form might have tempted Strindberg, *Swanwhite* is a remarkably successful and beautiful play. Inevitably though, as in *Advent*, he tends to sentimentalise his child heroine beyond both the credulity and the patience of his audience.

Swanwhite contains several ugly situations but they are larger-than-life nightmares in which tedium, the one implacable enemy of Strindbergian love, plays no part. Although the fairy play is a form in which Strindberg can conceive of love as heroic, he does not entirely lose himself in the fantasy. In Act 2, after the Gardener has sown discord between them, Swanwhite and the Prince bicker in a way that recalls the discordant scenes between Indra's Daughter and the Lawyer in *A Dream Play*. The very fact that they feel close to each other threatens their individuality and makes them behave selfishly: As long as they are tied to life on Earth, they feel separated even when they are physically together. This, though, is not quite the hell on earth portrayed in other post-Inferno plays; rather it is a Heraclitean universe. Flux predominates but instead of just being a process of change, it is a process of increasing decay in which love will turn to hate as youth becomes age and novelty becomes commonplace. Yet there is hope because, in the world of *Swanwhite*, this is fortunately the exception not the rule. Thus the Gardener must appear to sow discord since it does not grow naturally; and his influence which causes the lovers to vilify each other is soon overcome because it is an external imposition. According to Strindberg, on earth hatred issues naturally and inevitably from love and thus cannot be destroyed by it. So, not unnaturally, to escape this conclusion Strindberg writes his love idyll as a fairy play; as non-naturalistically as possible.

Both the theme and technique of *Swanwhite* are influenced by Maeterlinck's *The Princess Maleine* (1889). In his 'Fifth Letter to the Intimate Theatre', Strindberg admits Maeterlinck's stylistic and technical influence but asserts that his imagery is in the main either his own or the product of his own individual researches. Both in its mood and dramatic resource, *Swanwhite* is perhaps the most typically Maeterlinckian, as opposed to purely Symbolist, play Strindberg ever wrote.[3] By contrast, the biblical and Buddhist references of such obviously Symbolist plays as *Advent, Easter* and *A Dream Play* serve to differentiate them from *The Princess Maleine* and *Pelléas and Mélisande*. Unfortunately, *Swanwhite* shares an unfortunate characteristic of many of Maeterlinck's plays: its dramatic power does not really sustain its spiritual pretensions. Generally, its symbolism is too facile to communicate the spiritual understanding which both Strindberg and Maeterlinck emphasised so strongly. More often than not, the various symbols are used to evade the more difficult problems of dramatic realisation. They are not fully integrated into a thematic and psychological framework as they are in *To Damascus* and *A Dream Play*. Nevertheless, the delicacy and beauty of *Swanwhite's* imagery can excuse much of the shallowness of its emotional impact.

It would be an error to suppose that *Swanwhite* is little more than a sophisticated pantomime. In fact, the wicked stepmother of the play is authentically horrifying. With her steel whip designed to put on the neck of the recalcitrant Maid—'such a necklace that no young suitor will ever put his lips to it again' (p. 462)—her black witch-craft, her spiked cask and her horrifying transformation, she is a figure worthy of Hoffmann. Nor are Swanwhite and her Prince immune from the characteristically human failings of jealousy, pride and even malice. Moreover, the miraculous changes of scene, the skilful use of magic and the rejection of spatio-temporal laws are not gratuitous but are reflections of the spiritual world. In this respect, its style and technique are similar to *A Dream Play*. The Gardener, sower of discord and concord, clothed half in blue and half in green would fit into it quite easily: 'I sow, I sow' (p. 488). And the relationship between Swanwhite and her father is not unlike that between Indra and his Daughter in the Prologue to *A Dream Play*.

Little need be said of the themes of *Swanwhite* for they are not elusive. More interesting are the various techniques used by Strind-berg to define the play's moral categories and to imply the various emotional allegiances of its characters. In terms of technique it is a highly Wagnerian drama. Colour is used to represent moral values. Good and evil, innocence and corruption are depicted by white and black, red and blue, silver and gold motifs. Character is represented by a complex motif of bird life. The wicked stepmother's spies, who inform on Swanwhite while masquerading as her friends, are a peacock and two doves. Swanwhite herself has a bird identity and characterises her father, the Duke, as an oak tree in whose protective branches she would perch. Over the doorway of the castle apartment are the nests of two swallows. These swallows are instruments of good, working for Swanwhite's dead mother who returns to earth as a swan in order to protect her daughter. The sound of swans flying usually heralds the mother's presence. At the opening of Act 2 when she comes in the night to clothe Swanwhite in finery, the Stepmother's spies (the peacock and doves) are sleeping. In addition, Swanwhite's speech is full of bird imagery, for example, 'A brutal hand clutches at my breast like a bird of prey swooping on a dove' (p. 500). The effect of this is to clothe the play and the characters in a delicate unreality which suggests dimensions of tenderness and horror normally beyond the range of naturalistic psychological drama. In consequence, when the mundane does intrude into *Swanwhite* it recalls all the more powerfully how inevitably separated from the ideal of love and virtue are the sordid affairs of men and women.

Although *Swanwhite* is a fairy play, it is nonetheless describable in Swedenborgian terms. The predominant 'magical' forces in the play issue not from witches or fairies but from the spiritual afterlife. The mothers are dead souls who, as angels, possess powers for good. And, although the wicked stepmother is not a witch, she is controlled by evil spirits. Swedenborgian correspondences are articulated through a variety of objects; colours, birds, maids in pewter, clothes and fruit closets, magic horns and helmets. Spiritual suffering and hatred confronted by love are represented respectively by the greying of the Prince's hair, then that of the Stepmother and the three maids (cf. Alice in *The Dance of Death*). Like Balzac's Seraphitus, the Prince has a name which, once known, makes any woman fall in love with him. Swanwhite too resembles Balzac's ideal in that to the virtuous she appears beautiful, but to the brutal young King the reverse: 'You have no nose, my girl. You are cross-eyed and your lips are too thick . . . and blind and lame as well' (p. 501). He only sees her as she really is when he witnesses her love for the Prince (cf. p. 502). Conversely, all that is good appears beautiful to Swanwhite. She cannot hear the Young King because as Strindberg says in *A Blue Book* (p. 198) a good person cannot hear the conversation of a liar. In the presence of evil, Swanwhite cannot breathe and her roses wither, while the evil Stepmother is transformed by the presence of love. Good and evil cannot live together in this world as they can in real life. For Strindberg, this is a consolation that he had longed for most of his life; the conviction that good must eventually triumph. 'It is through the Flower Test in *Swanwhite* that the Prince wins her, for her desire is purer—and therefore stronger. The other is weakness.'[4]

Similarly, the corrupt Stepmother cannot speak the word 'love'. Nor can Swanwhite address her as mother until after her transformation. Moral values determine linguistic behaviour. The temporary transformation of the Stepmother and her Maids as they observe the love of Swanwhite and her Prince conforms to Swedenborg's view that physical appearance is a mirror of the soul. Indeed, he goes further: 'There is a sphere, as it were, of spiritual effluvia, which exhale and produce a perception of the life of one's mind. This sphere I recollect myself to have perceived and it has rarely if ever deceived me. Nor need this appear wonderful, when a shrewd and intelligent man is aware from the face, speech and actions of another, of what quality he is, whether simulated or sincere, and many other things which are manifest to a man's internal sense' (*The Spiritual Diary*, 1584).[5] Future producers of the fairy play, the *Damascus* trilogy, and *Easter* might strive for the appearance on stage of a 'sphere' distinctive for each major character.

In *Swanwhite*, Strindberg returns to his old theme of the mother ideal. Swanwhite and the Prince are protected by their respective mothers.[6] By contrast, the Stepmother is archetypically wicked. After showing her doll to the Prince, Swanwhite, wishing to invoke the worst of all possible horrors, remarks: 'I have beaten her, but that did not help either. Now I have thought of the worst punishment of all for her ... She shall have a stepmother' (p. 469). Only the Mothers and the Stepmother have unusual powers which they can use for good or evil in a stylised battle between nature and law, spirit and earthly sin. The Mothers represent love before which the Stepmother is powerless, but despite their help, Swanwhite and the Prince must endure much and so prove that only love, which can survive the misery of life, is precious.

Love even softens the heart of the Stepmother. Seeing the two lovers in each other's arms, she declares in a speech which resembles the last tableau of *The Pelican*:

> Never have I seen a sight more fair. Two roses blown together by the wind, two stars falling from heaven and joining, as they fall. This is beauty itself. Youth, beauty, innocence, love ... What memories this awakens, what sweet memories of the days when I lived in my father's house and was loved by him. (p. 495)

Her final transformation does not come entirely as a surprise; Strindberg carefully prepares its ground in Act 2. He makes her a plausible psychological figure as well as an allegorical one. Strindberg makes it clear that the love that destroys the evil in her is Christly love. As she is transformed, 'The Duke raises the cross-shaped hilt of his sword towards the Stepmother' (p. 508). It is this kind of love, symbolised by Swanwhite's final prayer, which can transcend death: 'Call the name of your beloved and lay your hand upon his heart. Then with the help of Almighty God *But only with His help*— your love will hear your voice—if you believe' (p. 511).

The types of love contrasted are not the poles of spiritual and sexual love. The latter plays no part in *Swanwhite*. The love between the heroine and her Prince is idealised and purified. Typically, it resembles the feeling Strindberg had for children which, unlike sensual attraction, did not always end in conflict. This innocent, childlike love is seen as the parallel on earth of the supreme love of God. Through this pure earthly emotion, man can discover a bridge to the spiritual love that is his salvation. Ultimately this, and not the idealisation of sexual or romantic love is the message of *Swanwhite*. Yet again Strindberg went beyond his initial intention; what was to be a dramatic love poem for Harriet Bosse became a declaration of mystical faith.

THE BRIDAL CROWN (1902)

Together with *Midsummer* and *The People of Hemso* (the play he adapted from his novel of the same name), *The Bridal Crown*[7] or *The Crown Bride* is perhaps the most locally coloured of all Strindberg's plays. The customs and landscape of the people of Calecarlia form its superstructure and determine the mood and style of its writing. As a detailed analysis of local milieu is outside the scope of this study, Bjorkman's excellent short introduction to his translation of the play can be recommended as preparatory reading.

More central to the present discussion is the influence of Maeterlinck's dramatic theory and practice. In a letter of February 1901, Strindberg described *The Crown Bride* as 'an attempt on my part to penetrate into Maeterlinck's wonderful realm of beauty, omitting analyses, questions and viewpoints, seeking only beauty in depiction and mood'.[8] To achieve this Strindberg created a spiritual allegory by reworking folk material. Symbolist techniques dominate the play. A hand loom rapping in waltz time (Scene 2), a waterwheel that acts of its own volition, fantastic shapes formed by chimney smoke, whirring grindstones, the file of ants, the Castle and the Church emerging from the frozen lake, as well as a host of allegorical figures serve to create a supernatural backcloth of magical, occult and spiritual correspondences. The similarities between Strindberg's comets, star showers and their trails ('their long-waving hair') as death symbols, and rain, red moon, fire and smashed windows portending disaster in Maeterlinck's *The Princess Maleine* are obvious.

Essentially the play is based upon a popular Swedish legend of two young peasants who fell in love whilst minding their parents' cattle on the mountain pastures. When the girl gave birth to a child, they cared for it themselves, communicating with each other by means of tunes played on an alpenhorn. To this Strindberg added a Montague-Capulet family strife and a variety of folk creatures such as the Neck, the Mewler and the Mocker. The ostensible conflict of the play centres upon Kersti's desire to wear the bridal crown at her wedding as a sign of her chastity. Because she is no longer a virgin, she feels guilty, but it is the fact that she has given her child to the demonic midwife that is the real obstacle to her future happiness. Her dishonesty about the crown, the wreath and the veil (bridal symbols) is but a formal expression of her mortal sin. This is expressed not primarily through psychological conflict but by the many folk correspondences of evil that invade Kersti's life and exacerbate her guilt feelings.

The Midwife is a wood spirit who takes human form but whose real identity is betrayed by her bushy fox tail. It is she who urges Kersti to sacrific her child for the sake of the crown. At first, Kersti resists her persuasions and threats, but eventually she yields. However, instead of being a Crown bride, she is in fact a Crown thief and her guilt relentlessly pursues her. The immensity of her sin, all the more revolting for Strindberg for whom mother love was an ideal, is expressed in a cameo which portrays a Child in White. This Christ Child mourns the loss of the innocent soul to the forces of evil as 'the grindstone [of fate] begins to whirl with a hissing sound'. We might suppose that this implies Kersti's eventual fate (cf. Luke 17:2), but *The Bridal Crown* is about the invincibility of love and the power of forgiveness,[9] not about vengeance.

Throughout the play, Kersti's guilt is emphasised by Brita, the witch-like sister of her lover, Mats. Aware that Kersti's marriage has not had the Blessing of God, Brita continually accuses her of dishonesty. These scenes are quite remarkable for their virulence. In addition to abusing Kersti, Brita reminds her of what her fate will be: 'Now I shall tell your fortune! . . . You get the mill, and the grist will be accordingly . . . The wages of sin is death' (Scene 2). Pointedly, she quotes the story of Shechem and Dinah (Genesis 34) a tale of seduction that ended in slaughter. Although she is vindictive, Brita is in the long run a force for good; another demonstration that out of evil can come good. Kersti's slender hope of redemption rests on the fact that encouraged by Brita she cannot forget her crime but continues to suffer her guilt to the full.

A third spiritual being who approaches her is perhaps the most curious of all; a figure from Swedish legend in the shape of a river spirit called the Neck. He is a fallen angel who is longing for the Paradise he has lost and is, in consequence, all the more conscious of the fruits of sin. The motif associated with him is the plea, 'I am hoping, I am hoping that my Redeemer still liveth', and he roams the world looking for evidence. Naturally, when he comes across such a case as Kersti's, he is driven to despair that neither he nor man will ever be forgiven. Together with the Child in White, he is one of the good spirits who serve to balance the evil influences surrounding Kersti so that her true nature may emerge. Neck is young, fair and brightly dressed, and like a former angel he sings of hope for mankind whilst accompanying himself on a golden harp or a fiddle with a bow of silver. Amidst the grotesqueries of the play, he is one of the few figures of physical beauty. Like the Child, he is aroused to anger only when Kersti sacrifices her baby and deceives Mats. To help her, he sings at the end of Scene 1 of his own fall from Grace, but Kersti pays no heed and puts out the fire, above which a vision of hell is being formed by the smoke. 'The smoke pours out in large quantities... forming a dark background against which appear fantastically shaped and vividly coloured snakes, dragons, birds etc'. On several other occasions Neck appears to remind Kersti of the loss of heaven and the threat of hell-fire; most notably in the mill when the wheel begins to turn backwards and the fireplace becomes a furnace. True to his words, he appears at her illicit wedding and causes her to drop the crown she has acquired under false pretences. When she is arrested for the murder of her child, Neck alters his plea to 'thy Redeemer', and the Child appears with spruce and flowers to comfort her. After Kersti's death has redeemed her, Neck can sing with renewed hope.

Two other supernatural creatures who play a decisive part in Kersti's development, the Mewler and the Mocker, are dual aspects of a single personality, also derived from Swedish folk sources. Their function is to warn the unmarried mother not to commit infanticide. The one is an apparition, the other a voice. The Mocker, assuming the voice of a child, echoes Kersti's lies and self-deceptions with devastating effect. Taking on the guise of the child, the Mewler ascends from the trap door in the mill floor, down which Kersti's child was thrown, to remind her of her crime. Kersti mistakes the Mewler for her child and the Midwife symbolically repeats its murder. Between them, these two ghostly figures represent Kersti's guilty memories of the murdered child.

Each of these supernatural forces serves to create an atmosphere of oppression that compels Kersti to face her personal reality; but it is the Child in White who plays the vital role in her conversion. At the end of Scene 4, he inspires her with new faith so that she 'know(s) that my Redeemer still liveth'. Henceforth, she will place herself in God's Hands and even reject the Midwife's offer to help her escape the Headsman. As the Child says, by doing so: 'Thy faith has saved thee! Out of faith has sprung hope. But the greatest of these be love —love, of all living things, great or small.' As a result, she is free to determine her own death and to avoid the shame and dishonour of ending her life as a criminal. The final scene depicts the ultimate penance. Kersti lives religiously in Krummedike Castle[10] ('I have found my saviour. His name is Jesus Christ') until one day she is drowned on her way to church. Only after her death can the Mill Folk and the Mewlings, the kinfolk respectively of Mats and Kersti, cease to slaughter each other and join together to open the White Church once again. While they were in dissension the Church was swamped by the lake, the symbol of their sins. When they make peace the 'church is seen rising out of the lake'. As this happens, they all give thanks to God as they kneel beside Kersti's body. Her death has served as a sacrifice not only for herself but for the whole neighbourhood, including the various spirits inhabiting it.

The subordinate, realistic characters in the play do not amount to much; with the possible exception of Brita and the Sheriff. Kersti's mother is a stock Strindbergian figure, stern, fatalistic, proud and highly moral, yet loving. Her function is to set the scene of mystical doom surrounding the protagonists. She senses her daughter's sin and the presence of evil spirits ready to exploit it and bring ruin on the family. Even Mats is nothing more than a decent young man who made one mistake and is prepared to 'do the right thing', until he finds himself mixed up in an intrigue beyond his comprehension. Yet the signs are there to be read; for example, the smoke from their pipes blows in different directions. Apparently their souls are intended for opposite destinations, but he, like Kersti, is in part the vitcim of their families' hatred, and though he seems remarkably insensitive to Kersti's troubles and also extremely ineffectual, he is intended by Strindberg to be a good lad. Perhaps his weakness is that he is too naive, too unthinkingly virtuous; such people are rarely of much use to their weaker brethren. The Sheriff is apparently a kindly man who tries to make friends with Kersti but because of his legal role and the Midwife's threats concerning him he only succeeds in upsetting her even more. It is not so much his behaviour that is at fault as Kersti's own guilty conscience; the Sheriff is a personification of her eventual retribution. All his remarks which are in intention innocent assume an ominously ambiguous tone to her. Such is the world mirrored through the girl's guilt.

Perhaps the strongest appeal of *The Bridal Crown* to contemporary producers is its theatrical potential. Few Symbolist dramas provide as many opportunities for innovations of set, design, costume and acting. Although its thematic concerns are unlikely to stimulate the modern imagination, its variety of atmospheric and visual effects as well as the richness of its folk tapestry would interest any producer.

11

The Chamber Plays

Strindberg wrote five Chamber Plays[1] which were to be his equivalent of the later Beethoven quartets. Their form and presentation closely resemble chamber music. In the small Intimate Theatre (seating only 161 people) these short plays, each lasting about an hour and a half, were staged simply, without intermissions and with reduced stage settings which could easily be transformed. When evaluating their dramatic resources, we must keep these limitations in mind. 'In drama we seek the strong, highly magnificent motifs, but with two limitations. We try to avoid in the treatment all frivolity, all calculated effects, places for applause, star roles, solo numbers.'[2] Unlike Strindberg's naturalistic work which aimed to present highly specified characters in their distinctive milieu, or his more *purely* expressionist plays in which the differentiated ego of the protagonist radiated obsessions, memories and subjective environment, or even the dreamlike plays which followed the amorphous structure of fantasy and unconscious impulse, the Chamber Plays are structured by *theme*. 'The author rejects all predetermined forms because the theme determines the form. Hence he has complete freedom in handling the theme as long as the unity and style of the original idea are not violated.'[3]

Such a conception of playwrighting gave Strindberg considerable scope as to form, structure and style which were only circumscribed by demands of economy and continuity.[4] 'A small motif treated in detail, a small cast, large issues, free imagination but based on observation, no unnecessary minor characters, no regular five actors or old saws, no pieces lasting the whole evening.'[5] Just as a composer can state, develop and *resolve* his theme through a series of repetitions within the classical sonata form, so the Chamber Plays are characterised by an outgrowth, and final rounding off, of a group of ideas, symbols and motifs. But this involves more than a set of loosely related variations on a theme, because Strindberg develops his themes in distinct ways that make the Chamber Plays as rule-governed as a

sonata. His variations are integrated to his theme. Nevertheless the
tone and texture of each play are important and are developed even
at the expense of *immediately* following thematic and formal
demands. Strindberg's dramatic intention in the Chamber Plays was
the converse of Brecht's Epic Theatre and the sentiments expressed in
the *Miss Julie* preface. He wished to entrance his audience and, at
least during the performance, suspend thought. 'Discussing a play
destroys the mood of it, the entranced senses regain control of themselves, becoming aware of what should remain lodged in the unconscious and the illusion that the playwright has been at pains to
create is broken.'[6] So the writing must be as tight as possible, with
a minimum of rhetoric and with precise visual and dramatic symbols
to carry both ideas and emotions. As a result, the Chamber Plays are
filled with symbolic impedimenta, powerful natural occurrences and
spiritual effects.[7] Climaxes become less important than sustaining an
oppressive mood; tension is regarded as continuous, not as being
based on some planned cycle.

As usual, Strindberg begins with a broadly based first scene or
act which is then developed in several directions to its logical conclusions. In the Chamber Plays he carries this practice to an extreme,
revealing the dominant ideas at the outset and being content to draw
them all together in the remaining scenes. Arguably, after the first
ten minutes and with a certain knowledge of Strindberg's obsessions
the themes and conclusions of the Chamber Plays are predictable.
This is especially true if we are familiar with musical forms, but
utterly unpredictable, as in a Beethoven quartet, are the startling
variations, both dramatic and symbolic, that he plays upon these
forms. In a movement of a classical symphony we know that
eventually the exposition after having its first theme in the 'home'
key moves into another key and in the next section develops or
expands the material already presented, and that the last section is
basically a varied repetition of the first. Yet this does not interfere
with our pleasure; indeed, it increases it, because we are able to
appreciate the skill with which the composer uses the form and
makes room for variety and manoeuvre within it to enrich both his
themes and (if it is a work of genius) the form itself. Similarly, in
the Chamber Plays, variety and dramatic skill are revealed in the
ways Strindberg develops form and theme through a complex range
of dramatic instrumentation and emotional tone-levels. Moreover,

these plays have key changes (e.g. the startling change between Scenes 2 and 3 of *The Ghost Sonata*) and pace variations (e.g. *The Ghost Sonata* climaxes most powerfully in Scene 2, *The Pelican* orthodoxly in Scene 3, *The Burned House* most strongly before it even begins—the play being, in one sense, the gradual development of an anti-climax) comparable with music.

The Chamber Plays are also collectively linked by an almost musical network of references to form a whole that is greater than each of the five plays taken separately. For instance, in some way or another, all the Chamber Plays treat life as a matter of bookkeeping in which any deficit must sooner or later be paid for in terms of suffering. The Old Gentleman in *Storm* is settling his account with life, which involves facing the one outstanding debt he owes to his wife and child. He is successful because basically he has been a victim and appeals to God's mercy. On the other hand, Hummel in *The Ghost Sonata*, whose purpose is much the same, fails because he arrogantly denies his own guilt and seeks to straighten out his accounts by accusing, and using, others.

Related to the web of guilt and suffering which connects all the characters in, say, *The Ghost Sonata* is the mass of lies and self-deceptions forming the biographical substructure of the community to be found in *The Burned House*.[8] There, social indulgence and complicity disperse guilt and makes community living just as false as family life. Again, the vampire element in *The Ghost Sonata* is developed virtually to its logical conclusion in *The Pelican*, where the comforts of domesticity are exposed as total sham. On their own none of these plays would quite warrant an attitude of complete misanthropy and extreme pessimism, but taken together they condemn every established source of human comfort and communication, with, of course, the significant exception of the Church. Collectively, they describe a number of ways in which man can approach death, sometimes resisting, sometimes welcoming, but always with the playwright insisting that this is the most important journey a man will ever make. For the road to death is the road to God, and it is the only way we can escape the hell that is life on earth.

Life is vilified in all the Chamber Plays. In *The Burned House* it is the Swamp; in *The Ghost Sonata* it is the House of Ghosts, and in *Storm* it is the bizarre house of transition where few know what is happening and an Old Man rots with his memories. Life is illusion, loneliness and suffering, which must be swept away by death or fire. A fire can uncover deception or destroy decay, sparing neither the old nor the young, for all are infected. One generation passes (or tries to pass) on its own corruption to the next. So deception is handed down in *The Burned House*, and the Young Girl in *The Ghost Sonata* and the Son and Daughter in *The Pelican* are drained of moral and physical strength by their parents. In contrast to the children of *Easter* or even those of such a deeply pessimistic play as *The Dance of Death*, the younger generations of the Chamber Plays seem etiolated. They are victims of the Nietzschean eternal recurrence defined in *A Blue Book*: 'We found a constant amid all variables, that is the instability of life, the transitoriness and mutability of all things. Everything is repeated; there are scarcely any surprises' (p. 163).

Particular links between the plays are numerous. A milkmaid appears in both *Storm* and *The Ghost Sonata*; silent and enigmatic. Also the alfresco first scenes of these two plays are strikingly similar. An attack on the law in *The Ghost Sonata*: 'Legal proof is of course a different matter. Two false witnesses provide complete proof of whatever they agree to say' is repeated almost word for word in *The Pelican*: 'One truthful witness proves nothing, but two false witnesses is proof positive' (p. 193). The vampire speeches of *The Ghost Sonata* (pp. 146 and 147) and *The Pelican* (pp. 182 and 187) are almost identical though by introducing an innocent cook into the later play to balance the earlier vampire cook, Strindberg makes it clear that this vice is not confined to one profession. When we examine them closely, there is not a great deal of difference between the Old Gentleman in *Storm* and the Mummy in Opus 3. In *The Ghost Sonata* a house collapses while, in *The Burned House* and *The Pelican*, houses are destroyed by fire.[9] Perhaps after the fire in the latter play, all the secrets of that family will likewise be exposed to public scrutiny. Many more examples of such ties (particularly similarities of props, music and lighting) are given by Brian Rothwell in his article 'The Chamber Plays'.[10]

Strindberg was not afraid of death though, in his later years, he saw it as the most important problem facing man. Having accepted that we must reconcile ourselves to suffering during life, he examined the 'curious' tenacity with which many men cling to their agony on earth. Pride, fear, sensuality and the desire for power, are all portrayed in his last Sonatas, together with the forms of behaviour they provoke; egotism, self-deception, incest, greed and vampirism. But now he does not rail wildly against man's sins, his paranoid hysteria has become muted, and he surveys man's stupidity with resigned contempt. Throughout these Chamber Plays, we are aware of the man waiting patiently for death to transport him to that pure existence intimated by his extra-sensory powers and by his Christianity. Meanwhile, to fill up the time left to him, he exposes the 'world of illusion'[11] and those follies of his species which hold him an unwilling victim.

This is the sublime and indulgent self-portrait which Strindberg had tried to project since the turn of the century. A useful corrective can be found in the *Occult Diaries* where it will be seen that, despite his deeply felt faith, he remained until the end a man of flesh and blood. This is a fact to be acknowledged gratefully, for in his flesh and in his blood were those anxieties, generosities, vulnerabilities antagonisms and open-heartedness that were his genius.

STORM (1907) OPUS ONE

Storm,[12] the first of the Chamber Plays, concerns old age and the desire of the elderly for peace and solitude in which to prepare for death. It proposes that living in memory, away from the ugliness and the complications of reality, is preferable to any other existence, because in isolation we can cherish what was beautiful and ignore what was painful. Through memory we can recreate life as we would have wished it to be. Unfortunately, we are rarely allowed to die so easily. Ghosts from the past return to make demands on us and to disturb our peace which is seen to be merely a calm before the storm.

The play's setting is 'the silent house', inhabited by ten families who live in complete isolation from each other. The Old Gentleman has retired there, in retreat from his wife, rarely speaking to anyone and rarely going out. He has 'lost the desire for movement' and is 'chained to the house by memories . . . Only in there can I find safety and peace' (p. 382). For ten years, he has watched couples who 'have come in bridal carriages and left in coffins', without the slightest desire to rejoin the turmoil of life. Mummified like the Colonel's wife in *The Ghost Sonata*, all he wants is to settle his account with life so that no-one can make any more demands on him. The Old Gentleman has outlived passion. Re-marriage does not appeal to him because he knows that he does not possess the stamina to prevent a wife from organising his life and disturbing his peace. Gently but firmly misanthropic, he speaks of 'this abyss which men call the human heart' (p. 399). Furthermore, his wife's slanders have made him misogynistic. This enables him to cut himself off from her entirely but by doing so he lives a life of illusion, in retreat from a reality which he must confront before he can be allowed to die. His desire for peace is shared by the Café Owner and by Louise who shows that even women can occasionally aspire to wisdom. The Gentleman's asexual relationship with her is seen as an ideal male–female relationship. The Café Owner too is getting old and does not 'seem able to get really angry nowadays. You lose it the way you do everything' (p. 389). When there is a fight upstairs, he does not interfere; he prefers peace.

Unfortunately their quiet is to be disturbed and the Gentleman is not to be allowed to remember only what was pleasant in his past, for we learn that his wife, Gerda, is living upstairs with her lover. She represents the selfishness of youth as well as the viciousness of the female sex. She has callously exposed her child to her lover's brutality and she has deliberately ruined her husband's reputation because he terminated their peculiar marital arrangement by leaving her, instead of allowing her to leave him. Hurt pride, hatred and self-interest motivate her behaviour. Yet her return is salutary because the Gentleman has become complacent: 'After one has reached a certain age, nothing changes, everything stays the same. Things just slide forward like a toboggan on a hill' (p. 396), and as Louise tells him: 'It isn't good to stay too long among memories . . . They turn pale and one fine day they may lose their colour' (p. 395). Gerda's disturbing presence is needed to prevent him from taking his solitude too much for granted. He has been in danger of allowing it to lose its savour. Even *he* admits that the 'peace of old age' may be beginning to pall. He has loved his wife and child and now he misses them. At last the tension of the thunderstorm, which has been building up throughout the play, is about to break. When Gerda and he meet, the encounter is harrowing; it is clear that she has not changed and so once again he rejects her. 'A thundercloud's just gone over, straight over our heads, but it didn't rain. False alarm' (p. 403). He is content that Providence has fittingly punished her by having her present husband, Fischer, run away with a younger woman, but when he learns that his daughter is in 'the hands of an adventurer', the clouds open, and he begins to understand that 'deafness can go too far and become dangerous' (p. 410).

As Scene 3 opens, the house is lit, the upstairs blinds drawn; the outside world has entered the cloister and all its secrets are brought out into the open. The shower is over, but it is not yet time for the lamplighter to light up their gas lamp; the symbol of normality.[13] Louise urges the Gentleman not to 'turn your back on danger, it will destroy you' (p. 412), but he believes, apparently correctly, that, having served its purpose of rousing him from his complacency, 'Everything solves itself, if you don't interfere'. There is nothing he can do anyway, and 'since she came in here and destroyed my memories . . . all my hidden treasures . . . I have nothing left' (p. 413). He feels empty, 'like a deserted house', and wants once more to rest: 'God please don't let them come back. I don't want them around my neck again' (p. 414). His prayers are answered and he is left in peace confident both of Gerda's calumny and the justice of this Swedenborgian universe which leaves an old man in peace. He has learned something from the experience and, when the lamplighter returns, he decides to 'Let our memories be put to bed' and concludes, 'This autumn I shall leave this silent house' (p. 419) (i.e. he will die). The past which it evokes no longer has any attraction for him. He has supposedly settled his accounts with his wife and now at last he can move out of this house of illusion, the symbol of the passive life he has been living, and prepare himself for death.

Like the rest of the Chamber plays, *Storm* does not exhibit any uniquely expressionistic qualities[14] but it differs from its successors in being dominated more by a preconceived form than in having a theme that determines its form. Themes, ideas and objects recur in developing patterns around the Gentleman's kaleidoscopic memories, like leitmotifs in a musical composition. Images of the storm, the lamplighter and the chess game impose upon events a structure of their own, with the result that the design of these patterns is more important than the events themselves. The climaxes and tensions of *Storm* are provided less by human emotions than by the *shape* of what happens. For once, the quality of a Strindberg play is largely formal. Perhaps, in the case of *Storm*, this is just as well because its theme is so antipathetic to the twentieth-century mind. Reared as we are on notions of authenticity and commitment, the suggestion that 'in order to depart content, we require religious resignation, complete irrevocable withdrawal from the world' (*A Blue Book*, p. 152) is likely to seem irrelevant at the very least. The Gentleman can easily appear a self-righteous coward who cares more for his own hurt pride and contentment than anything else. Whatever good reason there might have been, he deserted his wife and child, and the fact that they are ultimately released from Fischer's control is not any of his doing.

However, the play does not fail merely in our terms but in Strindberg's, because, although he appears to applaud the Gentleman's response, the presentation quite clearly does not demonstrate that. 'The object of the trials of old age is to adjust accounts, to finish up unsettled affairs, to see through the cheat of life, and to become weary of the incomplete, so that no backward longings may disturb the repose of the grave' (*A Blue Book*, p. 253). On the contrary, the Gentleman is a passive figure who solves nothing; all he does is whine, 'I just hope they don't come back, so I'll have them on my neck'. If, at the end, he has 'no backward longings', having put away his memories, it is not because of the wisdom of his old age but merely because the past has bludgeoned him to seek death. We certainly could not say of him that he 'know[s] everything beforehand, expect[s] no improvement, [is] no more deceived by false hopes, demand[s] nothing more of men, neither gratitude nor love, only some companionship in solitude (*A Blue Book*, p. 163). Thus *Storm* is too indulgently self-pitying to be admirable. Its most obvious virtue is the immense skill with which Strindberg has created a setting (in particular, the mysterious background figures in the shadows of the massive house), a mood of unnatural calm and humidity before the storm, and a leisurely pace ideally suited to depicting the uneventful life of a lonely old man. In addition, the gains in structural flexibility achieved by developing motifs within musical variations, lay the ground for the next three greater Chamber Plays.

Yet a marvellous chance seems to have been lost. Strindberg should have extended the musical rhythms, which are so apparent in his treatment of the flow of life within and without the house, to the mind and emotions of his protagonist. A move towards expressionism is badly needed to give the play power and point. As it is we have a situation in flux, as themes and external events conjure the whirl of life, but at the centre there is this static, witless figure who is supposed to hold together all the activity. It could be argued that Strindberg's purpose is to depict the sensible inertia of the aged within this useless turmoil of life, but even if this is so, it still does not explain why he portrays the Gentleman as cowardly instead of wise. Moreover, on Strindberg's own admission, the storm is something to be faced and transcended, but the Gentleman is merely buffeted to one side by it, content to whine until it abates of its own accord.

THE BURNED HOUSE[15] (1907) OPUS TWO

A one-storey house stands gutted by fire, its interior open to the public gaze. Gradually, as the neighbours gather to discuss the occasions, their secrets and those of the inhabitants of the house are revealed to the audience. By exploiting the mystery of the fire, and by analysing the affairs of this tightly knit community, Strindberg develops two related themes; the interconnection of human lives through a variety of family ties and shared past experiences in a great chain of being, and the predominance of deceit in human affairs. Men conspire to deceive themselves and other people as to their real natures, while striving to expose the sham of their neighbour's lives. In the normal course of events, the possibilities of playing such a dual role are extensive but when the chain of deception is interrupted, when some vital link is destroyed, such as the secrets of a house being revealed, everyone's hypocrisy is exposed. It is only when something like the fire (an Act of God) occurs that human knowledge can be anything but restricted and relative.

Strindberg's spokesman, who articulates the central thesis of the play and who also acts as its catalyst, is Arvid Valström, the Stranger. It is he who says:

> But think how our fates have interwoven with those of others . . . everywhere the same. When we were young we see the born being set up—parents, relatives, friends, acquaintances, servants; that's the warp. Later on in life we're aware of the weft, and the shuttle of fate weaves back and forth with the thread . . . sometimes it breaks, but it knits up again. The thud of the treadle forces the yarn into fabric and at last the pattern is there. In old age when the

eye can finally see, we discover that all the little curlicues form a design, a monogram, an ornament, hierogliphics which only now we can read: this is life. The world weaver wove it. (p. 68)

Wherever he goes, Arvid cannot escape the net of memories and acquaintances which make up his natural milieu. Events have an unnerving way of *recurring*. When the scandal of the Valströms' smuggling forbears comes to light, it makes an ironical comment on their relationship with the Eriksson brothers, whose parent was a custom officer. In the one case the *sins* of the father will be visited on the son, in the other case the virtues. Just as the tides return bodies and wrecks long since lost at sea, so time, by repeating itself, exposes secrets long forgotten (e.g. the apples stolen by Arvid's brother and the book from which Arvid's name has been erased). And now the fire has precipitated further revelations. As Arvid surveys the house with all its counterfeit possessions, he realises that: 'Everything in our house was stained with dye, so as not to be recognised. Everything in our house was counterfeit—the children's clothes were dyed and our bodies were always stained with dye . . . Ebony—humbug' (p. 79). Nothing can be accepted at face value, neither people, objects nor memories. So Arvid's conclusion is one of utter misanthropy and pessimism.

> You tiny Earth: densest and heaviest of planets—the most oppressive . . . Hard to breathe your atmosphere and hard to bear you . . . Your symbol is the cross—but it could have been a cap and bells or a straitjacket. World of illusion and lunatics . . . Eternal One! Is your Earth lost in space? Why does it whirl round and round so all your children are dizzy and lose their reason. Reason. We can only see what seems, never what is. (p. 80)

Such is this godless world in which any injustice can occur and blame is wholly man's. 'If we wanted to be just, we could put a rope around the neck of the whole family of man, but we don't want to. It's a terrible family; ugly, sweaty, stinking dirty linen, filthy socks with holes, sores, bunions, egh!' (pp. 82–3). These are Schopenhaurian sentiments not those of Kierkegaard or Swendenborg.

Where once Strindberg would have blamed the Powers, now he condemns man through the group of human beings whose neighbourhood is nicknamed the Swamp; an appellation which reminds

one of Gorki's *Lower Depths*. 'You have to be a pig to enjoy the
muck here' (p. 97). In common with the Stranger in *To Damascus*,
Arvid has returned to the scene of his youth 'to unpick his fabric'
and to settle his accounts with his brother, the Dyer, only to discover
that all his early life was illusion and that even he himself was not
blameless. But the experience has enlightened him and enabled him
to exorcise evil memories and forgive his transgressors.

The symbolic import of the fire is also religious; an act of God
which lights up the darkness of man's despair by showing him that
his life and values are illusions. After the fire in Scene 2, 'The garden
is fully visible, with daphne, dahlias, mexereum, deutzias, daffodils,
Easter lilies, narcissi, tulips etc in bloom' (p. 78). The Swamp and
the Garden can be taken as two visions of the world—the Golden
Age before the Fall and the present mire that man has made of it.
The Garden signals future hope which may or may not be realised,
for the Fire has forced the buds into blossom but a 'little early, I
guess . . . If we have a frost now' (p. 55). This Swedenborgian
contrast with the deceit and shadows of the Swamp is developed in
the second half, when Strindberg shows that, despite their failings,
some of the characters have good in them. The student is young
enough to survive his false arrest, the Stonecutter has a wry sense of
humour and the Wife a sense of shame. Moreover, a young couple is
to be married, so there is hope for the future, 'Now the garden will
grow better if only they don't build another bigger house' (p. 90).
Thus by implication Swedenborg's favourite abodes for good spirits
(beautiful gardens full of flowers and sunlight) are contrasted with
the natural destination of liars and hypocrites (dark caves and foetid
swamps).

In *Burned House*, Swedenborgian Providence rules with a firm
hand. The Dyer, who has falsified evidence against the Student, is
punished by losing his fortune. His guilt is symbolised by the colour
of his hands which are stained with dye—dye which Arvid has
already identified as the sham, the hypocrisy, of their lives. Similarly
and with appropriate irony, the Student is punished wrongly for the
Dyer's crime, but justly for his own crime of sleeping with the
Dyer's wife. Behind the apparent injustice of this world, there is a
definite design which, sooner or later, is revealed to the patient man.
Although the scene with the Painter makes it clear that Arvid too is
by no means free from arrogance, we can be certain that he is free

from the Swamp and will not be subjected to the baleful judgement of Providence. He is a man of the world who knows life and understands the hypocrisy of men, but he is also a spiritual man, possessed of greater insight and virtue than most of his fellows. Consequently, he believes in the retributive order of life and is unable to take this world of illusions seriously. Since the age of twelve, when he tried to hang himself, he has considered himself, in some sense, dead. Death, indeed, is a major motif in the play. Arvid married the niece of a suicide, his step-mother's father was 'a professional pall-bearer', there is a cemetery nearby and the local restaurant is called *The Coffin Nail*, 'where the hearses pull up and the condemned men used to get their last glass on the way to the gallows' (p. 67). After he had abortively hanged himself, Arvid awoke and found 'I had forgotten most of my previous life and had to begin a new one' (p. 74). So he had cast off Death, the Swamp and his guilt.

But, at the same time, he acquired new faculties. 'I could see through other people, read their thoughts, understand their motives (p. 74) (cf. the Student in *The Ghost Sonata*). In becoming weary of life to the point of wishing to leave it, he had transcended mere physical existence. Only *he* understands of life that 'Human beings didn't spin this web' (p. 98), and that we must submit to it however unjust it seems. Distinguished by his insight, he is a wanderer destined, like Strindberg himself, to find no lasting contentment with his fellow men, but, unlike other protagonists of the later plays, Arvid does not feel himself to be doomed and there is nothing morbid about his attitude. He is resigned to the condition of man but does not seem emotionally involved in it: 'I have no feelings for my fellow beings nor for myself. I just find it interesting to watch them' (p. 75). He lives in the hope of something better after death. As he tells his sister-in-law: 'And when you're fed up with the blue mist of illusion, turn your eyes inside out and look into your own soul— and you'll really find something to look at' (p. 97). Like the Stranger in *To Damascus* Part III, he has seen through life and come to the conclusion that the only reality (i.e. the only path to God) is through disciplined self-examination.

Of all the play's characters only Arvid's brother, the materialist Dyer, suffers unredeeming punishment. The Dyer is unable to forgive or humble himself, and looks for revenge. As Arvid says, he is 'Incorrigible! Unmerciful! Cowardly!' Thus is the Stranger allowed to pronounce judgement on his fellows. Finally, with his usual despondency, he places the wreath, intended for his parents' grave, on the ruins of the house as a sign that he considers his childhood memories to be as dead as his illusions about life. The mystery of human existence—'the cipher . . . the hieroglyph' remains unsolved, even though a single stone upturned has exposed such a confusion of deceit and lies. The Stranger alone understands that we must wait patiently for the time when we shall understand all. Meanwhile, we must endure the vanity, the corruption and the false illusions.

The Burned House is an extremely skilful piece. With a minimum of effects, Strindberg uncovers the deceptions of a whole community interrelating past, present and future intrigues as they centre upon the life of the Dyer's family. Apart from the themes we have discovered, he provides us with a series of sketches from parochial life reminiscent of Dickens. Taking full advantage of his new, flexible concept of theatre, allowing his characters to appear when they are needed thematically rather than when the plot warrants, he depicts with impressionistic brevity a detailed and authentic background. The result is undeniably cynical, but also effectively real. With its supple, indeed at times almost casual, sampling of social relations, it is the culmination of a tendency apparent in Strindberg's work since the *quart d'heure* plays. By different techniques, he achieved most of what the naturalists hoped to achieve through social documentation, yet with more economy and greater dramatic force.

THE GHOST SONATA (1907) OPUS THREE

The Ghost Sonata is the greatest of the Chamber Plays and one of the finest and most curious dramas Strindberg ever wrote, but it is also a very difficult play to analyse. Its style is clearly a mixture of symbolism and expressionism which anticipates surrealism, but its sense is highly elusive. The overall impression of the play is of a misanthropy so stark that it is barely redeemed by the final Christian/ Buddhist prayer. *The Ghost Sonata* is pervaded by the kind of blackness which does not admit of specific causes or targets but communicates an all-embracing disgust with self and others, with the living and the inanimate. Images of decay predominate and reflect most probably the influence of the Miss Haversham scenes in Dickens's *Great Expectations*, but distortion and symbol push

Strindberg's effects far beyond Dickensian realism to an approximation of surrealism. As its title suggests, it conforms to the classical
sonata form which is well analysed by Evert Sprinchorn in his
introduction and so need not be repeated here. There are several
specific literary and musical references (e.g. to *Faust* and Wagner)
but, as Sprinchorn argues, 'Regardless of how many bells these
allusions may set to ringing in our minds, none of them continues
to reverberate throughout the play' (p. xx). They are not followed
through but are used impressionistically to provide a musical background of themes which highlight particular sequences. They underline and emphasise, rather than set up a new, self-sufficient thematic
structure.

The Student and Hummel represent two opposing attitudes
towards life. Arkenholz can see the milkmaid as a figure of beauty
comforting him as he has comforted the victims of another ruined
house. Hummel, however, cannot see her physically but senses her
presence as the retributive force at the centre of life. She represents
the innocence he has resolutely destroyed. Depending upon the
moral qualities of the observer, she, the house and its inhabitants will
appear as objects of fear and squalor or hope and beauty. But Strindberg shows us that in time the idealism of the Student will be
frustrated by the horror and violence of life. And, although this does
not mean that he will become as cynical as Hummel, it does follow
that sadness will taint his optimism. In the end, he will be compelled
to admit his failure to save the Young Lady from the debilitating
influences of her surroundings. Arkenholz, the Student, is a Swedenborgian sensitive who has second sight and can see ghosts. He
represents the dutiful spiritual man who suffers his fate with
humility and patience. Heroically, he has saved the life of a child
when a house collapsed and 'spent the whole night bandaging
wounds and taking care of injured people' (p. 107). With typical
reticence, he has sought neither thanks nor reward for his courage.
He is a Sunday child (a Christ figure wandering the earth, doing
good and understanding more than the rest of us), born in 'the
middle of bankruptcy proceedings' initiated by Hummel against his
father. As Hummel's creditor, he expects nothing for himself; rather
he is a dreamer who can appreciate the natural joys of living.
However bitter experience in the house that represents death in life
will shortly cloud his youthful optimism.

It is his lack of experience that Hummel sets out to exploit. The Old Man has lived ruthlessly, manipulating people and situations for his own material advantage, driven by an insatiable demand for power. As a result, he has ruined Arkenholz's father, broken the heart of his former fiancée, now a crazy old woman, and has callously fathered an illegitimate child on the Colonel's wife (the Mummy). To the Student he pours out his rancour and cynically blackens the character of everyone who appears: 'I take a great interest in human destinies' (p. 112); that is, he wrecks them. Providence has repaid him in kind, physically crippling him as he has emotionally crippled others, but instead of learning from this, he refuses to discipline his own egotistical drives and arrogantly declares, 'I blame it all on life itself, with all its traps' (p. 110). However, recently he has received a sign that his sins must be repaid. The apparition of the Milkmaid reminds him that he is guilty of drowning her; a responsibility he tries to avoid by claiming that he once *saved* a girl from drowning. He knows that unless he does something to retrieve the balance of good in his account, he will suffer damnation. Unfortunately, his interest in Arkenholz is not a genuine response, a love of virtue for its own sake. It is a vampiristic seizing of goodness which issues from a fear of retribution and, thus, in the Providential scheme is inadequate to his salvation. Indifferent to such considerations, Hummel aims to use the Sunday Child as his spiritual guarantor through whom he might make amends, even though he does not yet feel the full weight of his sins. 'I've made people unhappy and people have made me unhappy; the one cancels out the other. But before I die I want to make you happy. Our destinies are tangled together through your father and other things' (p. 116).

Hummel's decision to purchase salvation is that of a doomed man who is compromising with death by seizing upon the life of an innocent youth. 'Let go of my hand—you are drawing all my strength from me—you're freezing me to death' (p. 116). He has no shame but rationalises even his sins. 'I saved your father from the worst possible misery, and he repaid me with all the terrible hatred of a man who feels obliged to be grateful' (p. 110). Hummel, the vampire, tries to make the Student feel responsible so that he can drain the life out of him, but the student has an ally in the Milkmaid (the symbol of purity and innocence), whose purpose is to save souls. Ultimately, Hummel punishes himself. The Milkmaid is a figment of his imagination and the Mummy plays on his feelings of guilt; 'Swedenborg speaks of being punished by imagination. That is what doctors generally call hallucination. He who suffers from persecution mania is persecuted' (*A Blue Book*, p. 146). What Hummel is really after is Power. 'All day long he rides around in his chariot like the great god Thor. He keeps his eye on houses, tears them down, opens up streets, builds up city squares. But he also breaks into houses, sneaks in through the windows, ravages human lives, kills his enemies and forgives nobody and nothing' (p. 121). Hardly surprisingly then the Opera to which he invites the Student is *Die Walküre*;[16] he has chosen the youth to substitute for him at death. 'Riding his war chariot, drawn in triumph by the beggars who don't get a cent for it, just a hint that something might come their way at his funeral' (p. 123).

This first scene is extremely similar to Durrenmatt's *The Visit*. Like Madame Zachanassian, Hummel 'steals people—in more ways than one . . . He literally stole me [i.e. his servant Johansson] out of the hands of the law. I made a little mistake—that's all—and he was the only one who knew about it. But instead of putting me in jail, he made me his slave. I slave for him just for my food' (p. 121). He will enslave Arkenholz if he can just as Madame Zachanassian, with the help of her bodyguards whom she saved from execution, traps her former lover. Nevertheless, Hummel is subtle; he doesn't deny that 'All my life I have *taken*—taken!', but professes to have reformed, 'Now I crave to give, to give! But nobody will take what I have to offer' (p. 117). Hummel sucks the life out of other people and, at the same time, leaves behind his poison in their blood stream. He accuses others, the Consul, the Old Woman and the Dead Man, of failings that are most noticeable in himself. He accuses the Colonel of being an ex-servant and yet later is himself revealed to have been a servant who dispossessed his master (now his servant, Bengtsson). Nothing about the man suggests remorse; he has yet to pass 'through the great purgatorial fire which burnt up the rubbish of my soul' (*A Blue Book*, p. 178).

Scene 2 takes place in the house where the 'Ghost supper' (the play's original title) will be enacted and justice will be administered. Seeking to gain control by means of economic exploitation, Hummel strips the Colonel of all his illusions and reduces him to the status of a slave.[17] Next we are introduced to the Colonel's Wife, Hummel's former mistress who, as a result of his mistreatment, has become almost literally mummified, spending most of her life in a cupboard. She cannot bear sunlight but, unlike the Judge in *Advent*, this is not because she is evil but because life is painful to her. Moreover, she chatters away like a parrot to avoid human conversation, by which she might reveal her feelings or discover the sickness of other people. 'She can't stand cripples . . . or sick people. She can't even stand the sight of her own daughter because she's sick' (p. 126). In a similar manner, the rest of the family has been drained of life. 'They all look like ghosts . . . This has been going on for twenty years—always the same people, always saying the same things. Or else keeping silent to avoid being embarrassed . . . And they crunch their biscuits and crackers all at once and all in unison. They sound like a pack of rats in an attic' (p. 126). Isolated in this house, their lives are a sham and their vitality has dried up. They are little more than ghosts; the living dead. The Mummy and the Japanese death screen define a limbo where the only relief is the obscurely glimpsed hyacinth room, the abode of innocence and youth in which the Young Lady sits reading. 'She feels she has to sit in the hyacinth room whenever she's in the house' (p. 135). Before the play ends, she must be rescued from the decay that surrounds and threatens to engulf her. This will be attempted by the Student, another innocent, who appears to have the vigour to save her from the fate of the Mummy. The only other dynamic character in the play is, of course, Hummel, but he is the promoter of decay and ruin; the 'black spider who will spin his web among the dust to trap those within'. By contrasting the beautiful marble statue of the Colonel's wife when young with the Mummy she has become, Strindberg emphasises the enormity of Hummel's crimes. He is a force of unrelenting vengeance. 'I was born unable to forgive until I have punished. I've always looked upon it as an imperative duty. And I still do' (p. 130). By marrying Arkenholz to the Young Lady, he hopes to spite the family, control his daughter and then redeem his past.

In the trial of strength that ensues between Hummel and the Mummy, he is defeated because he meets someone who sees through him and is so indifferent to life that she is immune to his attacks. Hummel uses the economic means of *this* world to win his battles but against someone who is already essentially dead, they are useless. The Mummy survives because she loves, and intends to protect, her daughter. Moreover, the Mummy is too strong for him because she has the spiritual strength of genuine humility and repentance on her side. 'I can wipe out the past and undo what is done. Not with bribes, not with threats—but through suffering and repentance' (pp. 137–8). In contrast with Hummel, she admits her own and the rest of the family's transgressions but asserts the basically Buddhist truth. 'At bottom we are better than ourselves since we abhor and detest our misdeeds.' Then turning on Hummel she teaches him the truth of dictum from *A Blue Book*. 'Every time that you rummage in the past of another, although it has been atoned for, the memory of your own evil deeds start up' (p. 47). 'But when you, Jacob Hummel, with your false name, come here to sit in judgement over us, that proves you are more contemptible than we. You are a slave trader, a stealer of souls!' (p. 138). So the woman of God destroys the man of evil, as the spectre of the Milkmaid appears to confirm the truth of the Mummy's indictment. Finally, his former master and servant, Bengtsson, exposes him as a vampire who steals the goodness from other men's food.

Hummel, who has been living the illusion that he is a great business man and can pay through the Student for whatever venial sins he has committed by the way, hears for the first time the truth about himself and cannot face it. Now Hummel has had the life drained out of him and he too becomes a parroting Mummy. Nothing is left for him but to kill himself because, unlike the Mummy, he has no spiritual strength or love for others to enable him to live on when all worldly attributes have been taken from him. He has relied totally on power and once that has been withdrawn, there is nothing left of him. The scene ends with his epitaph being sung by the Student and the Young Lady, the forces of life and virtue: 'Man reaps as he sows . . . kindness alone can make amends . . . the pure in heart have none to fear' (p. 140).

The final scene is located in the Hyacinth room ('The testing room. It's beautiful to look at, but it's full of imperfections') (p. 145); there the Student will try to restore the Young Lady to life, but tragically, youthful optimism will be defeated in the struggle to assert and preserve the beauty at the centre of life. Ultimately human weakness and corruption will triumph. Hyacinths are the young lady's symbol, purity, innocence and faithfulness her qualities, and confronted with them, Arkenholz feels humble. 'They deafen me, blind me, drive me out of my mind' (p. 141). Arkenholz, the spiritual sensitive, interprets the flower as 'an image of the whole cosmos' with Buddha sitting 'with the bulb of the earth in his lap'. The ornamentation of the room thus becomes a symbolic correspondence of Divine Mercy which ordains that 'this poor earth shall become a heaven' (p. 142).[18] Stimulated by these thoughts, the Young Lady soon reveals her feelings of spiritual kinship with him. This provides a poignant contrast to the Colonel and his Mummy wife who 'have nothing to say to each other, because they don't believe what the other says' (p. 143). Strindberg describes this marital paralysis perfectly in the section of *A Blue Book* entitled 'The Mummy Coffin' (cf. pp. 277-8).

Hummel's role is now taken over by the Cook. 'She belongs to the Hummel family of vampires' (p. 143), a bloated old woman who steals all the goodness out of their food. She is yet another expression of the family's inescapable debility; yet another of the evil spirits who torment them in their Kama-Loka. Another example is the infernal housemaid who, each day, sweeps away the piece of cork the Young Lady has placed under the foot of a writing table to prevent it from wobbling. The Lady is constantly plagued with minor irritations; she is awakened in the middle of the night and she is left with all the most unpleasant tasks to perform—'To sweep up after her, to dust after her and to start the fire in the stove after her . . . the drudgery of keeping oneself above the dirt of life' (p. 146).

The result of such treatment has been to make her ask if life is really worth the trouble. All that keeps her alive in fact are her illusions and, like Hummel, if she is stripped of them, she will die. But the Student believes in truth and light and proceeds to follow the example of his own father who told the truth and was declared mad. Acting on the principle that 'If you keep silent too long, stagnant water begins to accumulate and things begin to rot' (p. 150), he starts to lay a few ghosts. Although in this he appears to resemble Hummel, the Student is justified because he is honest and because he hopes selflessly to do good. Since everything has turned out to be illusion, he wants to introduce some reality into the house but unfortunately the Young Lady is too fragile to endure it. Escapism has become too entrenched. Arkenholz understands this but continues in his purpose because 'Now your flowers have poisoned me'. He is confronted by sensuality and he must resist. In despair, he asks 'why are beautiful flowers so poisonous and the most beautiful, the most deadly?' (p. 150). The Young Lady is a Sleeping Beauty who must be awakened even though it kills her, because to remain as she is would be a sin against Life and God. To live parasitically as she does is worse than death. The Student realises that life is a hell on earth but he cannot escape his essential goodness and his responsibility by tolerating evil: 'I cannot see what is ugly as beautiful and I cannot call what is evil good' (p. 151). Even when he feels most misanthropic, his spiritual virtues shine forth and illuminate the Young Lady's weakness, but his sense of reality is eventually too much for her and she dies, calling for the Japanese death screen. And so we must conclude that, in one respect at least, his idealistic optimism represents his personal failure since he has failed to save her.

Since she suffers through no fault of her own, no harm will come to her after death. Indeed, the fact of her death affirms the hope that in life after death the horror of this existence will be explained. J. R. Northam, in his perceptive study 'Strindberg's Spook Sonata',[19] attempts to provide a less pessimistic interpretation but there is little to show that 'the Young Lady's death is in part a triumph of innocence' and a great deal to suggest that she is an etiolated human spirit, beyond Arkenholz's invigorating influence. To paraphrase the song which serves to summarise the final scene—although she has done no evil, she does not appear to have done much good either. Arkenholz feels that he has to ask that she be treated mercifully by 'The Lord of Heaven'; he cannot assume it. The obvious spiritual ideal is not the Young Lady but the Student. While she dies, the Student prays for those who must live on in this Schopenhauerian world: 'Buddha, wise and gentle Buddha, sitting there waiting for a heaven to grow out of the earth, grant us the purity of will and the patience to endure our trials, that your hopes will not come to nought' (p. 151). When the Lady dies 'pure white light pours into the room' (p. 151) and she ('Child of this world of illusion and guilt and suffering') is transported to Boecklin's *Island of the Dead* where expectations will be better. The Student, who has delivered the antidote of truth to protect himself against the poison of the Young Lady's illusion, remains with strength to endure the sufferings of this world.

The structure of *The Ghost Sonata* is built up on a variety of correspondences which are in part Swedenborgian but also take the form of motifs. Hummel's wig and the Colonel's wig, Hummel at the ghost supper and the elder Arkenholz at the banquet, the two collapsed houses, the two deaths behind the Japanese screen, Hummel stealing the goodness out of the food and the Vampire Cook, Hummel and the Colonel, both former servants become masters, the statue and the Mummy, Hummel and the Student's attempt to save the Young Lady's life and Hummel and the Mummy become parrots. These together with Strindberg's liberal use of telepathy, apparitions, second sight, symbols and dopplegangers, present a tightly knit pattern of allusions to man's spiritual destiny as it issues from his condition in this life. As Martin Lamm has pointed out, these distorted elements are closer to the grotesque reflections of real people in a Hall of Mirrors than to the unreal world of a dream play in which 'anything can happen'. *The Ghost Sonata* is a profound intellectual achievement as well as a revolutionary dramatic enterprise.

Consider, for example, the skilful way in which Strindberg manages to integrate a complex biblical structure into the play. In his valuable article 'Strindberg's Biblical Sources for *The Ghost Sonata*',[20] Stephen C. Bandy has uncovered a wealth of allusions which provide a new dimension to the play. Briefly, he interprets the Milkmaid as the Woman of Samaria drawing water at the well, Hummel as Jacob, the Jewish Patriarch whose well it is and the Student as Christ. The Patriarch's wife Lia corresponds to Hummel's first wife, Amelia, the Mummy who is put aside in favour of her sister and who cannot bear sunlight ('tender eyed'). Both Jacob who is Israel and Jacob Hummel are lame and the former who prophesied the coming of the Messiah eventually rejected Christ. However, the Passion is inverted for the Student fails to redeem the Young Lady and, conforming to Strindberg's religious prejudices, Buddhist resignation triumphs over Christian missionary zeal. The decay produced by a Hummel continues beyond the grave.

This kind of superstructure was clearly intended by Strindberg, but although it extends the power and range of the play's reference, it is not essential to its understanding. Moreover, there are Swedenborgian parallels and surrealistic touches which cannot be accommodated within biblical mythology. However, Stephen Bandy has performed an important critical function if only to make clear yet again how carefully planned are the symbolic and theological references of Strindberg's plays.

THE PELICAN (1907) OPUS FOUR

Of all the Chamber Plays *The Pelican* has the most naturalistic psychological frame. Even though the theme is vampirism and its attendant corruption, *The Pelican* can be played on a straight psychological level. A spiritual world is certainly evoked but the behaviour of each character can be understood by reference to such everyday qualities as jealousy, meanness, greed, revenge and cruelty. The individuals depicted are not diabolic or beyond life like those in *The Ghost Sonata*. Certainly they exist in a limbo without purpose or vitality, but they are drained not deathly. The Mother alone is larger than life. Her vampirism, greed and capacity to persuade herself that her most callous behaviour is righteous typifies, rather than specifies, human qualities. Strindberg himself called her a Medea.[21] We can understand but not sympathise with her vanity in encouraging her son-in-law's attentions and the malice she shows against her dead husband, whose very decency is a constant reproach to her. Her character is best understood and defined by the Son, who is Strindberg's mouthpiece in the play. 'Always lying ... Father once said in anger that you were the greatest fraud ever perpetrated by nature ... you learned to be from the first word ... you always shirked your duty ... As soon as you heard an honest word you called it a lie ... How many times haven't I said of you 'She's so evil I feel sorry for her' (pp. 190–4).

She is, and is intended to be, an irredeemable monster, so habituated to greed and self-deceit that she can never be fully awakened to goodness. Her persistent rejection of the truth has crippled the personality of her daughter.[22] How a woman can bring herself to starve her children and keep all the food for herself, then conspire in her husband's death and the alienation of her son-in-law from her daughter, can be explained in non-spiritual terms. In *The Pelican* Strindberg once more reverts to a naturalistic and determinist account: 'And what do you suppose my childhood was like? Have you any idea what an ugly home I had, what evil things I learned there? It's all inherited. From whom? From generation to generation. From the first parents, it says in children's books, and that seems to make sense. So don't blame me, and I won't blame my parents, who won't blame theirs, and so on and on' (pp. 198–9). Here the emphasis on hereditary and environmental determinism revives memories of *The Father* and *Miss Julie*. However, Strindberg does not abnegate his religious views, he simply uses naturalistic determinism as another means of demonstrating the despair of man's earthly condition without God. If all we can accept is the reality of this life, then we are inevitably forced to deny freedom of will and admit that there is no hope, no purpose and no progress. As the daughter says: 'If that's true, I don't care to live. And if I'm forced to, I'd prefer to walk deaf and blind through this miserable existence, hoping for a better life to come' (p. 199).

The Mother then, represents a Zolaesque force struggling to survive in a world which will not accommodate her needs. She is continually harassed by spiritual forces; for example, the wind that sets her husband's rocking chair in motion[23] and the influence of her husband's letters and conversation even after he is dead. 'He rises from his grave and you can't shut him up' (p. 170). But while she is terrified by the Powers, they do not have any lasting salutary influence because she thinks within a different contextual framework. She is a materialist who denies her own freedom and thus, quite logically, acts solely in her own interest. So she can cheat and brutalise even her own flesh and blood for, without a dutiful belief in the Divine, she feels no moral responsibility towards anyone but herself. Thus we have the ironic image of her as a Pelican giving her life-blood to her young but really saving all the best nutriment for herself. As a subterfuge, she has built up a superstructure of illusions which can be destroyed only by a holocaust. So the fire started by the son is needed to burn up the rubbish of their lives, 'Everything had to burn up, otherwise we would never get out of here' (p. 200) and for the first time they feel warm in their comfortless dwelling. 'I'm no longer cold, listen to it crackling out there, everything old is burning up, everything old and mean and ugly' (pp. 200–1).

After the mother has jumped from the window to escape the fire, her son and daughter are apotheosised. By confronting the truth, they are released from the illusions of an unbearable earthly life.[24] Unlike the ending of *A Dream Play*, which constitutes an act of sacrifice for mankind, this holocaust can perhaps be related to von Hartmann's notion of cosmic suicide rather than to Heraclitus.

Here indeed we can say that only in their deaths do the characters achieve their finest moment and example. Nor are we to assume that their deaths are steps towards something finer. In the spirit of von Hartmann's pessimism, the act of sacrifice is to be valued for itself alone. Significantly, neither the son nor the daughter is strong enough to face reality and when they are enlightened (like the Young Lady in *The Ghost Sonata*) through their father's spiritual influence,[25] they die. Nevertheless, while the Mother dies in despair, they are happy at the end, remembering the good times with their father, and even those with their mother. They regress to childhood when their lives, uncomplicated by understanding, were full of joy, warmth and the promise of summer. We are left with the social conclusion that marriage is a means by which men and women torment each other and drain their children of vitality. At best, it is a system of illusions which allows each member of the family to evade the reality of his condition and to live a half life of lies and deceit.

Each of the three scenes of *The Pelican* is prefaced by a piece of music that sets the mood and indicates the theme. At the opening of Scene 1, Chopin's *Fantaisie Impromptu*, Oeuvre Posthume, opus 66 is being played. Not surprisingly this affirms the dream-like nature of the family's lives. They are surviving in an unreal gloom where fragments of external reality are only vaguely glimpsed but in which the actual decay of their household is clearly observed. Without any overall picture of either their past, present or destiny, they live from day to day, forgetting what is painful and improvising their behaviour to create for themselves situations in which their illusions might prosper. Even the son will not admit the full truth about his mother; for instance, he always stops short of accusing her of starving his sister and himself. Similarly, the daughter refuses to believe that her husband is utterly unreliable, and the Mother forces herself to accept that her son-in-law cares only for her, when it is clear that he cares for himself.

Significantly, Strindberg indicates that the Chopin Fantaisie is an 'Oeuvre Posthume' as indeed is this first scene. The characters are living during the stunned aftermath of the father's death. As Strindberg constructs his fantaisie on the various themes which are to dominate the play, we are aware that this is merely a prelude to the disclosures and disasters that will eventually follow upon the bereavement. (The father's death plays the role of the storm, the burned house, the ghost supper—it discloses all the family's secrets.) If we regard the play as a sonata, we shall be able to grasp how Scene 2 is an allegro which reveals the particular development of the themes outlined in the opening largo. As the pace gradually increases throughout the play (in contrast to *The Ghost Sonata*, for example), we are drawn into the climax of a frenzied presto.

Scene 2 has as its musical backing, the Berceuse from Godard's *Jocelyn*. A French cradle-song, this prefigures the sleep-walking theme (p. 177). As the action proceeds, the children gradually understand the full extent of their mother's corruption and *awaken* to the deception of their own lives. They realise that charity can often be another name for cowardice. 'It's best to overlook your neighbour's faults and weaknesses, no doubt of that. But the first thing you know you're flattering and fawning ... speak out' (p. 177). By the time that the final showdown is reached in Scene 3, a new musical theme is used, a waltz, 'Il me disait', by Wolf-Ferrari, the religious connotations of which reflect the ultimate religious turn of the last ecstatic sequence. Now awakened at last, they are called irresistibly, and calmly, to death. For them the waltz represents peace and acceptance, while, for the Mother, it revives the feelings of vanity she felt when the son-in-law danced with her rather than with her daughter. The children die almost joyfully as their Mother clings desperately to her life of selfish illusions. Strindberg's feelings of sympathy for those who suffer with humility, and of bitterness against those who are deaf to the Word, can be inferred from the way he uses this waltz in Scene 3. Symptomatic of the Mother's inevitable damnation is her blind interpretation of this spiritual waltz as a symbol of earthly pleasure, as if it were Viennese.

Since they all subscribe to similar family myths, the Mother can masquerade as the Pelican who gives her life's blood to her young. Only because each member of the family invests emotionally in this deception can she get away with her pretensions. A corollary of the naturalist thesis that she cannot be blamed for her behaviour is that the children cannot avoid being her victims. Yet, just as Strindberg asserted during his most extreme naturalistic phase that man has a margin of choice, albeit narrow, now he shows that, as a final resort, a weakling, presented with an impossible situation and an invincible adversary, can always destroy himself. We always remain responsible for continuing to survive in a predicament in which we are compelled to do evil. The alternative of suicide cannot be denied us, although, of course, for someone with Strindberg's religious views to choose such a course of action could only be justified as a necessity to opposing the Will of God.

The Pelican contains more than the resigned pessimism we have become familiar with in Strindberg's later plays. Like his earlier plays, it is infused with a vigorous Schopenhauerian bitterness which, in his later years, was only surpassed by *The Dance of Death*.[26] For a man within five years of his death, it was surprisingly vitriolic. Had we not known better, we might have thought that the author of so uncompromising a play would be extremely self-confident to imagine that his own life could withstand so stern an ethical scrutiny.

THE BLACK GLOVE (1909) OPUS FIVE

Although it was written approximately two years later than its four predecessors, *The Black Glove*[27] is generally regarded as the fifth Chamber Play. And, despite its being a lyrical fantasy which resembles a fairy tale in mood and style rather than the bleak sonatas Strindberg had written for the Intimate Theatre, it shares sufficient of the thematic obsessions of the Chamber Plays to be considered with them. Typical of these are the belief that life is a balance of payment whose debt must be paid for in suffering, the thesis that all human lives are linked in some great chain of being, guilt and destiny, and the notion that human beings are vampires.

In common with all the other Chamber Plays the dramatic action of *The Black Glove* takes place within and around a house: this time an apartment building. This is defined by the Gnome as 'A tower of Babel with many kinds of people and tongues of speech' (p. 337). Within this house of confusion a struggle between good and evil is taking place; the outcome of which will decide the spiritual destiny of its occupants. 'This mysterious house, where human fates are stacked, floor upon floor, the one above the other, and next door to each other' (p. 368). The characters' lives are linked to each other and each must be enlightened before they can welcome Christmas in a truly Christian spirit.

Evil, or rather human folly, is represented by the materialistic philosophy of the Old Man and by the uncharitable Mrs Hard. The former, a self-portrait of Strindberg, is a retired taxidermist, a pre-server of dead ideas and useless facts, who deludedly seeks for the meaning of life[28] while at the same time longing for the release of death. As he says: 'I stuff birds and fishes and insects but I can't preserve myself' (p. 333). Unlike the Janitor, who is 'sitting in the shadow of my Christmas tree with grateful memories of the past' (p. 344) he prefers *not* to remember, evades human involvement and persists in tormenting himself with the problem of life's purpose. Before he can enjoy Christmas, which for him means a peaceful death, he must learn that his knowledge is 'merely chaff', that intelligence, the 'system rules you, masters you, you are its slave' (p. 357), and become 'aware that life is spirit, though fettered in the body, in a thing or being' (p. 360). By showing him that dualism is as tenable a theory of the universe as his monism, the Gnome demon-strates that all materialist explanations are inadequate; 'Where formerly you saw but laws, you now shall meet the God Creator, and afterwards the Great Judge. Where once you saw but Nature and blind, haphazard devil's play, there you will not find spirits alike in nature to yourself . . .' (p. 354). When he has learned this lesson, he will be ready for death; he will have rejected reason, knowledge, money and be reconciled to life.

Mrs Hard, the other example of folly, is guilty of more human sins. Her inadequacy is emotional and vampiristic. She is miserly in refusing to pay her bills, distrustful (she accuses Ellen, her servant, of stealing her ring), harsh and intolerant. The only object of love in her life is her child whom she adores to the exclusion of everyone else. 'They [Mrs Hard and her daughter] both chirp in unison like canary birds . . . Believe me, the young lady is not so loving to the rest of us. She gives neither the janitor nor us (the servants) any Christmas presents. She says we are beasts' (p. 334). In some respects Mrs Hard is a milder version of the Mother in *The Pelican*. But she has her good side, 'now and then she can be like an angel' (p. 355), which makes Ellen pity her and think she is perhaps possessed by evil spirits. It is this evil which the Gnome and the Christmas Angel will purge from her by suffering.

Part of her trouble is that she lives an idle life; she has too much money, too much leisure, and so she lacks a genuine spiritual life. To reform her, the spirits remove the child upon which her egotism is built; 'grief will cure her sickness' (p. 339). At the same time she is made to realise that she has falsely accused Ellen of stealing her ring. When, through the insight of the Old Man this ring is discovered in the missing black glove, Mrs Hard breaks down and begs Ellen to *forgive* her. Her conceit is destroyed and she is redeemed, so that the Christmas Angel can say: 'I've heard the word that will atone for everything; Forgive!' (p. 369). Humility can atone for most human sins. So Mrs Hard is reunited with her daughter and can celebrate Christmas and look forward to the spring, the season of rebirth. Now at last she realises that her former life was 'a mere shadow life, a work of art, no doubt, and yet now flawless: too much the physical, too little soul' (p. 366).

The principal forces of good are spiritual beings; the Gnome who sows discord to disturb the residents' self-satisfaction. 'I chasten and I love, bring comfort, tidy up' (p. 337), and the Christmas Angel who prepares them for the season of Christian love, 'to help console and put things right is my chore' (p. 339). They are complementary Powers; the chastiser and the comforter. Between them they interfere with the natural life of the household so much so that the place acquires the nickname of 'the spooky house'. Their activities have a specifically moral purpose; to reward goodness, chastise evil, purge sins, stimulate self-criticism and to provide evidence of the workings of spiritual forces. The Gnome seeks particularly to teach the residents to live harmoniously together, to tolerate each others' minor failings and, above all, to 'practice patience'.

The theme of the conflict between good and evil is symbolised by the colour motif of the Hard's apartment; by black (the glove, Mrs Hard's hair, her gown) and white (the ice box, the mirror, silver brush, child's fur coat and bonnet). Similarly, the Old Man is dressed in a curious ensemble of black and white clothes. Reinforcing these is a subsidiary colour motif of blue (the child, the old man's ivory tower—lost illusion), yellow and green. The notion, common to all the Chamber Plays, of the existence of evil within good, ugliness within beauty[29] which applies both to the characters and to the house, is expressed through an extraordinary number of metaphorical contrasts. For example, Mrs Hard wears 'silken finery with sharp nails', the Janitor lives in basement darkness yet spreads light through the house, Mrs Hard is beautiful but stony-hearted, the Gnome keeps order by sowing disorder, the Christmas Angel consoles by causing suffering, the Christmas card is adorned with a thistle, 'sometimes hot water comes out of the cold water faucet . . .' (p. 347), the black glove conceals a pale hand (p. 349) and the ashes make things grow (p. 362).

As befits a Chamber Play, music is used liberally and effectively in *The Black Glove*. Strindberg quotes from four pieces during the play. Mrs Hard first hears Beethoven's Sonata 31, Opus 110 during her prolonged mime which superbly closes Scene 2 after the Gnome has extinguished the house lights. The mood created is fairly light and buoyant, though the visionary quality of the music prefigures the enlightenment which will be brought about by her impending tragedy. When, a few seconds later, she discovers the loss of the black glove which symbolises the loss of her child, Beethoven's funeral march is heard. Later when the Old Man is desperately searching for the riddle of life among his papers which have been muddled by the Gnome, we hear Beethoven's Sonata 29, Opus 106, andante sostenuto. The slow, extended rhythms emphasise the fatigue of the Old Man and the hopelessness of his task. Finally, as an indication of the impending enlightenment and spiritual rebirth of his central characters, Strindberg quotes from Sinding's *The Rustle of Spring*.

Apart from those already mentioned, *The Black Glove* is resonant with Maeterlinckian symbols. The transom-window of the apartment house has a heart painted on it, the Janitor provides physical light from the darkness as an analogue to the Powers who bring spiritual light; the two are compatible and complementary. Spiritual confusion and conflict is represented by the squeaking lift, roaring water pipes and voices through the walls.[30] Also, there are the print of Christ's Nativity which reaffirms the absence of Mrs Hard's child from its crib, the Old Man's 'spiritual' spectacles and the moral significance of the lost ring. Finally, of course, and most importantly, there is the black glove itself. This is defined by the Gnome: 'It holds its many secrets, and the dainty fingers have touched so many fates, and caused much harm, it stretches out its hand to you in friendship . . .' (p. 362). It is an ambiguous symbol; its loss is a cause of disharmony in the household, its return a means by which the Old Man can spread happiness. Essentially it becomes a symbol of giving; a token of peace rather than a gauntlet of challenge, but, more importantly, the lost black glove with the ring (the purpose of life) inside it represents the spiritual counterpart of its materialistic twin, which remains in Mrs Hard's possession. Like the Old Man she has 'lost' the spiritual meaning of life.

Having said all this, it must be admitted that *The Black Glove* is not a very good play. True, it contains some sensitive writing. Strindberg's use of verse in it is for the most part more successful than in any of the other post-Inferno plays, with the exception of *A Dream Play* and *The Great Highway*. The verbal depiction of Mrs Hard's madness (pp. 350–1) the Gnome's demolition of the Old Man's monistic philosophy, the latter's despairing reaction then his gradual reaffirmation of life (pp. 360–4) and Mrs Hard's monologue of mourning at the opening of Act 5, are all superbly realised. Nevertheless, the result seems highly schematic. It never achieves the cumulative organic variations on certain themes and styles which make the aforementioned two plays such masterpieces.

Apart from Mrs Hard, and to a lesser extent, Ellen, there is almost no attempt to develop character. The Old Man is a stock Strindbergian figure who is used simply to communicate an anti-materialist view of the world. The Janitor is of interest only for his role as the 'mountain king' who resides in the basement of the house, controlling its day to day running. Yet the implied comparison between him and the ubiquitous spiritual powers who dominate the lives of men, is powerfully evocative and might profitably have been developed. As it is, together with the Old Lady, he is left undeveloped and seems largely superfluous. Any philosophical contrast between him and the Old Man is unnecessary because this is provided adequately by the verbal criticisms of the Gnome. As for the Spirits themselves, they are probably all they need to be dramatically, though the context within which they work seems factitious because it appears to be set up for the sake of Strindberg's thesis. It is not a dramatically dynamic situation. The basic weakness of *The Black Glove* then is that it is merely a symbolist play of the Maeterlinckian type. Unlike *Easter* or *Advent*, it lacks a human centre which would provide a dramatic force, both centripetal and centrifugal, to its verbal and emblematic effects. It is symbol, without the emotion that at once grounds it and enables it to soar.

12

Final Play

THE GREAT HIGHWAY (1909)

In view of its exalted theme and its function as the summary of his spiritual convictions, it is fitting that Strindberg's last play should mark his return to verse. Both as a dramatic epitaph and as a spiritual manifesto *The Great Highway*[1] possesses a dignity and grandeur which demand the lyrical intensity of poetry. Although it is perhaps not as formally revolutionary as *A Dream Play* or *The Ghost Sonata* and surely not as profound as the *Damascus* trilogy, Strindberg's final play reveals clearly that, even at the end of his life, both his art and his philosophy were still developing. And perhaps more importantly, that however ascetic his temperament or serene his vision became, he retained until the end his passionate involvement in human affairs and his capacity to comment ironically upon them.

The Great Highway is described by the author as 'A Wayfaring Drama with Seven Stations', a clear reminder of the circular structure already used in *To Damascus* Part I. Dahlström even suggests that 'This play comes to us as a fourth part of "To Damascus" both by its form and its content',[2] as the retrospective conclusion to the prospective trilogy. But whatever Strindberg's intentions actually were, little is gained by regarding it in this light because the trilogy seems to be complete in itself.

The problem facing the Hunter, Strindberg's alter ego, is whether to strive upwards to heaven, a difficult route full of dangers, or to make the easy descent to earth which is superficially attractive but ultimately degrading and enervating. Clearly, he is willing to make the spiritual effort, but signs indicate that he is not yet ready, 'the signpost has thrown out his arms as if in warning of the upward way' (p. 639). The fact is that he has 'lived too long among humanity and (I) gave away my soul, my heart, my thoughts; the rest they took, they stole—' (cf. Indra's Daughter). He must, like the aged Strindberg, take stock of his life and character, while avoiding, as far as possible, further corrupting contact with mankind. 'I'm always fighting. Fighting to keep my personal independence . . .' (p. 655). When he comes close to earth, like Indra's Daughter, he is stifled.[3] This is because, as *The Imitation of Christ* puts it: 'The further a man advances in the spiritual life, the heavier and more numerous he finds the crosses, for his ever deepening love of God makes more bitter the sorrows of his earthly exile' (p. 86). To escape from life, 'I cast my moorings, threw overboard my ballast, all that weighed, however dear—and see I rose', where 'no breath breathed by another poison my blood' (p. 640). In this rarified environment of Schopenhauerian asceticism, the Hunter after truth 'who took *His* name in vain', 'Bow[s] . . . in shame, meanest of all before Thy mighty throne' (p. 640). But the earth, equated here with woman the temptress, draws him to her. To decide which direction he shall take, he allows his body and will to relax so that his natural inclination reveals itself; in this way he discovers that he is still earthbound. 'That's *his* will. Down, down to rest and breathe the breath of warm humanity and smell the fragrance of the clover fields . . .' (p. 641).

Immediately, the world in which he finds himself is straight out of Schopenhauer. Presented by Strindberg in a series of savagely satirical cameos, it is the upside down, mirror image reality of *A Dream Play*. Hypocrisy, injustice, wrongful arrest and lies masquerading as truths are the norm. There even the purest spirit is in constant danger of being corrupted, and the natural condition of man is so self-deluded that ordinary men and women rarely catch a glimpse of the Divine from birth to death. Small wonder then that both the Hunter and the Japanese long for the fresh clear air of the mountains, which is the first and the ultimate (the right) station of the wayfarer where the most tempting sin is *pride*. The inspirational nature of this recurrence, its function in creating and affirming man's faith in God, define it as Kierkegaardian.

The second station is the land of the Windmills, at which each of its inhabitants tilt. The two Millers, Adam and Eve, dispute about which of them has priority over the East Wind until one of them forgoes his claim so that he can have his supper, while the other proves himself to be a petty bureaucrat. Even the Hunter's companion, the Traveller, vainly asks if this valley of human *vanities* is en route for the Promised Land. The Traveller imagines he can read the history and character of the young girl with the assistance of his 'good portion of acquired acuteness' (p. 649). Wise beyond her years, she condemns his conceit and recognises in the Hunter a fellow critic of human delusions. Contrary to the Traveller's opinion, they know that 'one cannot *know* [people]. But one grows acquainted' (p. 651). The prerogative of knowing men belongs uniquely to God. Men are irredeemably separate and alone. 'For every language is a foreign one and foreigners we are, each to the other, all travelling incognito' (p. 651). Indeed, we are 'incognito even to ourselves'.

The third station is Assesdean where *conceit* is the major sin; where error masquerades as truth and fools are valued as wise men. The absurd Blacksmith is considered to be the leading intellectual of the community and has been made Mayor. The intelligent, ironic and humble schoolmaster is regarded as a clown and must act the part: 'I'm the only sane fellow in the place—therefore I must make myself out as an imbecile or else they'll shut me up' (p. 656). So he is reduced to talking nonsense and playing the role of Scapegoat. Here, as in *A Dream Play*, Strindberg ridicules the Academicians who suppose they can discover the meaning of existence; a feat which would demand the ability to read the Mind of God. As an introduction to his satire on the sterility of human logic,[4] Strindberg 'sends up' the inductive methods of Poe's Dupin; a creation he admired in his youth. The most pompous 'logician' is the Blacksmith who regards mathematics as his forte. But although he is a fool, he is by no means soft. On the contrary, he is a despot. In this topsy turvy world of ours, the rulers are buffoons and brutal buffoons at that. Savagely, Strindberg satirises the abilities and the aspirations of the pretentious Blacksmith which, as revealed in his conversation, as so absurd that if it were not for his arrogance, they would be pathetic. The dialogue between him and the Schoolmaster, so full of non-sequiturs, false information, verbal confusions, puns and specious logic, is a superb prototype of that inconsequential absurdist style which has become so popular today in the various forms developed by Beckett, Adamov, Ionesco, Pinter and Stoppard.

The Blacksmith is archly respectable; he pays his taxes and settles his disagreements 'behind the stable' (p. 658), but as he admits himself, he is a 'terrible despot' (p. 659), a symbol of earthly confusion, conceit and power. He has written a play to extol the dictator,

Charles XII, while the more sensible Schoolmaster characterises the world in a tragedy entitled 'Pondweed'; and things being what they are, the former takes first prize. In Assesdean, the ass is the wisest of animals and the owl a numbskull. The Blacksmith can say: 'I have public opinion on my side and a party. All right thinking, enlightened, un-deluded people (p. 663). So much for democracy. 'The highest right is the highest wrong' (p. 663).

The fourth station is at 'Tophet'[5] which is Hell, where men are corrupted by *commerce*. It was once the home of the Hunter who remarks, 'In this town one is never recognised if one washes' (p. 665). It is a competitive, egotistical place where Darwin's principle of the survival of the fittest is acted out to the letter. 'Is it true that all of you in this town are descended from a monkey?' (p. 666). Here, 'people lurk like robbers in the ditches ready to spring out upon each other', even the attractive girl who stares out at them from the café window and eventually ensnares the Traveller in her emotional net. 'Before long she would have robbed you of your friends, separated you from your family, ruined you with your superiors and patrons. In a word, she would have devoured you' (p. 667). There are in Tophet, murderers, seducers and profiteers who survive because the rest of the community are liars and hypocrites. Yet it is the one place that might have held the Hunter to earth, because it contains his past, his memories and his child. To resist its temptations, he appeals for the aid of Christ against 'That fire which never can be quenched, which burns, but does not warm, which burns, but does not burn away' (p. 670).

Providing a method of escape from the ties of earthly affections is the Japanese, an honest man who has been corrupted by living at Tophet. Conscience-stricken at his sins, he tries to commit *hara kiri*; to die honourably in order to escape a life of shame: 'Death alone can liberate me, for the evil is in my very flesh. My soul I have purified by suffering' (p. 671). Having purged his soul, he hopes that death will redeem him. And so he approaches death with the true optimistic fatalism, or rather resignation, of the Buddhist. If only the Murderer could do the same but all he wishes is to make the Hunter a scapegoat for his own crimes. The principal sins of Tophet are those of *dishonesty* and *avarice*. Injustice and self-contradiction are so rampant that the Hunter can say of the Murderer who represents the inhabitants at their worst: 'To think of anything as perverse, you would have first to stand on your head and then turn yourself back to front' (p. 575).

The fifth station is 'Outside the Crematorium' where the Japanese is to put an end to his life. Here human life is indicted and disgust and desire for release are forcefully articulated. Irrespective of the way we have lived, in death we 'all must be alike as dust resembles dust' (p. 675). For the Japanese life appears much as it did to Indra's daughter: 'A line with many coils like the image of a script on blotting paper. Back to front—forward and back and up and down—but in a mirror you can read the script' (p. 677). When one behaves virtuously, one is condemned, and when one is malicious and brutal, one is treated as a saint. 'And yet all that is nothing, nothing compared with life's own facts—the humiliation of living, a mere skeleton in a dress of flesh, set going with tendon strings, by a small motor in the chest's engine room, run by the heat the belly's furnace can get up. And the soul, the spirit sits there in the heart, like a bird in the bosom's cage, in a hencoop or a fish creel' (pp. 667–8). The central motif of this tirade is the soul's burdensome imprisonment in the flesh, which recalls to Strindberg the horrors of an untenable determinism. He was harassed by the sense that we are not free to rise above the sensual and that the only way 'you little bird . . . can fly to your own land' is by dying. But he could never persuade himself that suicide was a justifiable course. The Hunter too has found disillusion and disappointment. Having begun with youthful ideals, he has now to admit that 'Beauty does not exist in life, cannot materialise down here. The ideal is never found in practice' (p. 670), and yet one must believe in perfection for otherwise one can never aspire to God. It is this belief that will enable the Japanese to part from this life at peace and with genuine hope of something better after death.

Station Six is 'At the Last Gate' where the Hunter will be judged. He is alone with only himself to offer as a counterbalance to his sins. Like another Rimbaud, he can say of his life on earth, 'I grew conscious that I was shut up in a madhouse, a penitentiary, sanatorium, then I wished myself out of my mind, that no one should guess my thoughts . . . I desired, I desired to be mad!' (p. 680). As he reviews his past, only the innocence and spontaneity of childhood seem to redeem him. The happiness of the child's world is the closest we can come on a solely human level to the pure love of

Christ. However, Strindberg's temperament was too complicated to accept permanently what he saw as the simple emotional values of 'Little Lord Jesus'. The ambivalence, the harsh retributions and the alternating deep pessimism and stern exaltation of Jehovah were more appropriate to his life.

The child the Hunter meets in *The Great Highway*, presumably his own child, is significantly named Mary and displays the same precocious, self-conscious feyness as all Strindberg's children. She does not recognise the Hunter but meeting her gives him the strength to face his death. This brief flash of sunlight will light him through the darkness. And so his final station takes place in 'The Dark Wood', where he seeks death but cannot find it. Human existence is compounded of lies and hypocrisy, false ideals and un-realised ambitions but we must not reject it out of hand because it is part of us; it is our emblem by which God distinguishes us. More often than not Christ's spilt blood is wasted or misused but men need a scapegoat, even in the unworthy person of the Hunter (Ahasuerus the Wandering Jew). Whatever he has done has been misinterpreted but through his suffering, patiently borne, there is hope of atonement for himself and others.

At last, the Tempter enters to provide him with the final obstacle to a peaceful death. This emissary from Hell offers the Hunter wealth and fame in the service of the Grand Duke (Satan!) but this offer of employment in Hell is simply a reproduction of all that the Hunter has found false and worthless here on earth. He knows that Satan is 'not asking for my services, he's asking for my soul' (p. 687). Skilfully, Strindberg portrays Satan as a capitalist of souls and the Tempter as an entrepreneur who speaks the language of an estate agent and a stock marketeer. After he has resisted this ultimate temptation, the Hunter, like Indra's daughter, comes to the end of his 'walk . . . among the sons of man' and must return to the 'pure air' (p. 687). He has learned that life is one continuous pitfall and that, despite appearances and protestations, one remains irrevocably *alone* until it is time to receive and be received by God.

Those glimpses of truth and beauty which indicate the Divine Presence are most clear in the rarified atmosphere of the mountains. When we involve ourselves in human society we lose such insights and are in danger of being tainted by the failings of those around us. As an old man ready for death, Strindberg had felt the attractions of the life of the religious solitary, the hermit, even the ascetic. Now, in this final play, the purity of his own spiritual vision was most important, though never *all* important. He was not the kind of man ever to lose interest completely in his fellow men but it is of the greatest significance that *The Great Highway* is perhaps his only play on aspirational themes, in which there is no trace of the notion of redemption through woman. He is resigned to the disappointments of earthly life and no longer struggles to reform or convert society to more worthy codes of conduct. His remaining energies are directed to preserving and improving his own mystical understanding. Only with an effort can he resist the urge to withdraw into himself completely. He has ceased to rebel both against God and man and writes his own epitaph of submission.

> There with the hermit I will stay and wait for release . . . he fought a fight with God and did not cease to fight until laid low, defeated by His almighty goodness. O, Eternal One, I'll not let go Thy hand, Thy hard hand, till Thou bless me, whose deepest suffering, deepest of human suffering was this—I could not be the one I longed to be. (p. 689)

So his dramatic career closes on a note of submission. He learns with Thomas À Kempis that 'You must live a dying life' (*The Imitation of Christ*, p. 88). Perhaps it was the only end possible. Only madmen and automatons can sustain lonely and comprehensive hatred for a lifetime. 'Even hatred can't stay in one's mind for ever' (*Creditors*). Sooner or later, the most virulent of men will need some compensation for their failures, some security for their old age and some comfort for their loneliness and the prospect of their impending death. So, in his final vision of life as a context of suffering for all, Strindberg achieved a fellow feeling with his kind (albeit as companions in misery) which had evaded him throughout much of his past career. And curiously, when he experienced a sense of unity with his own species in this life, his constant wish was to leave it as swiftly as possible.

13

Strindberg's Influence on Modern Drama

This chapter is both brief and tentative. For the most part my discussion of one writer's influence upon future generations must be tentative. To take Strindberg's case, it is clear that for every O'Neill from whom there is personal testimony which enables us to quote chapter and verse of specific influences, there are a dozen dramatists who are in the Swede's debt but whose links with him cannot be established by concrete or testimonial evidence. More often than not later writers are influenced by ideas, techniques and forms which are 'in the air', which belong to an ideological and artistic climate partially created by a great or, as in the case of Jarry or Maeterlinck, a not so great original. Where this is so it is extraordinarily difficult to *prove* that the innovator has influenced later generations.

In view of this, it is wise to try to isolate those general tendencies stimulated by the writer's work which have survived in the writings of later dramatists. Provided that sufficient specific examples are given, at least by this means one may hope to establish the strong implication of influence. Given that too much is not claimed and that one's conclusions are offered tentatively this approach can be valuable in suggesting interesting parallels. In the absence of direct testimony or full-length comparative analyses, the alternative seems to be the kind of highly tendentious comparisons supplied by Anthony Swerling in *Strindberg's Impact in France* which reduces later writers either to plagiarists or to accidental acolytes.

Strindberg's contribution to the development of twentieth-century drama has been thematic, formal, stylistic and technical. While it is neither possible in most cases, nor fruitful in the rest, to separate these various elements of his work from each other, in this chapter we shall isolate a number of decisive innovatory contributions he made at each of these particular levels. However, it must be kept in mind that to say he made a contribution does not mean that the subsequent development would not have happened in any case, nor does saying that he influenced future drama in a certain way imply that particular dramatists were consciously influenced by him nor that he was the only such influence, nor that his influence was necessarily salutary.

Among the most far reaching debts the modern theatre owes to Strindberg is a more fluid and vigorous presentation of human character. Strindberg's notion of dramatic character developed and in some respects changed throughout his life but in several ways it has transformed the manner in which later generations have written for the theatre. His relatively early conception of the characterless character has been profoundly important in breaking down traditional notions of the stable ego. Whether in his naturalist days when he propounded, as in the preface to *Miss Julie*, the idea of multiple motives or later when he helped to originate the expressionist demand for a vision of reality radiated by the unfolding ego of the protagonist, he reviled what we might term the 'kernel' theory of human character. Both in his theoretical writings and in his dramatic practice, he rejected the model of human beings as consisting of a definable essence or core surrounded by a less determinate area, comprising the individual's potentiality for creative, innovatory, paradoxical or chaotic behaviour. In its place he substituted an image of human beings as creatures whose surface behaviour is amorphous and highly volatile. This conception has reverberated both inside and outside the theatre in this century. We can see its effect in the work of such disparate writers as the expressionists, D. H. Lawrence, the absurdists, Kafka and the existentialists, for whom he cleared ground even when he did not directly inspire them.

Through his attempts to portray human character as non-static, as a constant flow of thoughts and feelings, Strindberg opened the way for those dramatists who wanted to show that men and women are not neatly wrapped packages of emotions. 'Where is the self— which is supposed to constitute one's character? Here and there and every place at once. One's ego is not a unit in itself; it is a conglomeration of reflexes, a complex of urges, drives, instincts, alternately suppressed and unleashed' (*Son of a Servant*, p. 203). This vision of man Strindberg believed to be ultra-modern, and indeed in the theatre so it has proved. It is a commonplace to note the decline of the well-made play but it is equally true to note the decline of the well-made character throughout twentieth-century drama.

In recent years there has been a spate of dramatic characters who are notable for a lack of integration in, and a general amorphousness of, their emotional lives so that they more closely resemble bundles of attitudes than integrated personalities. We have become familiar in the work of O'Neill, Williams, Osborne and Albee with characters who adopt a series of attitudes or behavioural poses which are only loosely traceable to motives. When Jimmy Porter plays the social rebel and George and Martha indulge their marital fantasies we tend to remember Gustav and Edgar and Alice who are similarly un-motivated except in some highly general sense which says more about the concerns of the author or the demands of his ideology than about the protagonists. Or again when virtually any central character in an O'Neill or a Tennessee Williams' play responds in a highly exaggerated fashion which makes their so-called motivation quite inadequate but yet in no way mitigates their theatrical presence, we tend to remember how Strindberg used this technique in *Miss Julie*, *Creditors* and at one level in *The Dance of Death* to produce arche-typal dramatic conflicts.

A particiular form of this general type of dramatic character can be seen in the emergence, even the dominance, of the emotional exhibitionist, the compulsive self-dramatiser. Strindberg certainly seems to have played a part in popularising the protagonist whose affective nerves seem almost perpetually to be exposed. Particularly in the American Theatre of the last fifty years, the male and female neurotic has predominated. In this respect, with the possible excep-tion of *The Dance of Death*, *Miss Julie* has provided the character and context which have been most widely used as models. O'Neill's work provides numerous examples: the sexual situation in *Reckless-ness*, the effect of suggestion in *Diff'rent*, Lavinia in *Mourning Becomes Electra* and the characters of Julie and Emperor Jones.[1] Other interesting comparisons can be drawn between Julie and Silia in Pirandello's *The Game as it is Played*, Blanche Dubois in Tennessee Williams' *A Streetcar Named Desire* and even the highly self-consciously agonised male anti-heroes of John Osborne.

Also we can discern Strindberg's contribution to the decline of the well-made character in his later plays. In the subsidiary presences of *A Dream Play*, *To Damascus* and *The Ghost Sonata*, we can trace the stylistic sources of the surreal figures of the Theatre of the Absurd, while in the bizarre 'characters' of the greatest Chamber Play we can also probably detect the inspirational origins of such patchwork quilt protagonists as Durrenmatt's Madame Zachanassian and Albee's Tiny Alice. Again, in the Stranger of *To Damascus* and the Hunter of *The Great Highway*, there are anticipations of the epic theatre notion of character as consisting of an amorphous bundle of conflicting motives and interests; a view which is exemplified by Brecht's Mother Courage and Arden's Sergeant Musgrave. In their different ways each of these characters is strongly symbolic, but is far more fully developed dramatically than stock expressionist or surrealist types. They resemble Indra's Daughter[2] and the Hunter of *The Great Highway* in being both more realised in their formal aspects and less realised in their human aspects than conventional characters.

Connected with his notions of character is Strindberg's drive, in many of his plays, to compose dialogue that directly expresses his characters' immediate thoughts: dialogue as what people think instead of what they say. Once again this produces an emotional surface that is mercurial and often inconsistent but which can achieve also a greater naturalism, and *naturalness* of speech. This desire to write dialogue that was less a literary artefact and more an immediate expression of human thoughts and feelings remained with Strindberg throughout his life. Even in the later expressionist dramas it was entirely appropriate that he should attempt to compose speech which directly communicated the protagonists' fleeting thoughts. Of course he did write great set speeches (they litter *To Damascus*) and contrived literary monologues (e.g. the dream speeches of *Miss Julie*), but from *The Father* through *The Dance of Death* to *The Pelican* his concern with natural speech as he understood it is evident. In this respect, O'Neill, Tennessee Williams and John Osborne in *A Long Day's Journey Into Night*, *The Glass Menagerie* and *Inadmissible Evidence* are in his debt. In these plays, the protagonists exhibit an almost embarrassing emotional nakedness encapsulated in dialogue that is startlingly reminiscent of that of the Captain, Julie, Adolphe and Alice in being as revealing as soliloquy without lacking the naturalistic details of interpersonal communication.

Strindberg's attraction to 'direct thought dialogue' is merely one indication of his concern with reinvigorating stage speech. A further instance is his attempt to revitalise and 'naturalise' dramatic monologue in *The Stronger*, which has influenced a number of plays, including Beckett's *Krapp's Last Tape*, Cocteau's *Le Bel Indifferent* and O'Neill's *Before Breakfast* (here the influence is direct—indeed to the point of plagiarism). Furthermore, his experimentation with pauses, silences and contrapuntal dialogue in the Chamber Plays and in parts of *A Dream Play* has had a lasting influence on the Theatre of the Absurd (via Artaud) and by a complicated process on Beckett and Pinter. The result of this development has been to introduce a new and vigorous form of ordinary speech into the theatre which has, by common consent, revolutionised the way modern playwrights compose dialogue. This heightened version of ordinary dialogue which can be used for highly dramatic, indeed melodramatic purposes (for example in Pinter's *The Birthday Party*) is anticipated most clearly in the Deans' scene in *A Dream Play* and the ghost supper of *The Ghost Sonata*.

Perhaps Strindberg's most important and fertile *technical* achievement has been his develpment of mental or interiorised scenery. One might find other sources of this (Büchner and Jarry, perhaps), but in such plays as *To Damascus*, *A Dream Play* and *The Ghost Sonata*, Strindberg provided the most powerful and influential dramatic realisations of it. Particularly in the first two of these plays, stage settings and scenery constitute the mental furnishings of the protagonists. For example, the two Rose Room settings in *To Damascus I* differ because the moods and attitudes of the Stranger have changed. The two scenes define and express through their physical appearance his feelings and his beliefs. In general, throughout the trilogy, scenery is menacing *because* he is afraid, music has a joyful sound *because* he is happy, events happen slowly *because* he is weary, the people around him are drab *because* he is miserable. This is pathetic fallacy with a vengeance and through the expressionists, has had long-term effects on modern drama and cinema.

From the German expressionists, *The Cabinet of Dr Caligari* and O'Neill's *The Emperor Jones* to Tennessee Williams' *Camino Real* and Robbe-Grillet's *Last Year at Marienbad*, this innovation has borne fruit. Indeed, so much so that it has become a staple technique of contemporary cinema, quite assimilable by modern audiences. Even television dramatists appear to use it without too many qualms. However, in recent times, it was probably Arthur Miller in *Death of a Salesman* who used the device with greatest effect to depict the disintegration of Willy Loman. He experimented with it more radically yet still successfully in *After The Fall*, employing abrupt transitions, hallucinations, symbolic images, juxtapositions of time, place, mood and theme to portray inner conflicts in the same way that Strindberg does in the Convent and Banquet scenes of *To Damascus*.

The major advantage of this trend in the modern theatre has been to enable playwrights to portray the thought processes of their characters by means of purely notional devices. It has provided modern dramatists with a technique that is comparable with, though of course, not nearly as fertile as the novelist's device of interior monologue and direct psychological analysis. Yet there are two dangers. Writers who have taken over expressionistic techniques more from a desire for theatrical experiment than because they are either natural to their way of writing or necessary for their dramatic purposes have usually produced unsuccessful plays. Thus it is generally true that O'Neill's *Behind Life* plays, which he wrote in imitation of Strindberg were in these respects among his worst, while Tennessee Williams' uncharacteristic *Camino Real* is not among *his* best. The other danger has been the temptation for playwrights to introduce crypto first person ruminations on their own narrow personal obsessions. One could cite here among the best, David Mercer's *Ride a Cock Horse* and John Osborne's *Inadmissible Evidence*.

A major contribution made by Strindberg to the *form* of modern drama and one associated with the expressionists was his use of dream style and content. Here we can definitely pinpoint Strindberg and Freud with their great works of 1901, as the true, though not necessarily the first, precursors of this modern obsession. While it must be conceded that many of the resulting techniques can be explained by reference to *The Interpretation of Dreams*, it is their use in the novel which the symbolism of that book best explains. In the theatre, we can most successfully trace the influence back to playwrights of whom Strindberg is overwhelmingly the most important.

To understand the nature of the impact of *A Dream Play* and its Preface on later dramatists, we must not imagine that it is limited only to plays *about* dreams or dreaming. Certainly some are, such as Ernst Toller's *Die Wandlung* (1919), but the most important are not. The primary characteristics of Strindbergian and subsequent twentieth-century dream theatre are the disintegration of linear narrative, the introduction of time slips and dislocations, the rejection of spatial continuities and the development of fluid, often 'unreal' scenery, the replacement of observed, external reality with a symbolic representation of it, the use of optical illusions, absurdities, inconsequentialities and the blurring of a character's identity by means of masks, dopplegangers, types and transformations. The object of all this is to project a new and revealing way of looking at the world around us and of our place in it in order to expose with fresh dramatic clarity the delusions and irrationalities by which we live.

The influence of dream theatre on the Theatre of the Absurd is so apparent and has been so fully traced by Martin Esslin in his book of that title that little needs to be said here. It should be mentioned, however, that of the Absurdists probably only Arthur Adamov would admit to being consciously influenced by Strindberg. Nevertheless Adamov helped to define many of the movement's characteristically Strindbergian dream themes, man's isolation, the relativity of truth, the baffling strangeness of so-called ordinary events, the failure of reason to penetrate life's mysteries, and he provided in characteristically Strindbergian words what Esslin regards as a statement of its essence: 'What is there? I know first of all that I am. But who am I? All I know of myself is that I suffer. And if I suffer it is because at the origin of myself there is mutilation, separation. I am separated. What I am separated from—I cannot name it. But I am separated' (*The Confession*). Moreover, other writers associated with the movement has made statements of intention highly reminiscent of Strindberg's. For instance, Ionesco summed up the influence of dream theatre particularly well in the following personal declaration: 'Theatre is for me the outward projection on to the stage of an inner world; it is in my dreams, in my anxieties, in my obscure desires, in my internal contradictions that I, for one, reserve for myself the right of finding my dramatic subject matter.' Also Artaud—a notable precursor of Absurdist theatre—writes in *The Theatre and Its Double* that in his Theatre of Cruelty 'the reality of imagination and of dreams will here be seen on an equal footing with everyday life'. It is interesting to examine the plays of Jean Genet in the light of this remark, particularly *The Balcony*.

However, perhaps the most typically modern dreamplay which bears considerable similarity to Strindberg's work is Tennessee Williams' *Camino Real*. In it all the classic ingredients of the theatre of dreams are fused with those of expressionism. In fact, Williams wrote a foreword to *Camino Real* which echoes that of *A Dream Play* very closely. In it he uses such phrases as 'existence outside of time', 'a play of no specific locality', 'continually dissolving and transforming images of a dream', 'continual flow' and 'dream-like images'. In view of this, it is difficult to believe that he had not read Strindberg's preface and play.

On the thematic level, Strindberg's work served to popularise two themes or rather to popularise them in the particular guise in which he presented them. A notion of his which has sounded persistent echoes in twentieth-century literature is that of life as a kind of confinement. In *Easter*, *A Dream Play*, the Chamber Plays and *The Great Highway* earthly existence is depicted as claustrophobic, repetitive, meaningless, and human beings are shown as waiting for release (by apotheosis, death by fire or through enlightenment or resignation) from life's prison (symbolised by the house, marriage, human degradation, human intercourse). It is difficult to say to what extent Strindberg's pessimistic vision of life has directly influenced later writers but there is no doubt at all that remarkably similar themes are to be found in Kafka's novels[4] and the plays of Sartre, Beckett, Pinter and the Absurdists. Indeed, so prevalent is the trend with its sparse enclosed sets, its disorientated characters, waiting, pacing, procrastinating, circling around each other, menacing and feeling persecuted that Laurence Kitchin has coined the term Compressionism to describe it.[5]

Even a large-scale work of Strindberg's such as *The Dance of Death* possesses this claustrophobic mood and significantly, as in the plays mentioned above, the mood is reinforced by theme. Life is presented as a jail sentence in which human beings are condemned to torment each other. Sartre's vision of Hell in *Huis Clos* was far from being original; it was rather an explicit symbolic summation of a literary and dramatic tendency which had found its finest nineteenth-century expression in Strindberg.[6] Of course, Strindberg gave it spiritual dimensions by linking it to his notion of hell on earth but his treatment of the idea in domestic contexts with their reverberations of vampirism and internecine sexual conflict, his scenic and dialogue experiments in the trilogy, *A Dream Play* and the Chamber Plays, his presentation of central characters in *To Damascus*, *Easter* and *The Ghost Sonata* (who are hounded by often irrational forces and harassed by their own imaginations), all served to provide a paradigm of the genre.

Laurence Kitchin perceptively notes that 'the dynamics of claustrophobia can be enlisted by progressively filling the set with furniture or reducing the size of the set as the action goes forward. The line of development stretches from Ibsen and Strindberg by way of O'Neill and even *Journey's End* to Beckett and Pinter.'[7] When we think of the Banquet scene in *To Damascus*, the Quart D'Heures, the domestic scenes in *A Dream Play* and *The Ghost Sonata* as well as the other Chamber Plays, it is highly probable that the Swede's examples were far more seminal here than the Norwegian's.

A further element of compressionism which reinforces its claustrophobic quality is the manner in which characters hound or menace each other. Of course, Strindberg's characters are constantly persecuting or being persecuted by their fellows whether by suggestion or hypnotism, as in such early plays as *Miss Julie* and *Creditors*, or by the Powers or correspondences of guilt in such later plays as *Crimes and Crimes* and *Easter*. Even physical oppression which is so apparent in such compressionist plays as *Endgame* and *The Brig* is evident in the appropriate claustrophobic contexts of the Mummy in her closet of *The Ghost Sonata*. Indeed, together with the Young Lady in the Hyacinth Room, agoraphobically trapped, physically persecuted by the Cook and menaced by the housekeeper, we have perhaps the classic case of compressionist character relations.

However, there is one major respect in which Strindberg differs from virtually all modern compressionists and one which serves to make him a great playwright. This is that for him the notions that life is an incarceration of either the body or the spirit, or that life is hell on earth, are not premises as they appear to be for Kafka or Beckett. The Stranger and Indra's Daughter undergo a process of self-discovery and education through experience from which they learn compressionist 'truths'. There are few *a priori* truths in Strindberg's plays. He does not simply present an image of the way things are derived from certain ontological preconceptions. Instead, he provides a *dialectical inquiry* into the nature of human life which, by its very form, would appear to be more appropriate for dramatisation.

Closely linked with the idea of life as a form of imprisonment is a new topic or at least an old topic in a new guise explored by

Strindberg; that is the theme of marital hell, or marriage as a cannibalistic, destructive union. This image of marriage has constantly been used, as he used it, as a microcosm of life itself. Here there is no doubt that such plays as O'Neill's *Bread and Butter* and *A Long Day's Journey into Night*, Albee's *Who's Afraid of Virginia Woolf*, Osborne's *Look Back in Anger*, Anouilh's *Waltz of the Toreadors* and E. A. Whitehead's *Alpha-Beta* are derivative from *The Dance of Death* and perhaps also from *The Father*. Moreover there are representations of marital misery in Ionesco's *Amedée* and *Les Chaises* which seem very likely to owe something, respectively, to the scenes between Indra's Daughter and the Lawyer in *A Dream Play* and the supper scene in *The Ghost Sonata*. Incidentally to say this is not to criticise these authors or their plays, it is simply to state the facts.

Through this vision of marriage Strindberg has encouraged those representations, so widespread today, of sexual relationships as alternating between love and hatred, emotional masochism and sadism. Implicit in this portrayal is the identification of the sexual drive as something either destructive or grotesque. Inevitably, where marriage is seen as a battleground and heterosexual love a torment, the consequences to all men and women are bound to be bleak and degrading. Here Strindberg has close similarities with Artaud's Theatre of Cruelty and with such modern playwrights as Tennessee Williams and Edward Albee. The images of sexual horror or disgust that are prevalent in modern theatre derive at least partly from *The Father, Miss Julie, Creditors* and *The Dance of Death* which reflect Strindberg's sexual pessimism at its most unrelenting.

A particular genre fathered by Strindberg which has had a notable place in the theatre of the last sixty years or so is the Station drama. *To Damascus I* is an example and *The Great Highway* is actually described by Strindberg himself as 'a wayfaring drama with seven stations'. While Strindberg derived this dramatic form from the Calvaric Stations of the Cross and used it to portray his protagonist's gradual awakening to the spiritual nature of reality, the expressionist Georg Kaiser in *From Morn to Midnight* (1916) used it to satirise modern industrial civilisation.[8] Nevertheless, the expressionists took from Strindberg the idea of replacing conventional dramatic structures with a series of tableaux or stations which are symbolic. In addition, they included in their plays characters who are types performing actions that are symbolic in locales of no specific spatio-temporal identity. In common with Strindberg, they divide their plays into stations, having little external connection with each other, in order to plot the courses through which their protagonists are compelled by their inner drives to go. Again, like Strindberg, German expressionists frequently use the Station Drama to depict their own emotional spiritual traumas.

Without doubt, the finest developments of this genre, and the only ones to challenge comparison with Strindberg's own work, occur in the plays of Bertolt Brecht. It would be wrong to argue that Brecht was directly influenced by Strindberg,[9] but it is highly probable that through his involvement with the expressionist movement Brecht found prototypes for his epic theatre which had their embryonic origin in a play such as *The Great Highway* as well as in the early plays of Georg Büchner. From his early quasi-expressionist plays like *Baal* and *In the Jungle of the Cities* through the didactic plays of the thirties to the mature work of, for example, *The Caucasian Chalk Circle*, he experimented with the genre albeit in an innovatory manner. In more recent years, we can see traces of it in the work of such dramatists as John Arden and Edward Bond.

Finally, Strindberg has helped to introduce a new kind of protagonist—the anti-hero—into literature in general and the theatre in particular. Here, we must acknowledge immediately that in this respect Strindberg was just one of a number of innovators and not even the first. However, it is certainly true that in the theatre Strindberg most vividly portrayed the *religious* outsider. Faced with the irrational nature of life, the Strindbergian hero feels alienated from God and divided in himself. While he can discern patterns in the world around him and coherence in his own psychology, ultimately they fail to satisfy him. The result is that he feels that he has no identity and that his life is meaningless, though such despair is usually the prelude to a new, more real affirmation of religious belief.

The protagonists of plays like *To Damascus* and *The Great Highway* can therefore be seen as prototypes of such modern outsiders as Steppenwolf, Meursault, Antoine Roquentin and Kafka's K. Strindberg created characters who resemble those of the existentialist tradition in its Nietzschean and Kierkegaardian forms as well as characters who anticipate the anti-heroes of the Absurdists. No playwright in the history of the Western Theatre has so successfully invented and adapted dramatic form to project his own emotional and spiritual problems through first person protagonists as Strindberg. By doing so he provided an ideal model for those dramatists who have had similar drives. And since the desire to communicate a vision of the way things are, taking as its centre the artist's own personality, has become increasingly prevalent, Strindberg's influence here has been ubiquitous. Whether it has been on the whole salutary is another matter. The artist as tormented rebel, romantic outsider, has perhaps become the most tedious cliché in modern literature, and the pitfall of young writers everywhere. Strindberg, together with the German Romantics, Dostoievsky and the Expressionists, must take his share of blame for its predominance.

14
A Personal Epilogue:
Bizarre Ideas and 'Hysteria'

Strindberg's originality and importance as a writer cannot be assessed by considering his ideas in a purely theoretical light. As we have seen, most of his beliefs about life, society and God were culled from a wide variety of sources, and although the overall pattern of his thought is probably unique to himself, the individual views which make up that pattern are almost invariably second-hand. Consequently, on a solely philosophical level, it is more rewarding as well as more interesting to study Kierkegaard, Nietzsche and Swedenborg directly than Strindberg himself. Indeed, it is only when this Strindbergian hodge-podge of borrowed ideas is dramatised, when it is introduced to the catalyst of his artistic personality, with all its conflicts and contradictions, that something profoundly original results. It is not sufficient to define this simply as 'great drama'; it is more exactly the transmutation of social and religious philosophy into a powerful and persuasive body of dramatised thought and feeling that is instantly relevant not so much to the lives we all lead as to the human condition itself. Basically this has been the implicit thesis of the present book. Unfortunately, the implications of this thesis pose a dilemma for its author.

On the one hand, I am convinced that Strindberg is one of the world's major dramatists and that his plays, particularly those of the post-Inferno period, can only be understood and wholly appreciated in terms of his ideas. On the other hand, I am also convinced that most of the ideas he embraced are in themselves either absurd, distasteful or pernicious. Schopenhauer and Nietzsche seem to me to be indisputably great philosophers but their influence on Strindberg was not particularly salutary. Schopenhauer's work fed his growing morbidity and misanthropy, while his eventual acquaintance with Nietzsche's ideas encouraged his intolerance, his arrogance and his elitist prejudices. As for Kierkegaard, although he was undoubtedly a great social critic, he appears to me to be a man with a hypersensitive, even crippled temperament who elevated his own peculiar guilts and resentments into a universal religious philosophy. His ideas helped to increase Strindberg's anti-rationalism while appearing to justify the Swede's natural tendency towards masochistic self-abasement; in this case promoting a desperate posture of humility before God.

My response to the rest of Strindberg's ideological mentors is even more unfavourable. I find Swedenborgianism fascinating as mythology but absurd as a body of ideas with any pretension to truth. Thomas À Kempis's *The Imitation of Christ*, which Strindberg professed to love so much, seems to me to be repellent; being life-denying, humanly degrading and spiritually sycophantic. Moreover, I feel that I am under no obligation in the present context to make allowances for the age in which it was written. Finally, I find it difficult to say anything commendatory about the host of secondary ideological influences on the Swede's plays; for instance, Wagner, von Hartmann, Maeterlinck, Nordau, and his fairy-tale version of Hindu-Buddhism. In short, I feel that one of the most bewildering oddities about Strindberg's plays is that he was able to embody highly eccentric ideas, not to say medieval superstitions, in the most revolutionary dramatic forms and, moreover, to endow them with dramatic truth.

The point of making these personal declarations is that I imagine they would be accepted by many people today. In fact some would go further and deny that Strindberg was a philosophical dramatist at all. For instance, R. J. Kaufmann writes: 'Strindberg is the least philosophical of dramatists. There is no real thought going on his plays. True he busily collects ideas in the rain forests of the late nineteenth-century theosophising, but they are preserved in his plays only as dead, period decorations, preserved flowers in the crowded Victorian interiors of his scene.'[1] Those who do not share these or my opinions, of course, are not likely to have any crucial difficulties about appreciating the possibility that Strindberg's ideas are an important source of his dramatic achievement. But for those who do, I want to argue that it is possible to feel as I do and still maintain the greatness of Strindberg the dramatist and, moreover, of Strindberg the dramatist of ideas. First though, I need to explain how one can combine distaste for these ideas with a prolonged effort to discuss Strindberg's plays in terms of them; in the present case it does not seem to be sufficient to conclude, as does Birgitta Steene (albeit correctly): 'Certainly no Swedish writer before or after him has quite combined his creative vigor, linguistic versatility, or acute sense of drama with his encompassing vision of a transitional cultural epoch and his metaphysical probing.' While no one has quite matched the emotional intensity of his works—in that respect Strindberg's own words have remained true—'I do not have the greatest intellect, but the fire; my fire is the greatest in Sweden,'[2] at the end of a study as thematically orientated as the present one, it is well-nigh obligatory to ask why, if the ideas are so bad, spend so much time and space analysing them?

On one level this is an easy question to answer. As we have seen throughout this book, the changing philosophical and religious content of Strindberg's thought stimulated his constant experimentation with dramatic forms and styles. And ideas that we would probably call politically, socially or morally reactionary were capable of doing so because there is no necessary connection between the impact of an idea and the nature of the form best adapted to express it. It is just as likely that reactionary as well as progressive ideas will require new dramatic forms and styles to embody them. All that is desirable is that in some way they are new or strange. Only the ideologically commonplace is, by its nature, unlikely to generate anything theatrically revolutionary, and whatever may be said about Strindberg's curious bundle of ideas, it was *not* commonplace.

Then again, the dottiness of many of his ideas is frequently transformed as they are filtered by his artistic sensibility. As we have often seen in the foregoing pages, the intrusion of his emotional problems into his work served to provide a paradigmatic account of man's attempt to make sense of his life and to make peace with his own drives. Looked at from this point of view, his dramatised thought reveals a complex personality undergoing a crucial and life-long existential struggle. In the dramatic context, we can examine his thought as it is forged by the emotional demands of a profoundly contradictory human being attempting first to conquer, and later to come to terms with, a recalcitrant world.

Initially, this struggle is important because the artistic personality is interesting and is compelled to adopt fascinating strategies to extricate itself from, or reconcile itself to, conflicts that are archetypal. Among the latter are issues which are universal as well as others which have been crucial to modern culture; God and man, men versus women, illusion and reality, rebellion or submission, duty and desire, faith or reason, conscience and egotism, sexual licence or restraint, liberty and determinism, self and the other, guilt and redemption and so on. Of all modern ideological antitheses, perhaps only those concerning class issues were not dealt with in any depth by Strindberg in his *plays*. Those that were generally transcend the particular philosophical and religious theories through which they are expressed, for instance, one notably *modern* aspect of this lifelong struggle is the articulation of a variety of attitudes and concepts which are recognisably existentialist. 'Alienation', 'dread', 'choice', 'rebellion', 'bad faith', 'despair', 'authenticity', 'absurdity', are some of the terms we have come to associate with the *broad* existentialist movement that spans Kierkegaard and Dostoievsky, Heidegger and Camus,[3] and although we cannot place Strindberg's work in a tradition with which his differences are as great as his similarities, it is undeniable that all the concepts listed above apply in some sense to the *central* concerns of his work. While he did not think in terms of 'being' and 'consciousness' and so on, he formulated and faced the problems crucial to existentialists in a manner that offers a unique perspective on them.

Faced with a universe that is resistant to one's needs and hopes, which is painfully inadequate to one's spiritual yearnings, cruelly destructive of one's social and sexual integrity and constantly indifferent to one's desire for emotional fulfilment, there are two possible, extreme responses; resignation and rebellion, that of Job and that of Jacob. The significance of Strindberg's protagonists is the manner in which they alternate between the two so as to reveal the common ground between them. Although finally and often grudgingly his central characters retreat from the world, we can never feel that their conflicts have ceased. Only death will finally release them. From Lucky Peter to the Hunter of *The Great Highway*, they pass through a series of social and religious temptations which define the precariousness of human life. As they curse mankind and blaspheme against God, Strindberg's protagonists teach us the irresolvable difficulty of matching human demands to the realities of life. They teach us above all the necessity of seeking experience of all kinds, of passing through the vale of sorrows, if we are ever to be able to reject this world of illusions and adjust to some more profound conception of reality. And, by the latter, is not meant invariably a sterile or escapist religiosity but an appreciation of life in all its dimensions and, in particular, in the context of its all pervading and intimate connections with the spiritual world. For Strindberg, as for the Christian existentialist, the only authentic life is one in which we strive for self-fulfilment in the full realisation of the spiritual presence within and around us. Whenever his protagonists achieve, or retreat into, an attitude of resignation or acceptance, it is after 'trying out' life to the full. Almost always, they have earned the right to their pessimism and world weariness.

Erik O. Johanneson makes a generalisation about the novels which would apply equally well to the plays: 'Strindberg's novels, if read in sequence, create a gigantic Bildungsroman depicting the modern writer's quest for a set of values that will give order and meaning to his world.'[4] Each of Strindberg's heroes must make his journey, resist his temptations, endure the misery of existence and learn the lessons of his life, before he can understand the design of God's universe and his own place in it. Taken together they practically exhaust all the existential strategies available to men who are conscious that they are inhabiting a spiritual world. But more broadly, Strindberg's dramatic corpus works through the matrix of possibilities confronting those who are aware of the seemingly irresolvable disharmonies in our lives. It demonstrates that understanding and personal peace must be fought for and that the struggle is continuous, for there are no such things as *a priori* knowledge or intrinsic goodness in Strindberg's world; except possibly in his child characters who are for the most part dramatic failures. His heroes are existential seekers; they create, mar and fulfil themselves through their choices. Thus the existentialist dimension of his thought transcends or rather substructures the particular philosophical doctrines in which he expressed it.

So the particular philosophical tactics deployed by Strindberg in his dramatic debates do not crucially affect the wider existential, moral or theological strategy. But this, of course, once again raises the question of why we should concern ourselves with the philosophical tactics. Would it not have been better to have gone straight to the strategical discussion? I think there are two reasons why this was not advisable. First of all, it would have meant omitting a considerable amount of detail which adds depth and subtlety to the wider, more basic debates. Secondly, the specific theorising makes intelligible much of the narrative and technical development of the plays.

Despite what has been said so far we must remember that, however philosophically inclined a dramatist is, the ideological content of his work should not be considered in the same light as philosophical theories themselves. Our primary concern in this area is not with truth values or even with rationality, but rather with the manner in which a particular idea can be used to illuminate a range of experience. Even in the most ascetic, theoretical plays ideas will be developed, pulled out of shape, blurred or made vivid by being expressed through the medium of plot and character. Indeed, if the drama is at all successful in its realisation of life, it will not be possible to produce a complete description of its ideas without referring to the situations in which they are developed.

For instance it is clear that Swedenborgian themes as they appear in *To Damascus* and *The Great Highway* differ at least to the extent that the Stranger is a rebel who demands understanding, while the Hunter is a man of resignation who seeks peace and rest. In the trilogy Strindberg uses the Swedenborgian stages to present a redemptive vision of human life, in his dramatic epilogue he uses them to create a transcendent vision. Again, the Hindu–Buddhist notion of Karma permeates both *A Dream Play* and *The Ghost Sonata*, but the mood and mesage of the plays are quite different. As it emerges in the very different worlds of Indra's Daughter and the Student and Young Lady, it acquires distinct and often unique resonances. So while it is possible to classify these plays together as sharing a common ideology, it is never possible to give a full description of them in terms of this ideology.

There is a simple yet powerful argument to show why this should be so. In successful dramas, philosophical ideas are expressed through well-realised characters and situations. In such plays the characters and situations form the medium but the ideas only constitute part of the message. The reason for this is that the medium conditions the message; the former elaborates and enriches the latter by making it concrete. Unlike abstract codes or symbolism, characters and situations in plays are not ideologically neutral. An idea expressed in two different symbolisms or even in two different languages (say, French and German) remains essentially as it is, but an idea expressed in two different scenes not only acquires characteristics peculiar to each scene, but becomes an integral part of each scene. To remove that idea from the two scenes would be to divorce it from those implications and resonances which give it significance in them. On the other hand, to describe it within the context of each scene would involve us in the task of detailing those implications and resonances. Now since these latter are dependent upon the situations and characters which presumably differ in the two scenes, the idea as it appears in one scene would be distinct from the way in which it appears in the other. Thus in both cases it would hardly be possible to isolate the idea or offer a neutral definition of it, adequate to accounting for its role in different scenes.

So it appears that an idea is transmuted by the scene in which it occurs and is, in some important sense, inseparable from it. In view of this it is not at all inevitable that a philosophically odd idea should be a dramatically odd idea or that pernicious ideas viewed philosophically should be pernicious in plays. If they are transmuted by the dramatic context, it is at least possible (in practice probable) that the contribution of the medium will either make them less absurd or less pernicious or even not absurd or pernicious at all.

Nevertheless, in attempting to say why we should bother with Strindberg's philosophy, I have not yet faced the basic problem. This is that despite the experimental vigour and his undoubted dramatic talent, to many people his plays seem undisciplined, hysterical, pious, humourless, morbid, self-obsessed, bigoted and even diseased or fascist. And much of the most obvious evidence for such views can be found among the strange philosophical and religious ideas that influenced him. Certainly there seems to be little point in denying that most if not all of the adjectives listed above are applicable to his work at various times. Indeed the only plausible way to defend his work is to admit his faults. This has been one aim of the present book, another has been to show that his virtues are often related to his faults.

The three objections to his work which are heard most frequently are those of character incredibility, emotional obsessiveness or one-sidedness and an almost hysterical lack of dramatic control. I have tried in my discussion of the pre-Inferno plays to absolve Strindberg from the first charge, while in my discussion of the later symbolist-expressionist plays I have tried to show that their presentation of character raises a different range of problems and demands from those of realism. In other words, it is not entirely appropriate in a play that reflects the world through the often distorted mental universe of its tormented protagonist to demand that its characters resemble those we encounter in everyday life. Unfortunately this will not satisfy those who feel that Strindberg's characters are not so much unbalanced as that their reactions and dialogue change to the point at which they become blatantly contradictory.

I must confess that, on the surface, this is quite true. After we have provided all possible theoretical justifications for Strindberg's fluid treatment of character, there still remains a residue of doubt. It seems that fundamentally he depicted people as volatile and contradictory because that is how he was himself and hence how he imagined others to be. Ultimately there is something highly idiosyncratic, even wayward, about Strindberg's presentation of human beings, but we can concede this and still argue that his characters do not lack consistency; that, at a deeper level, they are perfectly intelligible. It is merely that the logic of their behaviour is to be grasped by penetrating beneath the conscious surface; and this does not mean just to the conventional level of 'hidden motives or drives' but to the deep structures of their psychology; to the layers of their unconscious mind. Complex, subtle and elusive as they are, the characters of the Captain, Julie, Edgar and the Stranger do yield to this kind of depth analysis. Such a response demands effort from an audience and expertise from actors, but not noticeably more than is required in order to understand our fellow men at their least predictable moments. For the most part our responses are habitual, only occasionally do we innovate, responding 'out of character'— creatively or chaotically. In his desire for compression and economy and in his expressionistic dramas, Strindberg leaves out most of the habits and concentrates on these rarer occasions when people are at their most vulnerable and revealing: when, as if by some kind of behavioural free-association, they expose their deepest feelings and desires.

The second criticism—that of one-sidedness and obsessiveness— has in part been dealt with both in respect of the pre- and post-Inferno plays. I have shown how the depiction of the sex war in the great naturalistic plays is far from bigoted and that the religious obsessions in his later plays spring not from dogma but from a complex and varied response to life as he experienced it.[5] Yet might we still not say that he is guilty as charged since we know that in virtually any play of his the misogynistic tirade will be introduced and that sooner or later his protagonist will lapse into morbid pessimism? To do so would I think be unreasonable in view of the variety of sources and types of the former and the complex, indeed comprehensive, searches that precede the latter. To illustrate the richness of his misogynistic treatment of marriage, for example, we can compare the manner in which he portrays the growth of marital disillusion, the decline of love into domestic routine, in any of his naturalistic plays, with Act 3 Scene 3 of *To Damascus* III and the marriage scene between Indra's Daughter and the Lawyer in *A Dream Play*. Each is utterly different from the other yet each deals with essentially the same situation. Nor should we assume that his despair is either final or easily come by. It invariably represents the conclusion of a lengthy search for values and is closer to weariness than to pessimism, since the search is always liable to be resumed as soon as either his energies or his inspiration returns. To this degree, his plays do not have conclusions, merely resting places— hence their circular structure. In sum, it is not the fact that Strind- berg, in common with Dante or Milton, Tolstoy or Dostoievsky, Proust or Kafka, has obsessions that is crucial but what results from them.

The third point about dramatic control is fundamental in Strind- berg's case. The analyses contained in this book have shown that he had a powerful awareness of theatrical styles—their scope and limita- tions, that he developed themes and projected ideas with considerable rigour and precision and that he had a lifelong appreciation of how to exploit dramatic forms to meet the demands of content. Moreover, as can be seen from his theoretical writings, these achievements were fully intended and testify to his ability to put his dramatic ideas into practice. Even in those cases where his intentions (e.g. in the *Miss Julie* preface) were not fulfilled in the play he actually wrote, we can generally find that his artistic sense triumphed over sterile theory. Whatever we might think about Strindberg's best twenty plays, we cannot plausibly argue that *generally* he did not achieve in them what he wanted. The argument and analysis contained in the present book testify to this fact and represent an answer to criticisms of his dramatic control.

On the general question of Strindberg's hysteria, it is illuminating to contrast his work with Ibsen's. It is quite understandable to argue that *Miss Julie* is almost hysterical in contrast with, say *Hedda Gabler* or that *When We Dead Awaken* is a far more economical and technically well-made play than *The Great Highway*. Again we could be excused for believing that *Peer Gynt* and *Brand* are both more magnanimous and intellectually clear than *The Road to Damascus*. But precisely what have we said when we have made such comparisons? I would suggest that we have said nothing more than that we do not understand Strindberg's work. At best we have said we do not like Strindberg because he is not Ibsen and this is an expression of taste not of judgement. It may very well be that the one is less restrained, less precise and less lucid than the other, but to say this does not, of necessity, say anything about their respective aesthetic merits. To underline this point we might go on to suggest that, even if we grant the 'deficiencies' attributed above to Strindberg's three plays, nowhere in Ibsen's corpus can we find anything like the emotional vigour and colour of *Miss Julie*, the theatrical inventiveness and symbolic mastery of *A Dream Play* or the intellectual complexity of *To Damascus*. That we tend to value such qualities as restraint and economy so highly says more about the liberal-humanist tradition than it does about drama itself. We might, with equal justice, applaud emotional directness, iconoclasm, primitivism, high invention and uncompromising innovation. Of course, even better, we might refuse to accept that such alternatives are, as as they perhaps appear to be at first sight, mutually exclusive. And, I would argue, that if we do and examine Strindberg a little more closely, we might discover that he is romantic on the surface and classical at a deeper level, while Ibsen is the reverse.

Now this again does not *necessarily* make Strindberg a better playwright than Ibsen any more than the latter's capacity for restraint and naturalistic authenticity *necessarily* makes him superior. Indeed no single quality can define a writer's stature and Ibsen shares many of Strindberg's virtues, just as Strindberg's plays as we have seen, are generally only ostensibly uncontrolled. At a deeper level, they reveal an astonishingly complex intellectual structure. The point of contrasting the two men's work was to suggest that if Ibsen gains and Strindberg loses when viewed from one point of view, from another their positions are reversed. Unfortunately, though, for

Strindberg the virtues of technical fluency and balance, which are so obvious in Ibsen's work, are those which are most highly prized in traditional Western theatre. Strindberg's obsessions, however accomplished in their execution, with characterless characters, multiplicity of motives, rejection of linear narrative, the representation of immediate thoughts in dialogue, were not only dramatic innovations, but run contrary to most of the dramatic demands of our still largely realistic theatre.

In the last analysis, I do not believe we can attribute the survival of Strindberg's work simply to his literary ability or his theatrical flair. A great dramatist, even more than a great novelist or a great poet, must possess an intrinsic sense of emotional rightness or psychological proportion. Beneath their surface excesses, Strindberg's plays do, more often than not, possess an ineradicable sense of dramatic perspective or balance which enables him to present eccentric ideas and often bizarre human characters in concrete situations which illuminate our shared experience. This dramatic sense is what anchors the rhetoric, the symbolism and the occult fantasies and what enables him to develop apparently sterile or absurd ideas with human understanding and originality. Nowhere perhaps is this more perfectly demonstrated than in *The Ghost Sonata* where pantomime characters, melodramatic events and weird ideas are superbly balanced and somehow 'grounded' by the totally credible integrity of the existential situation with its very real moral and spiritual conflicts. So philosophical ideas are successfully incarnated and while they do not cease to be bizarre they do serve as material to be deployed within the behavioural strategies of credible characters.

Essentially then, Strindberg's plays remain vital and important today because they represent certainly the most persistent, and probably the most profound, dramatic investigation yet achieved in the modern theatre of three themes that are of perennial and central human concern. Most basically, he sought a reason and justification for man's existence. By doing so he tried to find a way of coping with our essential alone-ness, the inexplicability of our lives and the seemingly unbridgeable gulf between ourselves and any intelligible end or God. Secondly, by inventing new theatrical techniques, he analysed and exposed the false methods men use to cope with these problems; the numerous, insidious illusions by which men live. Finally, he relentlessly explored the nature of self and identity by means of his newly found expressionistic and dream theatre techniques.

Whether or not the answers he provided are acceptable or the philosophical and religious theories he employed to reach them palatable is less important than what remains. This is an image of man or of what man ought to be. The Strindbergian protagonist while alive, and prepared to remain so, is a restlessly questing spirit refusing to be content with answers, let alone with palliatives. He is always ready to probe, to try out new solutions, to test his ideas and his illusions against often bitter experience. He lives his life head on. He is constantly 'available' to whatever ideas or encounters might promise some hope either of understanding or, by contrast, of escaping from the awful dilemma of being a self-conscious, speculative creature. The results of such searching are inevitably inadequate but Strindberg shows that for himself, and for us, the quest must be pursued resolutely to its end, if we are to come to terms with our human condition.

In conclusion, then, we can say that the contexts in which Strindberg's ideas are embodied inevitably transforms them, though the relationship is reciprocal; they also determine the overall strategies employed. So if we treat the philosophical ideas as serving some more basic intellectual design, as content of profound existential struggles, then the absurdity of many of those ideas will not be seen to undermine the dramatic quality of the plays. This is the case because, while the ideas provide material for the variations among the strategies adopted by Strindberg's protagonists to face and deal with their emotional and religious difficulties, the structure of these strategies itself remains constant. Yet to uncover this general structure, we must examine the ideological content of the plays, because this structure is imposed or expressed through the ideas. In Marxist jargon, the existential problems form a base or substructure; the particular ideologies constitute a superstructure. The particular dramatic contents of the plays are an elaboration of the superstructure which is determined by the base. The constant factors in the development of the numerous characters' life styles represent an elaboration of the base problems which are approached in various ideological (superstructural) ways. So one method of apprehending the existential base (and perhaps the most effective since it involves tracing causal links) is by analysing the ideological superstructure.

Finally, I feel that taking into account Strindberg's emotional instability which at least appears to affect the surface of his work and in view of his odd ideas, it is a powerful testimony to his dramatic power and skill that his plays have survived. We might have imagined that it would be easy to dismiss or ignore them, but this has not proved to be the case. They have remained with us as more than curiosities, both for themselves and through their influence, and his reputation as a major dramatist has remained for many people uncomfortably resilient. What is more, there is every reason to believe that it will endure and grow as a more balanced assessment of theatrical developments in the twentieth century is achieved.

Checklist of Strindberg's Social
and Religious Plays

1882	Lucky Peter's Travels	*1900*	Midsummer
1886	The Comrades	*1900*	Casper's Shrove Tuesday
1887	The Father		
1888	Miss Julie	*1900*	Easter
1888	Creditors	*1900*	The Dance of Death I
1888–9	The Stronger	*1900*	The Dance of Death II
1889	The Pariah	*1901*	Swanwhite
1889	The People of Hemso	*1901*	The Bridal Crown
1889	Simoon	*1901*	The Road to Damascus III
1892	The Key of Heaven		
1892	The First Warning	*1901*	A Dream Play
1892	Debit and Credit	*1902*	The Dutchman
1892	In Face of Death	*1903*	The Storm
1892	Mother's Love	*1907*	The Burned House
1892	Playing with Fire	*1907*	The Ghost Sonata
1892	The Bond	*1907*	The Pelican
1898	The Road to Damascus I	*1907*	Totel Insel
		1908	Abu Casem's Slippers
1898	The Road to Damascus II	*1909*	Black Glove
		1909	The Great Highway
1898	Advent		
1899	There are Crimes and Crimes		

Notes

Introduction

1 *Strindberg's Dramer*, i, 19, translated by Dahlström in *Strindberg's Dramatic Expressionism*, p. 89. Unfortunately, Lamm's two-volume classic has not been translated in full.
2 'Notes to the Members of the Intimate Theatre', translated by Evert Sprinchorn in *The Chamber Plays*, p. 205.
3 Letter to Adolf Paul, 6 January 1907, quoted by Sprinchorn, *Chamber Plays*, p. viii.
4 Review of Gunnar Brandell's *Strindberg in Inferno, Times Literary Supplement*, 20 December 1974.
5 Quoted by Lamm, *August Strindberg*, p. 63 (translated by Harry G. Carlson).
6 Translated by Andrew Melrose.

1 General Introduction to the Pre-Inferno Plays

1 Among the important French literary influences on Strindberg during his pre-Inferno period were Alphonse Daudet, Maupassant, Dumas *fils*, the Goncourts and Henri Becque.
2 Zola, *The Experimental Novel and Other Essays*, translated by B. M. Sherman, pp. 25-6.
3 Ibid., pp. 20-1.
4 Ibid., p. 18.
5 Translated, in part, by Madsen in *Playwrights on Playwriting*, ed. Toby Cole.
6 Zola, *The Experimental Novel*, pp. 53-4.
7 A concept derived from the work of the French psychologist Théodule Ribot (1839-1916).
8 See Chapter 5.
9 H. Maclean's article 'Expressionism' in *Periods of German Literature*, ed. J. M. Ritchie.
10 There are major concessions to biographical criticism in this section.
11 Quoted by Walter Johnson in *The Pre-Inferno Plays*, p. 4.
12 Letter to Hedlund, November 1895, quoted by Sprigge in *The Strange Life of August Strindberg*, p. 165.

13 Quoted by Lamm, *Strindberg*, pp. 533–4. This passage is not included by Field in his translation of selections from *A Blue Book*, published as *Zones of the Spirit*. All other quotations in the present work from *A Blue Book* are cited from the Field translation.

14 See Ollen's *August Strindberg* (pp. 11–12) for an excellent summary of Strindberg's love affairs.

15 *A Madman's Defence*, translated by Evert Sprinchorn, p. 189. His self-understanding, particularly of his sexual psychology, in this book is as astonishing as his capacity for self-deceit.

16 *Thus Spake Zarathustra*, translated by R. J. Hollingdale, p. 91.

17 Letter to Edward Brandes, 22 January 1887, quoted by Michael Meyer in his introduction to his translation of *The Father*.

18 Ibid.

19 Sprinchorn's translation.

20 Sprigge's translation.

21 The following discussion of philosophical influences on Strindberg's work during his pre-Inferno period must be cursory in view of the range of his reading.

22 Marx and Freud are not included here in the class of philosophers.

23 Strindberg formally renounced Nietzsche's philosophy after the Inferno crisis. Certainly his influence is much stronger in the earlier period but there are frequent Nietzschean resonances in his later work, as we shall see.

24 In his authoritative study *Nietzsche's Influence on Swedish Literature*; also compare Lamm, *Strindberg*, p. 259.

25 *The Strange Life of August Strindberg*, p. 145. Also see Lamm, *Strindberg*, Ch. 12 for further evidence of Strindberg's attraction towards Nietzsche's writings.

26 *Essays and Aphorisms*, translated by R. J. Hollingdale, p. 42.

27 Nietzsche's letter to Overbeck, 21 May 1884.

28 *Kierkegaard's Journals*, p. 474, quoted in Ronald Grimsley's *Kierkegaard*, p. 41.

29 *The Anti-Christ*, translated by R. J. Hollingdale, p. 115.

30 *Zarathustra*, p. 64.

31 Introduction to his translation of *Thus Spake Zarathustra*, p. 23.

32 Lamm, *Strindberg*, p. 260.

33 *Essays and Aphorisms*, p. 82. Strindberg certainly read Schopenhauer's *Metaphysics of the Love of the Sexes*.

34 Ibid., p. 83. A plausible summation of the central themes of *Creditors* and *The Father*?

35 Ibid., p. 85. Compare Gustav's speech in *Creditors*—see p. 79 below.

36 *Zarathustra*, pp. 83–4.

37 Ibid., p. 92.

38 Ibid., p. 95.

39 The basic text for this discussion is B. G. Madsen's *Strindberg's Naturalistic Theatre*. This section relies heavily on Madsen's work.

40 Translated by J. R. McIlraith.

41 From *Vivisections*, quoted by Madsen, *Strindberg's Naturalistic Theatre*, p. 49.

42 Ibid., p. 50.

43 What he was to call his 'exteriorised sensibility', his seventh sense (see Lamm, *Strindberg*, p. 513).

2   Two Early Plays

1 Translated by E. Classen and C. D. Locock.

2 In *The Flower and the Castle*.

3 The Father is a victim of the Powers. An early example of a later Strindbergian archetype.

4 Translated by Edith and Warner Oland in *Plays by August Strindberg*, vol. ii.

5 Though one would hardly accept Madsen's description of it (p. 42) as 'drawing room comedy'.

6 Not surprisingly Strindberg had originally intended to entitle the play *Marauders*.

7 This notion of a lazy breed of women usurping men's hard-earned scientific and artistic achievements over the centuries does not appear in any of the later misogynistic plays.

3   The Great 'Naturalistic' Plays

1 Michael Meyer's translation. Page references are to *Strindberg: the Plays*, vol. i.

2 However, as we shall see, *The Father* cannot be described as naturalistic in many other respects.

3 In this last sentence, the Captain specifically denies that he has a military vocation. This underminds Lucas's objection that he behaves incredibly for a soldier.

4 The Greek influence is most apparent in Strindberg's observance of the unities.

5 This would also conform to Kierkegaard's demand that tragedy should not arise from the exigencies of fate or external circumstances but from within the hero himself.

6 Strindberg, quoted by Johnson, *The Pre-Inferno Plays*, p. 6.

7 Michael Meyer's translation. Page references are to *Strindberg: the Plays*, vol. i.

8 The notion that intellectual and cultural sophistication is debilitating (as in *The Father*), that intelligent people are vulnerable to those who have low animal cunning and that social refinement can be accompanied by hysterical or morbid symptoms (as in *Miss Julie*) are probably traceable to the influence of Eduard von Hartmann. See Chapter 5.

9 Strindberg first read Dickens in 1878.

10 Translated by Barbara Foxley.

11 Lamm, *Strindberg*, p. 216.

12 This has been interpreted as Jean killing Julie's spirit. In ancient lore a bird was frequently the symbol of the human spirit.

13 However, in the Preface, Strindberg argues that his use of monologue and mime are realistic because they are motivated. What he says about the realistic possibilities of these two styles is plausible but unfortunately the content of his actual monologues makes his case irrelevant to *Miss Julie*.

14 'Strindberg and the Naturalistic Tragedy', *Scandinavian Studies*, 30 (February 1958), p. 18.

15 Michael Meyer's translation. Page references are to *Strindberg: the Plays*, vol. i.

16 *Zarathustra*, p. 137.

17 Ibid., p. 92.

18 Ibid., p. 83.

19 'Creditors Re-examined', *Modern Drama*, 5 (1962–3), pp. 281–90.

20 *Zarathustra*, p. 91.

21 Walter Johnson, 'Creditors Re-examined', p. 282.

22 *A Madman's Defence*, p. 175.

23 *Zarathustra*, p. 96.

4 Miscellaneous Plays (1889–1892)

1 *Strindberg*, p. 224.

2 He achieved a more subtle and satisfactory solution to the problem of dramatic economy in the Chamber Plays by use of interlocking 'musical' motifs.

3 Strindberg read Poe in December 1888.

4 Edwin Bjorkman's translation in *Plays of August Strindberg*, second series.

5 There are perhaps influences of Dostoievsky's *Crime and Punishment* here.

6 *Ibsen and Strindberg*, p. 439.

7 Michael Meyer's translation. Page references are to *Strindberg: the Plays*, vol. i.

8 Introduction to his translation of *The Stronger*, p. 221.

9 An interpretation shared by Lamm (with reservations).

10 *Strindberg's Impact in France 1920–1960*, pp. 15–16.

11 'Strindberg's *The Stronger*', *Scandinavian Studies*, 42 (1970), pp. 297–309.

12 This was Strindberg's own view of the conflict (cf. Lamm, *Strindberg*, p. 226).

13 Michael Meyer's translation. Page references are to his *Strindberg: the Plays*, vol. i.

14 Compare the Lady in *To Damascus* Part II who dresses the Stranger in the style of the Doctor, her former husband.

15 Ironically, the father's proverbs which, in 1892, were intended as self-condemnatory credentials might have come from Strindberg's own *Blue Book* written fifteen years later.

16 Elizabeth Sprigge's translation. Page references are to *Twelve Plays of Strindberg*.

17 It is also explicitly portrayed in the story 'For Payment' in *Getting Married*.

18 Whether she is referring to heterosexual or mother love here is a moot point.

19 Arvid Paulson's translation in *Eight Expressionist Plays by August Strindberg*. Page references are to this volume.

20 A notion that informs *To Damascus*, *A Dream Play* and *The Ghost Sonata* much more profoundly.

21 Figuratively, a fool's paradise.

22 Cf. 'No more love! No more money-making! No more honour! The Way of the Cross, the only one that leads to Wisdom' (*Inferno*, p. 41).

5 A General Introduction to the Post-Inferno Plays

1 There is some controversy about the exact nature of Strindberg's introduction to Swedenborg's thought. 'Ultimately Balzac [i.e. his *Seraphita*] led Strindberg to Swedenborg who in turn influenced the symbolic structure of the later drama', R. B. Vowles, 'A Cook's Tour of Strindberg Scholarship', p. 260.

2 *Essays and Aphorisms*, p. 41.

3 Ibid., pp. 47–8.

4 Ibid., pp. 105–6.

5 *The World As Will and Idea*, translated by R. B. Haldane and J. Kemp, i, pp. 506–7. Pp. 488–514 are highly relevant to a study of Strindberg's ideas.
6 Ibid., i, p. 493.
7 Strindberg assisted in translating von Hartmann's book in 1877–8. See *A Madman's Defence*, p. 44.
8 Swedenborg too dated the separation within man of the Soul and the Intellect at the time of the Fall. Before then all knowledge was contained *a priori* in the Soul.
9 It should be mentioned that this view of Hartmann added a dimension to Strindberg's pre-Inferno evolutionary ideas. So in *The Father* high intelligence makes the Captain vulnerable to low female cunning, and in *Miss Julie* social sophistication results in the heroine's hysteria, morbidity and lack of self-discipline.
10 Like Strindberg, Kierkegaard was the 'son of a servant' (his father married a servant in his house after his first wife's death), he had suspicions of his own illegitimacy and was plagued subsequently by feelings of guilt and sexual inadequacy. Whether Strindberg was aware of any of these facts is not known.
11 *Concluding Unscientific Postscript*, translated by D. F. Swenson and W. Lowrie, p. 182.
12 *The Concept of Dread*, translated by W. Lowrie, p. 55.
13 Despair takes far more forms and is far more complex than the present account suggests.
14 *Either-Or*, ii, p. 175.
15 Ibid. ii, p. 189.
16 *Repetition*, p. 35.
17 Quoted by Steene, *The Greatest Fire*, p. 82.
18 He claimed to have replaced Swedenborg's influence with that of Thomas À Kempis's *The Imitation of Christ*. This was indeed important and will be mentioned where relevant.
19 No attempt will be made here to analyse the coherence of Swedenborg's ideas.
20 Balzac's *Seraphita*, Ch. 2.
21 This has proved to have been Swedenborg's most powerful influence upon literature. Compare for example, Blake, Baudelaire and the Symbolists. It is of particularly profound importance to an understanding of Strindberg's symbolist and expressionistic drives.
22 Strindberg, by contrast, frequently found correspondence between objects on the same ontological level.
23 'The Infinite and the Final Cause of Creation', quoted in *Swedenborg and the New Cosmology* by Clifford Harley.

24 Each of these conflicts is dramatised by Strindberg as a stage in the gradual development of the Stranger in *To Damascus.*
25 Frequently, Strindberg transposes the experiences discussed below to life on earth.
26 Quoted by Lamm, *Strindberg*, p. 296.
27 Swedenborg, quoted by Strindberg in *A Blue Book*, p. 88.
28 Strindberg's allusions to Divine Retribution were probably stimulated by his reading of Linnaeus's *Nemesis Divina*. In Swedenborg, punishment is for guidance.
29 Compare the poems of Ernst Stadler, the theoretical work of Kurt Hiller and the writings of Frans Werfel.
30 'Origins of Strindberg's Expressionism', *Scandinavian Studies*, 34 (February 1962), p. 45.
31 'Expressionism' in *Periods of German Literature*, ed. Ritchie, p. 261.
32 H. Maclean, op. cit.
33 Quoted in Grimsley, *Kierkegaard*, p. 104.
34 *Emanuel Swedenborg: Scientist and Mystic*, p. 345.
35 In the Strindberg issue of *Modern Drama*, 5 (December 1962), p. 315. It should be mentioned that Strindberg later condemned French Symbolism in *Talks to the Swedish Nation*, cf. Lamm, *Strindberg*, p. 520.
36 'If one may believe Swedenborg, I am a damned soul in hell, and the Powers punish me ceaselessly and mercilessly' (*Legends*, p. 25).
37 *The Sandman*, translated by Michael Bullock.
38 *The Symbolist Movement in Literature*, p. 154.
39 *The Treasure of the Humble.*

6 The Road to Damascus

1 All quotations, unless otherwise stated, are from Graham Rawson's translation.
2 *Strindberg's Dramatic Expressionism*, p. 65.
3 Ronald Gaskell, *Drama and Reality*, p. 46.
4 Despite Strindberg's acknowledged debt to Swedenborg throughout *Inferno, From an Occult Diary, A Blue Book, Fair Haven and Foul Strand* etc. there is no analysis of the trilogy in English which is prefaced by an account of Swedenborg's thought.
5 Kierkegaard maintained that Dread is consciousness of Original Sin.
6 'Origins', p. 45.
7 An image of Kierkegaardian choice or decision.
8 When the Stranger is daydreaming he doodles in the sand with his cane. This refers to John 8:6: 'But Jesus stooped down and with his

finger wrote on the ground as though he heard them not'. F. L. Lucas quotes a letter in which Strindberg gives it a specific expressionistic purpose. 'The instinct of the ego's expansion, its tendency to set itself up as the axis of the world' (*Ibsen and Strindberg*, p. 414).

9 Cf. 'You thought that you were looking upon the divine wonders of Nature with reverence and pious admiration, but by embarking on a wanton enquiry into every detail of the causes and conditions of these wonders, you destroyed that reverence, and the knowledge after which you strove became a mere phantom, deceiving you like inquisitive and impertinent children.' E. T. A. Hoffman, *Meister Floh*.

10 A recurring motif of his intellectualism is the corrupting influence of his books (cf. p. 30).

11 Also an alter ego of the Stranger. When the Mother identifies the Stranger as her new son-in-law, the Dominican remarks: 'Singularly like the first' (p. 119).

12 Compare Ibsen's reason for having Strindberg's portrait in his study, 'The man fascinates me—he is so subtly, so delicately mad.'

13 Ironically, here man tempts woman to sample the Tree of Knowledge.

14 Cf. the Doctor's curse: 'When you sit at your work I shall come with a poppy, invisible to you, that will put your thoughts to sleep and confuse your mind so that you'll see visions you can't distinguish from reality' (p. 132).

15 A symbol of Kierkegaardian recurrence and also a Swedenborgian instrument of faith. See R. B. Vowles, 'Strindberg and the Symbolic Mill', *Scandinavian Studies*, 34 (May 1962).

16 The result of struggling like Jacob with God. 'Evil spirits and not good, wrestled with Jacob, for by wrestling is signified temptation and temptation is never wrought by good spirits but by evil' (Swedenborg, *Arcana Coelestia*, no 4 307). Or again, 'When the avenging spirits see an evil act or the intention to commit a wrong, they punish by inflicting pain in the foot, the hand or the neighbourhood of the diaphragm' (Swedenborg quoted by Strindberg in *Legends*, p. 46).

17 Translated by Leo Sherley-Price.

18 The curse of Deuteronomy had included the words: 'The Lord shall cause thee to be smitten before thine enemies; thou shalt go out one way against them, and flee *seven* ways before them and shall be removed into all the kingdoms of the earth' (*To Damascus*, p. 83).

19 *Strindberg*, p. 312.

20 Strindberg frequently cast himself in the role of Job.

21 Cf. 'Are you visiting women? Do not forget your whip' (*Zarathustra*, p. 93).

22 Compare Part I, Scene 2, pp. 88, 117 and 163 of *To Damascus.*
23 Compare Act 4 Scene 3 of *Erik XIV* and the Last Supper sequence of Buñuel's film *Viridiana.*
24 This odour signifies the presence of evil spirits. 'According to Swedenborg's doctrine of correspondences, good men exhale sweet perfume and bad men a stench like that of corpses' (*A Blue Book*, p. 178). The evil man referred to would be the Doctor.
25 Compare Swedenborg's distinction between spiritual and natural suns.
26 Now we're on the other side of the river and have life beneath us, behind us', p. 217. Before he crosses he has to give away his gold and receives, in exchange, a glass of wine for last Communion.
27 For Swedenborg, severe temptations are the way to conquer real (inner) evils.
28 As usual F. L. Lucas misses the point. 'Indeed the Tempter appears to my diabolic mind to talk far better sense than any other character in the whole trilogy' (*Ibsen and Strindberg*, p. 432). To tempt a subtle man, one must needs be subtle oneself.
29 Swedenborg, *Conjugal Love*, no 476.
30 She has married unhappily for a third time and her meeting with the Stranger who is similarly unhappy in love, is an example of the notion of recurrence which dominates the trilogy.
31 Kierkegaard writes of a confessionless Christianity.
32 Translated by Mary Sandbach.

7   Hybrid Plays

1 Elizabeth Sprigge's translation. Page references are to *Twelve Plays of August Strindberg.*
2 Letter to Schering, September 1902, quoted by Dahlström, *Strindberg's Dramatic Expressionism*, p. 165.
3 A suggestion of repetition of child 'murders'?
4 Cf. 'No man can live in the public eye without risk to his soul' (*The Imitation of Christ*, p. 50).
5 Compare the descriptions of the Luxembourg Gardens in *Legends*, pp. 157 ff.
6 'Symbol and Meaning in Strindberg's *Crimes and Crimes*', *Modern Drama*, 9 (1966–7), pp. 62–73.
7 Elizabeth Sprigge's translation. Page references are to *Twelve Plays of August Strindberg.*
8 The expressionistic form of their marriage is illuminated by comparing it with a later expressionistic battle of the sexes in a play that

it probably influenced, Oscar Kokoschka's *Murderer Hope of Woman Kind* (1907).

9 F. L. Lucas's description of Edgar as 'simply a sadistic Caliban ... an incurable neurotic unable to free his feet from the hated wife' (p. 388) is partly inadequate because it naively humanises him.

10 As C. V. Spivack points out, the hell of *The Dance of Death* is existential. It is the condition of marital existence ('The Many Hells of August Strindberg', *Twentieth Century Literature*, 9 (1963–4), pp. 10–16).

11 The dance of death itself.

12 'Don't you realise we go through the same rigmarole every day' (p. 353). The concept of recurrence here is more Nietzschean than Kierkegaardian: that is, it is not a condition of spiritual growth, on the contrary it is enervating.

13 Typically both feel they have married beneath them and criticise each other's family to prove the point.

14 Alice best describes his fatal weaknesses: 'For this man no laws exist; he doesn't recognise any rules or regulations. He's above everything— everybody; the universe is created for his private use; the sun and the moon revolve to carry his praises to the stars' (p. 381). And, as we read in *A Blue Book*: 'Fortunately godlessness is an hallucination imposed on haughty blockheads as a punishment (p. 204).

15 *Strindberg*, p. 373.

16 However the immediate motivation of his behaviour here is presumably that he has discovered that Alice has informed the authorities about his embezzling Army funds.

17 This hair symbolism probably derives from Maeterlinck's *The Princess Maleine* (Gerard Harry's translation).

18 Darkness of one kind or another is a leitmotif of the play. The Captain, in particular, fears it, i.e. death.

8 'Christian' Plays

1 Edwin Bjorkman's translation, third series. Lamm mentions that the play was published together with *Crimes and Crimes* under the collective title *Before a Higher Court* (*Strindberg*, p. 317).

2 Letter of Geijerstam, 1889, quoted by Lamm, *Strindberg*, p. 319.

3 An Ibsenesque symbol of their cruelty and sanctimoniousness. It stands on Gallows Hill and houses ghosts.

4 William White, *Emanuel Swedenborg: His Life and Writings*, i, p. 412.

5 This is substantially the basic notion that Strindberg found in Thomas À Kempis's *The Imitation of Christ*.

6 Direct Maeterlinckian influence at this time must be asserted tentatively. Strindberg had read him but confessed in his Fifth Letter to the Intimate Theatre 'that Maeterlinck was like a closed book to me'.

7 Fittingly the Old Lady is allowed to reveal *her* sins of pride and vanity in a ghostly ballroom where corpse-like musicians play funeral music.

8 Clearly based on Balzac's Seraphitus-Seraphita.

9 Possibly the influence of Maeterlinck. The symbol of the sun that burns the wicked and comforts the good probably derives from *The Princess Maleine*.

10 E.g. silver cups which turn black in the Judge's possession, food tasting of carbolic acid, the Judge's Caul, the bust of Pan: these 'symbolist' techniques point forward to the fully-fledged Symbolist dramas culminating in *A Dream Play*.

11 Elizabeth Sprigge's translation in *Twelve Plays of August Strindberg*.

12 *Strindberg's Dramatic Expressionism*, p. 170.

13 From the point of view of Strindberg's psychology, it is not surprising he chose a girl to represent Christ because the orthodox Christ figure did not appeal to him. 'The Holy Mother and Child greeted me with a gentle smile. The figure on the cross, incomprehensible as always, left me cold' (*Inferno*, p. 35).

14 'Strindberg's *Easter*: A Musical Play', *University Review of Kansas* (Spring 1967), pp. 219–25.

15 Though this has a dual reference: peace and chastisement.

16 'She suffers with all living things: in other words she manifests Christ in Man. Therefore she is kin to Balzac's Seraphitus-Seraphita, Swedenborg's niece' (Letter to Harriet Bosse, 8 February 1901, quoted in Lamm, *Strindberg*, p. 368).

17 Intimations of Kierkegaardian despair.

18 Her story of the rat buzzard exactly parallels Swedenborg's account of the punishment of damned souls in Hell. Both are tormented by their own failings.

19 It does not, as in the case of the Stranger in *To Damascus*, issue from arrogance.

20 *Strindberg's Dramatic Expressionism*, p. 160.

21 Strindberg's injunction that 'the old man should be good-natured and good-hearted and only pretend to be irascible' does not mean that he is not a menacing, even terrifying, figure for Elis.

22 This symbol of suffering reappears in the flagellating sound of

Lindkvist's galoshes which so torments Elis. *Easter* is the purest symbolist drama Strindberg ever wrote.

9   A Dream Play

1 Elizabeth Sprigge's translation. Page references are to *Twelve Plays of Strindberg.*

2 In this preface and in *A Dream Play* itself, we can trace anticipations of the subjective time of Bergson and Proust, the dream and unconscious symbolism of surrealism, the notion of stream of consciousness, absurdist and aleatory art.

3 *Modern Drama*, 5 (December 1962), p. 356.

4 'Strindberg almost certainly never read a word of Freud . . . There is no mention of Freud in Strindberg's 20,000 surviving letters which are full of references to what he was reading, nor is there any work of Freud's in Strindberg's library . . . Strindberg had probably never heard of Freud's name' (Michael Meyer, *Henrik Ibsen: the Making of a Dramatist 1828–64*, p. 199).

5 Maya, the creative power, came to mean illusion.

6 Translated by Mary Sandbach.

7 For a more detailed analysis of the Hindu, Christian and alchemical references, see Leta Jane Lewis, 'Alchemy and the Orient in Strindberg's *Dream Play*', *Scandinavian Studies*, 35 (1963).

8 The plays' constant refrain, 'Mankind is to be pitied', lacks Strindberg's usual bitterness. Compare Maeterlinck's remark about men: 'They are certainly to be pitied' (*The Intruder*, p. 224). Also compare *Pelléas and Mélisande*, Act 4 Scene 2.

9 This symbol is echoed by the Officer's imprisonment in the Castle.

10 Agnes = Agni = fire, God and heavenly messenger. Suitably at the end of the play she is consumed by fire.

11 Compare the symbol of the growing castle with Maeterlinck's growing cemetery—'it is eating into the very gardens of the castle' (*The Princess Maleine*, p. 41).

12 For a repeated condemnation of this vice we can turn to Thomas À Kempis's *The Imitation of Christ*, e.g. 'Take no pleasure in your own ability or cleverness lest you offend God, who has himself bestowed on you all your natural gifts' (p. 34). This particularly applies later to the conduct of the Academic Deans.

13 Yet another Swedenborgian seer based on Strindberg's former mother-in-law, Maria Uhl.

14 The Officer remarks that everyone at the Opera likes fishing because the fish are mute and cannot be their rivals.

15 Translations taken from Bertrand Russell's *History of Western Philosophy* Part I, Ch. 4. For further details see G. S. Kirk and J. E. Raven, *The Pre-Socratic Philosophers*, Ch. 6.

16 'I saw on the pavement a tin-coated piece of iron in the shape of a clover leaf. What does that signify? The Trinity, that is clear. And further?' (*Legends*, p. 193).

17 In many respects similar to the novel *The Cloister*.

18 Almost a prophetic parody of a modern health farm!

19 The roadstead six miles east of Cape Matala at which St Paul wished, after having had a premonition of a hurricane, to rest on the sea journey to his captivity in Rome. His pleas, however, were ignored, the Divinely chosen Fair haven was left behind and the ship was wrecked in Malta.

20 Her Bach toccata represents the spiritual as opposed to the worldly waltz of the dancers. Eventually Edith's music triumphs by drowning the sound of the other.

21 Like *To Damascus*, it could be argued that *A Dream Play* is an example of pure expressionism with only one character, i.e. the Dreamer.

22 'Bringing the reader and the audience back to the same environment where the action began strengthens one's feeling of having experienced a dream sequence from the time of going to sleep until awakening' (letter to Geijerstam, 13 March 1898, quoted in Brandell, *Strindberg in Inferno*, p. 270. Also compare Part I of *To Damascus*, his 'earlier dream play'.

23 Heraclitus associates the divine with fire and strongly implies that the soul returns to the fiery aether at the death of the body.

10   Folk and Fairy Plays

1 Elizabeth Sprigge's translation. Page references are to *Twelve Plays of August Strindberg*.

2 Letter to the actress Anna Flygare, October 1908, quoted by Lamm, *Strindberg*, p. 383.

3 Lamm disagrees and offers rather strange reasons for his conclusion: That *Swanwhite* does not have much in common with Maeterlinck's dramas despite the similarity in themes is due to its bright mood and the recurrent folk ballad phrases . . .' (*Strindberg*, p. 382).

4 Letter to Harriet Bosse, Palm Sunday 1901, quoted by Elizabeth Sprigge, *Twelve Plays*, p. 456.

5 Cf. Swanwhite's premonition of the evil young King's arrival (p. 500).

6 Swanwhite's mother washes her feet with tears—recalling Christ and Mary Magdalene.
7 Edwin Bjorkman's translation, fourth series.
8 Quoted in Haskell M. Block, 'Strindberg and Symbolist Drama', *Modern Drama*, 5 (1962), p. 320.
9 It seems that, in common with Maeterlinck, Strindberg rejected the idea that any particular sin or even group of sins could irredeemably condemn a person. Repentance is always possible but it must be genuine. 'Remorse is impotence, it will sin again. Only repentance is strong; it can end everything (Balzac, *Seraphita*, Ch. 3).
10 Even Bjorkman confesses to being unable to throw any light on this choice of name.

11   The Chamber Plays

1 With the exception of *Storm* and *The Black Glove* the translations are by Evert Sprinchorn, Seabury Quinn jr and Kenneth Petersen. Page references are to their volume *Chamber Plays*.
2 *Open Letters to the Intimate Theatre*, translated by Walter Johnson, p. 19.
3 'Notes to Members of the Intimate Theatre' in Sprinchorn, *The Chamber Plays*, p. 27.
4 Scenic and plot economy had been one of Strindberg's obsessions since his earliest days.
5 Letter to Adolf Paul, 6 January 1907, quoted by Gunnar Ollén, *August Strindberg*, p. 102.
6 'Note to Members of the Intimate Theatre', p. 207.
7 Evert Sprinchorn has plausibly suggested that Strindberg found a musical form essential because 'Instead of causes he saw correspondences' (Introduction in *Chamber Plays*, p. x).
8 'This is the way the Weaveress of the World weaves the fates of men, there are that many secrets in *every* home' (Letter to Schering, 29 March 1907, quoted by Lamm, *Strindberg*, p. 479).
9 Houses are so important in the Chamber Plays that the Swedish critic Sven Rinman has maintained that 'houses, not people... are the central characters'. Although this is a half truth, it is sufficiently apposite to be revealing.
10 In *Essays on Strindberg*, pp. 29–38.
11 Each of the Chamber Plays contrasts reality with illusion. The House as the outer shell concealing man's sordid secrets—people's external behaviour hides the rapacity of their characters.
12 Michael Meyer's translation. Page references are to *Strindberg: the Plays*, vol. i.

13 Strindberg's original title was *The First Lamp*.
14 *The Ghost Sonata* is more precisely a surrealistic development.
15 Also translated as *After the Fire* and *The Burned Site*.
16 The Young Lady is to be the Student's Brunnhilde.
17 The exposure of the Colonel extends to showing that even his hair, his teeth, indeed, his very existence, is false.
18 'The only consolation given me, I receive from Buddha, who tells me, quite frankly, that life is a phantom, an illusion which we will only see in its right perspective in another life' (Letter to Harriet Bosse, 4 October 1905, quoted in Rheinhert (ed.), *Strindberg: Critical Essays*, p. 9.
19 In *Essays on Strindberg*, pp. 39–48.
20 *Scandinavian Studies*, 40 (August 1968).
21 'The Pelican is very definitely a modern version of Choephori. Frederick and Gerda, the two dispossessed children, are Orestes and Electra, swearing vengeance on their mother for the 'murder' of their father. The Aegisthus . . . is Axel, the mother's second husband and co-conspirator' (Robert Brustein, *The Theatre of Revolt*, p. 106).
22 In many ways the situation and characters resemble a mature re-writing of the earlier play *Mother's Love*, though Lamm says the family of *The Pelican* is the one left behind by the dead teacher of *Totel Insel*.
23 Cf. Maeterlinck, *The Princess Maleine*, p. 114.
24 According to Lamm, Strindberg considered calling the play *The Sleepwalker* which is exactly what all the characters, with the exception of the son-in-law, are.
25 Unlike *The Ghost Sonata* in which some characters are expressionist types, spiritual forces are depicted in *The Pelican* through inanimate objects, e.g. the rocking chair ('which was always like two chopping blades when he sat there and hacked at my heart'), the cold house (death) and the red sofa cloth (blood-guilt). Strangely Lamm denies the presence of spirits in the play.
26 Walter Johnson has suggested that the play was intended as a sequel to *The Dance of Death*, Part II.
27 Arvid Paulson's translation. Page references are to *The Strindberg Reader*, pp. 332–70. It was written as a Christmas play.
28 Brian Rothwell acutely observes: 'The Tower of Babel becomes (in good Swedenborgian fashion) the ideas of the Old Man, false schemes to climb to heaven' ('The Chamber Plays' in *Essays on Strindberg*, p. 33).
29 I.e. the 'flowers from filth' motif of *A Dream Play*.
30 These are taken from Strindberg's own Inferno delusions.

12   Final Play

1 Elizabeth Sprigge's translation. Page references are to *Twelve Plays of August Strindberg.*
2 *Strindberg's Dramatic Expressionism,* p. 157.
3 Many of the characters in the later plays have difficulty breathing. This obsession probably derives from Strindberg's stomach cancer and the claustrophobic pressures caused by it, so fully reported in *From an Occult Diary.*
4 Generally speaking Strindberg was not contemptuous of the powers of reason. He had too much scientific ambition for that. His position was rather, 'as soon as I believe in an Almighty God who can suspend the few natural laws we know and brings into operation the countless host of laws which we do not know, I must believe in miracles' (*A Blue Book,* p. 195).
5 'Place in Valley of Hinnom near Jerusalem used for idolatrous worship and later for depositing refuse, for consumption of which fires were kept burning' (*Concise Oxford Dictionary*). It is therefore a biblical hell (cf. Spivak, 'The Many Hells of August Strindberg').

13   Strindberg's Influence on Modern Drama

1 A complete chapter could be written on Strindberg's influence on O'Neill. Consider, for instance, the parallels between the coal heaver scene in *A Dream Play* and *The Hairy Ape,* the use of Strindbergian symbolic backgrounds in *The Emperor Jones* and *Beyond the Horizon,* the notion of Hell on earth in *A Long Day's Journey into Night,* the Strindbergian protagonist of *More Stately Mansions,* O'Neill's Nietzschean proclivities, his bitch women and idealised females. Consider the following testimony of artistic indebtedness: 'It was reading his plays . . . that above all else, first gave me the vision of what modern drama could be. If there is anything of lasting worth in my work, it is due to that original impulse from him' . . . the precursor of all modernity in our present theatre (O'Neill, programme note to *The Ghost Sonata* 1926).
2 *Mother Courage* is similarly written on by experience while remaining in part untouched by it.
3 Compare O'Neill's use of these in *Great God Brown* and *Days Without End.*
4 'Strindberg is tremendous. This rage, these pages won by fist fighting' (Kafka, *The Diaries 1914–23,* p. 78).
5 *Mid-Century Drama,* pp. 115ff.

6 'All those who nowadays believe that man is no more than his life have something to learn and profit from Strindberg's drama' (Sartre, quoted by Swerling in *Strindberg's Impact in France*, p. 93).

7 *Drama in the Sixties*, p. 63.

8 Further orthodox expressionist examples of the genre are to be found in Ernst Toller's plays *Transfiguration* (1919) (in thirteen stations) and *Man and the Masses* (1920).

9 Yet Brecht certainly regarded him highly: 'He [Wedekind] did not seem mortal . . . he belonged with Tolstoy and Strindberg among the great educators of the new Europe' (quoted by Frederick Ewen in *Bertolt Brecht*, p. 66).

14 A Personal Epilogue: Bizarre Ideas and 'Hysteria'

1 'Strindberg: the Absence of Irony' in Strindberg: *Critical Essays*, ed. Otto Rheinhert, p. 67.

2 *The Greatest Fire*, p. 157.

3 'He [Strindberg] is the guardian and the witness of individual revolt. The great adventure of the mind is perpetuated in him as in every great artist' (Camus, quoted by Swerling in *Strindberg's Impact in France*, p. 105).

4 *The Novels of August Strindberg*, p. 10.

5 George Bernard Shaw, however, would not have agreed: 'Strindberg was a great genius . . . one of the greatest. But his sense of the miraculous was so overpowering that he failed as an artist to give adequate place to the ordinary world of common sense' (Interview given to Paul Green in 1928, quoted in Margery M. Morgan in 'Strindberg and the English Theatre', *Modern Drama*, 7 (September 1964).

Selected Bibliography

Translations of Strindberg

A Blue Book, trans. as *Zones of the Spirit* by Claud Field, George Allen and Co (London 1913).

The Cloister, ed. C. G. Bjurstrom and trans. Mary Sandbach, Secker and Warburg (London 1969).

Chamber Plays, trans. Evert Sprinchorn, Dutton (New York 1962).

Dramas of Testimony, trans. Walter Johnson, Washington University Press (Seattle 1976)

A Dream Play and The Ghost Sonata, trans. Carl Richard Mueller, Chandler (San Francisco 1965).

A Dream Play and Four Chamber Plays, trans. Walter Johnson, Washington University Press (Seattle 1973).

Easter and Other Plays (The Dance of Death, The Ghost Sonata A Dream Play), trans. E. Classen, C. D. Locock, and Erik Palmstierna and James Bernard Fagan, Jonathan Cape (London 1929).

Easter, trans. Elizabeth Sprigge, Duckworth (London 1951).

Eight Expressionist Plays, trans. Arvid Paulson and John Gassner, Bantam Books (Toronto 1965).

Eight Famous Plays by Strindberg, trans. Edwin Bjorkman and N. Erichsen, Duckworth (London 1949).

Fair Haven and Foul Strand (no trans. given, McBride, Nast and Co (London 1914).

From an Occult Diary, trans. Mary Sandbach, Icon Books (London 1966).

Getting Married, trans. Mary Sandbach, Gollancz (London 1972).

Inferno, Alone and Other Writings, trans. Evert Sprinchorn, Doubleday (New York 1968).

Legends, no trans. given, Andrew Melrose (London 1912).

Letters of Strindberg to Harriet Bosse, trans. Arvid Paulson, Thomas Nelson (London 1959).

Lucky Peter's Travels and other Plays, trans. E. Classen, C. D. Locock, Elizabeth Sprigge and Claude Napier, Jonathan Cape (London 1930).

A Madman's Manifesto, trans. Anthony Swerling, Trinity Lane Press (Cambridge 1969).

A Madman's Defence, trans. Evert Sprinchorn, Jonathan Cape (London rev. ed. 1969).

Miss Julie and Other Plays (The Ghost Sonata, Creditors, The Stronger), trans. Max Faber, Heinemann Drama Library (London 1960).

Miss Julie and Other Plays (The Creditor, The Stronger, Woman, Motherly Love, Pariah, Simoon), no trans. given, Modern Library series (New York 1918).

Miss Julie. A Naturalist Tragedy, trans. Michael Meyer, Methuen (London 1967).

One Act Plays, trans. Arvid Paulson, Washington Square Press (New York 1969).

Open Letters to the Intimate Theatre, trans. Walter Johnson, Peter Owen (London 1967).

Pariah, Simoon: Two Plays by August Strindberg, trans. H. B. Samuel, Hendersons (London 1914).

The People of Hemso, trans. Elspeth Harvey Schubert, Jonathan Cape (London 1959).

Plays Vol. i and iii, trans. Edith and Werner Oland, Luce and Co. (Boston 1912–14).

Plays Vol. ii, trans. Edith and Werner Oland, Frank Palmer (London 1913).

Plays, trans. Edwin Bjorkman, 4 vols, Duckworth (London 1912–16).

The Plays, trans. Michael Meyer, Secker and Warburg Vol. 1 (London 1964), Vol. 2 (London 1975).

Pre-Inferno Plays, trans. Walter Johnson, Washington University Press (Seattle 1970).

Psychic Murders, trans. Walter Johnson, *Tulane Drama Review*, 13 No 2 (Winter 1968).

The Red Room, trans. Elizabeth Sprigge, Dent (London 1967).

The Road to Damascus: A Trilogy, trans. Graham Rawson, Jonathan Cape (London 1958).

The Scapegoat, trans. Arvid Paulson, W. H. Allen (London 1967).

Selected Plays and Prose, ed. R. Brustein, Holt, Rinehart and Winston (New York 1965).

The Son of a Servant, trans. with introd. and notes by Evert Sprinchorn, Jonathan Cape (London 1967).

Strindberg's One Act Plays, trans. Arvid Paulson, Washington Square Press (New York 1969).

Strindberg Reader, ed. Arvid Paulson, Phaedra (New York 1968).

Tales, trans. L. J. Potts, Chatto & Windus (London 1941).

Three Experimental Plays, trans. F. R. Southerington, University of Virginia Press (Charlottesville 1975).

Three Plays (The Father, Miss Julie, Easter), trans. Peter Watts, Penguin Books (London 1958).

Twelve Plays, trans. Elizabeth Sprigge, Constable (London 1963).

Books on Strindberg

Berendsohn, Walter A. *The Oriental Studies of August Strindberg*, trans. Rudolf Loewenthal, Central Asian Collectianea (Washington 1960).

Bjarnson, Loftur L. *Categories of Kierkegaard's Thought in the Life and Writings of August Strindberg*, Stanford University Ph.D. thesis (1951).

Brandell, Gunnar. *Strindberg in Inferno*, trans. Barry Jacobs, Harvard University Press (Cambridge, mass. 1974).

Bulman, Joan. *Strindberg and Shakespeare*, Jonathan Cape (London 1933).

Campbell, G. A. *Strindberg*, Duckworth (London 1933).

Dahlström, C. E. W. L. *Strindberg's Dramatic Expressionism*, Michigan University Press (1930).

Harman, M. *Strindberg and O'Neill: a study in influence*, New York University Ph.D. thesis (1960).

Heller, Otto. *Prophets of Dissent*, Kennickat Press Inc. (New York 1918).

Howard, Gordon S. *Strindberg's Use of Irony in his Post-Inferno Dramas*, Minnesota University Ph.D. thesis (1969).

Jarvie, Raymond. *Strindberg's Post-Inferno Dramas and Music*, Washington University Ph.D. thesis (1970).

Johannesson, Eric O. *The Novels of August Strindberg: a study in theme and structure*, California University Press (Berkeley and Los Angeles 1968).

Johnson, Walter. *Strindberg and the Historical Drama*, Washington University Press (Seattle 1963).

—. *August Strindberg*, Twayne World Authors Series (Boston 1976).

Lamm, Martin. *August Strindberg*, trans. and ed. Harry G. Carlson, Benjamin Blom (New York 1971).

Lind af Hageby. *August Strindberg*, The A.K. Press (London 1938).

—. *August Strindberg: Spirit of Revolt*, Stanley Paul (London 1913).

Lucas, F. L. *Ibsen and Strindberg*, Cassell (London 1962).

Madsen, B. G. *Strindberg's Naturalistic Theatre*, Washington University Press (Seattle 1962).

McGill, V. J. *August Strindberg, the Bedevilled Viking*, Noel Douglas (London 1930).

322 *Selected Bibliography*

Mortensen, B. M. E. and Downes, B. W., *Strindberg: an introduction to his life and work*, Cambridge University Press (1949).

Ollén Gunnar. *August Strindberg*, World Dramatist series, Frederick Unger Publishing Co. (new York 1972).

Palmblad, H. V. E. *Strindberg's Conception of History*, Cornell University Press (New York 1927).

Passerini, Edward M. *Strindberg's Absurdist Plays. An Examination of Expressionistic, Surrealistic and Absurd Elements in Strindberg's Drama*, Virginia University Ph.D. thesis (1971).

Rapp, E. E. *Strindberg's Reception in England and the United States*, Colarado University Ph.D. thesis (1940).

Rheinhart, Otto (ed.). *Strindberg: Critical Essays*, Twentieth Century View series Prentice Hall (New York 1971).

Smedmark, Carl R. (ed.). *Essays on Strindberg*, Strindberg Society (Sweden 1966).

Sprigge, E. *The Strange Life of August Strindberg*, Macmillan (London 1949).

Steene, Birgitta. *The Greatest Fire: a study of August Strindberg*, Southern Illinois University Press (1973).

Swerling, Anthony. *Strindberg's Impact in France 1920–60*, Trinity Lane Press (Cambridge 1971).

Uddgren, Gustaf. *Strindberg the Man*, trans. Johan Axel Uppvall, Four Seas Co (Boston 1920).

Uppvall, Johan Axel. *August Strindberg: a psychoanalytic study with special reference to the Oedipus Complex*, The Gorham Press (Boston 1920).

Valency, Maurice. *The Flower and the Castle*, Macmillan (New York 1963).

Articles on Strindberg

Adler, Henry. 'To Hell with Society', *Tulane Drama Review*, 14 (May 1960).

Ahman, Sven, 'Episodes and Epistles', *American Swedish Monthly*, 56 (March 1962).

Allen, James L. (Jnr.). 'Symbol and Meaning in Strindberg's *Crimes and Crimes*', *Modern Drama*, 9 (1966–7).

Bandy, Stephen C. 'Strindberg's Biblical Sources for *The Ghost Sonata*', *Scandinavian Studies*, 40 (1968).

Benson, Adolph B. 'Humour and Satire in Strindberg's *The Island of Paradise*', *Scandinavian Studies*, 26 (1954).

Benston, Alice N. 'From Naturalism to the *Dream Play*', *Modern Drama*, 7 (1965).

Bergmann, S. A. 'Strindberg's Symbolic Drama', *The Norseman* (London), 15 (March, April 1957).

Bergson, David M. 'Strindberg's *Easter*: A Musical Play', *University Review of Kansas*, 33 (Spring 1967).

Block, Haskell M. 'Strindberg and the Symbolist Drama', *Modern Drama*, 5 (1962–3).

Borland, H. H. 'The Dramatic Quality of Strindberg's Novels', *Modern Drama*, 5 (1962–3).

Bronsen, D. '*Dance of Death* and the possibility of Laughter', *Drama Survey*, 6 (Spring 1967).

Brustein, Robert. 'Male and Female in August Strindberg', *Tulane Drama Review*, 7 (Winter 1962).

—. '*Creditors*', *New Republic*, 146 (February 1962).

Burnham, Donald L. 'Restitutional Functions of Symbol and Myth in Strindberg's *Inferno*', *Psychiatry*, 36 (1973).

Carlson, Harry G. 'Ambiguity and Archetypes in Strindberg's Romantic Organist', *Scandinavian Studies*, 48 (1976).

Dahlström, C. E. W. L. 'Strindberg's *The Father* as Expressionistic Drama', *Scandinavian Studies*, 16 (1940–1).

—. 'Strindberg and the Problems of Naturalism', *Scandinavian Studies*, 16 (1940–1).

Dahlström, C. E. W. L. 'Theomancy: Zola, Strindberg and Andreyev', *Scandinavian Studies*, 17 (1942–3).

—. 'Strindberg's Naturalistika Scorgespel and Zola's Naturalism', *Scandinavian Studies*, 17 (1942–3).

—. 'Strindberg's Naturalistika Sorgespel and Zola's Naturalism', *Scandinavian Studies*, 18 (1944–5).

—. 'The Parisian Reception of Strindberg's Plays', *Scandinavian Studies*, 19 (1946–7).

—. 'August Strindberg 1849–1912: Between Two Eras', *Scandinavian Studies*, 21 (1949).

—. 'Strindberg's '*The Father* as Tragedy', *Scandinavian Studies*, 27 (1955).

—. 'Strindberg and Naturalistic Tragedy', *Scandinavian Studies*, 30 (1958).

—. 'An Approach to Tragedy', *Modern Drama*, 1 (1958).

—. 'Origins of Strindberg's Expressionism', *Scandinavian Studies*, 34 (1962).

Davidson, Clifford. 'Indra's Daughter and the Growing Castle', *Laurentian University Review*, 3 (1970).

Deer, Irving. 'Strindberg's Dream Vision: Prelude to the Film', *Criticism*, 14 (1972).

Dukore, Bernard F. 'Strindberg: The Real and Surreal', *Modern Drama*, 5 (1962–3).

Eaton, W. K. 'Contrasts in the Representation of Death by Sophocles, Webster and Strindberg', *Jacobean Drama Studies*, 17 (1975).

Fleisher, Frederic. 'Strindberg and O'Neill', *Symposium*, 10 (1956).

Fletcher J. 'Bergman and Strindberg', *Journal of Modern Literature*, 3 (1973).

Freedman, Morris, 'Strindberg's Positive Nihilism', *Drama Survey*, 2 (1962).

Gassner, John. '*Creditors*'. *Educational Theory Journal*, 14 (1962).

—. 'The Influence of Strindberg in the U.S.', *World Theatre*, 11 (1962).

Gravier, Maurice. 'Strindberg and French Drama', *World Theatre*, 11 (1962).

Grew, E. M. 'Strindberg and Music', *Music Quarterly*, 14 (1933).

Hamilton, Mary G. 'Strindberg's Alchemical Way of the Cross', *Mosaic*, 7 (1974).

Harrison, C. A. '*Miss Julie*: Essence and Anomaly of Naturalism', *Central States Speech Journal*, 21 (1970).

Hauptman, Ira. 'Strindberg's Realistic Plays', *Yale Theatre*, 5 no. 3 (1974).

Hayes, Stephen G. and Zentner, Jules. 'Strindberg's *Miss Julie*: Lilacs and Beer', *Scandinavian Studies*, 45 (1973).

Hildeman, Karl Ivar. 'Strindberg, *The Dance of Death* and Revenge', *Scandinavian Studies*, 35 (1963).

Holtan, Orley I. 'The Absurd World of Strindberg's *The Dance of Death*', *Comparative Drama*, 1 (1967–8).

Jacobs, Barry. 'Psychic Murder and Characterisation in Strindberg's *The Father*', *Scandinavica*, 8 (1968).

Janzen, Assar. 'The Title of Strindberg's Last Drama', *Scandinavian Studies*, 34 (1962).

Jarvi, Raymond. '*A Dream Play*; A Symphony for the Stage', *Scandinavian Studies* 44 (1972).

—. 'Strindberg's *The Ghost Sonata* and Sonata Form', *Mosaic* 5 (1972).

Johnson, Walter. 'Strindberg and the Danse Macabre', *Modern Drama*, 3 (1960).

Johnson, Walter, '*Creditors* Re-examined', *Modern Drama*, 5 (1962–3).

—. '*A Dream Play*: Plans and Fulfillment', *Scandinavica*, 10 (1971).

Jorgenson, Theodore. 'August Strindberg', *Christian Liberty*, 1 (1953).

Kaufmann, R. J. 'Strindberg: The Absence of Irony', *Drama Survey*, 3 (1964).

Kristensen, S. M. 'Strindberg's *Damascus*', *Orbis Literarium*, 22 (1966–7).

Lamm, Martin. 'Strindberg and the Theatre', *Tulane Drama Review*, 6 (1961).

Lapisardi, Frederick S. 'The Same Enemies: Notes on Certain Similarities Between Yeats and Strindberg', *Modern Drama*, 12 (1969–70).

Lawson, Stephen R. 'Strindberg's *Dream Play* and *Ghost Sonata*', *Yale Theatre* 5 no. 3 (1974).

Lewis, Leta Jane. 'Alchemy and the Orient in Strindberg's *Dream Play*', *Scandinavian Studies*, 35 (1963).

Lide, Barbara A. B. 'Strindberg's Comic Spirit', *Dissertations Abstracts International*, 36:6107A–08A.

Lyons, Charles R. 'The Archetypal Action of Male Submission in Strindberg's *The Father*', *Scandinavian Studies*, 36 (1964).

Madsen, B. G. 'Strindberg as a Naturalistic Theorist', *Scandinavian Studies*, 30 (1958).

—. 'Strindberg's Cynical Tragedy, *The Bond*', *Modern Drama*, 5 (1962–3).

Mays, Milton A. 'Strindberg's *Ghost Sonata*: Parodied Fairy Tale', *Modern Drama*, 10 (1967–8).

Melchinger, Siegfried. 'German People Face to Face with Strindberg', *World Theatre*, 11 (1962).

Milton, John R. 'The Aesthetic Fault of Strindberg's Dream Plays', *Tulane Drama Review*, 4 (1960).

—. 'Strindberg in The Inferno', *Modern Drama*, 5 (1962–3).

Morgan, Margery M. 'Strindberg and the English Theatre', *Modern Drama*, 7 (1964).

Mudford, P. G. 'The Theatre of Trance: A View of the Consistency of Strindberg's Dramatic Craft', *Theatre Review*, 11 (1971).

Nilsson, N. A. 'Strindberg, Gorky and Blok', *Scando-Slavica* (Copenhagen), 4 (1958).

Oster, Rose-Marie G. 'Hamm and Hummel: Beckett and Strindberg on the Human Condition', *Scandinavian Studies*, 41 (1969).

Parker, Gerald. 'The Spectator Seized by the Theatre: Strindberg's *Ghost Sonata*', *Modern Drama*, 14 (1971–2).

Paulson, Arvid. 'Strindberg's Pilgrimage Dramas', *The Chronicle*, I (1954–5) II (1955).

Plasberg, E. 'Strindberg and the New Poetics', *Modern Drama*, 15 (1972).

Rapp, Esther H. Bibliographies, *Scandinavian Studies*, 23 (1951).

Redwood, Chris. 'Delius and Strindberg', *Music and Letters*, 56 (1954).

Reinhardt, N. S. 'Visual Meaning in Strindberg's Theatre', *Dissertations Abstracts International*, 36:3224A.

Scanlon, David. '*The Road to Damascus Part I*: A Sceptic's Everyman', *Modern Drama*, 5 (1962–3).

—. 'The Traditional Comic Form in Strindberg's Naturalistic Plays', *Dissertations, Abstracts International*, 31:3697A.

Scharbach, Alexander. 'German Militarism in *The Nightingale of Wittenberg*', *Scandinavian Studies*, 29 (1957).

Scobie, Irene. 'Strindberg and Lagerkvist', *Modern Drama*, 7 (1964).

Senelick, Lawrence. 'Strindberg, Antoine and Lugné-Poë, a Study in Cross Purposes', *Modern Drama*, 15 (1973).

Spivak, C. V. 'The Many Hells of August Strindberg', *Twentieth Century Literature*, 9 (1963–4).

Sprinchorn, Evert. 'The Logic of *A Dream Play*', *Modern Drama*, 5 (1962).

—. 'Zola of the Occult: Strindberg's Experimental Method', *Modern Drama*, 17 (1974).

—. 'Strindberg and the Wit to go Mad', *Scandinavian Studies*, 48 (1976).

—. 'Hell and Purgatory in Strindberg', *Scandinavian Studies*, 50 (1978).

Steene, Birgitta. 'Shakespearean Element in the Historical Plays of Strindberg', *Journal of Comparative Literature*, 11 (1959).

—. 'The Ambiguous Feminist', *Scandinavian Review*, 64 (1976).

Steiner, Donald L. 'August Strindberg and Edward Albee: Dance of Death', *Dissertations Abstracts International*, 33:766A.

Stenberg, Peter A. 'Servants of Two Masters: Strindberg and Hofmannsthal', *Modern Language Review*, 70 (1975).

Stockenstrom, Goram. 'The Journey from the Isle of Life to the Isle of Death: The Idea of Reconciliation in *The Ghost Sonata*', *Scandinavian Studies*, 50 (1978).

Tornquist, Egil. 'Strindberg's *The Stronger*', *Scandinavian Studies*, 42 (1970).

—. 'Miss Julie and O'Neill', *Modern Drama*, 19 (1976).

Uppvall, A. J. 'Strindberg in the Light of Psycho-Analysis', *Scandinavian Studies*, 21 (1949).

Vincenta, Sister M. 'Wagnerism in Strindberg's *The Road to Damascus*', *Modern Drama*, 5 (1962–3).

Vowles, R. B. 'Tennessee Williams and Strindberg', *Modern Drama*, 1 (1958).

—. 'Strindberg and the Symbolic Mill', *Scandinavian Studies*, 34 (1962).

—. 'A Cook's Tour of Strindberg Scholarship', *Modern Drama*, 5 (1962).

Weinstock, John. 'Strindberg and Women's Lib', *Germanic Notes*, 2 (1971).

Wescher, Paul. 'Strindberg and the Chance-Images of Surrealism', *Art Quarterly*, 16 (1953).

White, Kenneth S. 'Visions of a Transfigured Humanity: Strindberg and Lenormand', *Modern Drama*, 5 (1962–3).

Williams, Raymond. 'Strindberg and the New Drama in Britain', *World Theatre*, 11 (1962).

Winther, S. K. 'Strindberg and O'Neill', *Scandinavian Studies*, 31 (1959).

Young, Vernon. 'The History of *Miss Julie*', *Hudson Review*, 8 (1955).

Other Books

Artaud, Antonin. *Collected Works* 1 and 2, trans. V. Corti, Calder and Boyars (London 1968 and 1970).

Balzac, Honoré de. *Seraphita*, trans. Clara Bell, Macmillan (New York 1901).

Bentley, Eric. *The Playwright as Thinker*, Methuen (London 1955).

Bernheim, H. *Suggestive Therapeutics*, trans. C. A. Herter, Y. J. Pentand (Edinburgh & London 1890).

Borland, Harold H. *Nietzsche's Influence on Swedish Literature*, Kungl (Goteborg 1956).

Brown, N. O. *Life Against Death*, Sphere Books (London 1968).

Brustein, Robert. *The Theatre of Revolt*, Methuen (London 1965).

Charcot, J. M. *Lectures on the diseases of the Nervous System*, New Sydenham Society (London 1877)

Chernishevsky, N. G. *What Is To Be Done*, trans. N. H. Dale and S. S. Skidelsky, Thomas Crowell and Co (New York 1886).

Cohn, Ruby. *Currents in Contemporary Drama*, Indiana University Press (Boomington 1969).

Cole, Toby (ed.). *Playwrights on Playwriting*, MacGibbon and Kee (London 1960).

Esslin, Martin. *The Theatre of the Absurd*, Eyre and Spottiswoode (London 1962).

Ewen, Frederick. *Bertolt Brecht*, Caldar and Boyars (London 1970).

Freud, Sigmund. *The Interpretation of Dreams*, Standard edition, Vols. 4 and 5, Hogarth Press (London 1953).

Gascoigne, Bamber. *Twentieth Century Drama*, Hutchinson (London 1963).

Gassner, John. *Directions in Modern Theatre and Drama*, Holt Rinehart and Winston (New York 1965).

Gaskell, Ronald. *Drama and Reality: the European Theatre since Ibsen*, Routledge and Kegan Paul (London 1972).

Grimsley, Ronald. *Kierkegaard*, Studio Vista (London 1973).

Gustafson, Alrick. *History of Swedish Literature*, Minnesota University Press (Minneapolis 1961) .

Harley, Clifford. *Swedenborg and the New Cosmology*, Missionary Society of the New Church (London 1951).

Hinchliffe, Arnold P. *The Absurd*, Methuen (London 1969).

Hoffman, E. T. A. *The Sandman*, trans. M. Bullock, New English Library (London 1962).

—. *Tales of Hoffman*, ed. J. M. Cohen, Bodley Head (London 1951).

—. *Master Flea*, trans. G. Sloane in *Specimens of German Romance*, Vol. 2, T. Carlyle (London 1826).

Hollingdale, R. J. *Nietzsche*, Routledge and Kegan Paul (London 1973).

Huysmans, J. K. *En route*, trans. C. Kegan Paul, Trench Trubner and Co (London 1896).

Kafka, Franz. *The Diaries 1914–23*, ed. Max Brod, trans. Martin Greenberg, Schocken Books (New York 1949).

Kaufmann, Walter. *Nietzsche: Philosopher, Psychologist, Antichrist*, Vintage Books (New York 1968).

Kempis, Thomas A. *Imitation of Christ*, trans. Leo Sherley-Price, Penguin (Harmondsworth 1952).

Kermode, Frank. *Romantic Image*, Routledge and Kegan Paul (London 1957).

Kierkegaard, Soren. *Concluding Unscientific Postscript*, trans. D. F. Swensen and W. Lowrie, American-Scandinavian Foundation (London 1941).

—. *Either–Or*, trans. D. F. Swenson, L. M. Swenson and W. Lowrie, Princeton University Press (1944).

—. *The Concept of Dread*, trans. W. Lowrie, Princeton University Press (1944).

—. *Repetition: an essay in experimental Psychology*, trans. W. Lowrie, Princeton University Press (1941).

—. *The Sickness Unto Death*, trans. W. Lowrie, Princeton University Press (1951).

Kirk, G. S. and Raven, J. E. *The Presocratic Philosophers*, Cambridge University Press (1975).

Kitchin, Laurence. *Mid-Century Drama*, Faber (London 1960).

—. *Drama in the Sixties*, Faber (London 1966).

Klaf, Franklin S. *Strindberg: Origin of Psychology in Modern Drama*, Citadel Press (New York 1963).

Lamm, Martin, *Modern Drama*, trans. Karen Elliott, Basil Blackwell (Oxford 1952).

Laver, James. *The First Decadent* (Life of J. K. Huysmans), Faber (London 1954).

Lavrin, Janko. *Studies in European Literature*, Constable (London 1929).

Lehmann, A. G. *Symbolist Aesthetics in France 1885–95*, Basil Blackwell (Oxford 1968).

Lumley, Frederick. *Trends in Twentieth-Century Drama*, Barrie and Rockliff (London 1960).

Maeterlinck, Maurice. *The Princess Maleine* and *The Intruder*, trans. Gerard Harry, Heinemann (London 1892).

—. *The Treasure of the Humble*, trans. Alfred Sutro, Arthur L. Humphreys (London 1897).

Matthews, Honor. *The Primal Curse*, Chatto and Windus (London 1967).

Meyer, Michael. *Henrik Ibsen: the Making of a Dramatist 1828–64*, Rupert Hart-Davis (London 1967), *Farewell to Poetry 1864–1882* and *The Top of a Cold Mountain*, Rupert Hart-Davis (London 1971).

Moore, Harry T. *Twentieth Century German Literature*, Heinemann Educational (London 1971).

Nietzsche, Friedrich. *The Anti-Christ*, trans. R. J. Hollingdale, Penguin (Harmondsworth 1968).

—. *Beyond Good and Evil*, trans. R. J. Hollingdale, Penguin (Harmondsworth 1972).

—. *Case of Wagner*, trans. W. Kaufmann, Vintage Books (New York 1967).

—. *Thus Spake Zarathustra*, trans. R. J. Hollingdale, Penguin (Harmondsworth 1968).

—. *Twilight of the Gods*, trans. R. J. Hollingdale, Penguin (Harmondsworth 1968).

Nordau, Max. *Paradoxes*, trans. J. R. McIlraith, Heinemann (London 1906).

Praz, Mario. *Romantic Agony*, trans. A. Davidson, Oxford University Press (1970).

Ritchie, J. M. (ed.). *Periods in German Literature*, Oswald Wolff (London 1966).

Rousseau, Jean Jacques. *Emile*, trans. Barbara Foxley, Dent (London 1969).

Russell, Bertrand. *History of Western Philosophy*, Allen and Unwin (London 1957).

Schopenhauer, Arthur. *Essays and Aphorisms*, trans. R. J. Hollingdale, Penguin (Harmondsworth 1970).

—. *World as Will and Idea*, trans. R. B. Haldane and J. Kemp, Routledge and Kegan Paul (London 1950).

Sigstedt, C. S. *The Swedenborg Epic*, Bookman Associates (New York 1952).

Steiner, George. *The Death of Tragedy*, Faber (London 1961).

Stromberg, Roland M. (ed.). *Realism, Naturalism and Symbolism*, Macmillan (London 1968).

Styan, J. L. *The Elements of Drama*, Cambridge University Press (1960).

—. *The Dark Comedy*, Cambridge University Press (1968).

Swedenborg, Emanuel. *The Animal Kingdom, Arcana Coelestia, Conjugal Love, The Divine Love and the Divine Wisdom, Heaven and Its Wonders and Hell, The New Jerusalem, The Spiritual Diary, The True Christian Religion*. All published in translations by the Swedenborg Society, London.

Symons, Arthur. *The Symbolist Movement in Literature*, Constable (London 1911).

Taylor, John Russell. *Anger and After*, Methuen (London 1969).

Toksvig, S. *Emanuel Swedenborg: Scientist and Mystic*, Faber (London 1948).

Trobridge, George. *A Life of Emanuel Swedenborg*, Swedish Society (London 1920).

Weinstock, John M. and Ravinsky, Robert (eds.). *The Hero in Scandinavian Literature from Peer Gynt to the Present*, Texas University Press (Austin 1975).

Wellwarth, George E. *The Theatre of Protest and Paradox*, New York University Press (1964).

White, William. *Emanuel Swedenborg, his life and writings*, 2 vols. Simpkin Marshall (London 1867).

Williams, Raymond. *Drama from Ibsen to Eliot*, Chatto and Windus (London 1961).

—. *Modern Tragedy*, Chatto and Windus (London 1966).

Yeats, W. B. *Uncollected Prose by W. B. Yeats*, ed. J. P. Frayne and C. Johnson, Macmillan (London 1975).

Zola, Emile. *The Experimental Novel and other essays*, trans. Belle M. Sherman, Cassell (New York 1893).

Index